MUSASHI #9

volume 6

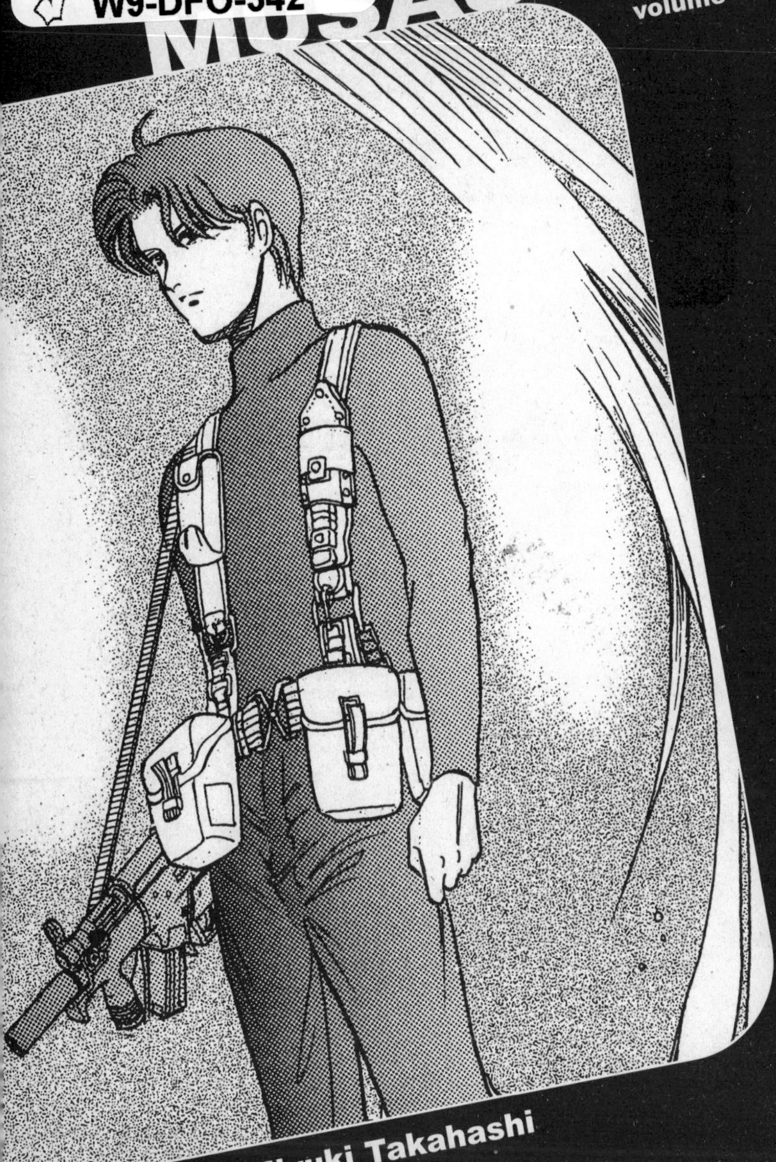

by Miyuki Takahashi

The history of mankind has
been one of wars. Race.
Religion. Philosophy.
The causes are untold.

The combatants have their own
justifications, but on occasion,
some create a volatile
situation that threatens to
destroy the world.

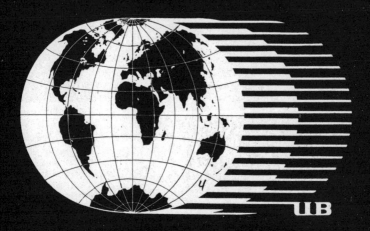

Ultimate Blue.
An organization shrouded in
complete secrecy. Also known
as "the other United Nations."
Nobody knows when it was
created. Nobody knows
where it is based.

The Blue of the Seas.
The Blue of the Skies.
The Blue of the Earth.

The last line of defense against chaos.

The story so far...

The history of mankind has been one of wars. Relentless warfare would have doomed the planet to annihilation were it not for Ultimate Blue, a secret organization also known as the "other United Nations," and its team of super agents.
Musashi Nine is one of them.
Musashi masquerades as a boy and goes undercover at a high school to find evidence that would destroy a gun-smuggling organization called "White Dragon." She befriends Tachibana Shingo, who has unwittingly come across that evidence, and together they bring down the organization. The mission should have ended there except Lau survives White Dragon's demise and vows revenge.
Now, Musashi must protect Shingo.
However, Shingo's affection has grown into an uncontrollable fire that threatens them both!

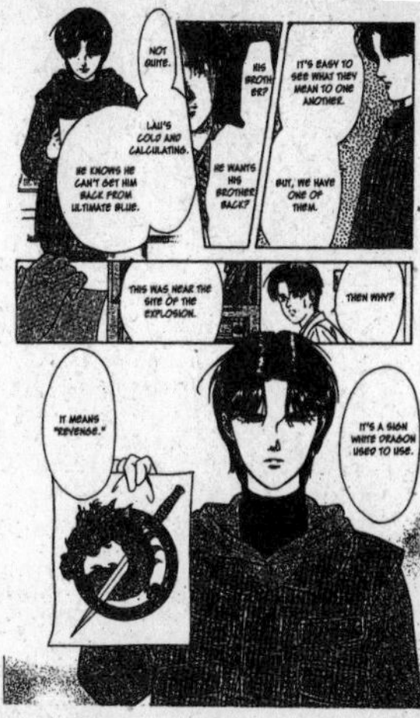
IT'S EASY TO SEE WHAT THEY MEAN TO ONE ANOTHER.
BUT, WE HAVE ONE OF THEM.
HIS BROTHER?
HE WANTS HIS BROTHER BACK?
NOT QUITE.
LAU'S COLD AND CALCULATING.
HE KNOWS HE CAN'T GET HIM BACK FROM ULTIMATE BLUE.
THEN WHY?
THIS WAS NEAR THE SITE OF THE EXPLOSION.
IT'S A SIGN WHITE DRAGON USED TO USE.
IT MEANS "REVENGE."

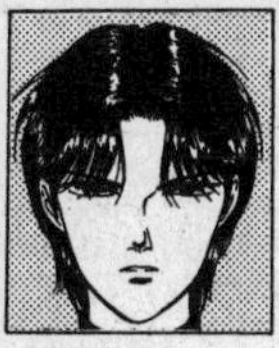
MUSASHI

Ultimate Blue agent Number Nine. A.K.A. Shinozuka Kou,
Is undercover at a boys' school, but is actually a girl. Single-digit agents like her have the power to change the world. Until now, she has not shown any emotions, but...

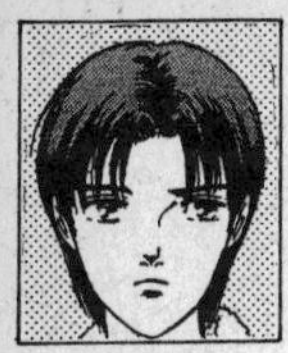
TACHIBANA SHINGO

A hot-headed teenager befriended by Musashi when they avenged his best friend. He knows Musashi will leave when the mission is over and is deeply troubled over that.

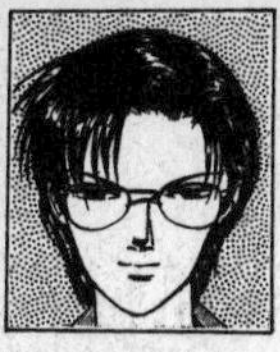
No.19

Ultimate Blue agent.
He assists Nine in her missions as her lieutenant and at times as her double. While sympathizing with Shingo about his feelings toward Musashi, he tries to suppress them.
Nicknamed one-niner by Shingo.

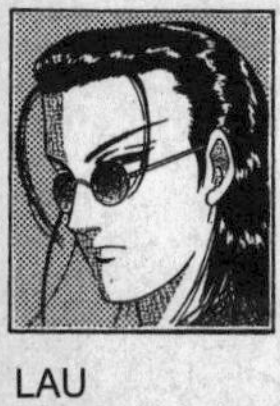
LAU

Survived Ultimate Blue's dismantling of White Dragon.
Explosives expert.
Despises Ultimate Blue because they captured his brother.

contents

MUSASHI #9

6

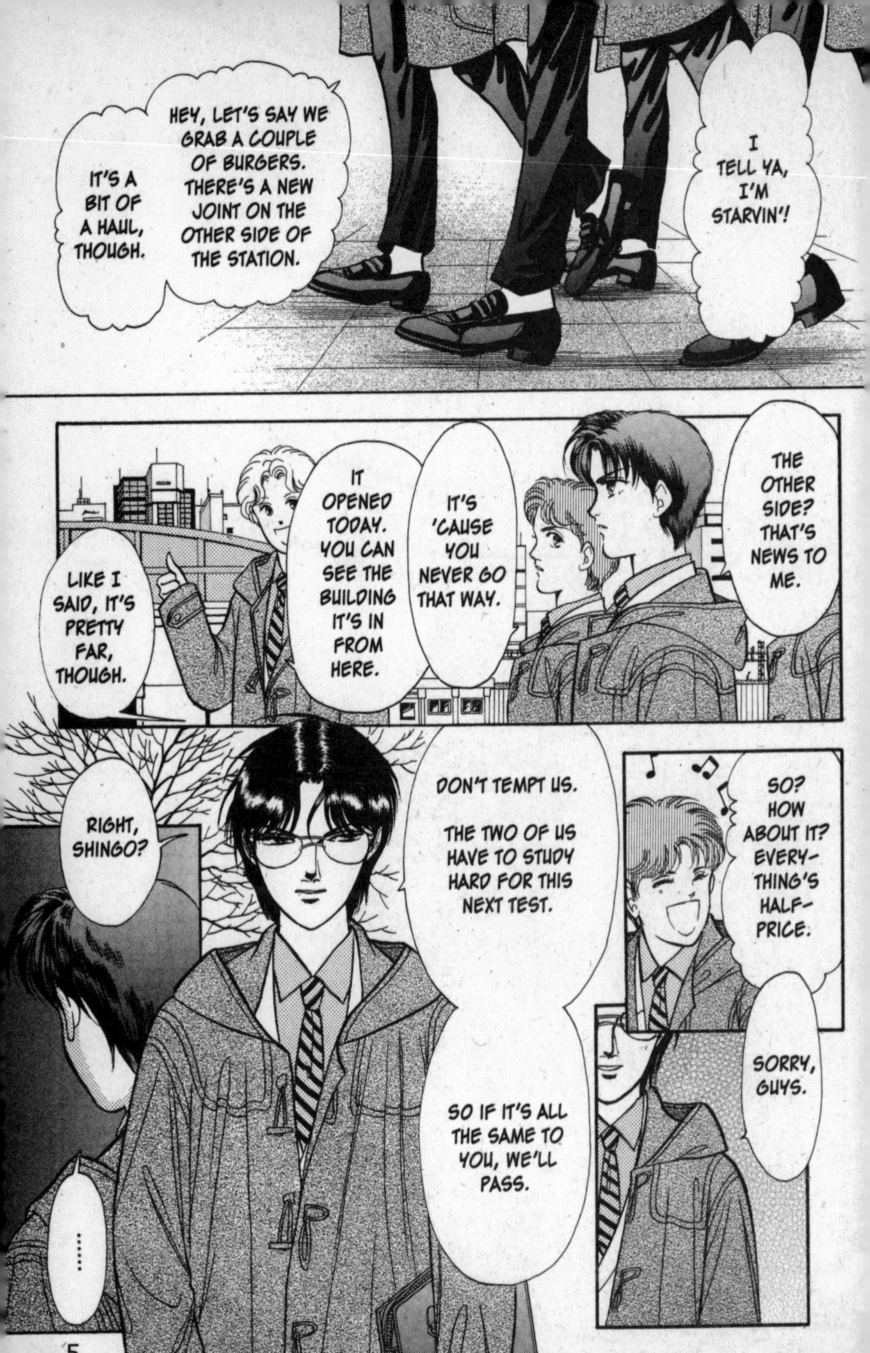
I TELL YA, I'M STARVIN'!
HEY, LET'S SAY WE GRAB A COUPLE OF BURGERS. THERE'S A NEW JOINT ON THE OTHER SIDE OF THE STATION.
IT'S A BIT OF A HAUL, THOUGH.
THE OTHER SIDE? THAT'S NEWS TO ME.
IT'S 'CAUSE YOU NEVER GO THAT WAY.
IT OPENED TODAY. YOU CAN SEE THE BUILDING IT'S IN FROM HERE.
LIKE I SAID, IT'S PRETTY FAR, THOUGH.
SO? HOW ABOUT IT? EVERYTHING'S HALF-PRICE.
SORRY, GUYS.
DON'T TEMPT US.
THE TWO OF US HAVE TO STUDY HARD FOR THIS NEXT TEST.
SO IF IT'S ALL THE SAME TO YOU, WE'LL PASS.
RIGHT, SHINGO?
......

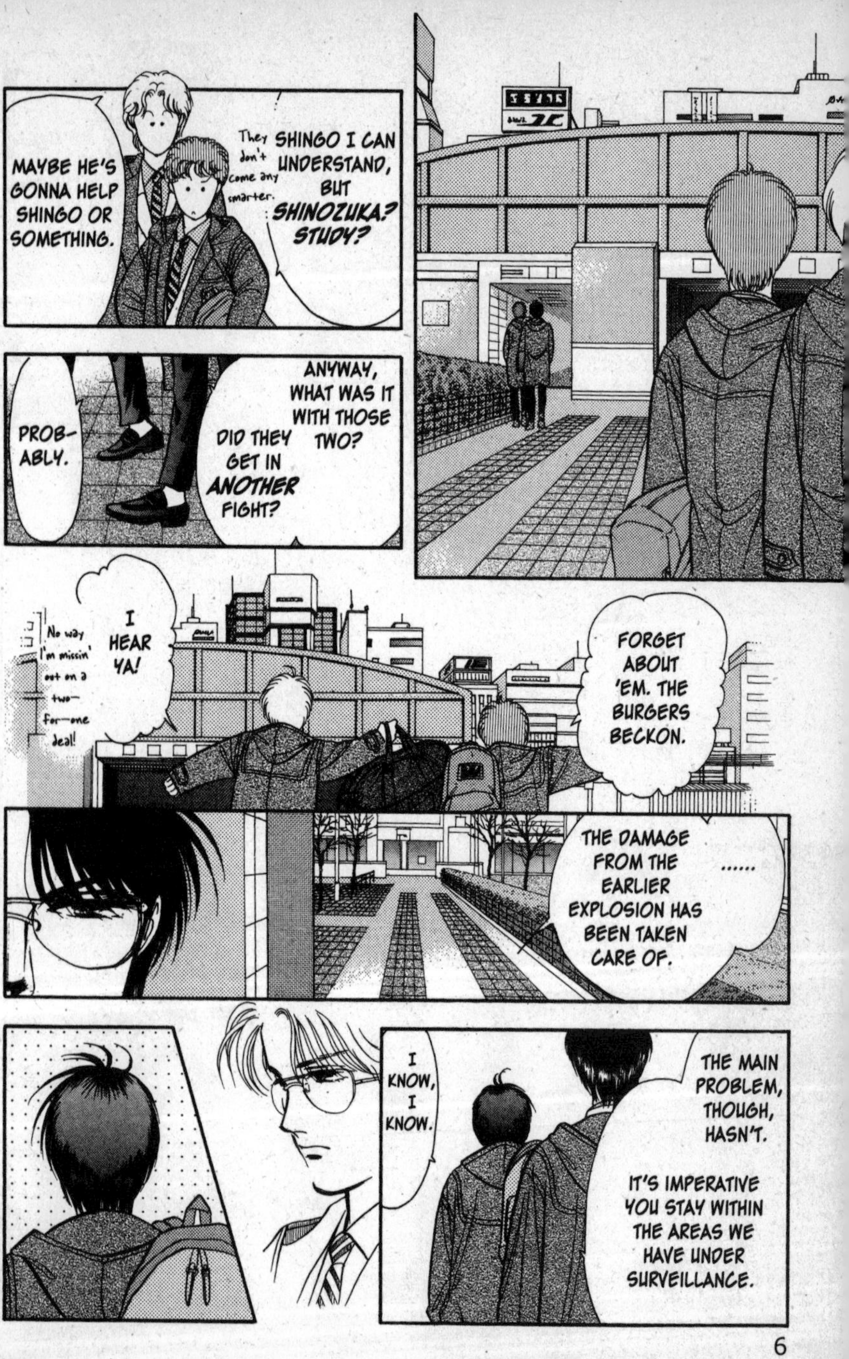
SHINGO I CAN UNDERSTAND, BUT SHINOZUKA? STUDY?
They don't come any smarter.
MAYBE HE'S GONNA HELP SHINGO OR SOMETHING.
ANYWAY, WHAT WAS IT WITH THOSE TWO?
DID THEY GET IN ANOTHER FIGHT?
PROB-ABLY.
FORGET ABOUT 'EM. THE BURGERS BECKON.
I HEAR YA!
No way I'm missin' out on a two-for-one deal!
......
THE DAMAGE FROM THE EARLIER EXPLOSION HAS BEEN TAKEN CARE OF.
THE MAIN PROBLEM, THOUGH, HASN'T.
IT'S IMPERATIVE YOU STAY WITHIN THE AREAS WE HAVE UNDER SURVEILLANCE.
I KNOW, I KNOW.

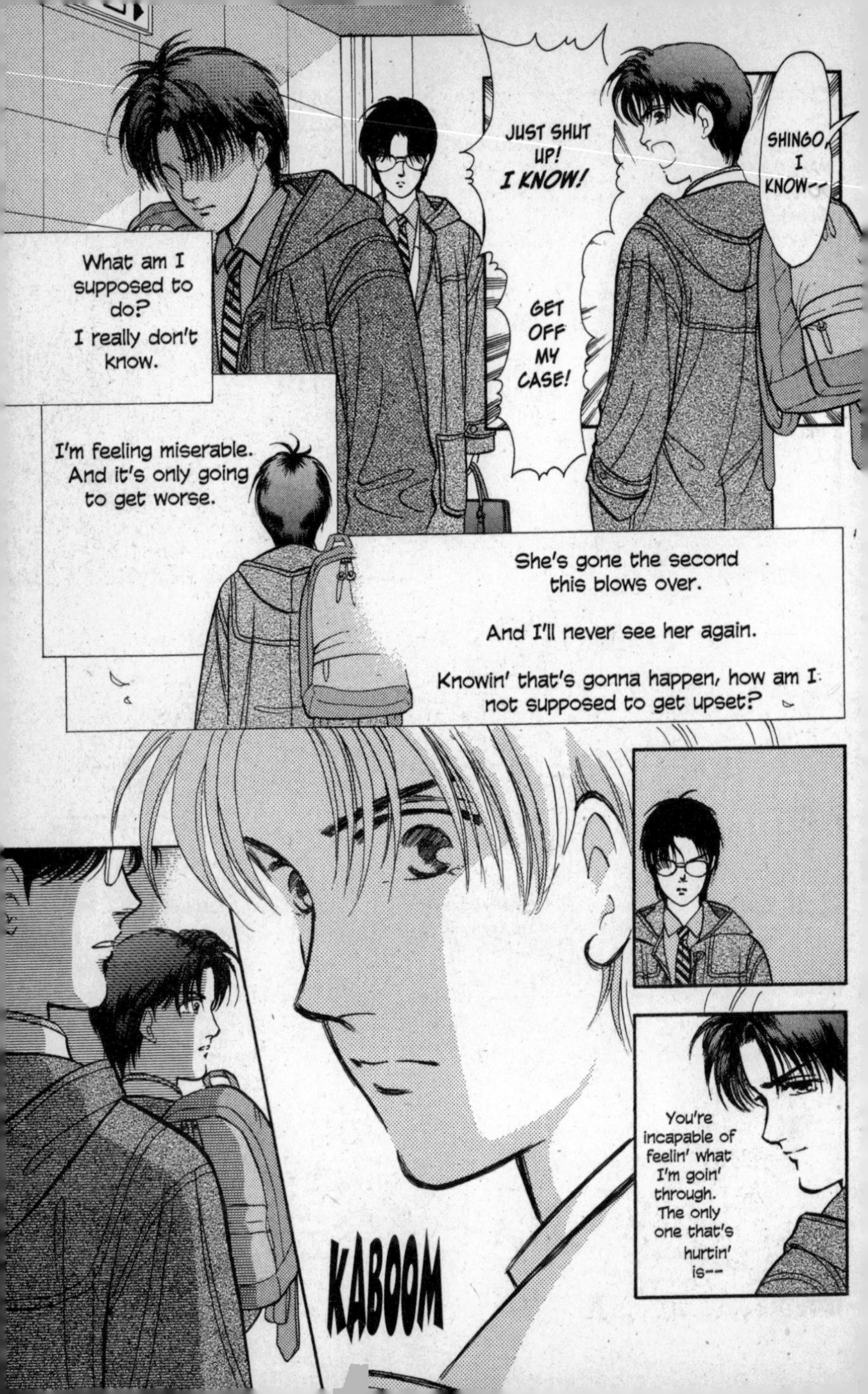
SHINGO, I KNOW--
JUST SHUT UP! I KNOW!
GET OFF MY CASE!
What am I supposed to do? I really don't know.
I'm feeling miserable. And it's only going to get worse.
She's gone the second this blows over.
And I'll never see her again.
Knowin' that's gonna happen, how am I not supposed to get upset?
You're incapable of feelin' what I'm goin' through. The only one that's hurtin' is--
KABOOM

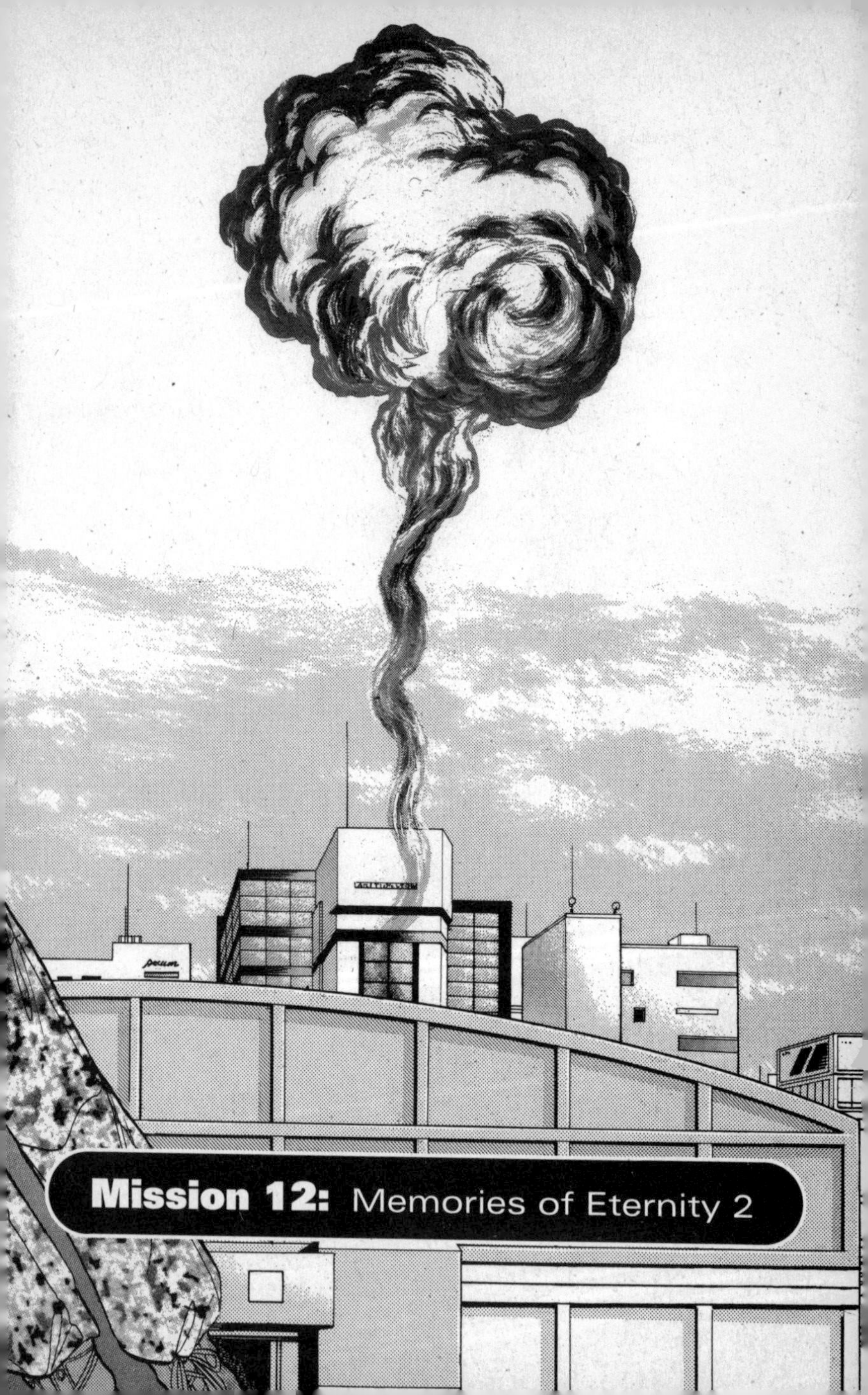
Mission 12: Memories of Eternity 2

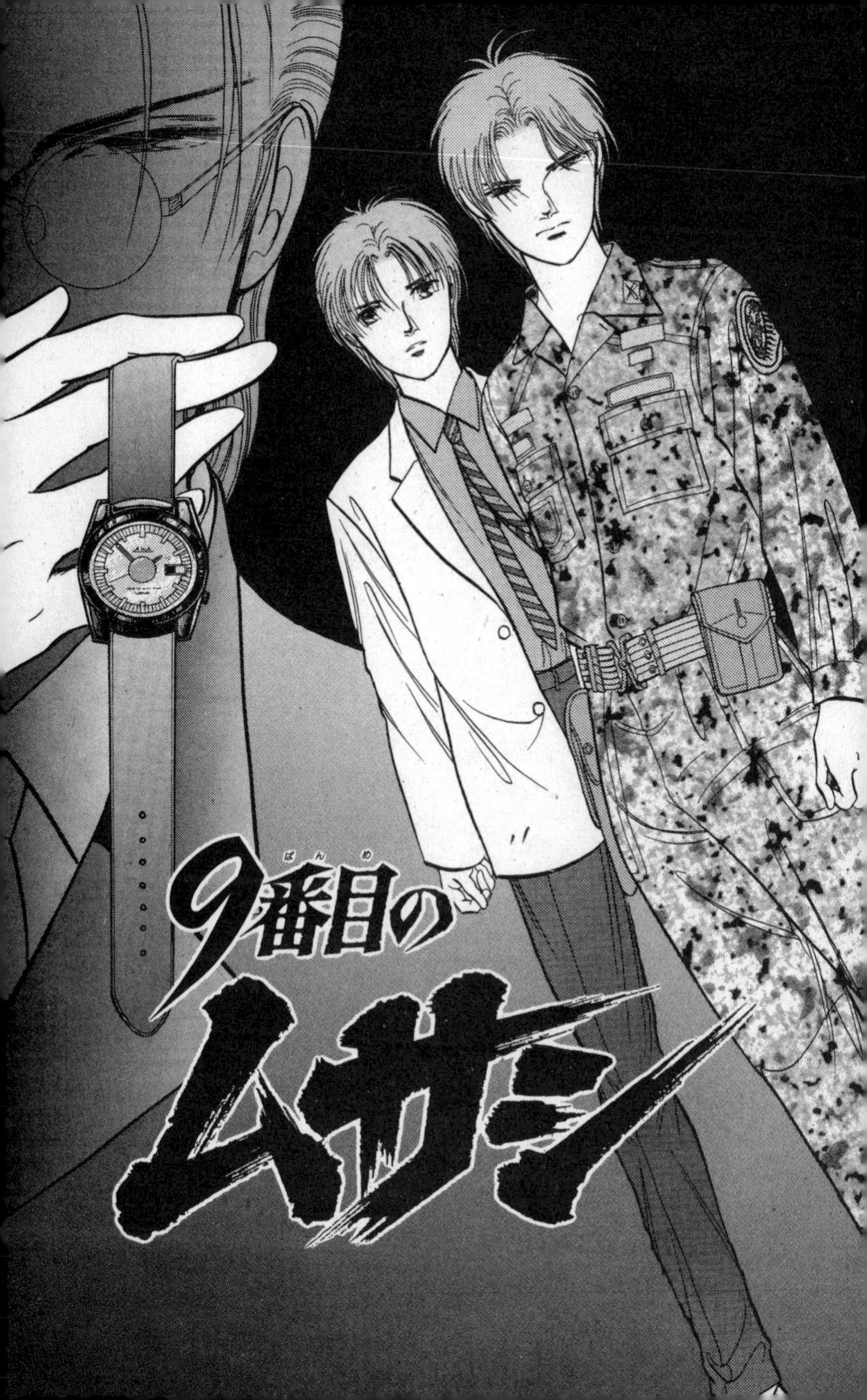
9番目のムサシ

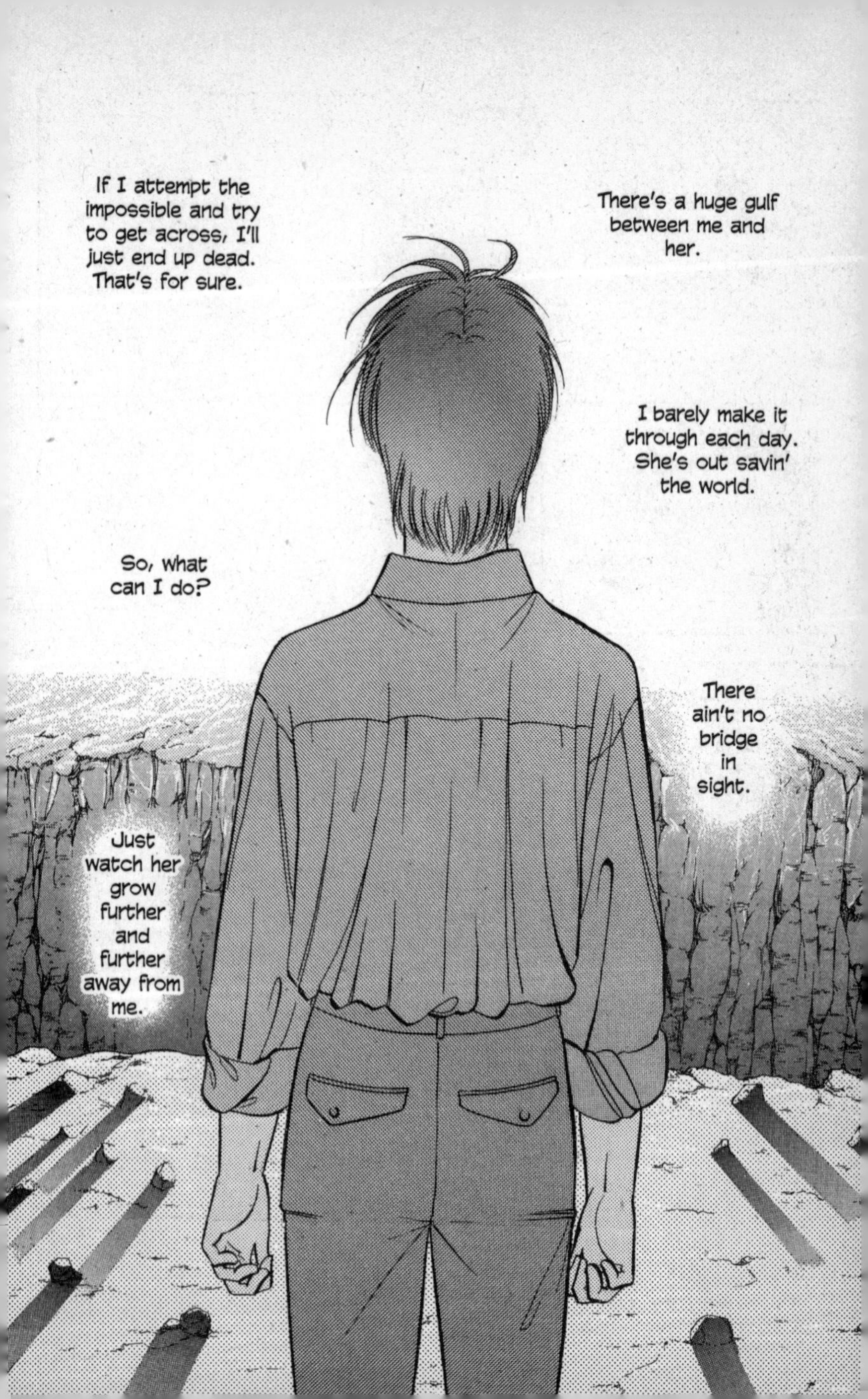
There's a huge gulf between me and her.
If I attempt the impossible and try to get across, I'll just end up dead. That's for sure.
I barely make it through each day. She's out savin' the world.
So, what can I do?
There ain't no bridge in sight.
Just watch her grow further and further away from me.

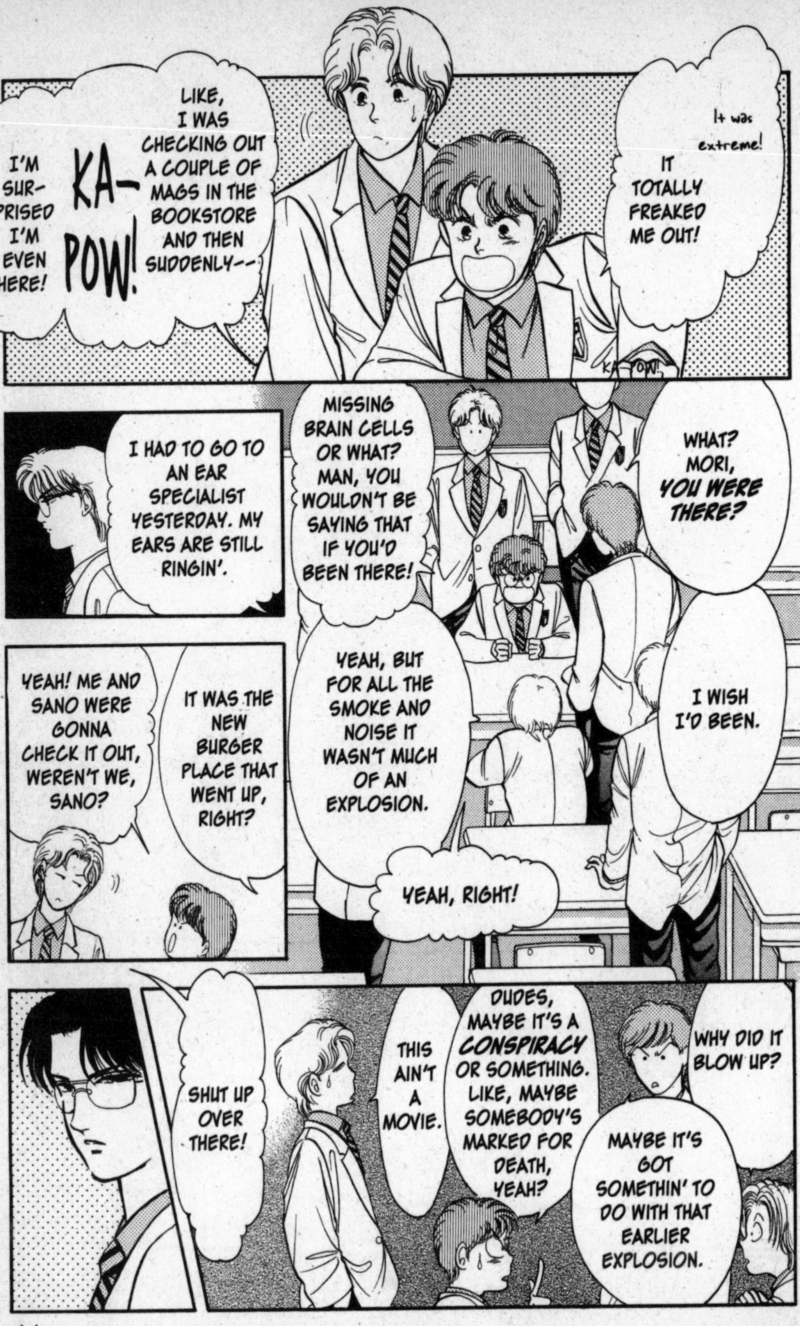
It was extreme!
IT TOTALLY FREAKED ME OUT!
LIKE, I WAS CHECKING OUT A COUPLE OF MAGS IN THE BOOKSTORE AND THEN SUDDENLY--
KA-POW!
I'M SURPRISED I'M EVEN HERE!
WHAT? MORI, *YOU WERE THERE?*
MISSING BRAIN CELLS OR WHAT? MAN, YOU WOULDN'T BE SAYING THAT IF YOU'D BEEN THERE!
I WISH I'D BEEN.
YEAH, BUT FOR ALL THE SMOKE AND NOISE IT WASN'T MUCH OF AN EXPLOSION.
YEAH, RIGHT!
I HAD TO GO TO AN EAR SPECIALIST YESTERDAY. MY EARS ARE STILL RINGIN'.
IT WAS THE NEW BURGER PLACE THAT WENT UP, RIGHT?
YEAH! ME AND SANO WERE GONNA CHECK IT OUT, WEREN'T WE, SANO?
WHY DID IT BLOW UP?
MAYBE IT'S GOT SOMETHIN' TO DO WITH THAT EARLIER EXPLOSION.
DUDES, MAYBE IT'S A *CONSPIRACY* OR SOMETHING. LIKE, MAYBE SOMEBODY'S MARKED FOR DEATH, YEAH?
THIS AIN'T A MOVIE.
SHUT UP OVER THERE!

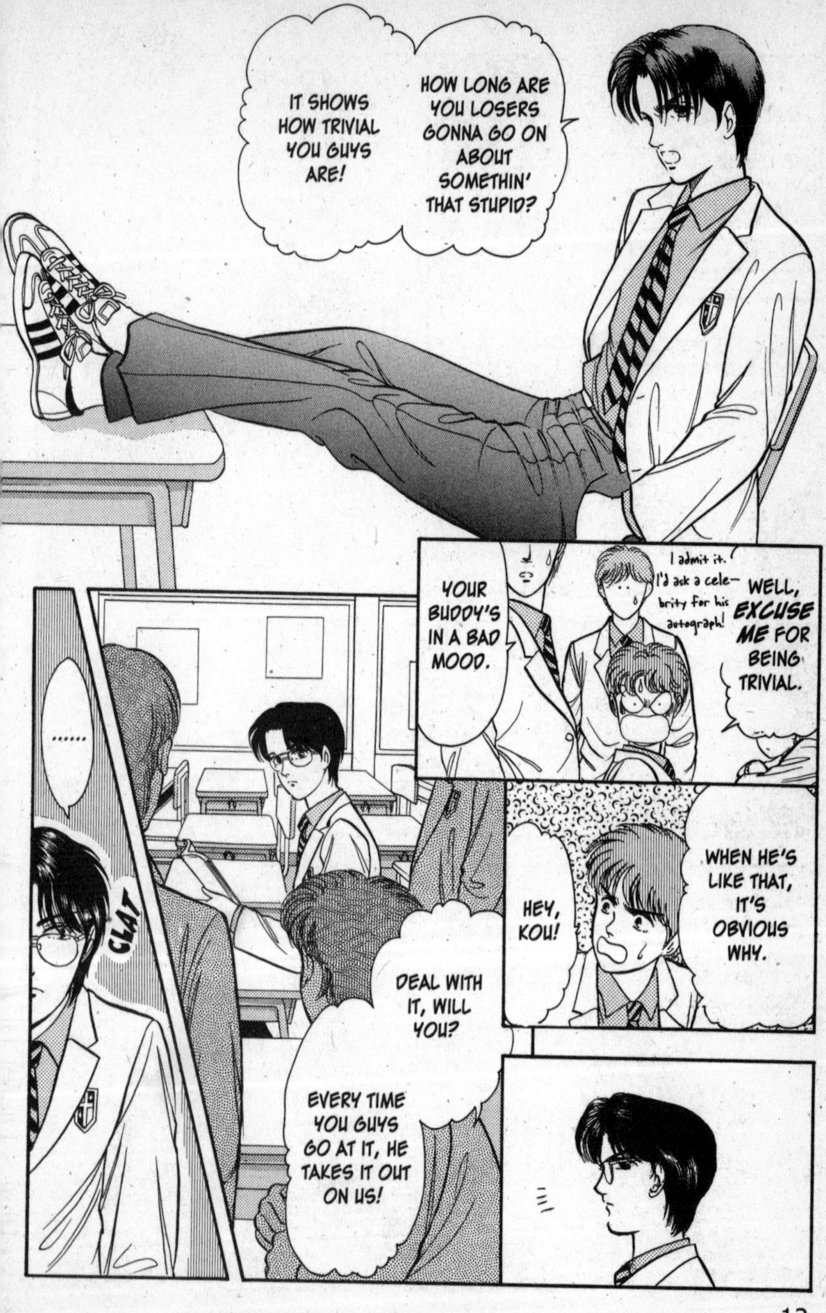
HOW LONG ARE YOU LOSERS GONNA GO ON ABOUT SOMETHIN' THAT STUPID?
IT SHOWS HOW TRIVIAL YOU GUYS ARE!
WELL, EXCUSE ME FOR BEING TRIVIAL.
I admit it. I'd ask a celebrity for his autograph!
YOUR BUDDY'S IN A BAD MOOD.
WHEN HE'S LIKE THAT, IT'S OBVIOUS WHY.
HEY, KOU!
DEAL WITH IT, WILL YOU?
EVERY TIME YOU GUYS GO AT IT, HE TAKES IT OUT ON US!
......
CLAT

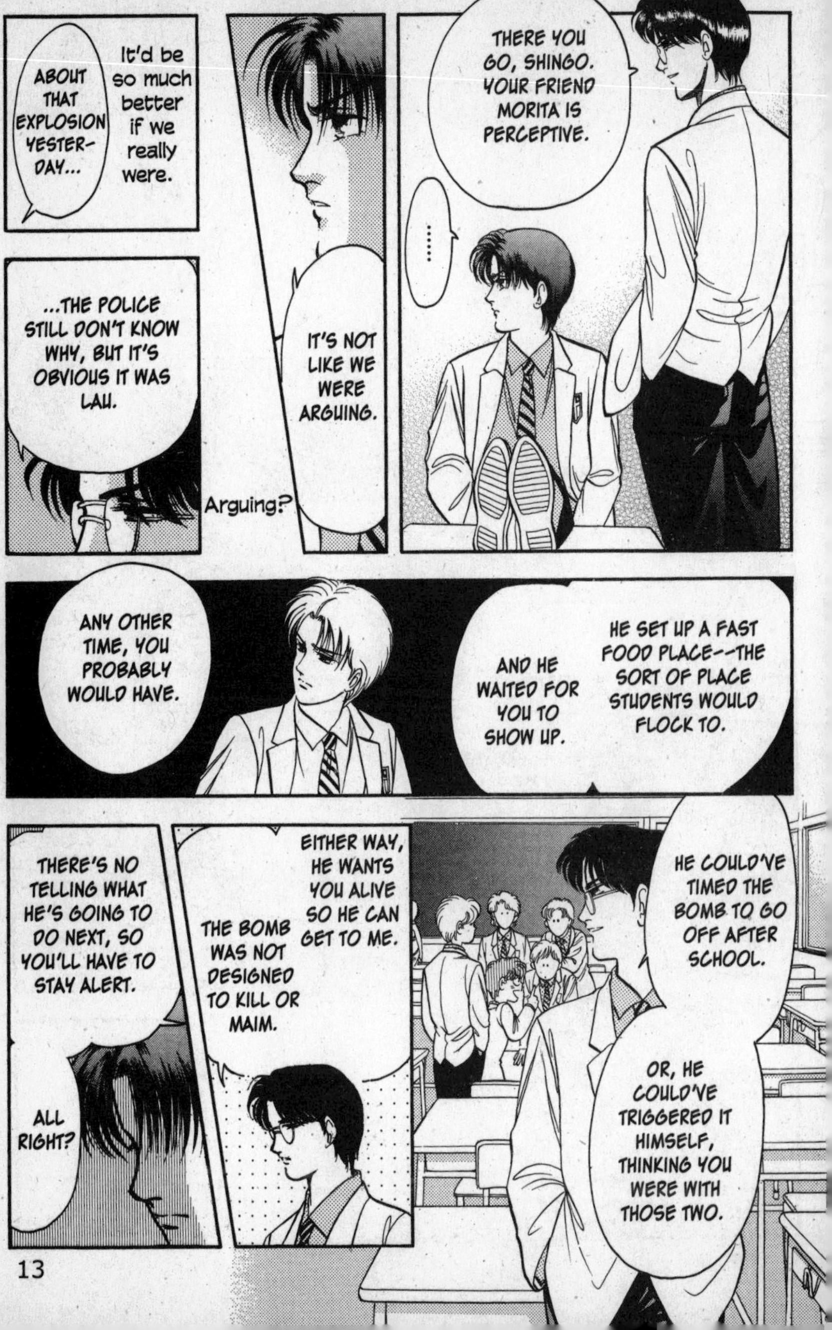
THERE YOU GO, SHINGO. YOUR FRIEND MORITA IS PERCEPTIVE.
......
IT'S NOT LIKE WE WERE ARGUING.
Arguing?
It'd be so much better if we really were.
ABOUT THAT EXPLOSION YESTER-DAY...
...THE POLICE STILL DON'T KNOW WHY, BUT IT'S OBVIOUS IT WAS LAU.
HE SET UP A FAST FOOD PLACE--THE SORT OF PLACE STUDENTS WOULD FLOCK TO.
AND HE WAITED FOR YOU TO SHOW UP.
ANY OTHER TIME, YOU PROBABLY WOULD HAVE.
HE COULD'VE TIMED THE BOMB TO GO OFF AFTER SCHOOL.
OR, HE COULD'VE TRIGGERED IT HIMSELF, THINKING YOU WERE WITH THOSE TWO.
EITHER WAY, HE WANTS YOU ALIVE SO HE CAN GET TO ME.
THE BOMB WAS NOT DESIGNED TO KILL OR MAIM.
THERE'S NO TELLING WHAT HE'S GOING TO DO NEXT, SO YOU'LL HAVE TO STAY ALERT.
ALL RIGHT?

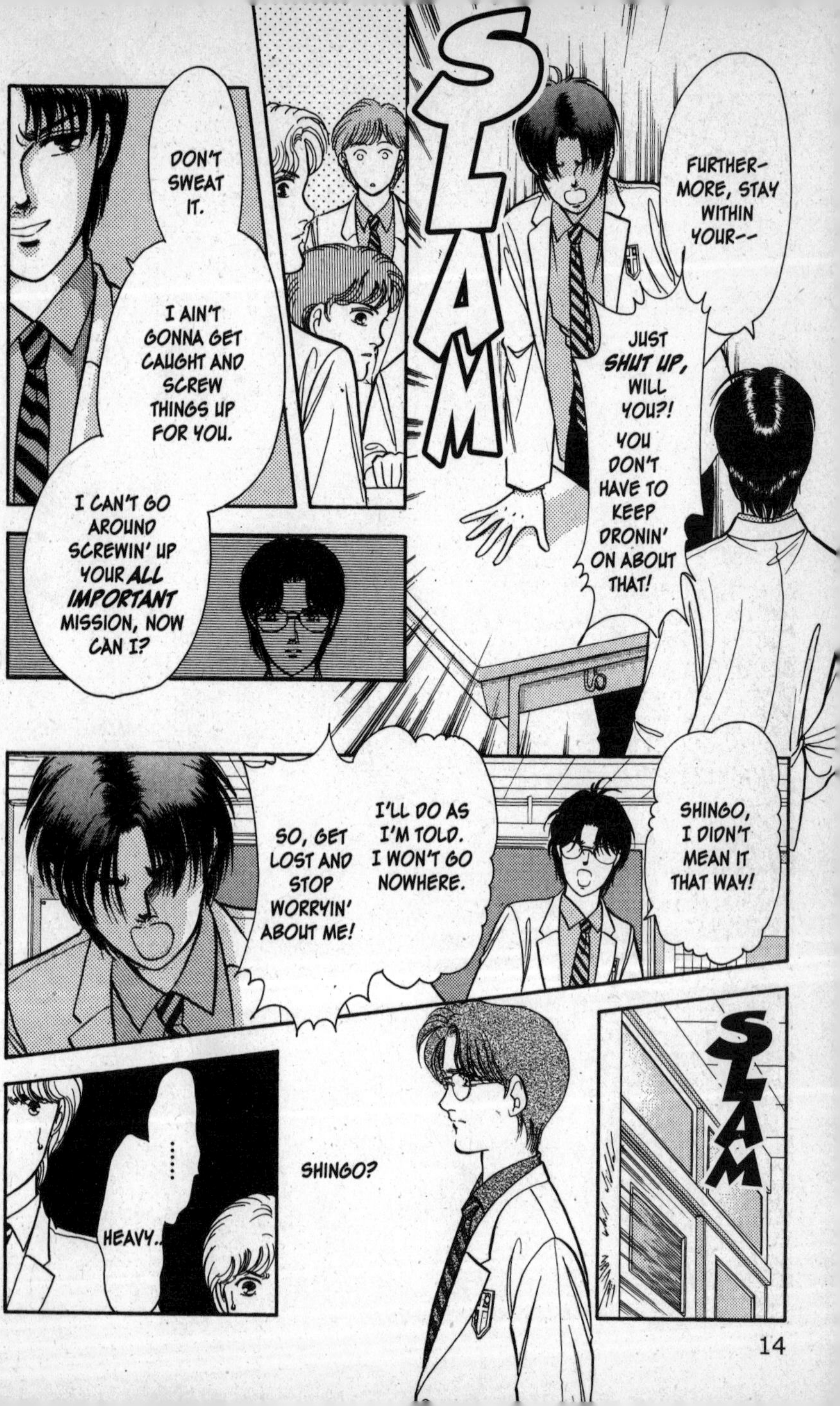
SLAM
FURTHER-MORE, STAY WITHIN YOUR--
JUST SHUT UP, WILL YOU?!
YOU DON'T HAVE TO KEEP DRONIN' ON ABOUT THAT!
DON'T SWEAT IT.
I AIN'T GONNA GET CAUGHT AND SCREW THINGS UP FOR YOU.
I CAN'T GO AROUND SCREWIN' UP YOUR ALL IMPORTANT MISSION, NOW CAN I?
SHINGO, I DIDN'T MEAN IT THAT WAY!
I'LL DO AS I'M TOLD. I WON'T GO NOWHERE.
SO, GET LOST AND STOP WORRYIN' ABOUT ME!
SLAM
SHINGO?
......
HEAVY..

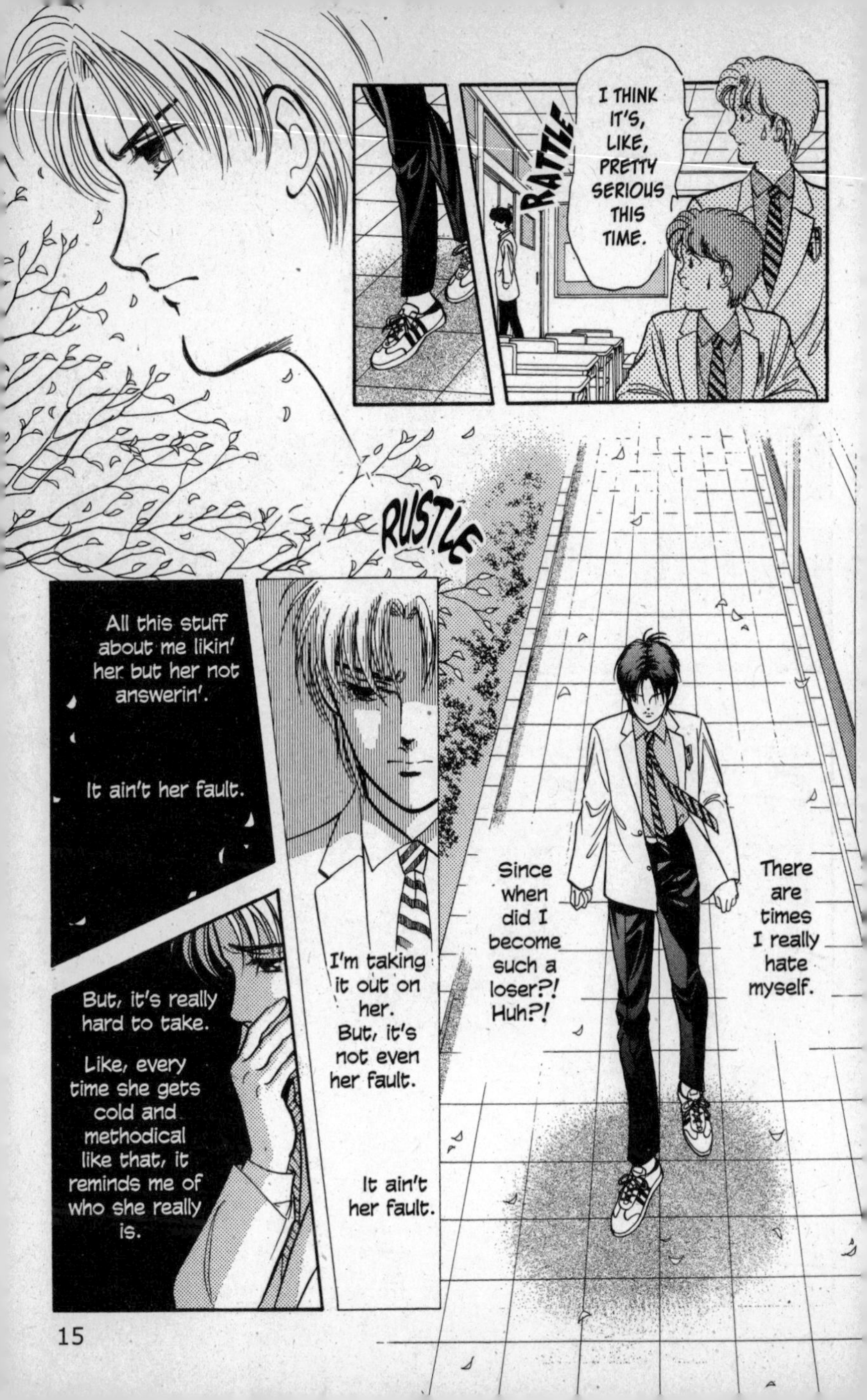
I THINK IT'S, LIKE, PRETTY SERIOUS THIS TIME.
RATTLE
RUSTLE
There are times I really hate myself.
Since when did I become such a loser?! Huh?!
I'm taking it out on her. But, it's not even her fault.
It ain't her fault.
All this stuff about me likin' her but her not answerin'.
It ain't her fault.
But, it's really hard to take.
Like, every time she gets cold and methodical like that, it reminds me of who she really is.

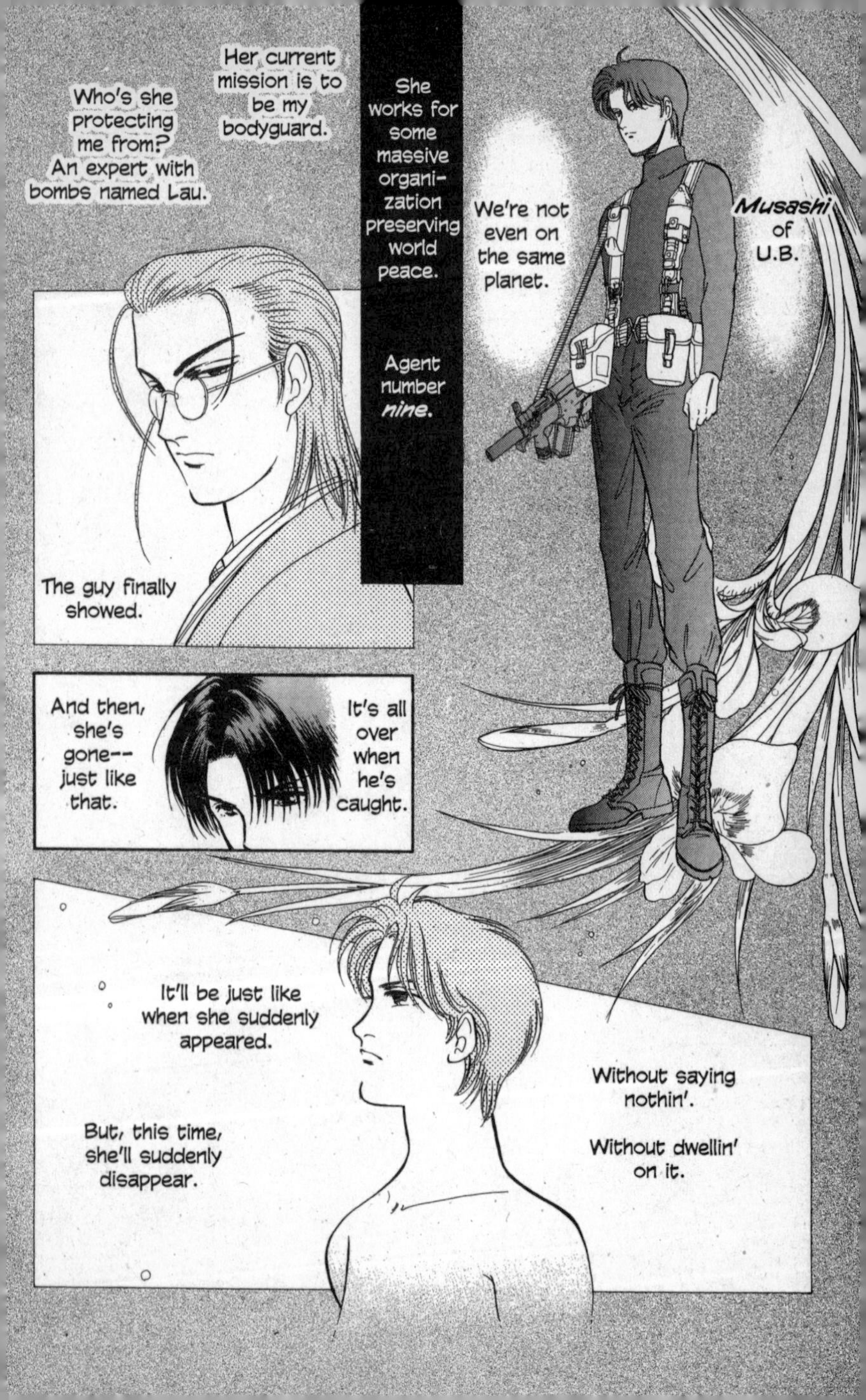
Musashi of U.B.
We're not even on the same planet.
She works for some massive organi- zation preserving world peace.
Agent number nine.
Her current mission is to be my bodyguard.
Who's she protecting me from? An expert with bombs named Lau.
The guy finally showed.
It's all over when he's caught.
And then, she's gone-- just like that.
It'll be just like when she suddenly appeared.
But, this time, she'll suddenly disappear.
Without saying nothin'.
Without dwellin' on it.

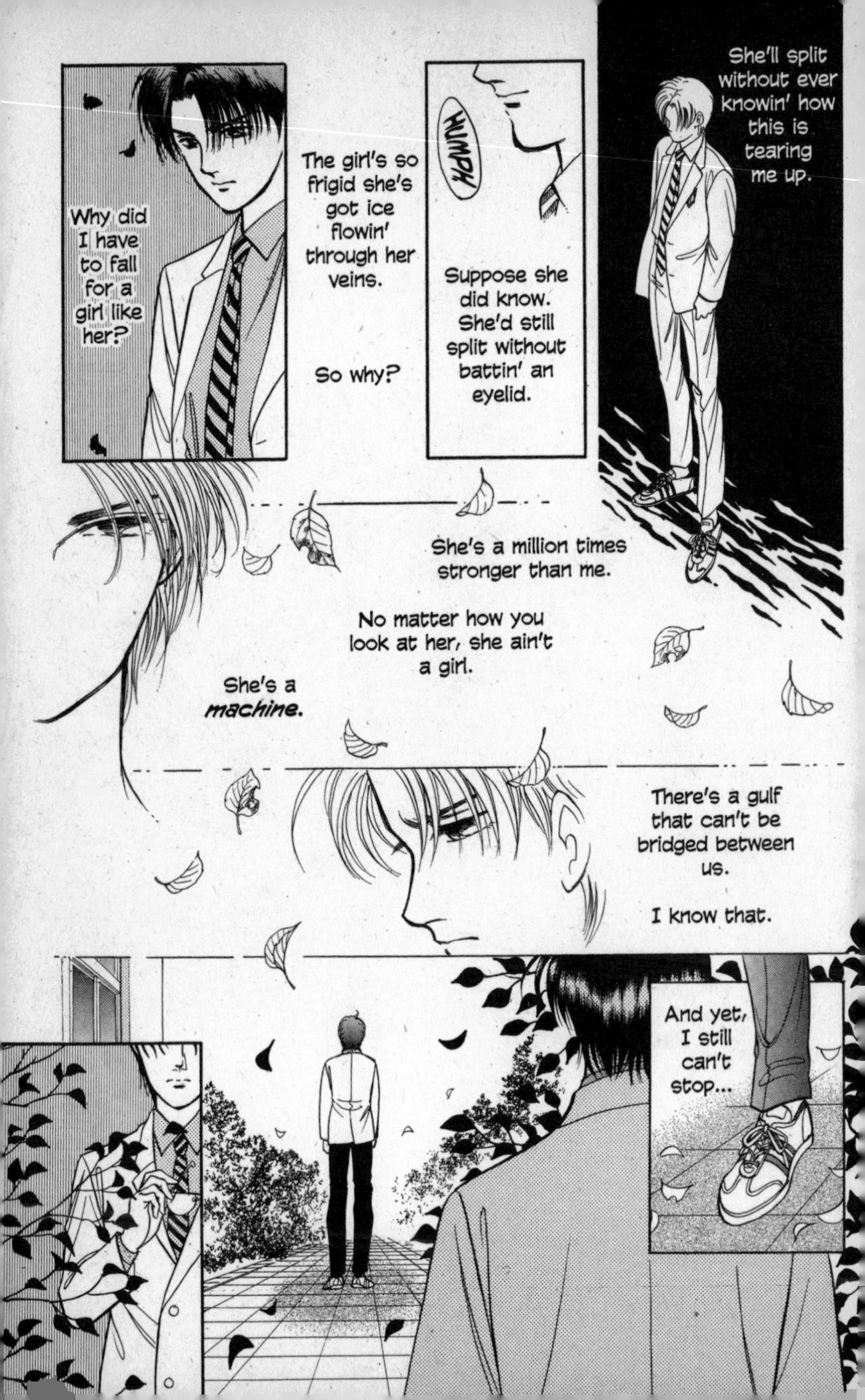
She'll split without ever knowin' how this is tearing me up.
HUMPH
Suppose she did know. She'd still split without battin' an eyelid.
The girl's so frigid she's got ice flowin' through her veins.
So why?
Why did I have to fall for a girl like her?
She's a million times stronger than me.
No matter how you look at her, she ain't a girl.
She's a *machine*.
There's a gulf that can't be bridged between us.
I know that.
And yet, I still can't stop...

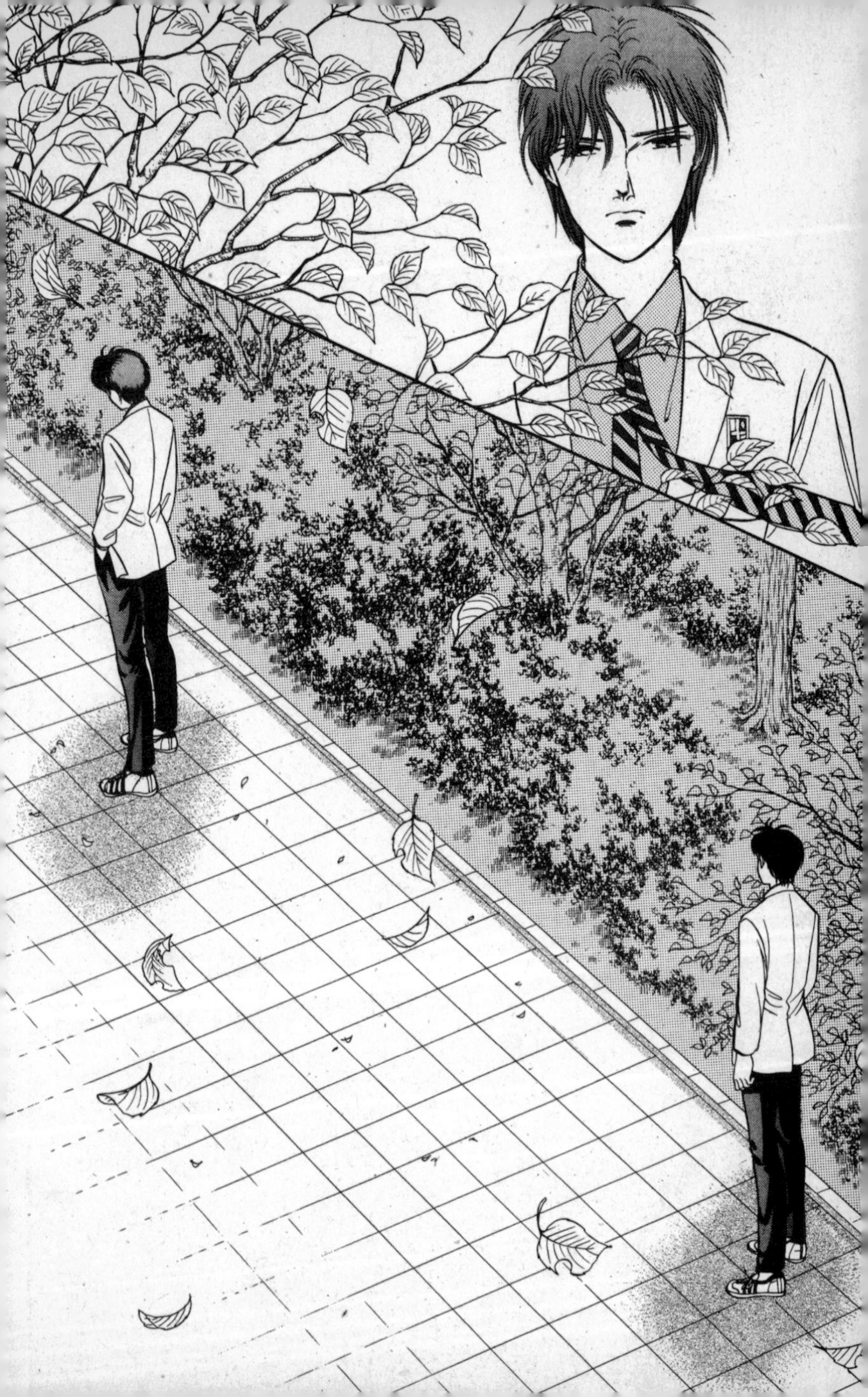

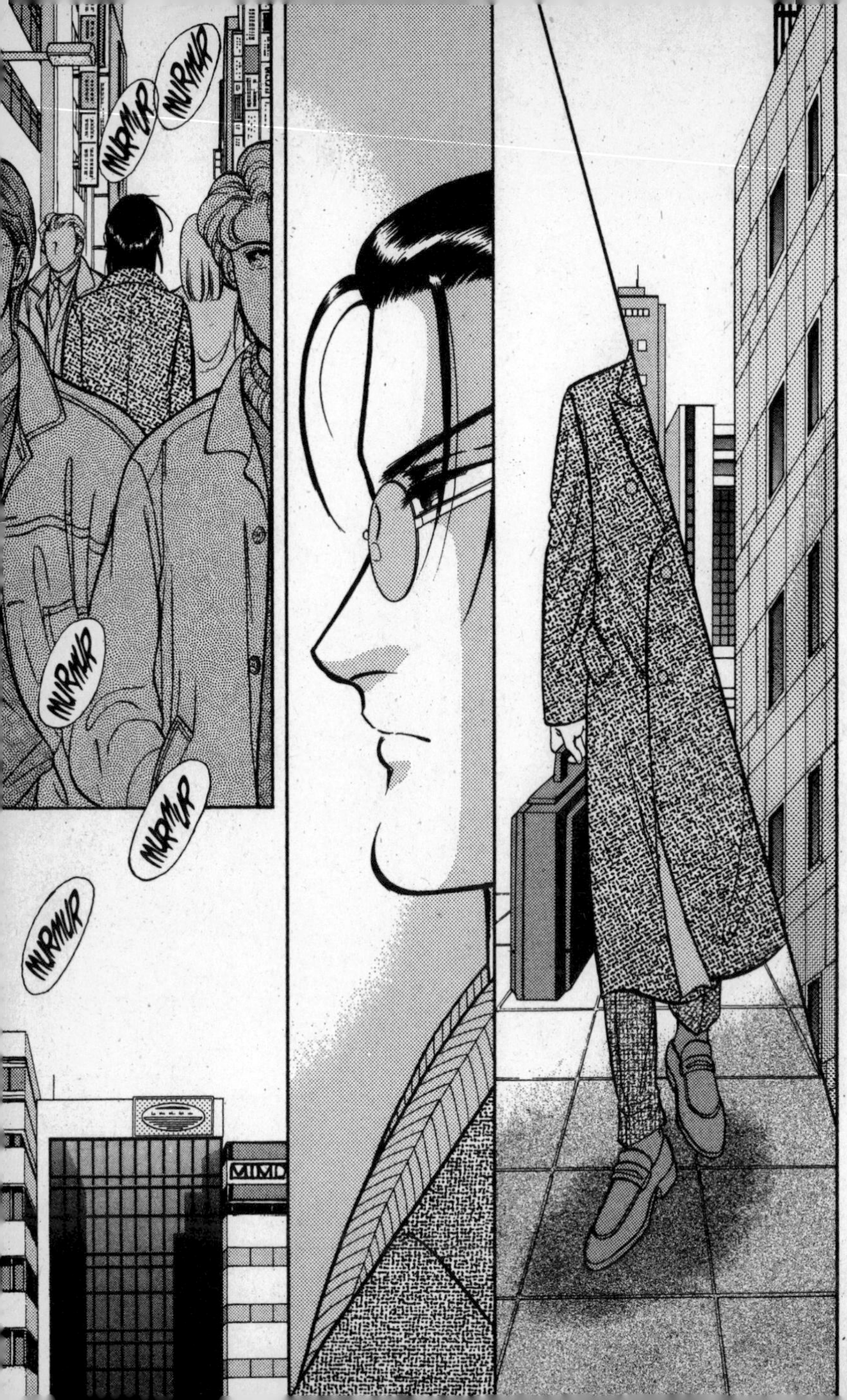
MURMUR
MURMUR
MURMUR
MURMUR
MURMUR

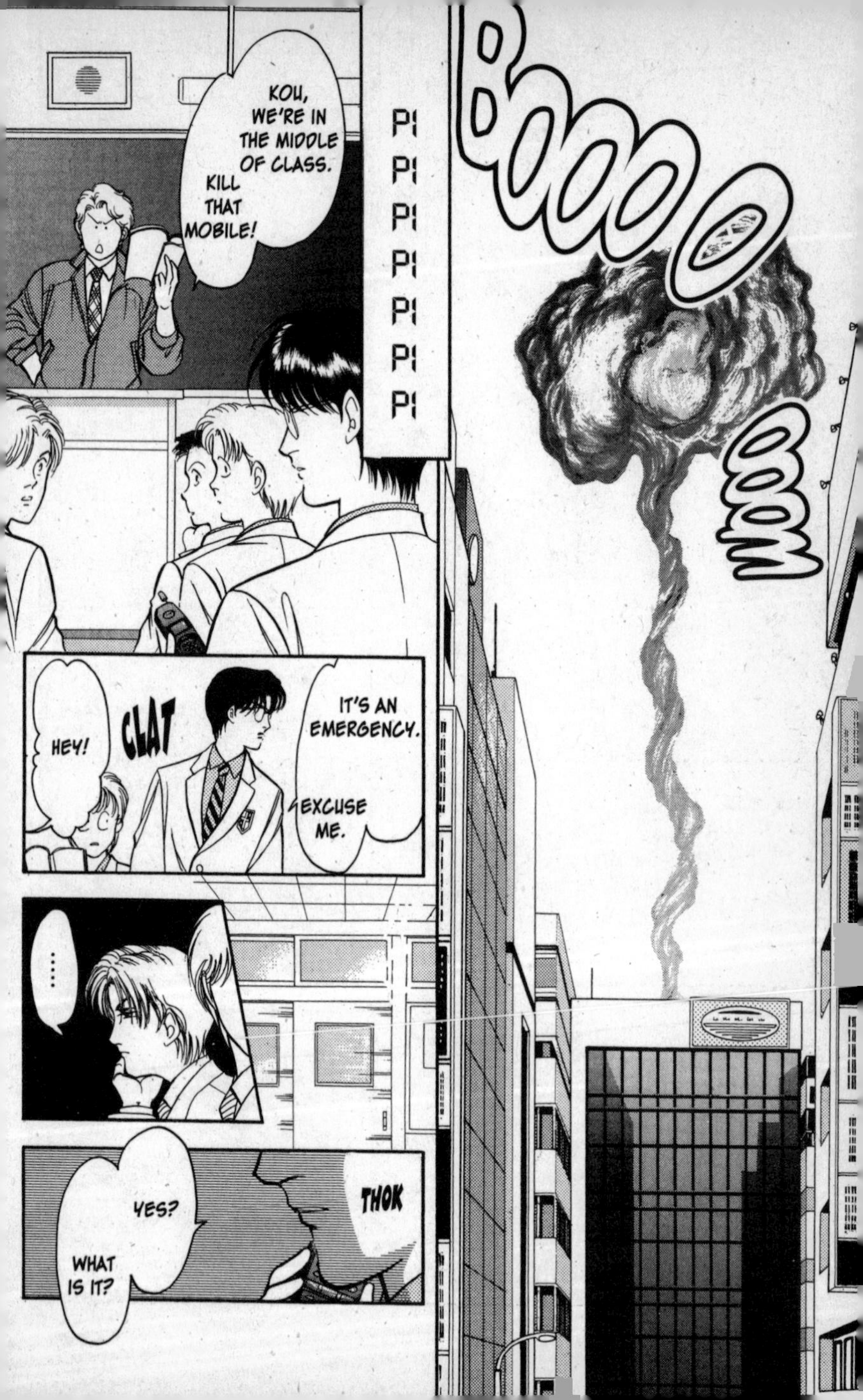
BOOOOOOOOM
PI PI PI PI PI PI PI
KOU, WE'RE IN THE MIDDLE OF CLASS.
KILL THAT MOBILE!
IT'S AN EMERGENCY.
EXCUSE ME.
CLAT
HEY!
.....
THOK
YES?
WHAT IS IT?

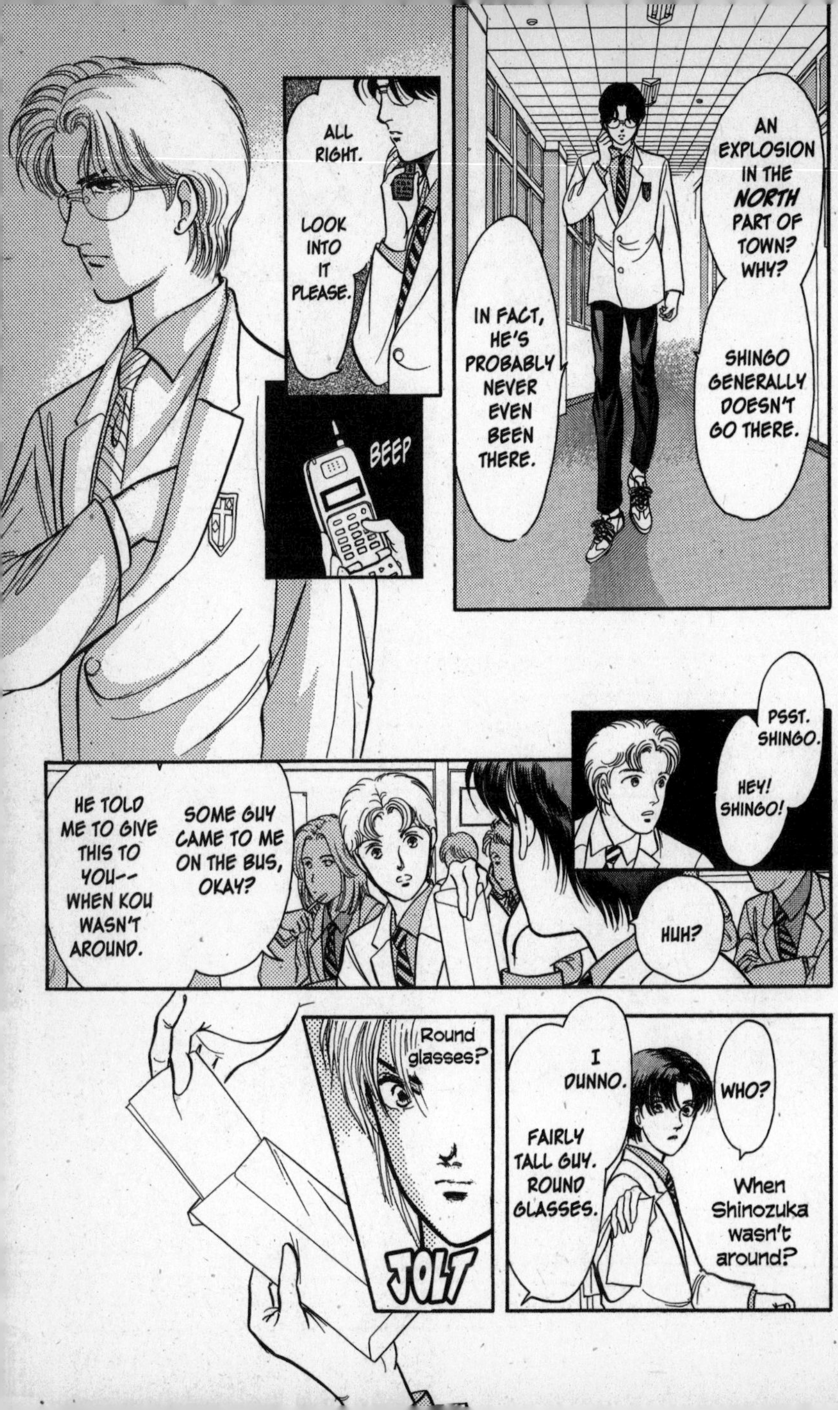
AN EXPLOSION IN THE NORTH PART OF TOWN? WHY?
SHINGO GENERALLY DOESN'T GO THERE.
IN FACT, HE'S PROBABLY NEVER EVEN BEEN THERE.
ALL RIGHT.
LOOK INTO IT PLEASE.
BEEP
PSST. SHINGO.
HEY! SHINGO!
HUH?
SOME GUY CAME TO ME ON THE BUS, OKAY?
HE TOLD ME TO GIVE THIS TO YOU-- WHEN KOU WASN'T AROUND.
WHO?
When Shinozuka wasn't around?
I DUNNO.
FAIRLY TALL GUY. ROUND GLASSES.
Round glasses?
JOLT

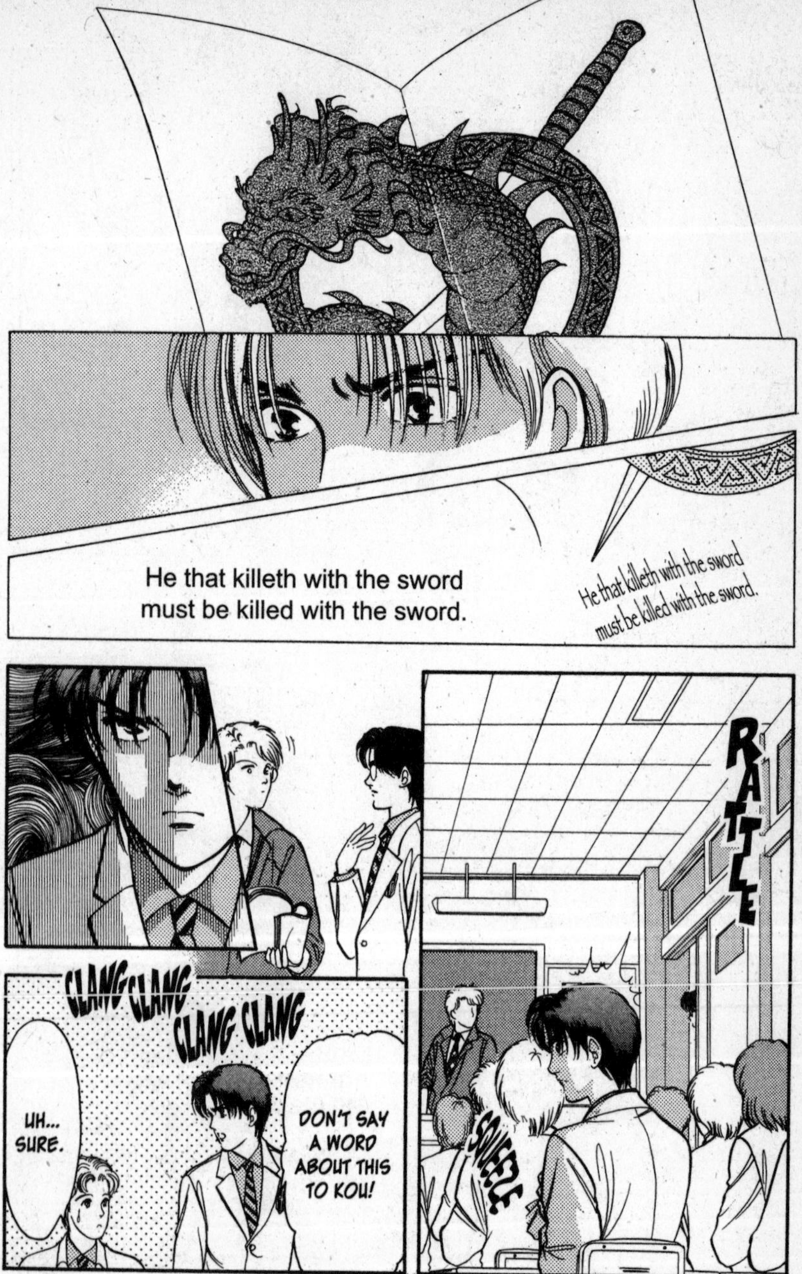
He that killeth with the sword must be killed with the sword.
He that killeth with the sword must be killed with the sword.
RATTLE
SQUEEZE
CLANG CLANG CLANG CLANG
DON'T SAY A WORD ABOUT THIS TO KOU!
UH... SURE.

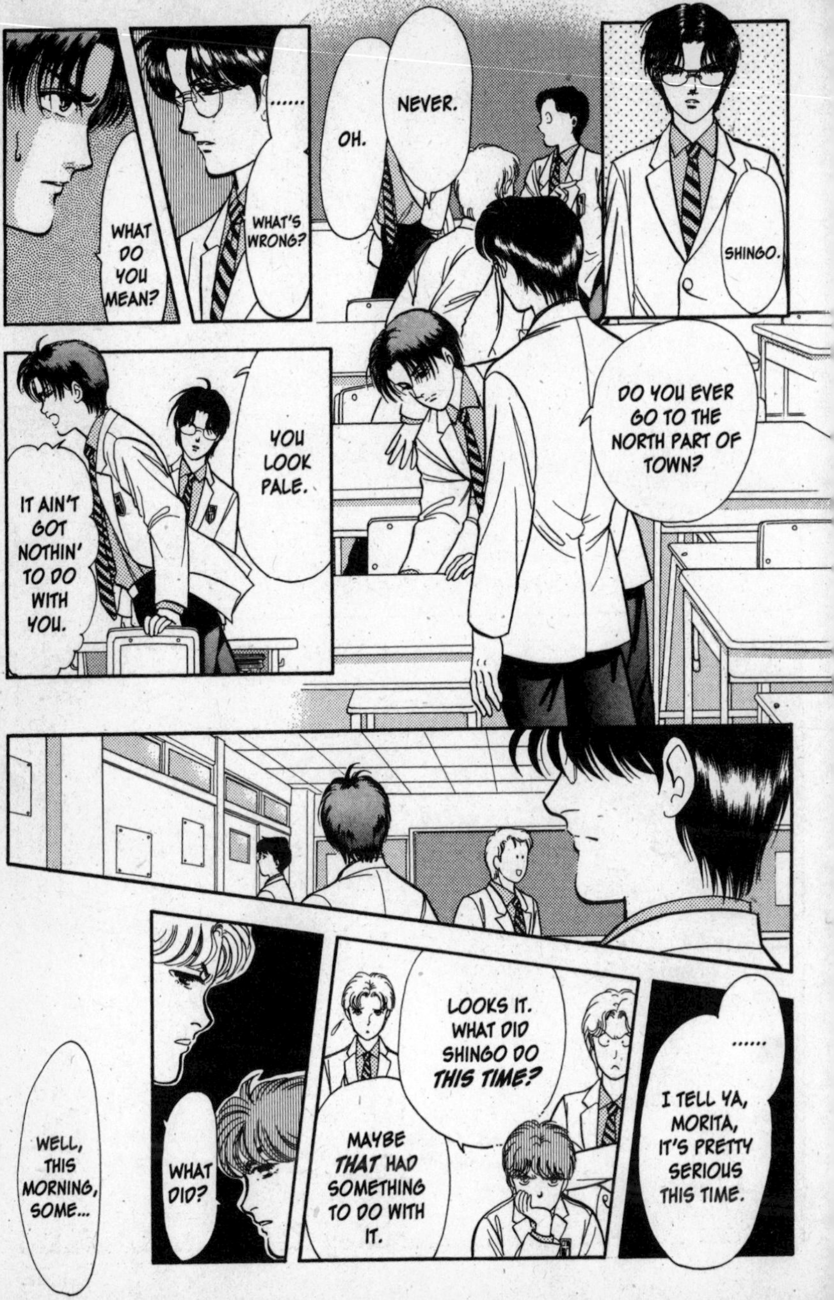
SHINGO.
DO YOU EVER GO TO THE NORTH PART OF TOWN?
NEVER.
OH.
......
WHAT'S WRONG?
WHAT DO YOU MEAN?
YOU LOOK PALE.
IT AIN'T GOT NOTHIN' TO DO WITH YOU.
......
I TELL YA, MORITA, IT'S PRETTY SERIOUS THIS TIME.
LOOKS IT. WHAT DID SHINGO DO THIS TIME?
MAYBE THAT HAD SOMETHING TO DO WITH IT.
WHAT DID?
WELL, THIS MORNING, SOME...

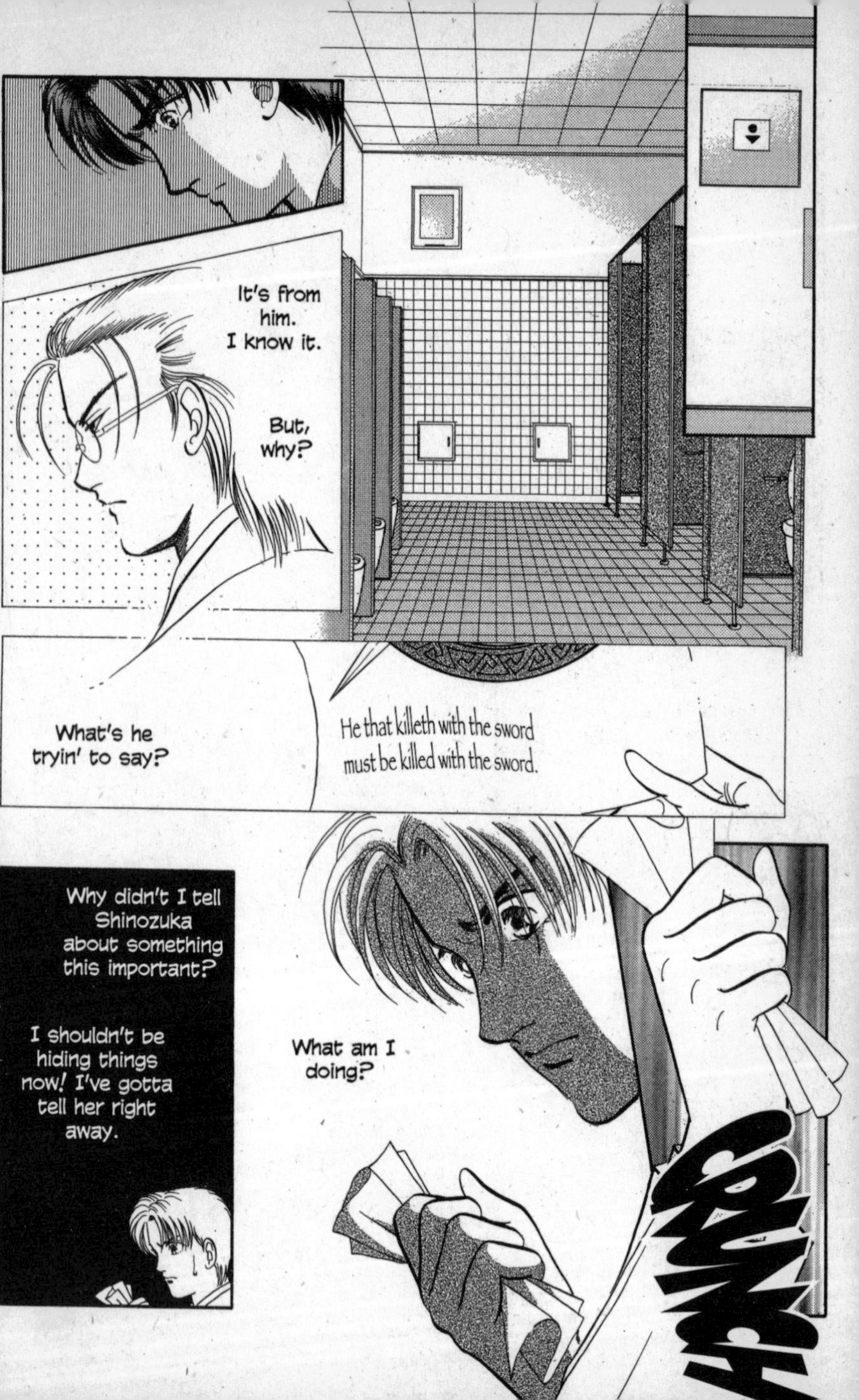
It's from him. I know it.
But, why?
He that killeth with the sword must be killed with the sword.
What's he tryin' to say?
What am I doing?
CRUNCH
Why didn't I tell Shinozuka about something this important?
I shouldn't be hiding things now! I've gotta tell her right away.

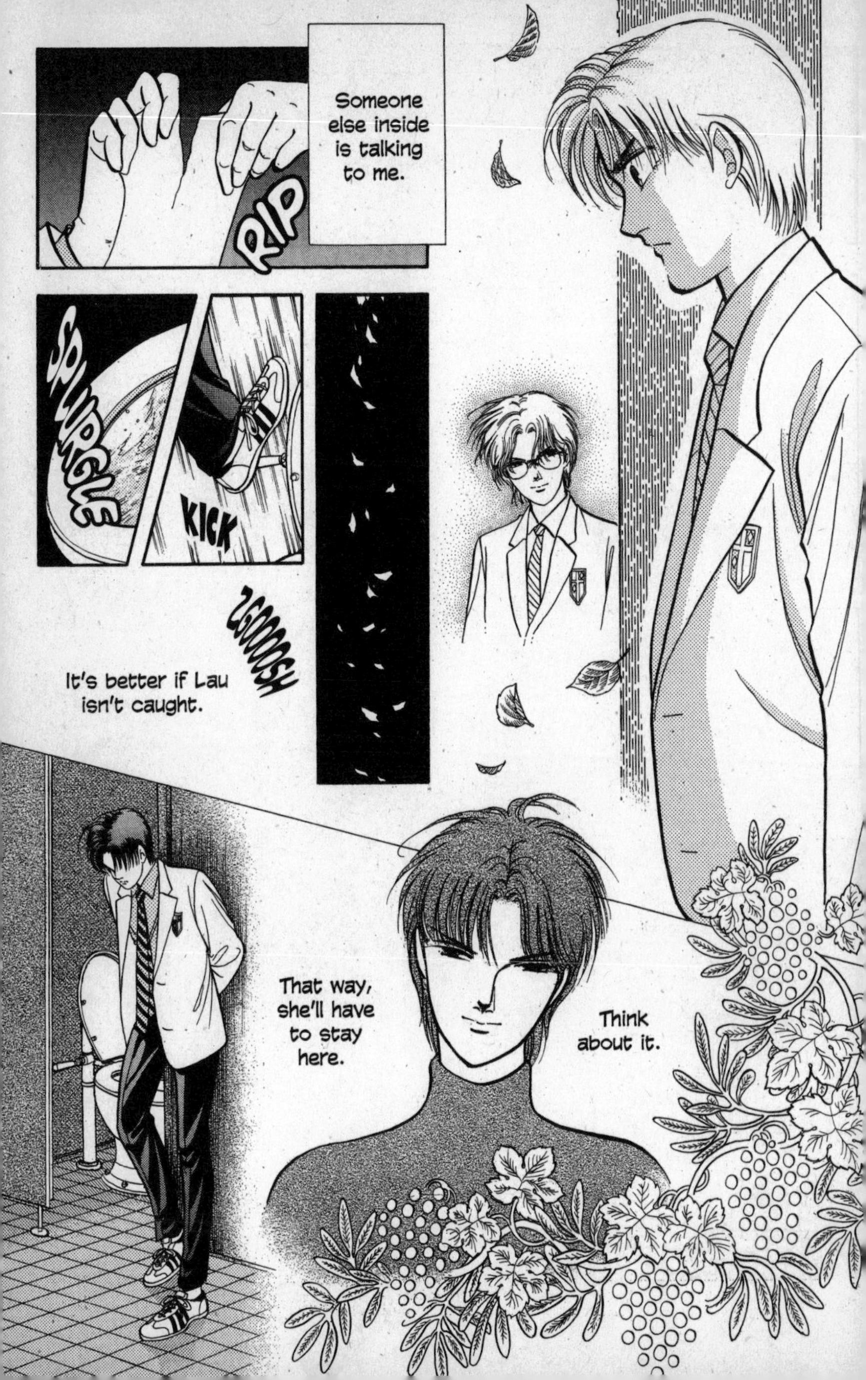
Someone else inside is talking to me.
RIP
KICK
SPLURGLE
ZGOOOOSH
It's better if Lau isn't caught.
Think about it.
That way, she'll have to stay here.

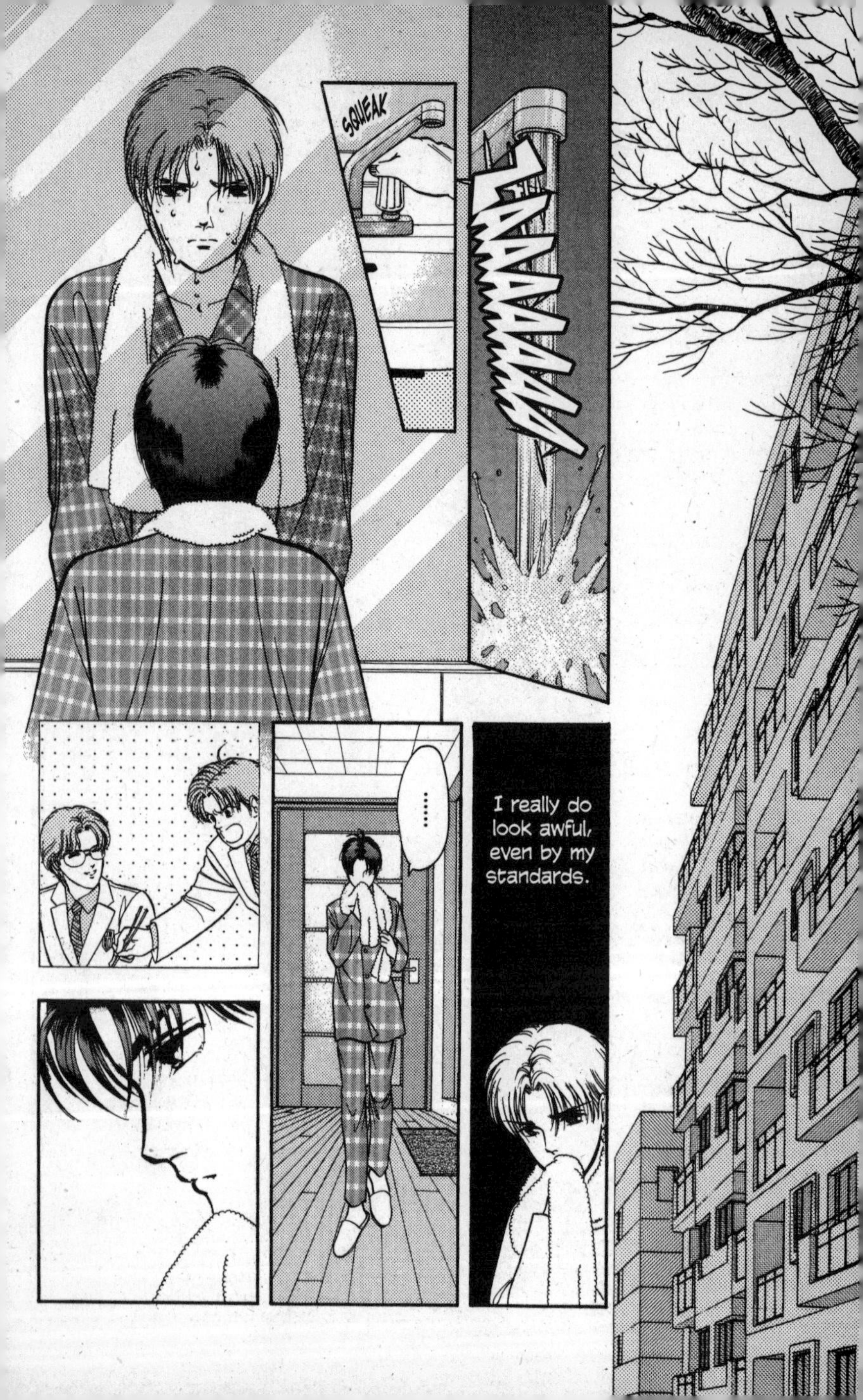
ZAAAAAAA
SQUEAK
I really do look awful, even by my standards.
......

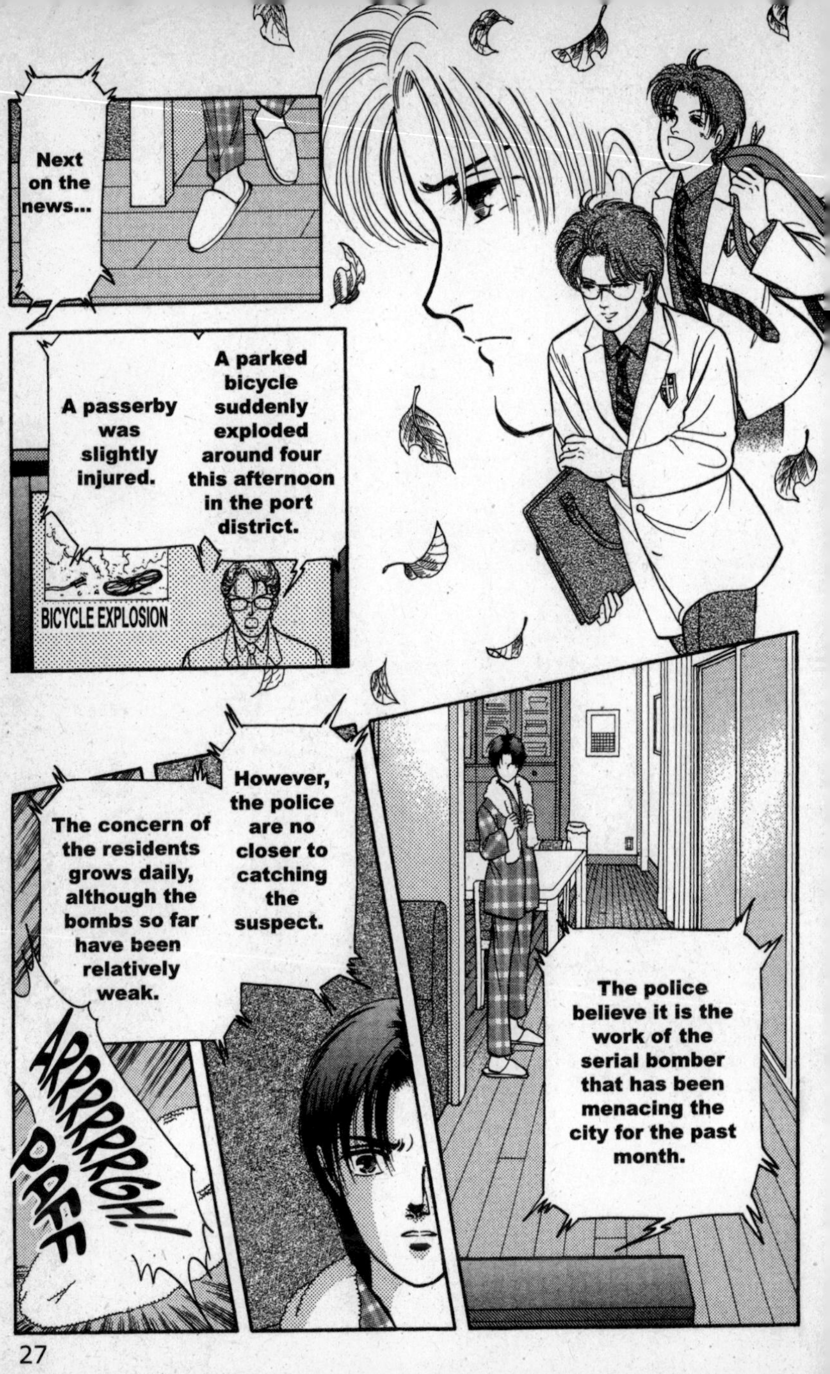
Next on the news...
A parked bicycle suddenly exploded around four this afternoon in the port district.
A passerby was slightly injured.
BICYCLE EXPLOSION
The police believe it is the work of the serial bomber that has been menacing the city for the past month.
However, the police are no closer to catching the suspect.
The concern of the residents grows daily, although the bombs so far have been relatively weak.
ARRRRRGH!
PAFF

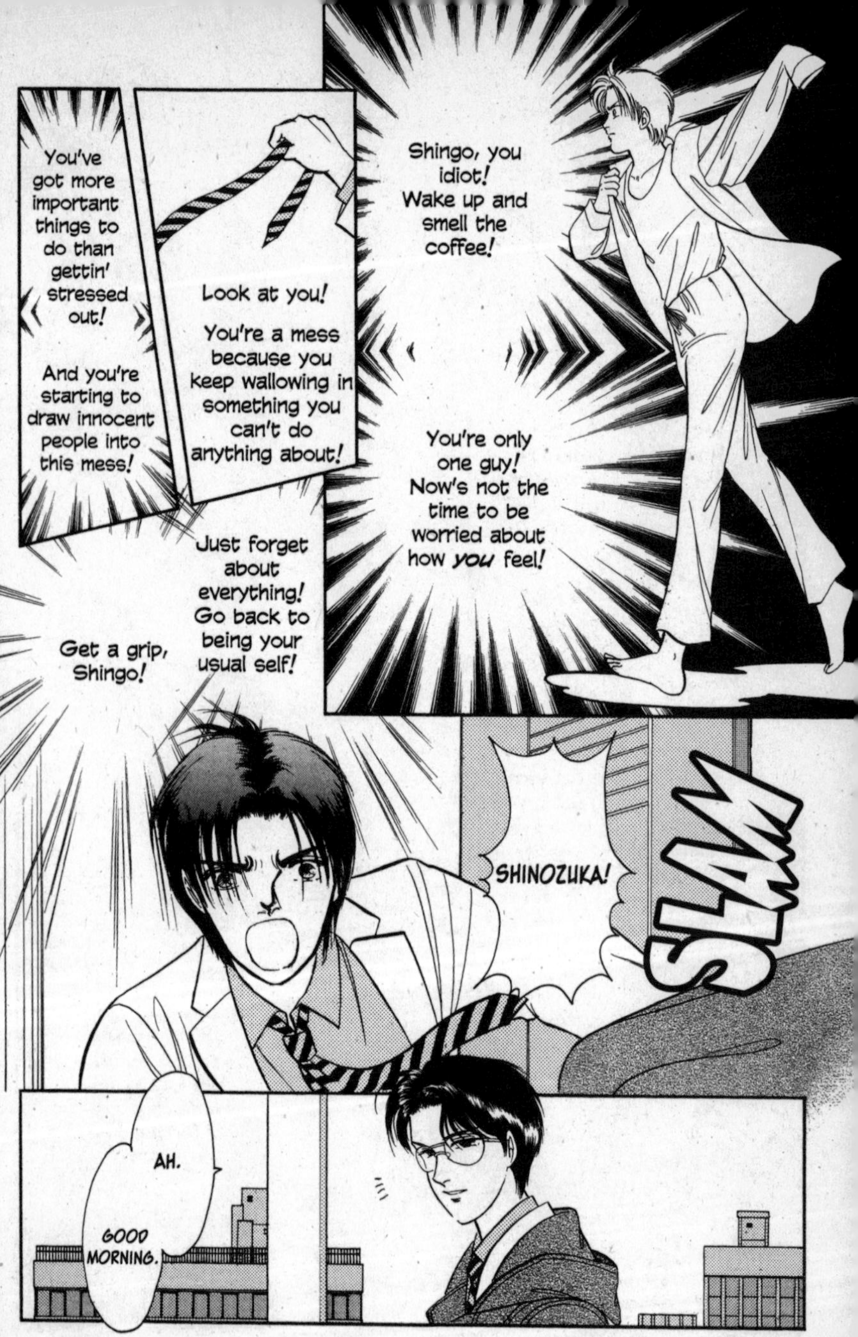

Shingo, you idiot! Wake up and smell the coffee!
You're only one guy! Now's not the time to be worried about how *you* feel!
Look at you!
You're a mess because you keep wallowing in something you can't do anything about!
You've got more important things to do than gettin' stressed out!
And you're starting to draw innocent people into this mess!
Just forget about everything! Go back to being your usual self!
Get a grip, Shingo!
SHINOZUKA!
SLAM
AH.
GOOD MORNING.

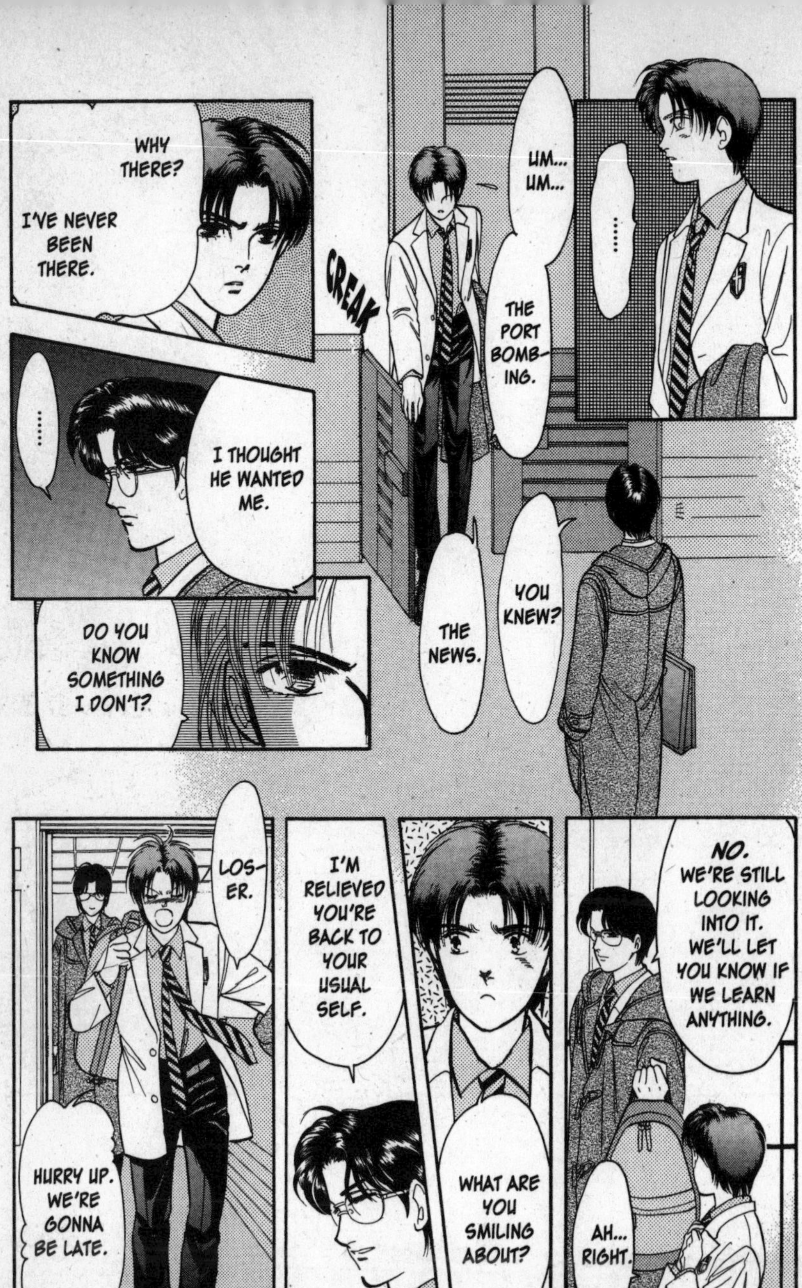
......
UM... UM...
CREAK
THE PORT BOMB-ING.
YOU KNEW?
THE NEWS.
WHY THERE?
I'VE NEVER BEEN THERE.
......
I THOUGHT HE WANTED ME.
DO YOU KNOW SOMETHING I DON'T?
NO. WE'RE STILL LOOKING INTO IT. WE'LL LET YOU KNOW IF WE LEARN ANYTHING.
AH... RIGHT.
WHAT ARE YOU SMILING ABOUT?
I'M RELIEVED YOU'RE BACK TO YOUR USUAL SELF.
LOS-ER.
HURRY UP. WE'RE GONNA BE LATE.

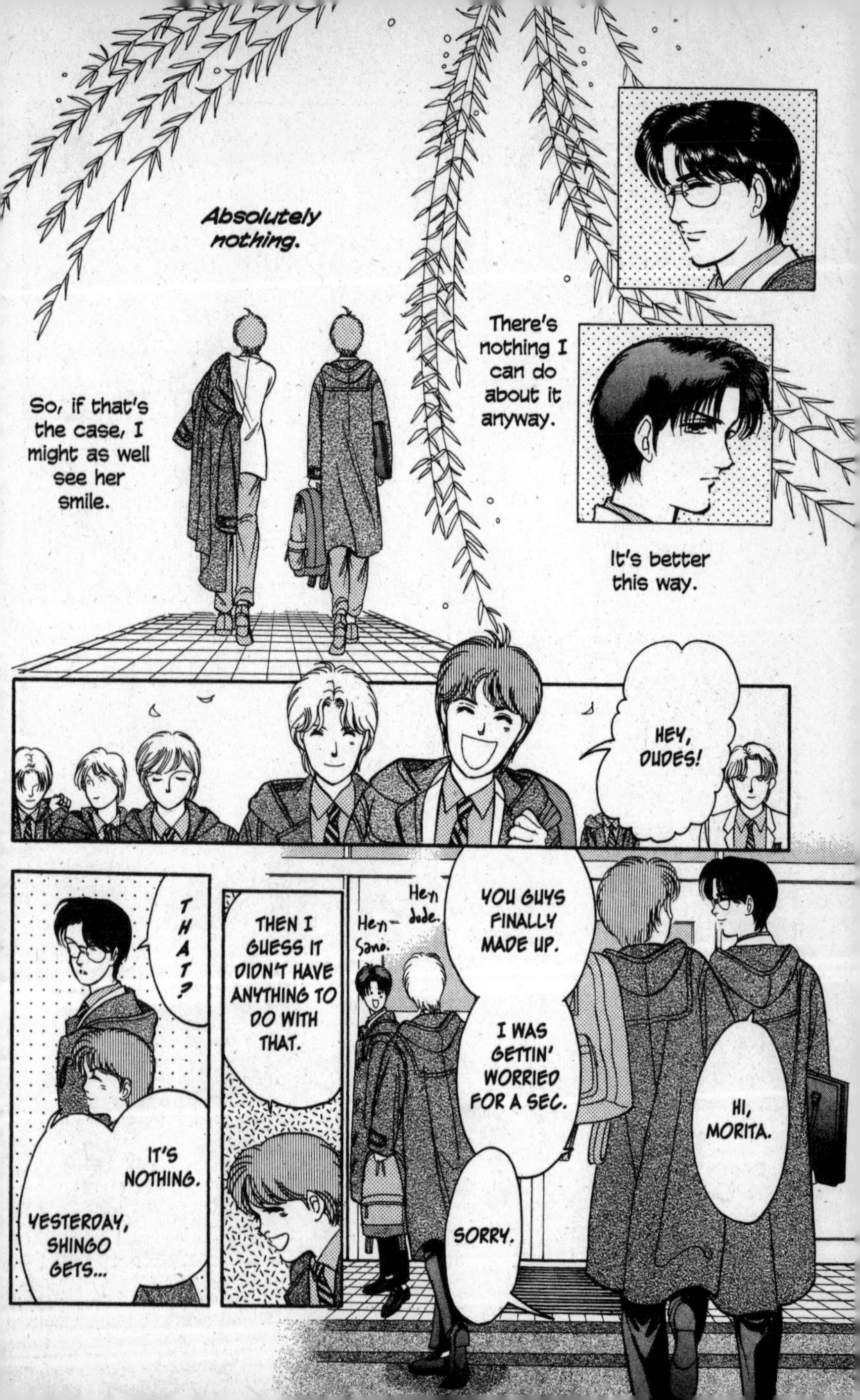
There's nothing I can do about it anyway.
Absolutely nothing.
It's better this way.
So, if that's the case, I might as well see her smile.
HEY, DUDES!
YOU GUYS FINALLY MADE UP.
I WAS GETTIN' WORRIED FOR A SEC.
SORRY.
HI, MORITA.
Hey, dude.
Hey- Sano.
THEN I GUESS IT DIDN'T HAVE ANYTHING TO DO WITH THAT.
THAT?
IT'S NOTHING.
YESTERDAY, SHINGO GETS...

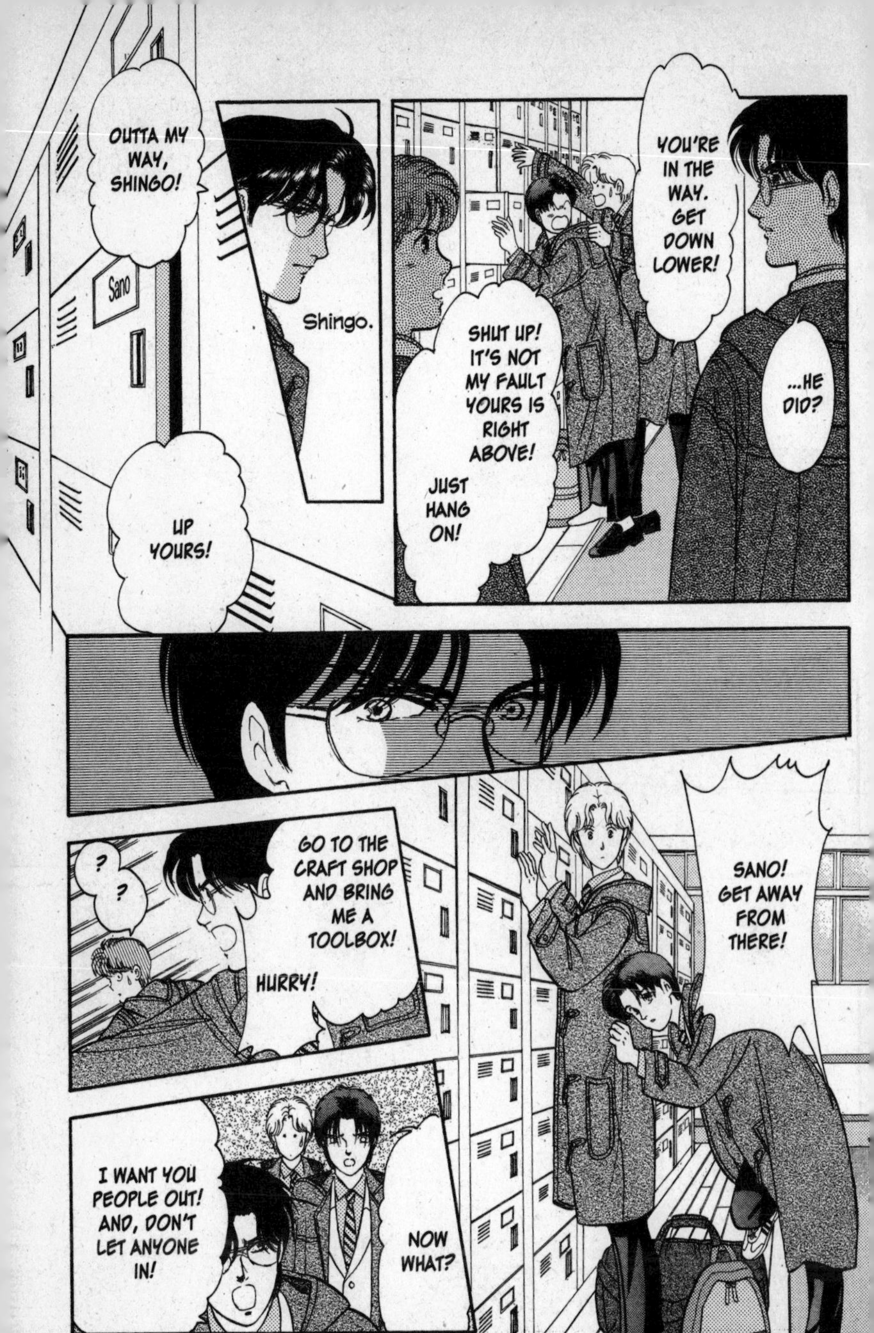

YOU'RE IN THE WAY. GET DOWN LOWER!
SHUT UP! IT'S NOT MY FAULT YOURS IS RIGHT ABOVE!
JUST HANG ON!
...HE DID?
OUTTA MY WAY, SHINGO!
Sano
Shingo.
UP YOURS!
SANO! GET AWAY FROM THERE!
? ?
GO TO THE CRAFT SHOP AND BRING ME A TOOLBOX!
HURRY!
NOW WHAT?
I WANT YOU PEOPLE OUT! AND, DON'T LET ANYONE IN!

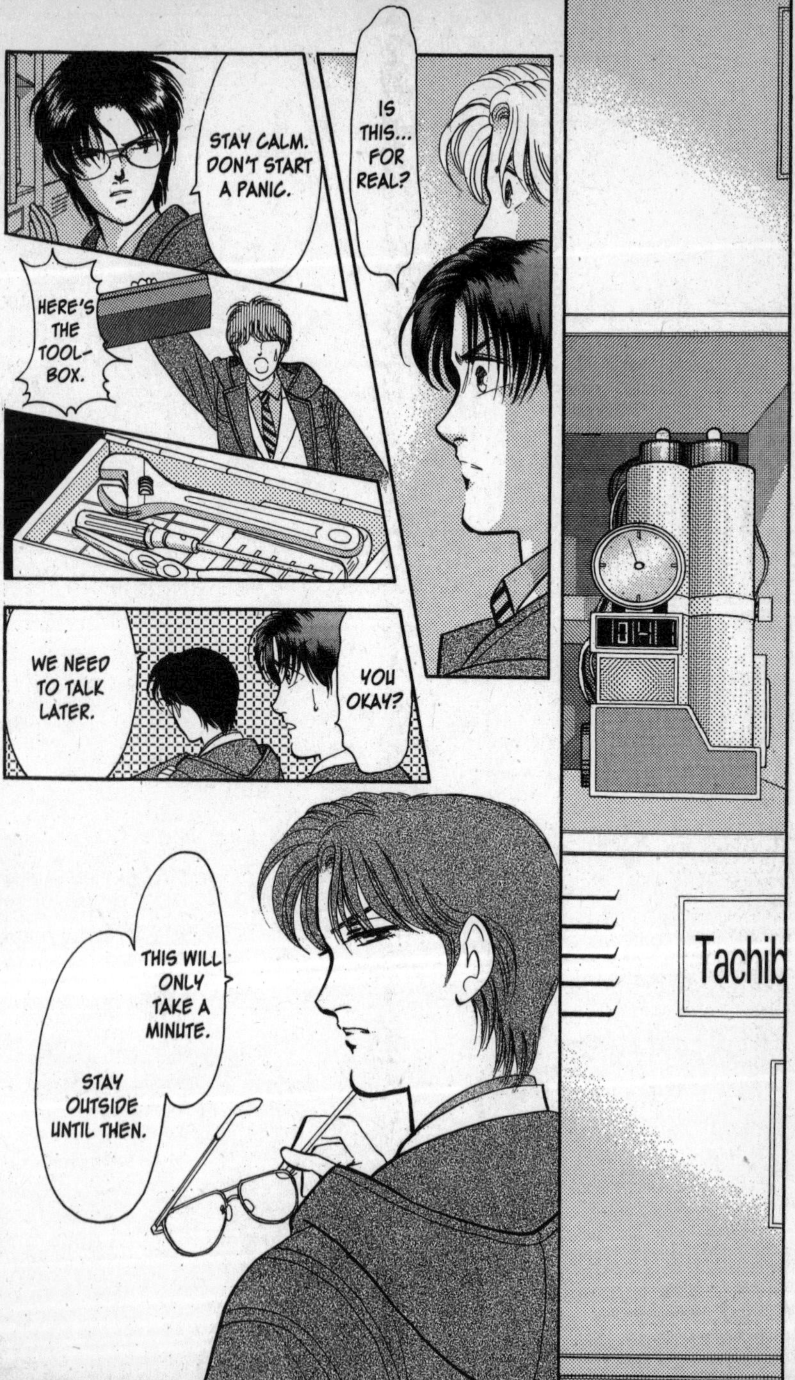
Tachib
IS THIS... FOR REAL?
STAY CALM. DON'T START A PANIC.
HERE'S THE TOOL-BOX.
YOU OKAY?
WE NEED TO TALK LATER.
THIS WILL ONLY TAKE A MINUTE.
STAY OUTSIDE UNTIL THEN.

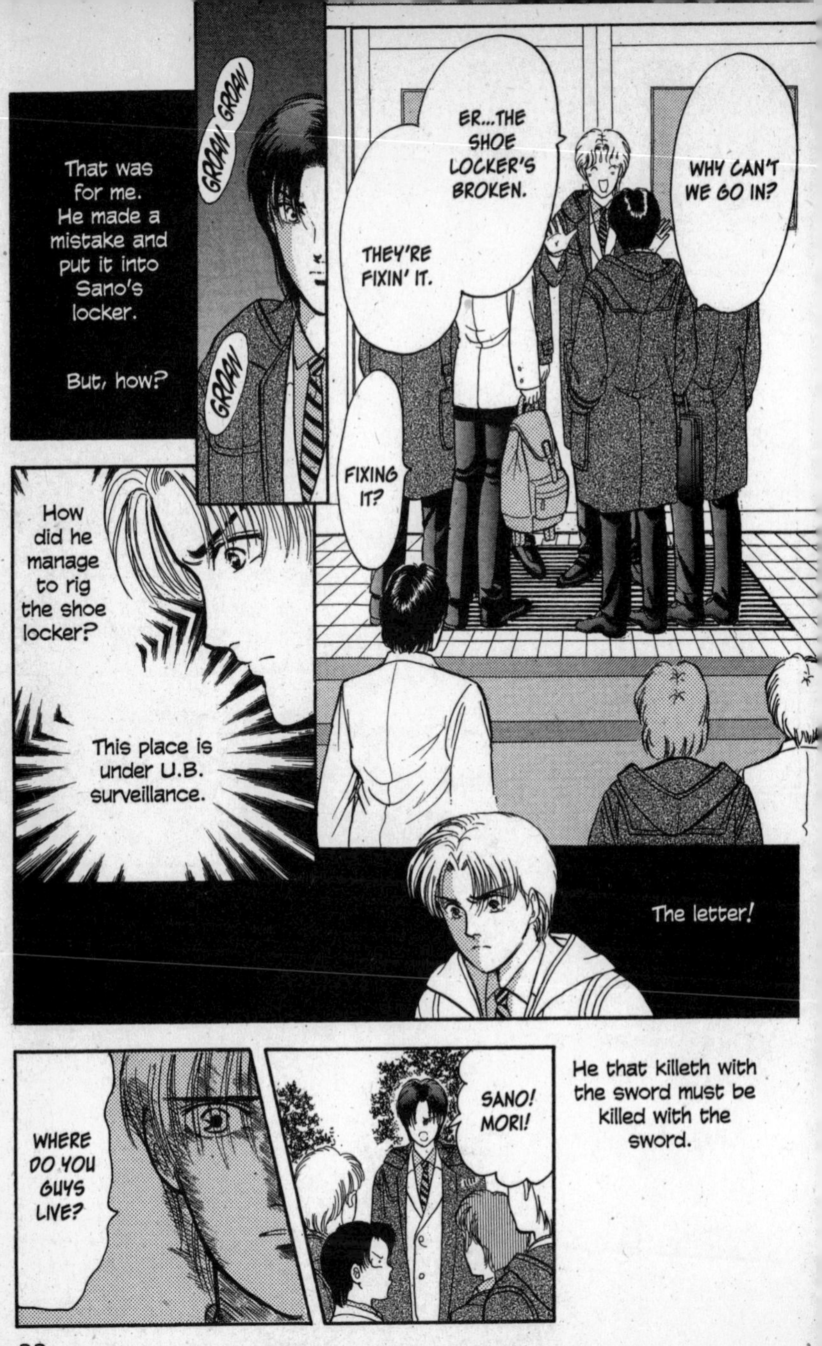
WHY CAN'T WE GO IN?
ER...THE SHOE LOCKER'S BROKEN.
THEY'RE FIXIN' IT.
FIXING IT?
GROAN GROAN
That was for me. He made a mistake and put it into Sano's locker.
But, how?
GROAN
How did he manage to rig the shoe locker?
This place is under U.B. surveillance.
The letter!
He that killeth with the sword must be killed with the sword.
SANO! MORI!
WHERE DO YOU GUYS LIVE?

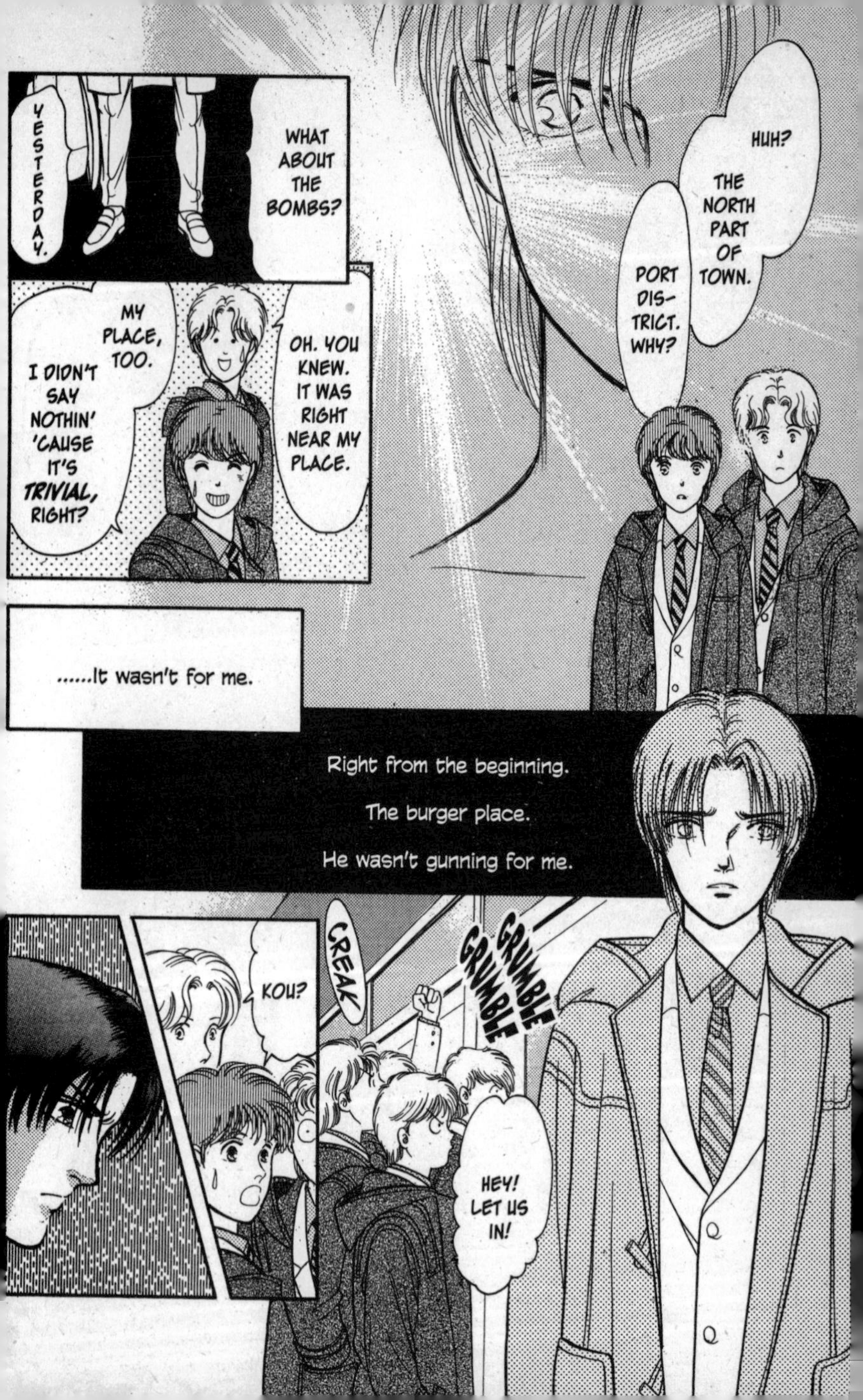
HUH? THE NORTH PART OF TOWN.
PORT DISTRICT. WHY?
WHAT ABOUT THE BOMBS?
YESTERDAY.
OH. YOU KNEW. IT WAS RIGHT NEAR MY PLACE.
MY PLACE, TOO.
I DIDN'T SAY NOTHIN' 'CAUSE IT'S *TRIVIAL*, RIGHT?
......It wasn't for me.
Right from the beginning.
The burger place.
He wasn't gunning for me.
GRUMBLE GRUMBLE
CREAK
HEY! LET US IN!
KOU?

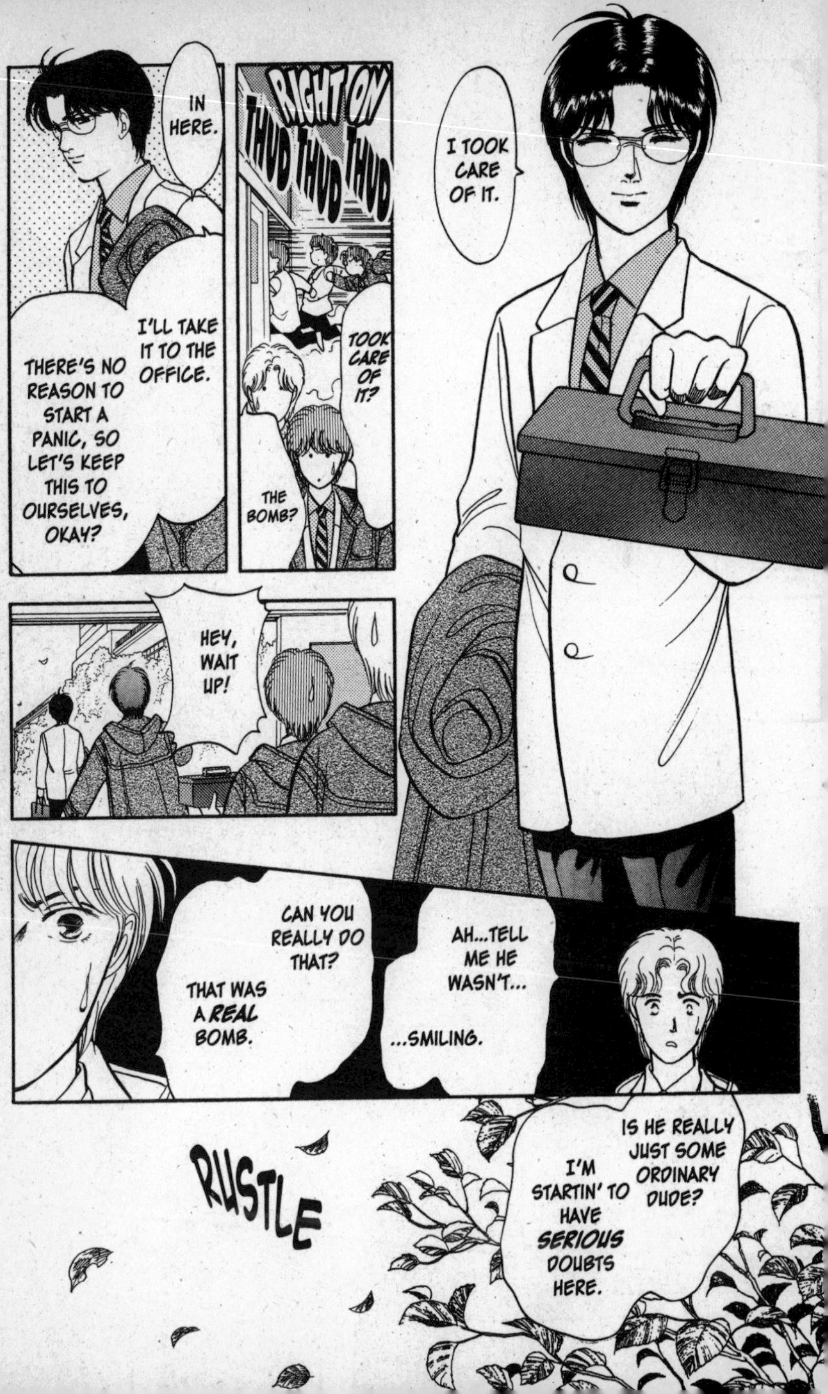
I TOOK CARE OF IT.
RIGHT ON
THUD THUD THUD
TOOK CARE OF IT?
THE BOMB?
IN HERE.
I'LL TAKE IT TO THE OFFICE.
THERE'S NO REASON TO START A PANIC, SO LET'S KEEP THIS TO OURSELVES, OKAY?
HEY, WAIT UP!
AH...TELL ME HE WASN'T...
...SMILING.
CAN YOU REALLY DO THAT?
THAT WAS A *REAL* BOMB.
IS HE REALLY JUST SOME ORDINARY DUDE?
I'M STARTIN' TO HAVE *SERIOUS* DOUBTS HERE.
RUSTLE

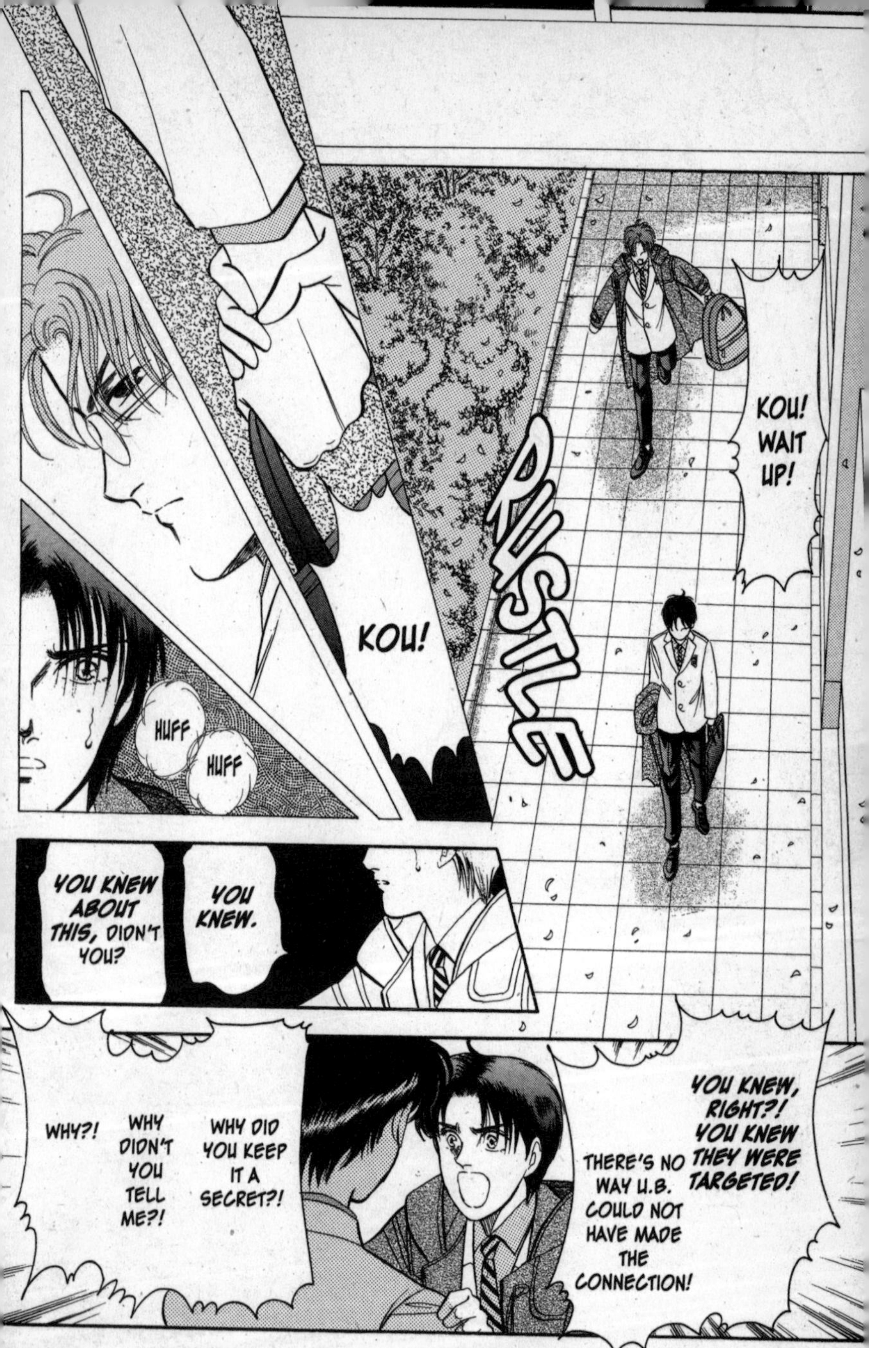
KOU! WAIT UP!
RUSTLE
KOU!
HUFF
HUFF
YOU KNEW.
YOU KNEW ABOUT THIS, DIDN'T YOU?
YOU KNEW, RIGHT?! YOU KNEW THEY WERE TARGETED!
THERE'S NO WAY U.B. COULD NOT HAVE MADE THE CONNECTION!
WHY DID YOU KEEP IT A SECRET?!
WHY DIDN'T YOU TELL ME?!
WHY?!

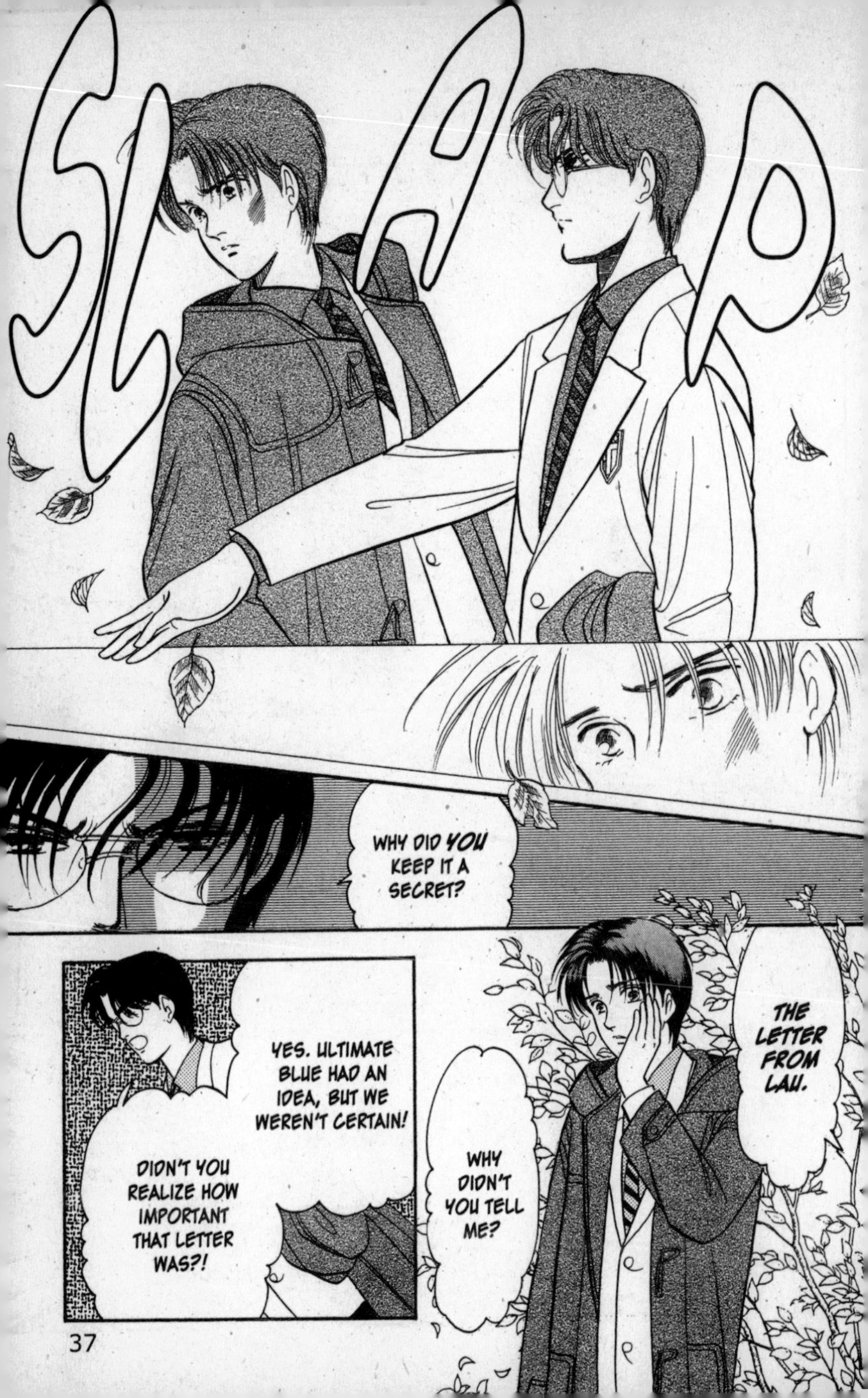
SLAP
WHY DID YOU KEEP IT A SECRET?
THE LETTER FROM LAU.
WHY DIDN'T YOU TELL ME?
YES. ULTIMATE BLUE HAD AN IDEA, BUT WE WEREN'T CERTAIN!
DIDN'T YOU REALIZE HOW IMPORTANT THAT LETTER WAS?!

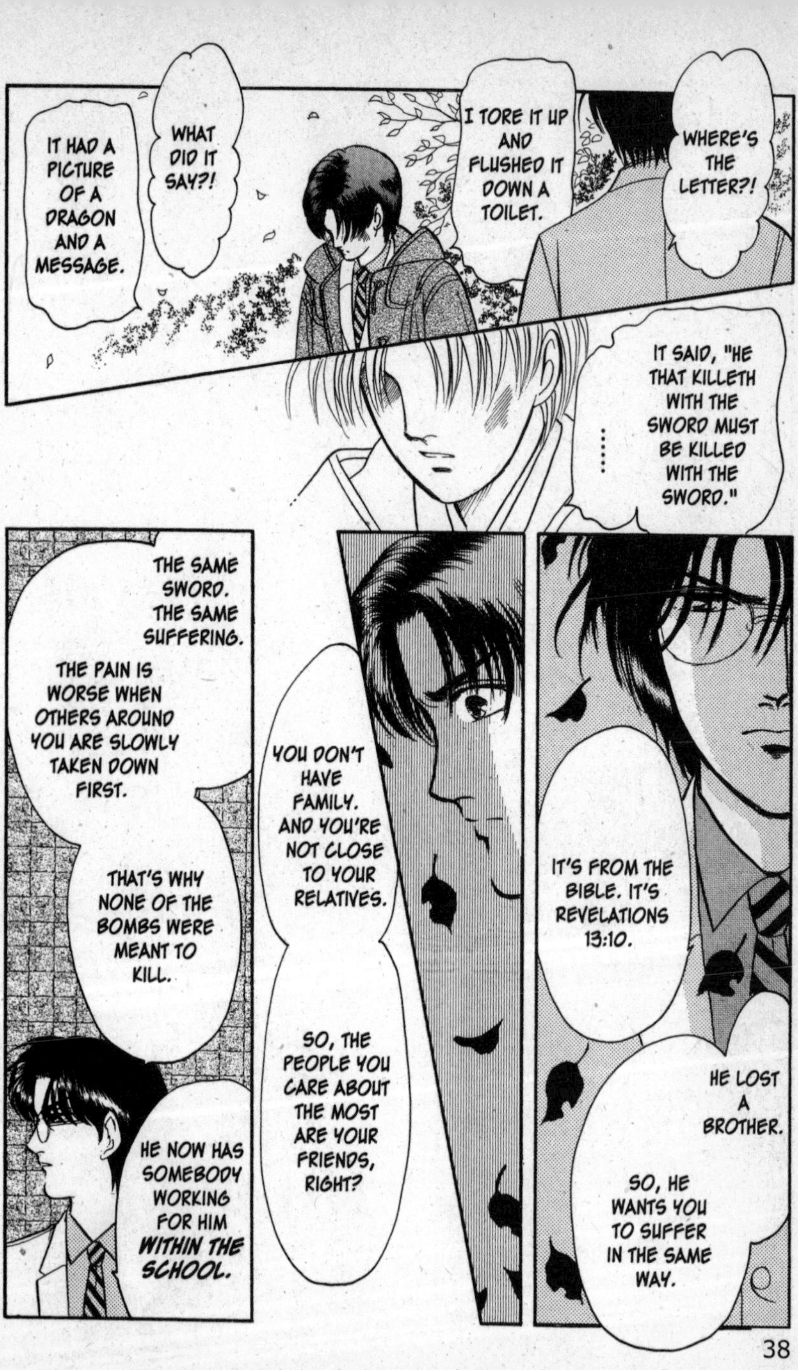
WHERE'S THE LETTER?!
I TORE IT UP AND FLUSHED IT DOWN A TOILET.
WHAT DID IT SAY?!
IT HAD A PICTURE OF A DRAGON AND A MESSAGE.
IT SAID, "HE THAT KILLETH WITH THE SWORD MUST BE KILLED WITH THE SWORD."
......
IT'S FROM THE BIBLE. IT'S REVELATIONS 13:10.
HE LOST A BROTHER.
SO, HE WANTS YOU TO SUFFER IN THE SAME WAY.
YOU DON'T HAVE FAMILY. AND YOU'RE NOT CLOSE TO YOUR RELATIVES.
SO, THE PEOPLE YOU CARE ABOUT THE MOST ARE YOUR FRIENDS, RIGHT?
THE SAME SWORD. THE SAME SUFFERING.
THE PAIN IS WORSE WHEN OTHERS AROUND YOU ARE SLOWLY TAKEN DOWN FIRST.
THAT'S WHY NONE OF THE BOMBS WERE MEANT TO KILL.
HE NOW HAS SOMEBODY WORKING FOR HIM *WITHIN THE SCHOOL.*

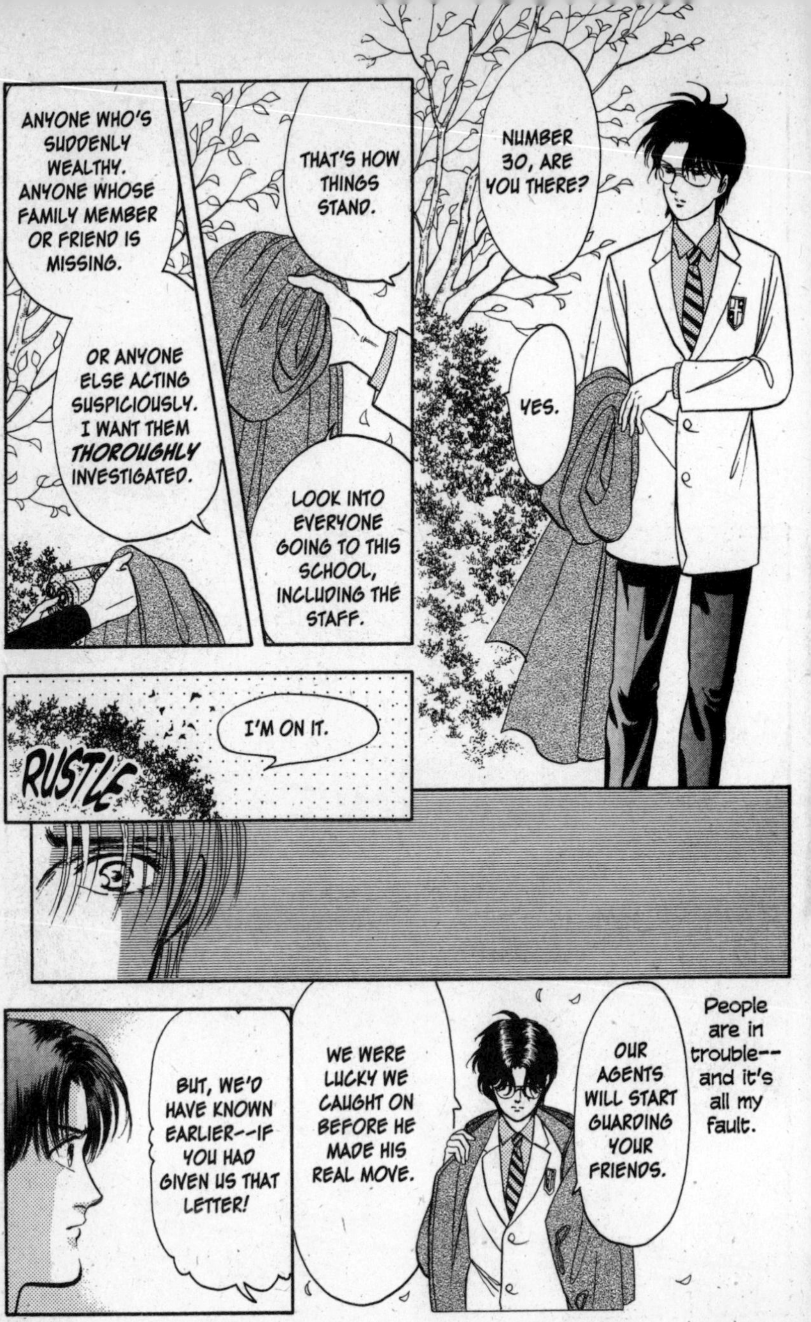
NUMBER 30, ARE YOU THERE?
YES.
THAT'S HOW THINGS STAND.
LOOK INTO EVERYONE GOING TO THIS SCHOOL, INCLUDING THE STAFF.
ANYONE WHO'S SUDDENLY WEALTHY. ANYONE WHOSE FAMILY MEMBER OR FRIEND IS MISSING.
OR ANYONE ELSE ACTING SUSPICIOUSLY. I WANT THEM *THOROUGHLY* INVESTIGATED.
I'M ON IT.
RUSTLE
People are in trouble--and it's all my fault.
OUR AGENTS WILL START GUARDING YOUR FRIENDS.
WE WERE LUCKY WE CAUGHT ON BEFORE HE MADE HIS REAL MOVE.
BUT, WE'D HAVE KNOWN EARLIER--IF YOU HAD GIVEN US THAT LETTER!

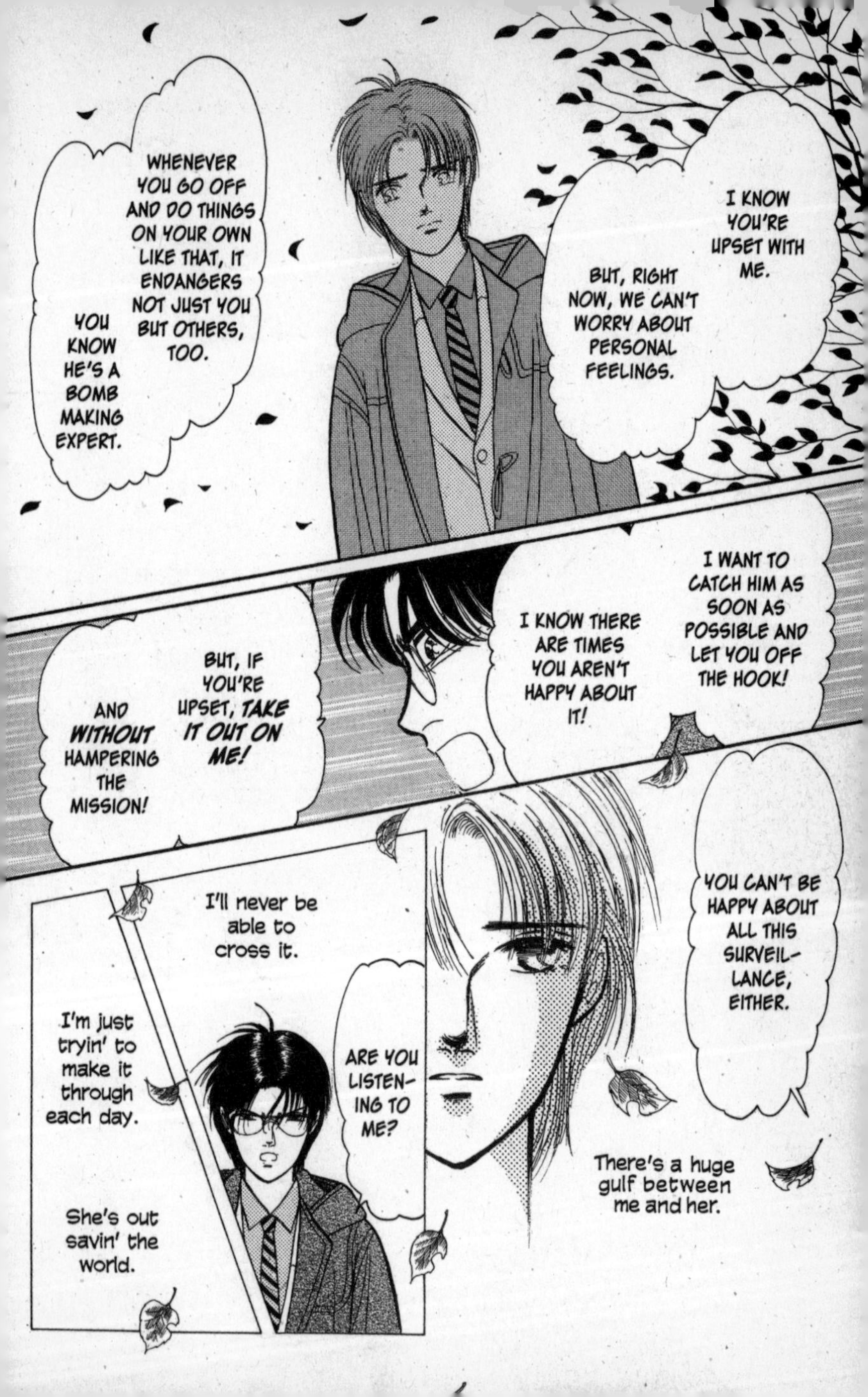
I KNOW YOU'RE UPSET WITH ME.
BUT, RIGHT NOW, WE CAN'T WORRY ABOUT PERSONAL FEELINGS.
WHENEVER YOU GO OFF AND DO THINGS ON YOUR OWN LIKE THAT, IT ENDANGERS NOT JUST YOU BUT OTHERS, TOO.
YOU KNOW HE'S A BOMB MAKING EXPERT.
I WANT TO CATCH HIM AS SOON AS POSSIBLE AND LET YOU OFF THE HOOK!
I KNOW THERE ARE TIMES YOU AREN'T HAPPY ABOUT IT!
BUT, IF YOU'RE UPSET, *TAKE IT OUT ON ME!*
AND *WITHOUT* HAMPERING THE MISSION!
YOU CAN'T BE HAPPY ABOUT ALL THIS SURVEIL-LANCE, EITHER.
There's a huge gulf between me and her.
I'll never be able to cross it.
ARE YOU LISTEN-ING TO ME?
I'm just tryin' to make it through each day.
She's out savin' the world.

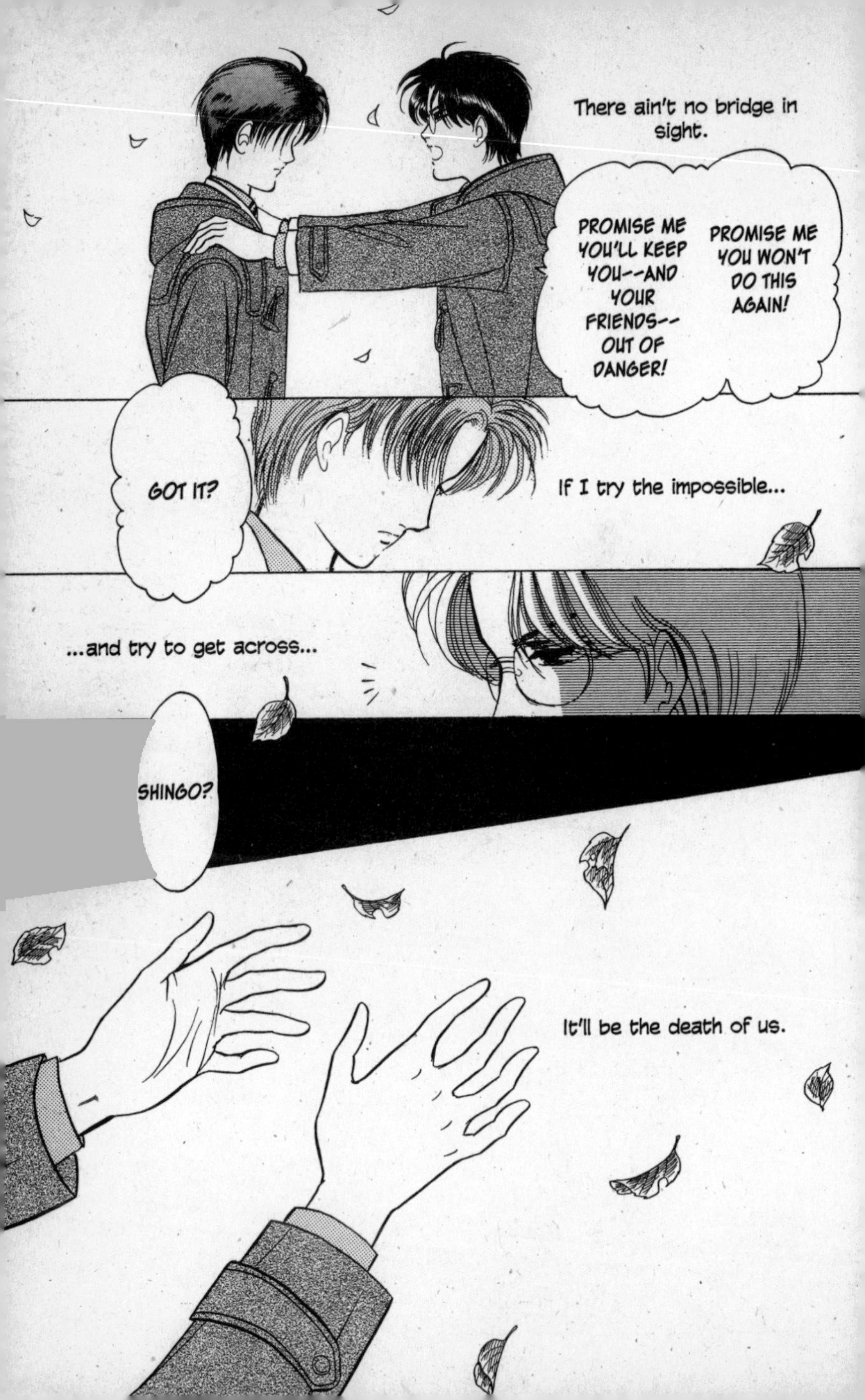
There ain't no bridge in sight.
PROMISE ME YOU WON'T DO THIS AGAIN!
PROMISE ME YOU'LL KEEP YOU--AND YOUR FRIENDS--OUT OF DANGER!
If I try the impossible...
GOT IT?
...and try to get across...
SHINGO?
It'll be the death of us.

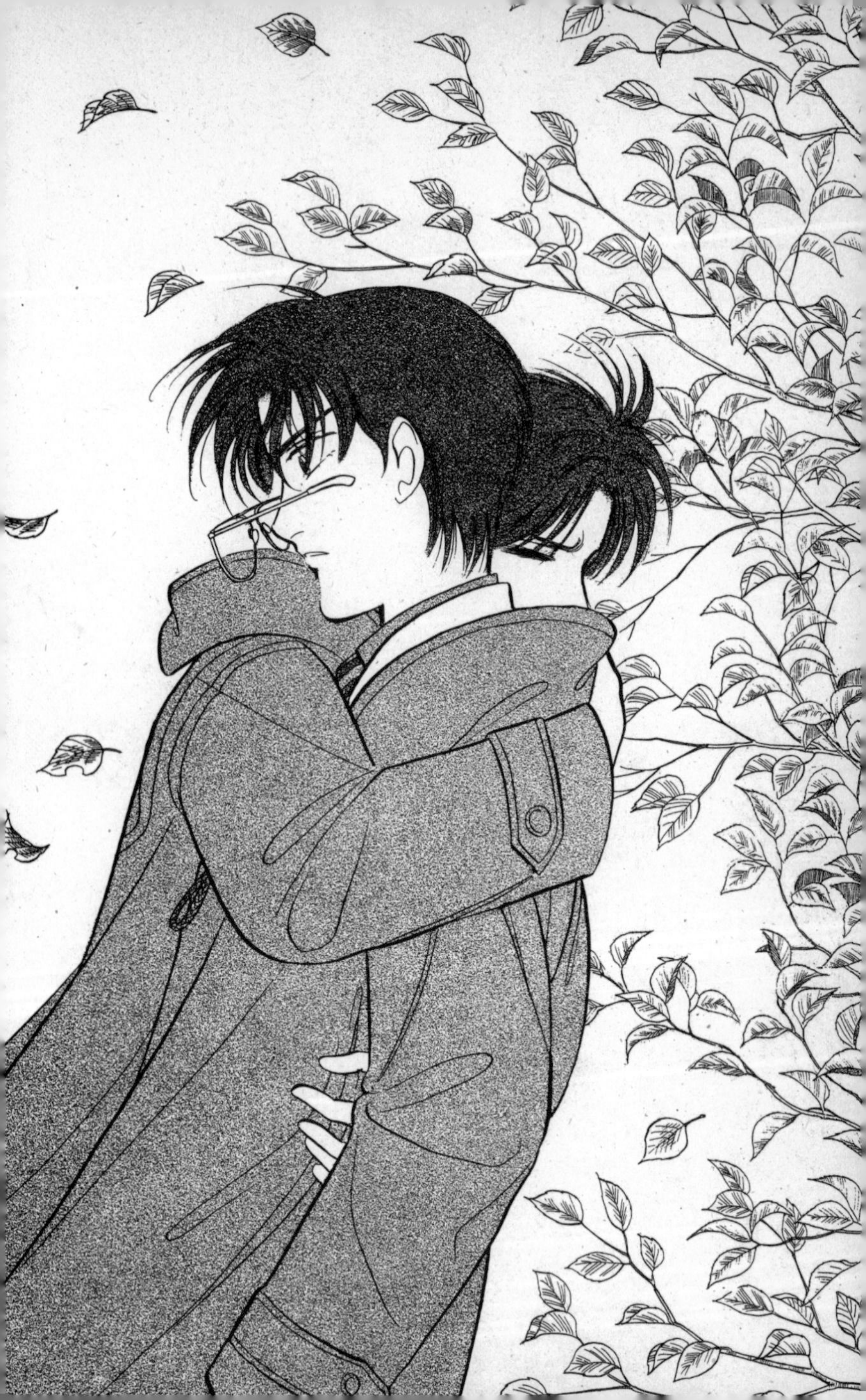

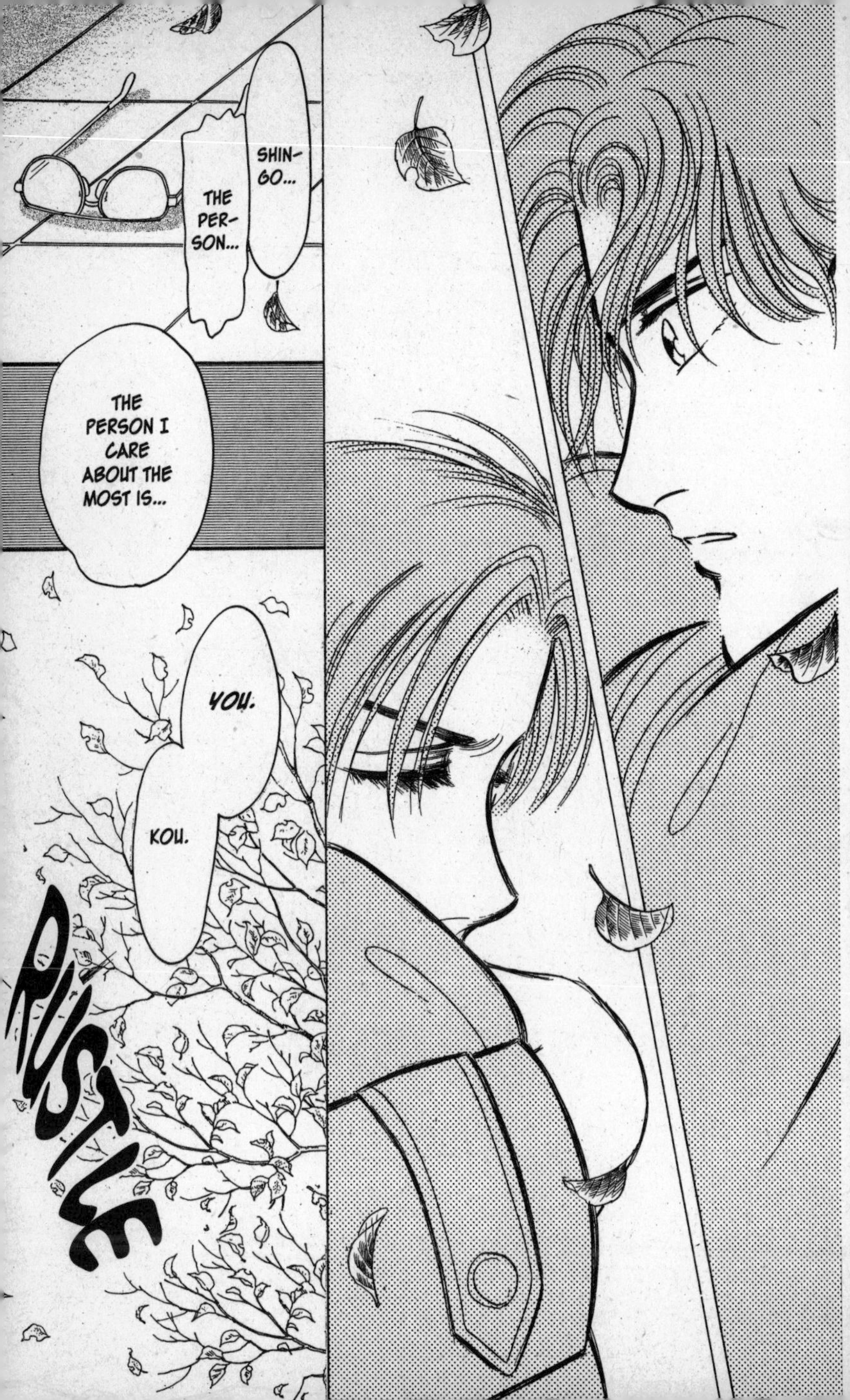
SHIN-GO...
THE PER-SON...
THE PERSON I CARE ABOUT THE MOST IS...
YOU.
KOU.
RUSTLE

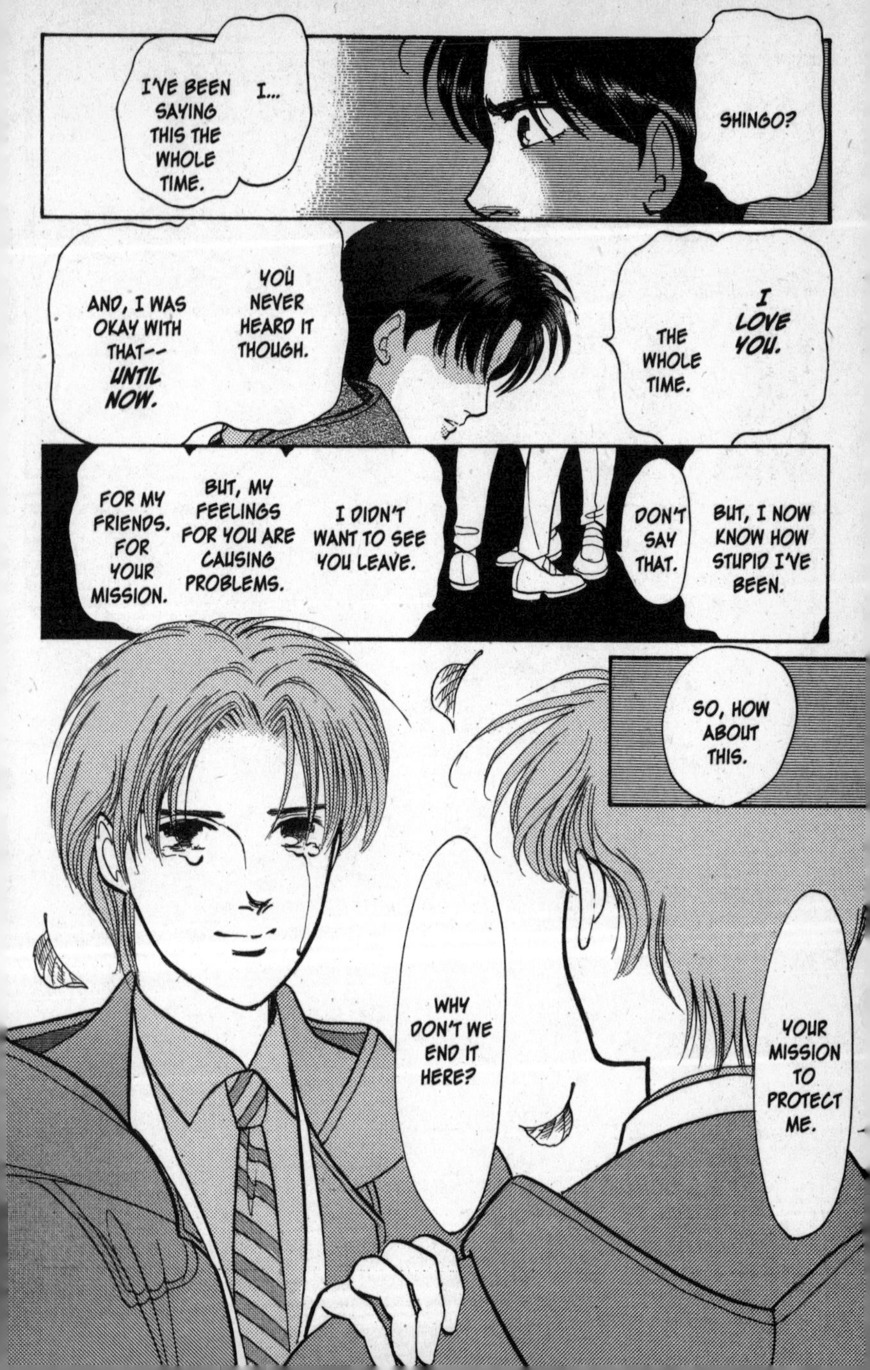
SHINGO?
I...
I'VE BEEN SAYING THIS THE WHOLE TIME.
I LOVE YOU.
THE WHOLE TIME.
YOU NEVER HEARD IT THOUGH.
AND, I WAS OKAY WITH THAT-- *UNTIL NOW.*
BUT, I NOW KNOW HOW STUPID I'VE BEEN.
DON'T SAY THAT.
I DIDN'T WANT TO SEE YOU LEAVE.
BUT, MY FEELINGS FOR YOU ARE CAUSING PROBLEMS.
FOR MY FRIENDS. FOR YOUR MISSION.
SO, HOW ABOUT THIS.
YOUR MISSION TO PROTECT ME.
WHY DON'T WE END IT HERE?

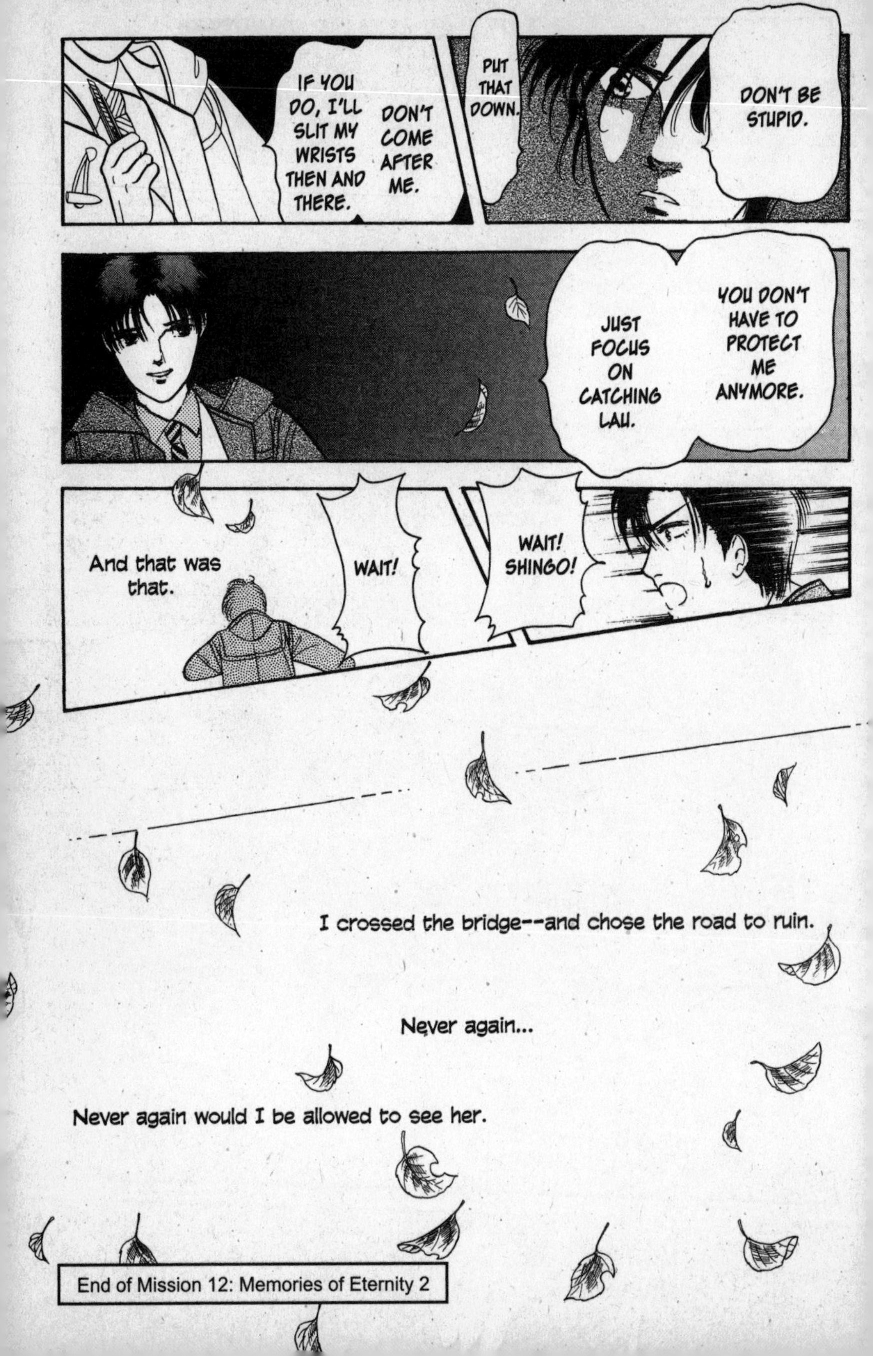
DON'T BE STUPID.
PUT THAT DOWN.
DON'T COME AFTER ME.
IF YOU DO, I'LL SLIT MY WRISTS THEN AND THERE.
YOU DON'T HAVE TO PROTECT ME ANYMORE.
JUST FOCUS ON CATCHING LAU.
WAIT! SHINGO!
WAIT!
And that was that.
I crossed the bridge--and chose the road to ruin.
Never again...
Never again would I be allowed to see her.
End of Mission 12: Memories of Eternity 2

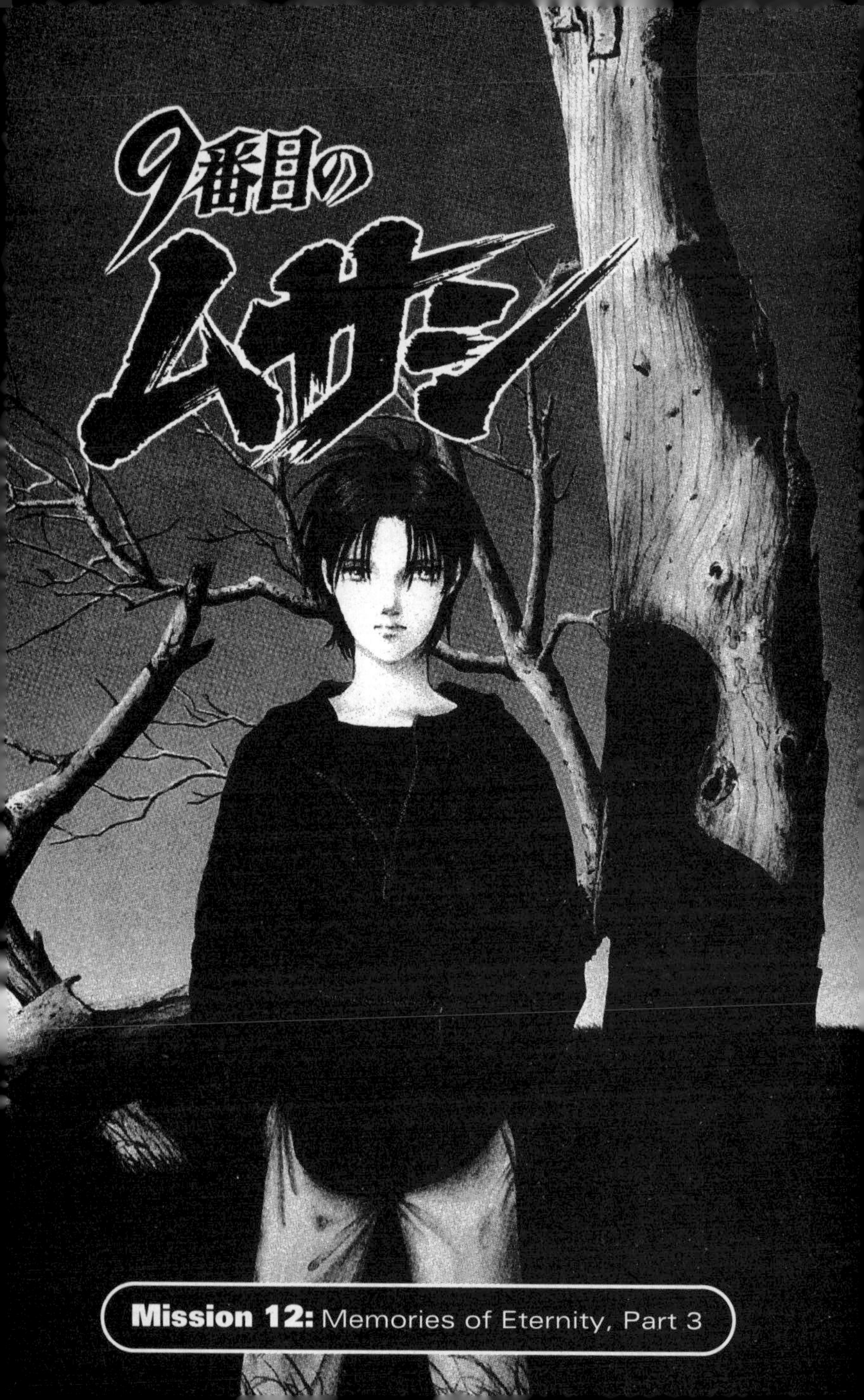
9番目のムサシ

Mission 12: Memories of Eternity, Part 3

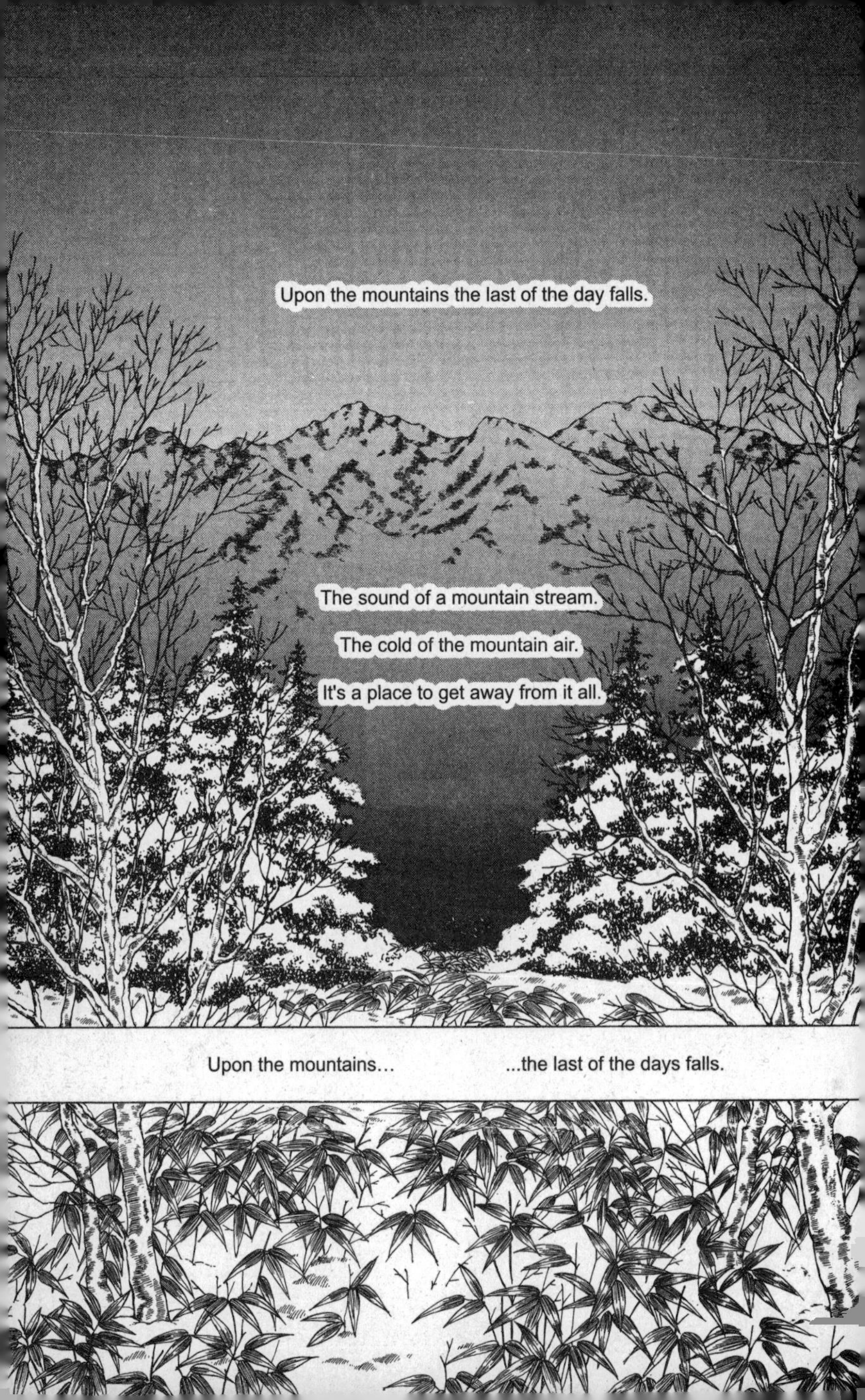
Upon the mountains the last of the day falls.
The sound of a mountain stream.
The cold of the mountain air.
It's a place to get away from it all.
Upon the mountains…
...the last of the days falls.

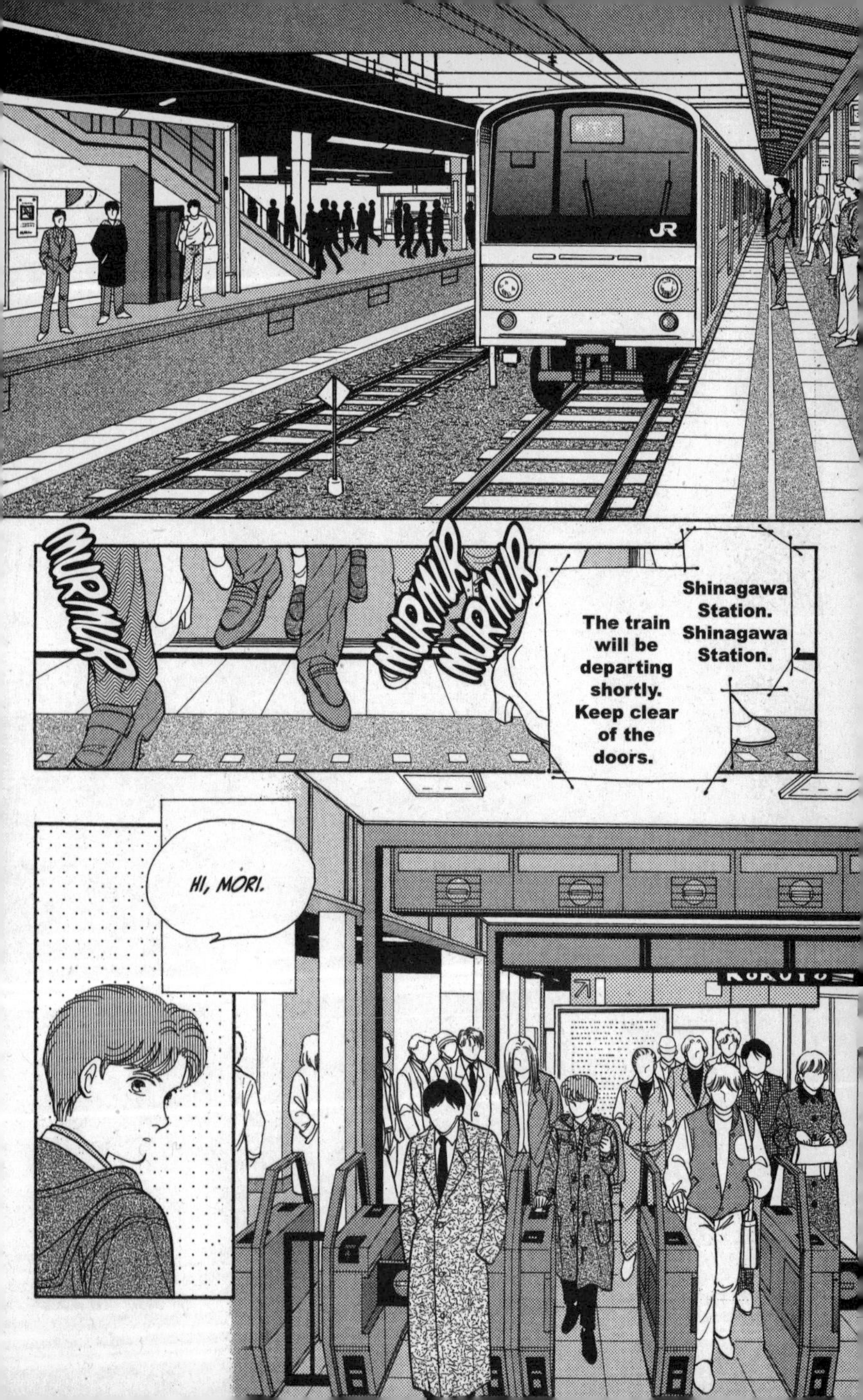
Shinagawa Station. Shinagawa Station.
The train will be departing shortly. Keep clear of the doors.
MURMUR MURMUR
MURMUR
HI, MORI.

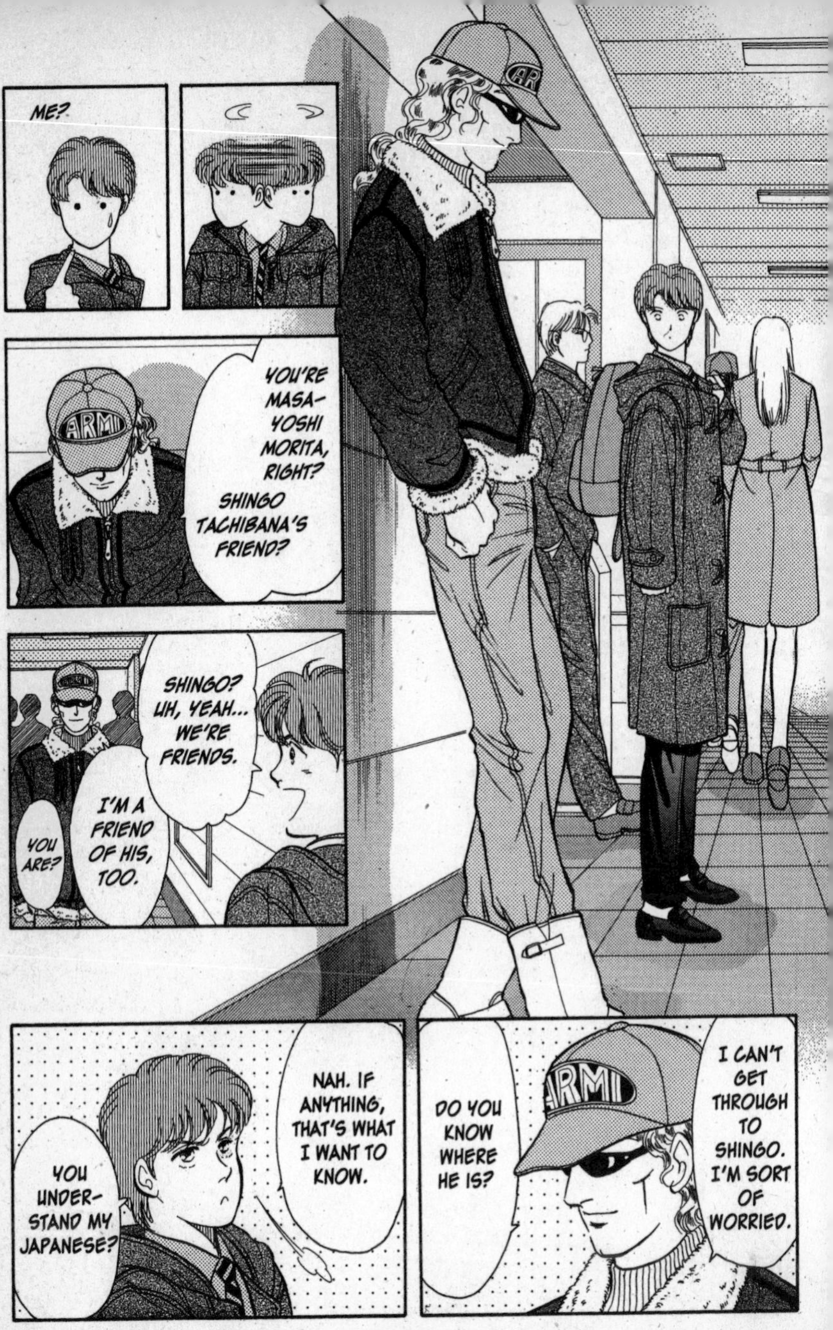
ME?
YOU'RE MASA-YOSHI MORITA, RIGHT? SHINGO TACHIBANA'S FRIEND?
SHINGO? UH, YEAH... WE'RE FRIENDS.
I'M A FRIEND OF HIS, TOO.
YOU ARE?
I CAN'T GET THROUGH TO SHINGO. I'M SORT OF WORRIED.
DO YOU KNOW WHERE HE IS?
NAH. IF ANYTHING, THAT'S WHAT I WANT TO KNOW.
YOU UNDER-STAND MY JAPANESE?

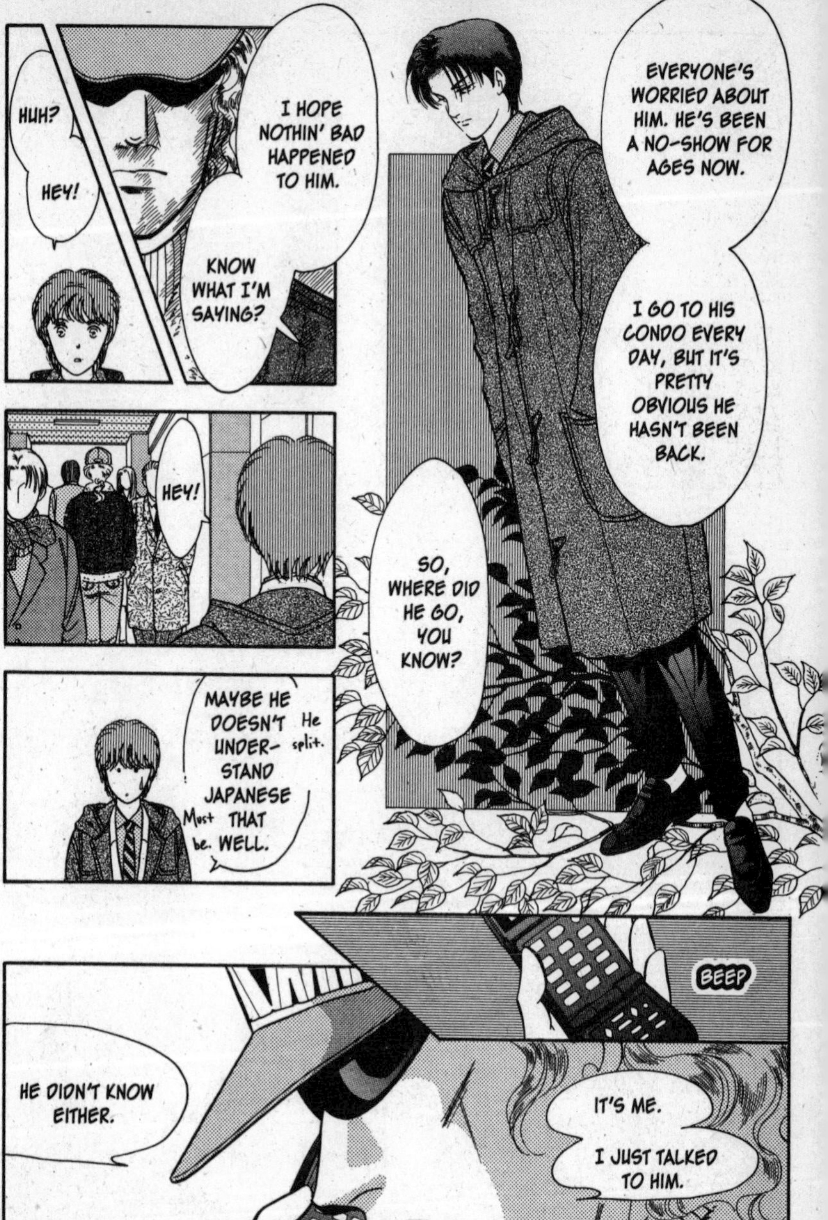
EVERYONE'S WORRIED ABOUT HIM. HE'S BEEN A NO-SHOW FOR AGES NOW.
I GO TO HIS CONDO EVERY DAY, BUT IT'S PRETTY OBVIOUS HE HASN'T BEEN BACK.
SO, WHERE DID HE GO, YOU KNOW?
I HOPE NOTHIN' BAD HAPPENED TO HIM.
KNOW WHAT I'M SAYING?
HUH?
HEY!
HEY!
MAYBE HE DOESN'T UNDER-STAND JAPANESE THAT WELL.
He split.
Must be.
BEEP
IT'S ME.
I JUST TALKED TO HIM.
HE DIDN'T KNOW EITHER.

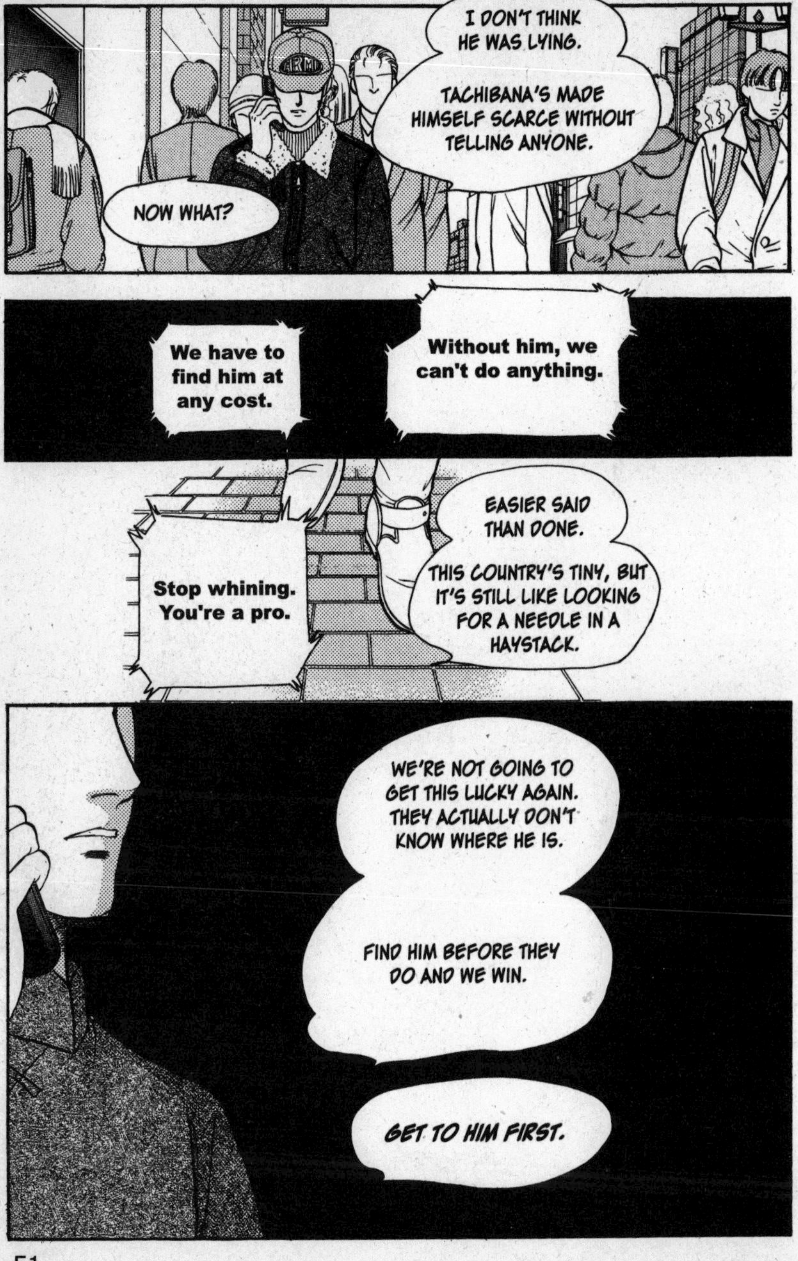
I DON'T THINK HE WAS LYING.
TACHIBANA'S MADE HIMSELF SCARCE WITHOUT TELLING ANYONE.
NOW WHAT?
Without him, we can't do anything.
We have to find him at any cost.
EASIER SAID THAN DONE.
THIS COUNTRY'S TINY, BUT IT'S STILL LIKE LOOKING FOR A NEEDLE IN A HAYSTACK.
Stop whining. You're a pro.
WE'RE NOT GOING TO GET THIS LUCKY AGAIN. THEY ACTUALLY DON'T KNOW WHERE HE IS.
FIND HIM BEFORE THEY DO AND WE WIN.
GET TO HIM FIRST.

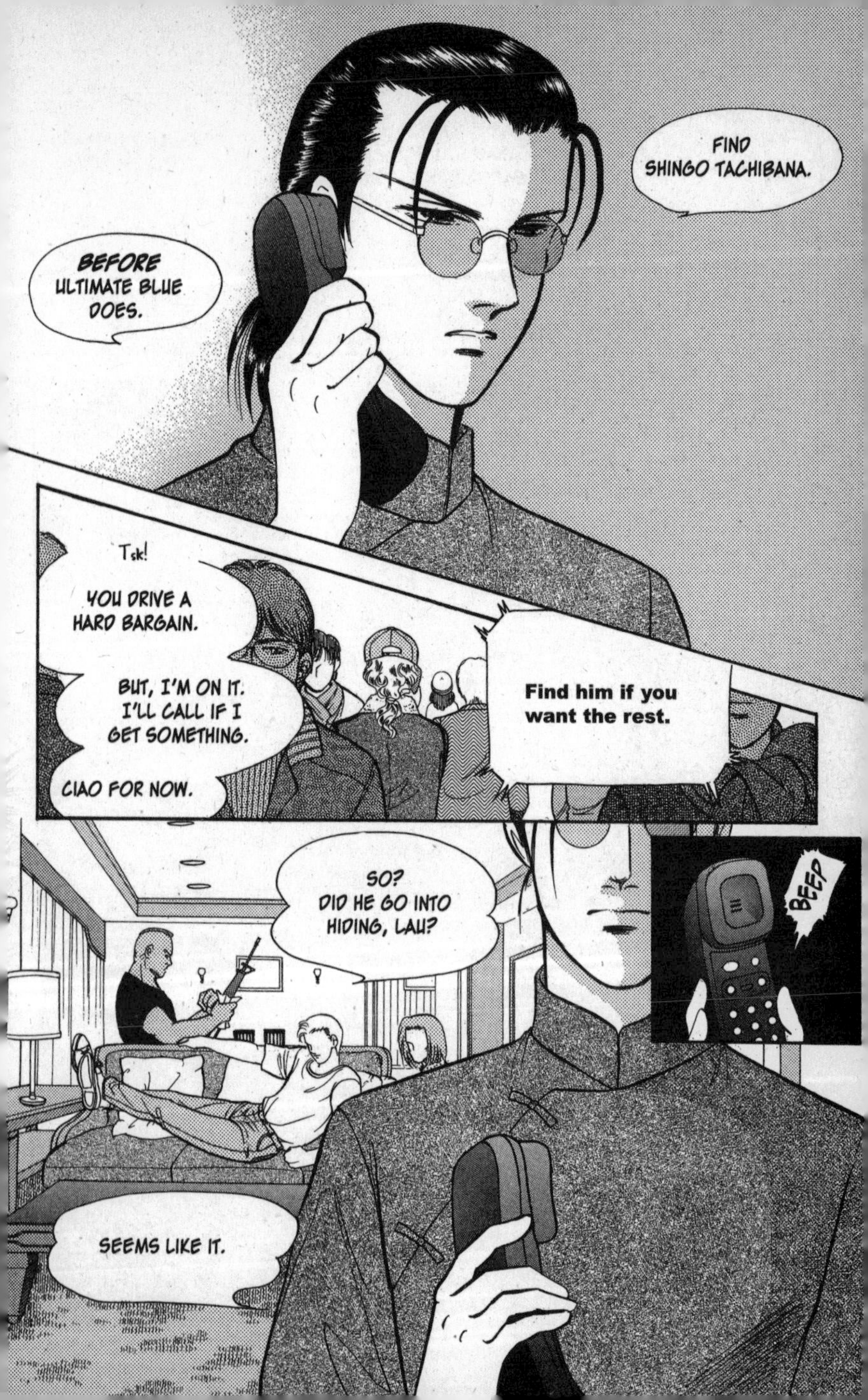
FIND SHINGO TACHIBANA.
BEFORE ULTIMATE BLUE DOES.
Find him if you want the rest.
Tsk!
YOU DRIVE A HARD BARGAIN.
BUT, I'M ON IT. I'LL CALL IF I GET SOMETHING.
CIAO FOR NOW.
BEEP
SO? DID HE GO INTO HIDING, LAU?
SEEMS LIKE IT.

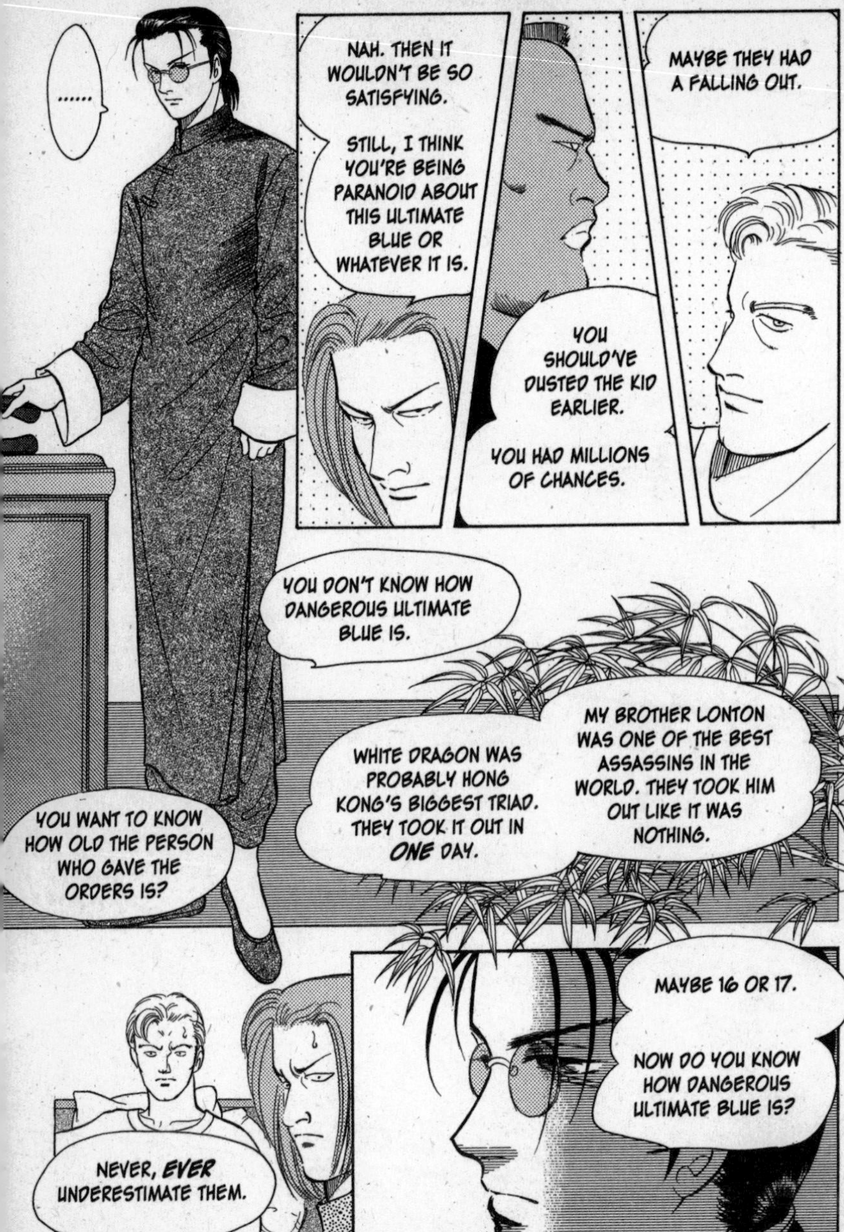
MAYBE THEY HAD A FALLING OUT.
YOU SHOULD'VE DUSTED THE KID EARLIER. YOU HAD MILLIONS OF CHANCES.
NAH. THEN IT WOULDN'T BE SO SATISFYING. STILL, I THINK YOU'RE BEING PARANOID ABOUT THIS ULTIMATE BLUE OR WHATEVER IT IS.
......
YOU DON'T KNOW HOW DANGEROUS ULTIMATE BLUE IS.
MY BROTHER LONTON WAS ONE OF THE BEST ASSASSINS IN THE WORLD. THEY TOOK HIM OUT LIKE IT WAS NOTHING.
WHITE DRAGON WAS PROBABLY HONG KONG'S BIGGEST TRIAD. THEY TOOK IT OUT IN ONE DAY.
YOU WANT TO KNOW HOW OLD THE PERSON WHO GAVE THE ORDERS IS?
MAYBE 16 OR 17. NOW DO YOU KNOW HOW DANGEROUS ULTIMATE BLUE IS?
NEVER, EVER UNDERESTIMATE THEM.

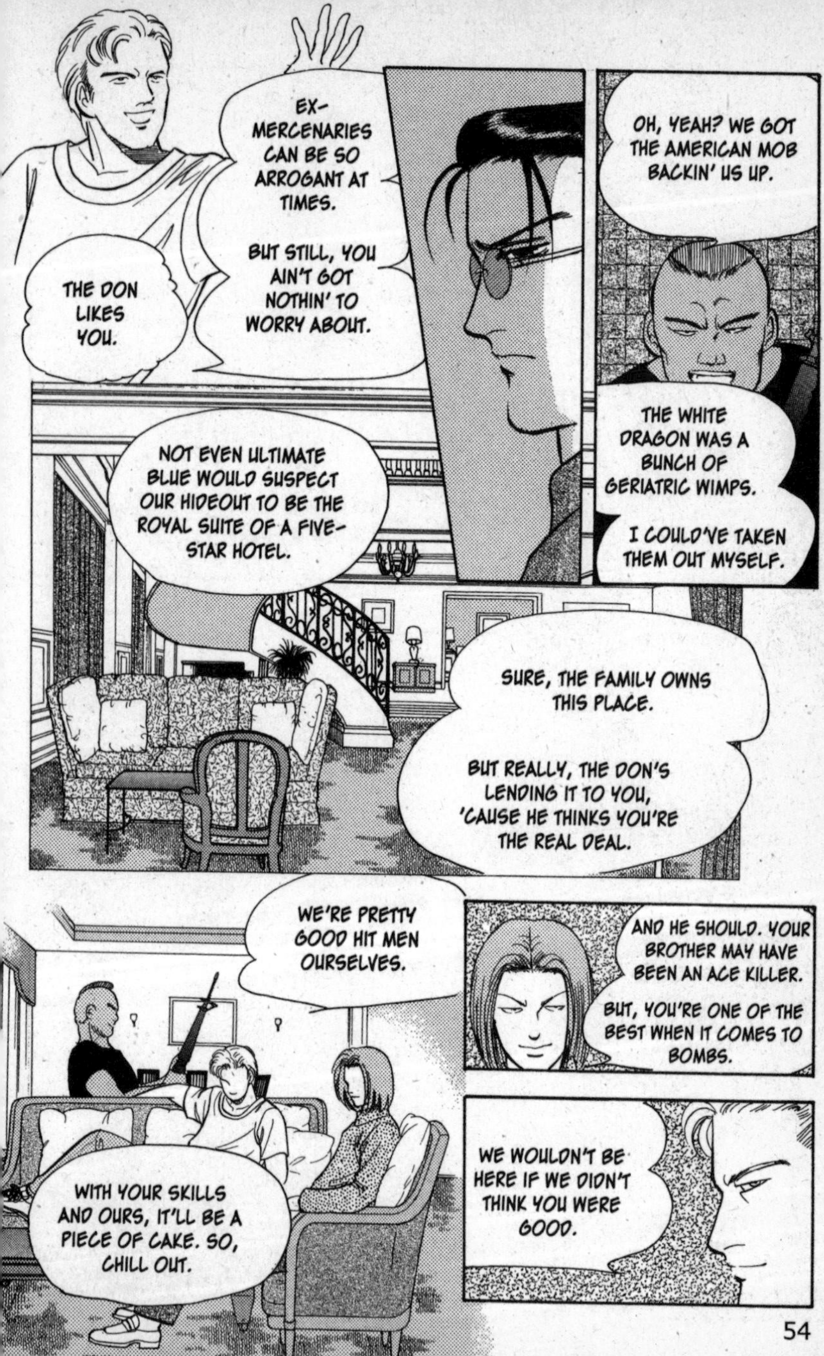

OH, YEAH? WE GOT THE AMERICAN MOB BACKIN' US UP.
THE WHITE DRAGON WAS A BUNCH OF GERIATRIC WIMPS.
I COULD'VE TAKEN THEM OUT MYSELF.
EX-MERCENARIES CAN BE SO ARROGANT AT TIMES.
BUT STILL, YOU AIN'T GOT NOTHIN' TO WORRY ABOUT.
THE DON LIKES YOU.
NOT EVEN ULTIMATE BLUE WOULD SUSPECT OUR HIDEOUT TO BE THE ROYAL SUITE OF A FIVE-STAR HOTEL.
SURE, THE FAMILY OWNS THIS PLACE.
BUT REALLY, THE DON'S LENDING IT TO YOU, 'CAUSE HE THINKS YOU'RE THE REAL DEAL.
AND HE SHOULD. YOUR BROTHER MAY HAVE BEEN AN ACE KILLER.
BUT, YOU'RE ONE OF THE BEST WHEN IT COMES TO BOMBS.
WE WOULDN'T BE HERE IF WE DIDN'T THINK YOU WERE GOOD.
WE'RE PRETTY GOOD HIT MEN OURSELVES.
WITH YOUR SKILLS AND OURS, IT'LL BE A PIECE OF CAKE. SO, CHILL OUT.

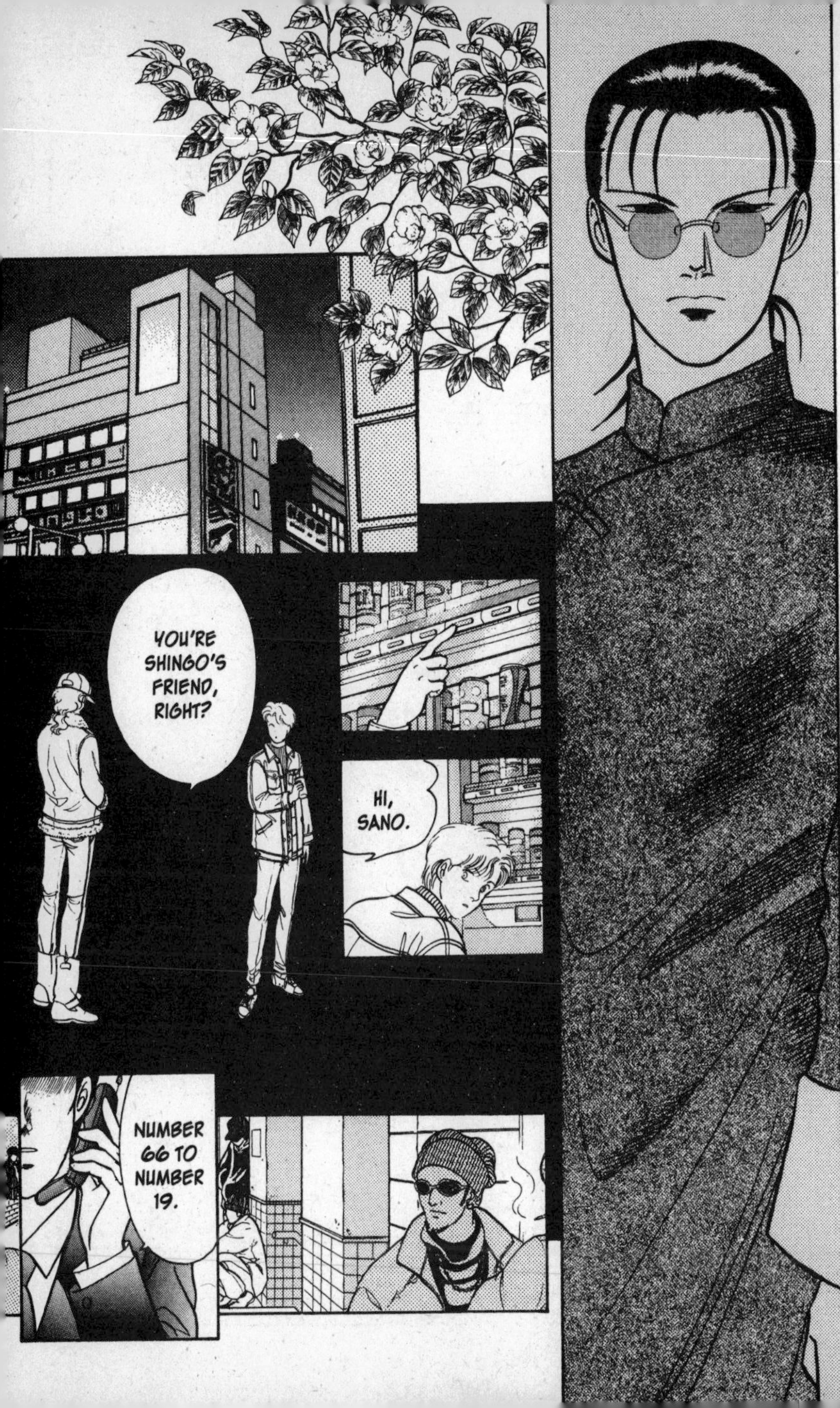
HI, SANO.
YOU'RE SHINGO'S FRIEND, RIGHT?
NUMBER 66 TO NUMBER 19.

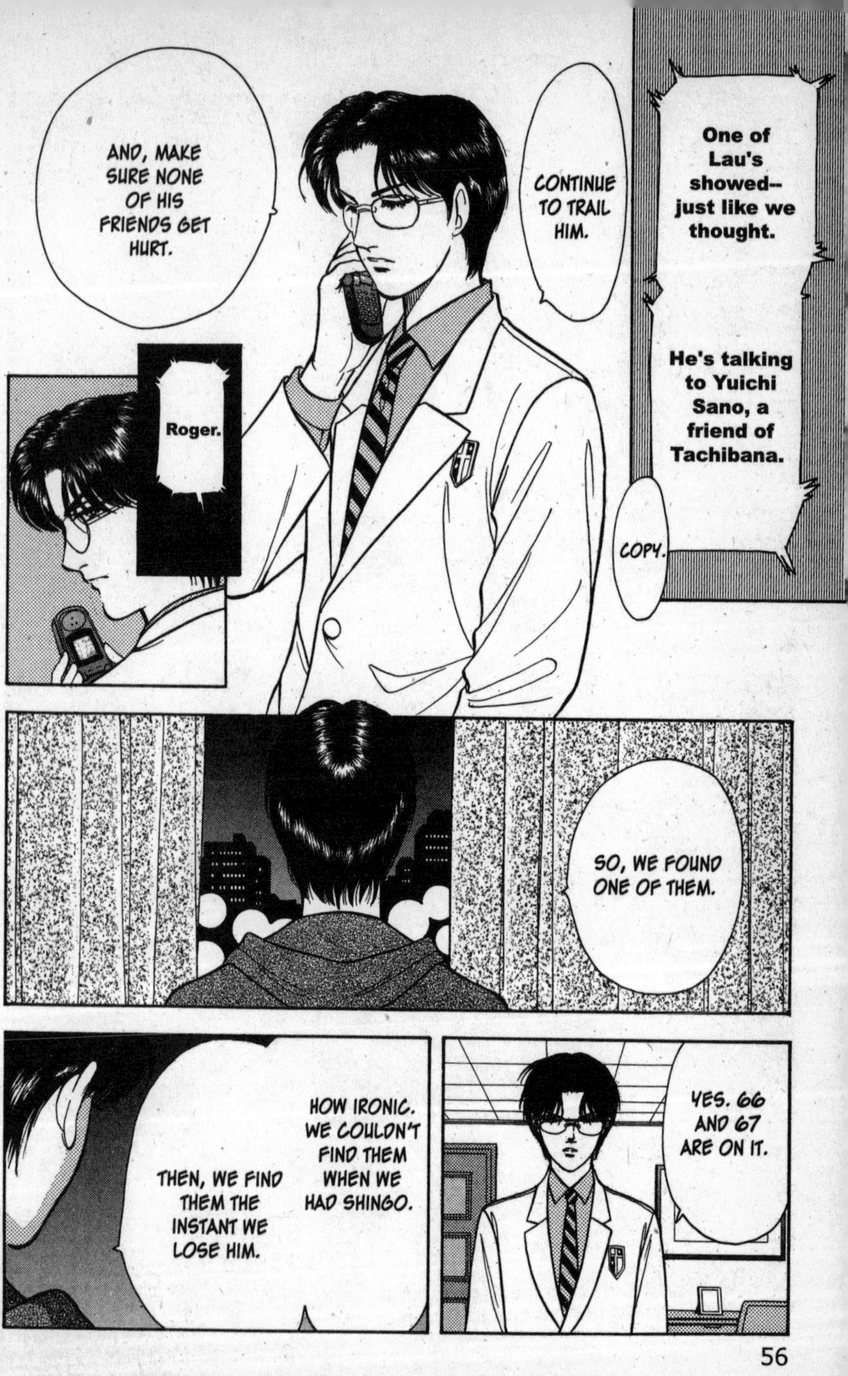
One of Lau's showed-- just like we thought.
He's talking to Yuichi Sano, a friend of Tachibana.
CONTINUE TO TRAIL HIM.
AND, MAKE SURE NONE OF HIS FRIENDS GET HURT.
COPY.
Roger.
SO, WE FOUND ONE OF THEM.
YES. 66 AND 67 ARE ON IT.
HOW IRONIC. WE COULDN'T FIND THEM WHEN WE HAD SHINGO.
THEN, WE FIND THEM THE INSTANT WE LOSE HIM.

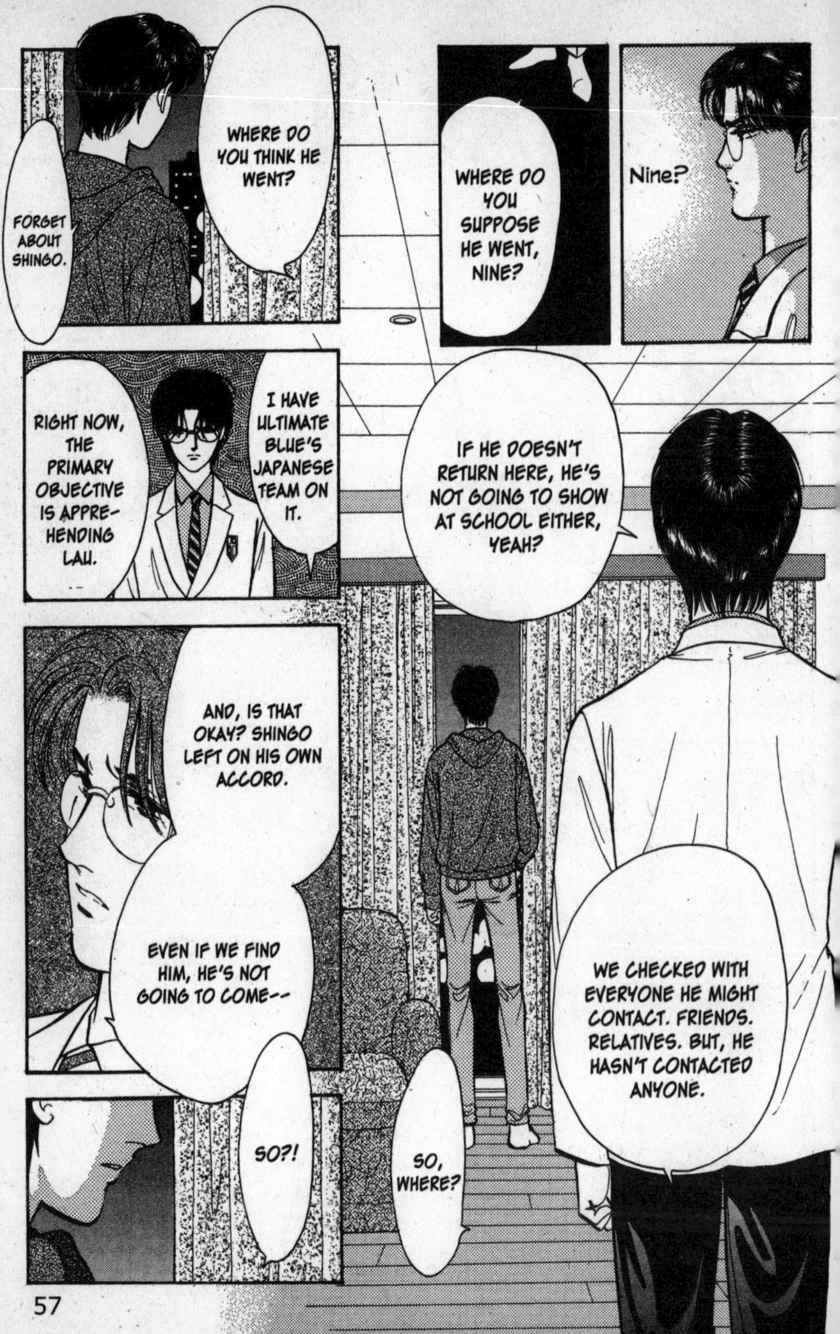
Nine?
WHERE DO YOU SUPPOSE HE WENT, NINE?
WHERE DO YOU THINK HE WENT?
FORGET ABOUT SHINGO.
IF HE DOESN'T RETURN HERE, HE'S NOT GOING TO SHOW AT SCHOOL EITHER, YEAH?
WE CHECKED WITH EVERYONE HE MIGHT CONTACT. FRIENDS. RELATIVES. BUT, HE HASN'T CONTACTED ANYONE.
SO, WHERE?
I HAVE ULTIMATE BLUE'S JAPANESE TEAM ON IT.
RIGHT NOW, THE PRIMARY OBJECTIVE IS APPREHENDING LAU.
AND, IS THAT OKAY? SHINGO LEFT ON HIS OWN ACCORD.
EVEN IF WE FIND HIM, HE'S NOT GOING TO COME--
SO?!

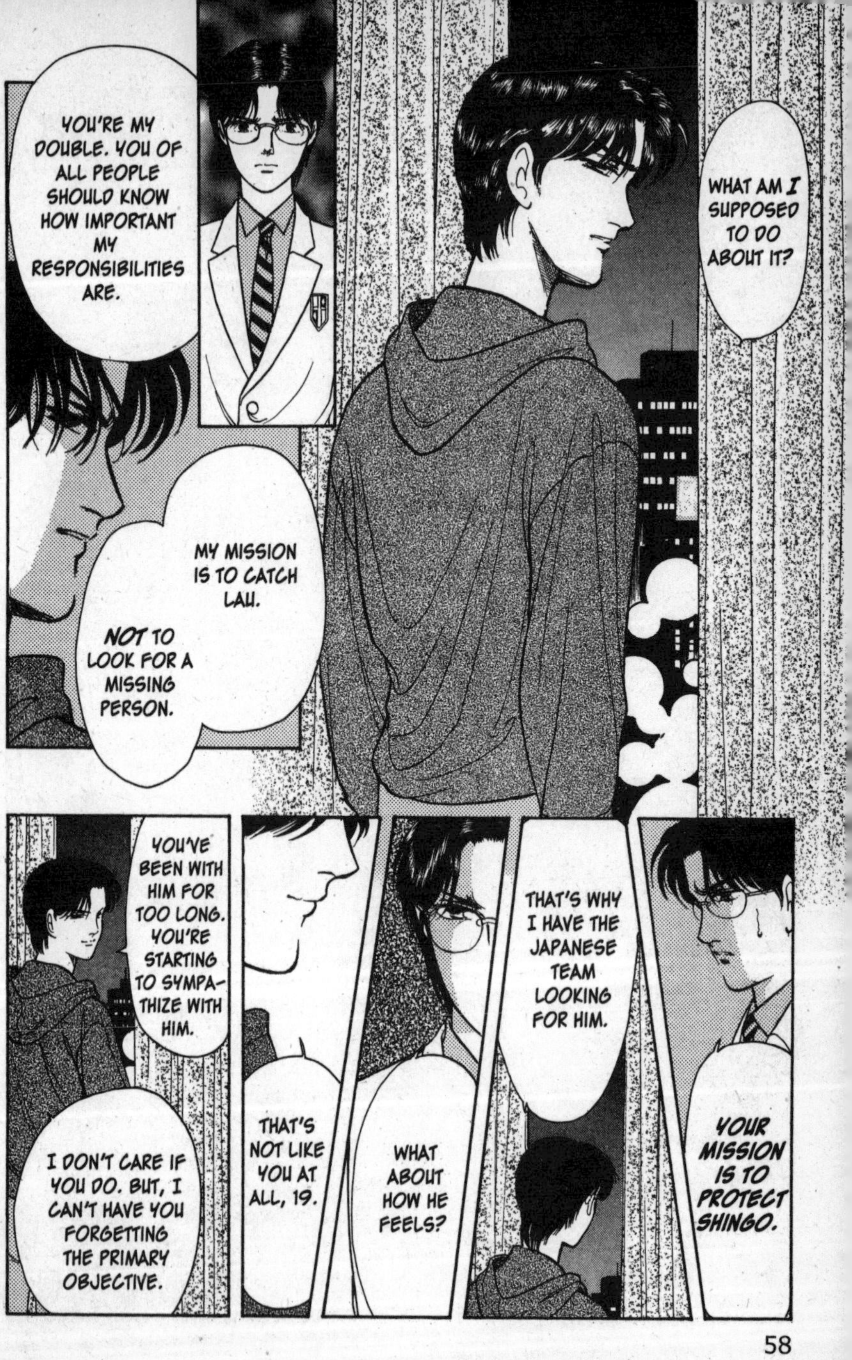
WHAT AM *I* SUPPOSED TO DO ABOUT IT?
YOU'RE MY DOUBLE. YOU OF ALL PEOPLE SHOULD KNOW HOW IMPORTANT MY RESPONSIBILITIES ARE.
MY MISSION IS TO CATCH LAU.
NOT TO LOOK FOR A MISSING PERSON.
YOUR MISSION IS TO PROTECT SHINGO.
THAT'S WHY I HAVE THE JAPANESE TEAM LOOKING FOR HIM.
WHAT ABOUT HOW HE FEELS?
THAT'S NOT LIKE YOU AT ALL, 19.
YOU'VE BEEN WITH HIM FOR TOO LONG. YOU'RE STARTING TO SYMPA-THIZE WITH HIM.
I DON'T CARE IF YOU DO. BUT, I CAN'T HAVE YOU FORGETTING THE PRIMARY OBJECTIVE.

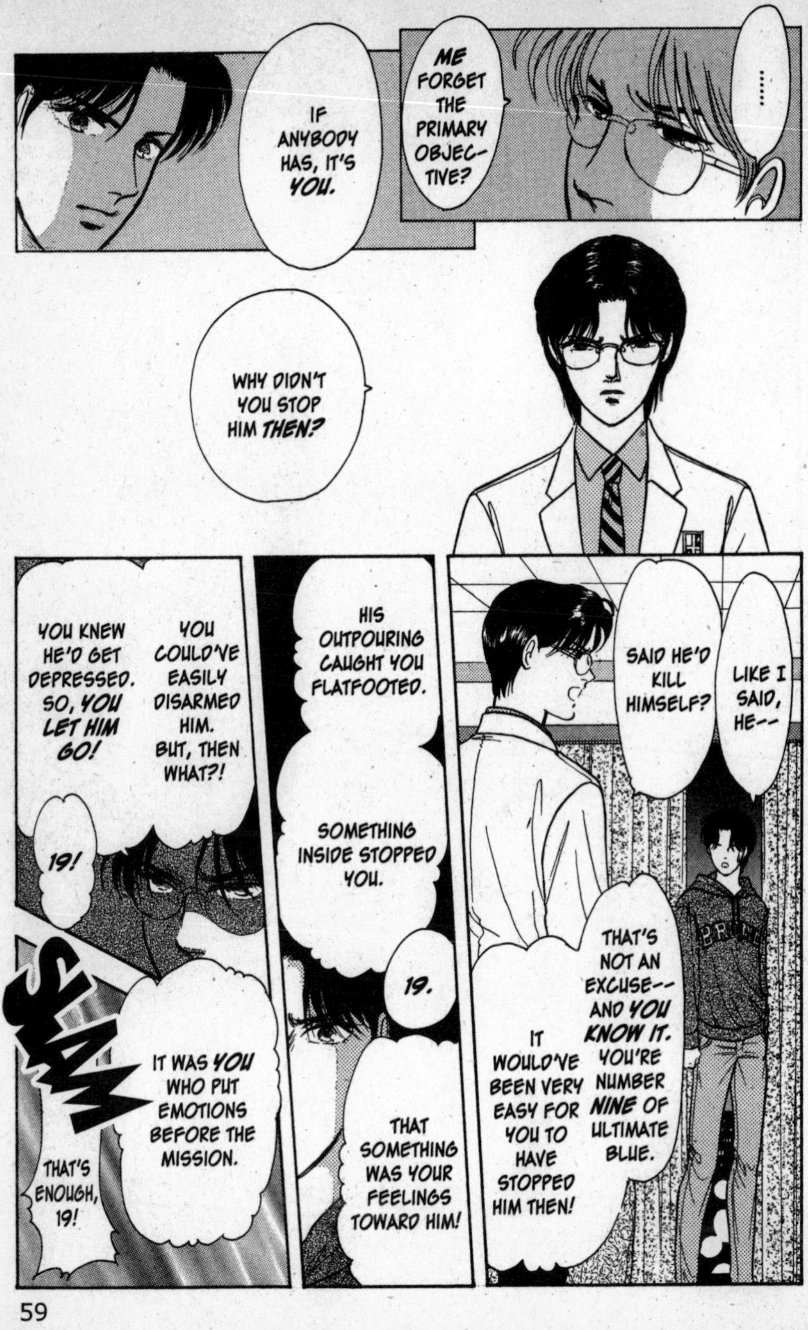
......
ME FORGET THE PRIMARY OBJEC- TIVE?
IF ANYBODY HAS, IT'S YOU.
WHY DIDN'T YOU STOP HIM THEN?
LIKE I SAID, HE--
SAID HE'D KILL HIMSELF?
THAT'S NOT AN EXCUSE-- AND YOU KNOW IT. YOU'RE NUMBER NINE OF ULTIMATE BLUE.
IT WOULD'VE BEEN VERY EASY FOR YOU TO HAVE STOPPED HIM THEN!
HIS OUTPOURING CAUGHT YOU FLATFOOTED.
SOMETHING INSIDE STOPPED YOU.
19.
THAT SOMETHING WAS YOUR FEELINGS TOWARD HIM!
YOU COULD'VE EASILY DISARMED HIM. BUT, THEN WHAT?!
YOU KNEW HE'D GET DEPRESSED. SO, YOU LET HIM GO!
19!
IT WAS YOU WHO PUT EMOTIONS BEFORE THE MISSION.
SLAM
THAT'S ENOUGH, 19!

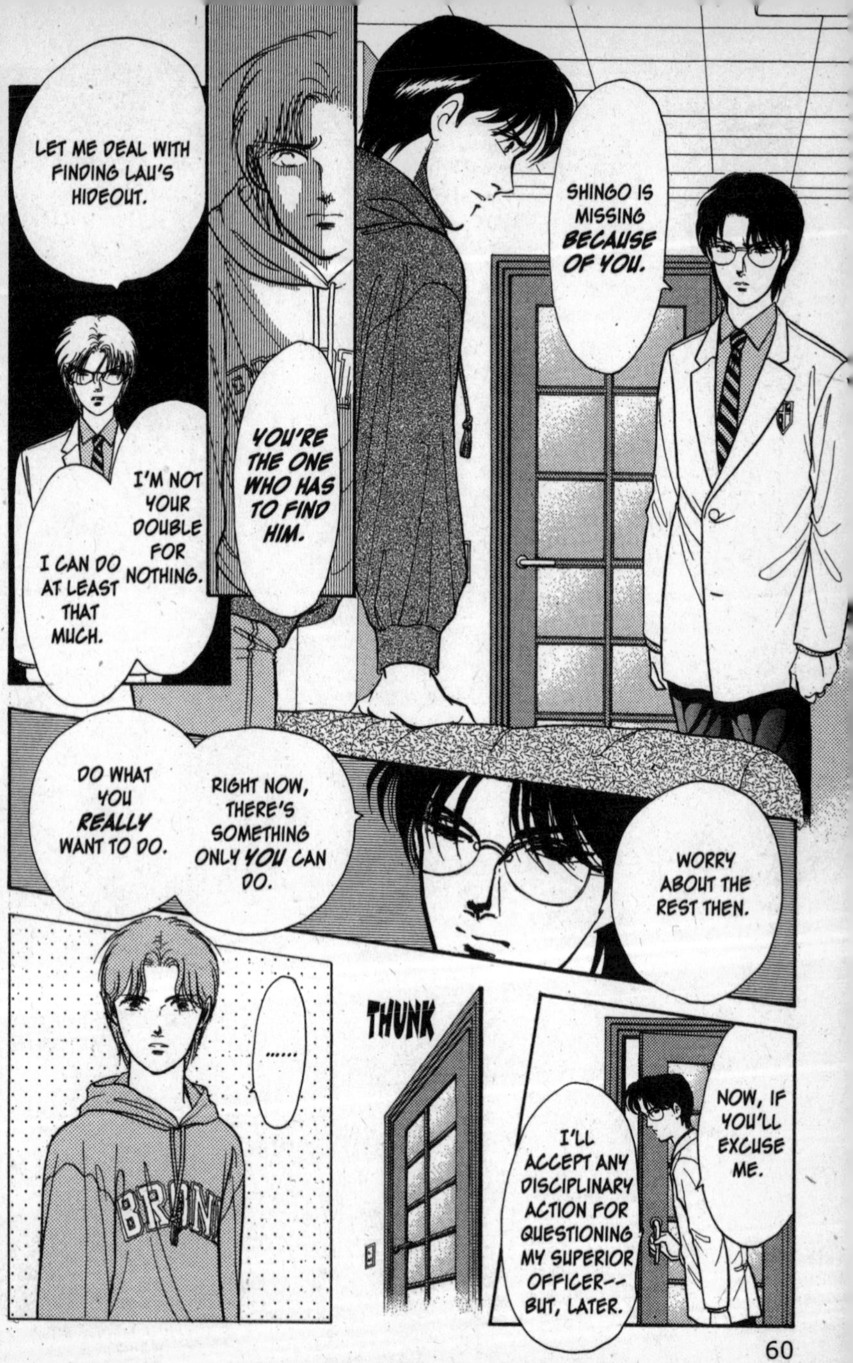
SHINGO IS MISSING *BECAUSE OF YOU.*
YOU'RE THE ONE WHO HAS TO FIND HIM.
LET ME DEAL WITH FINDING LAU'S HIDEOUT.
I'M NOT YOUR DOUBLE FOR NOTHING.
I CAN DO AT LEAST THAT MUCH.
WORRY ABOUT THE REST THEN.
RIGHT NOW, THERE'S SOMETHING ONLY *YOU* CAN DO.
DO WHAT YOU *REALLY* WANT TO DO.
NOW, IF YOU'LL EXCUSE ME.
I'LL ACCEPT ANY DISCIPLINARY ACTION FOR QUESTIONING MY SUPERIOR OFFICER--BUT, LATER.
THUNK
......

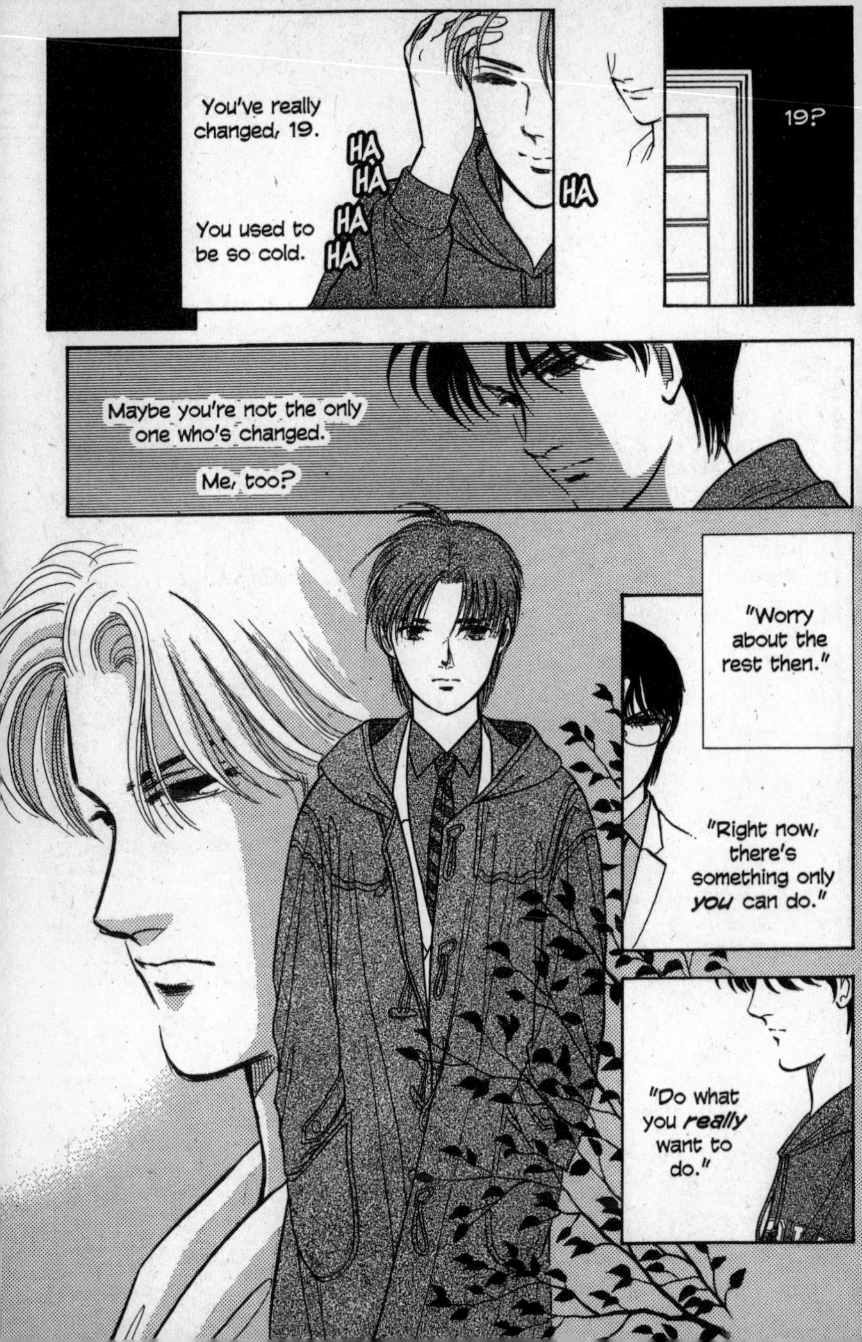
19?
HA
You've really changed, 19.
HA HA HA HA
You used to be so cold.
Maybe you're not the only one who's changed.
Me, too?
"Worry about the rest then."
"Right now, there's something only *you* can do."
"Do what you *really* want to do."

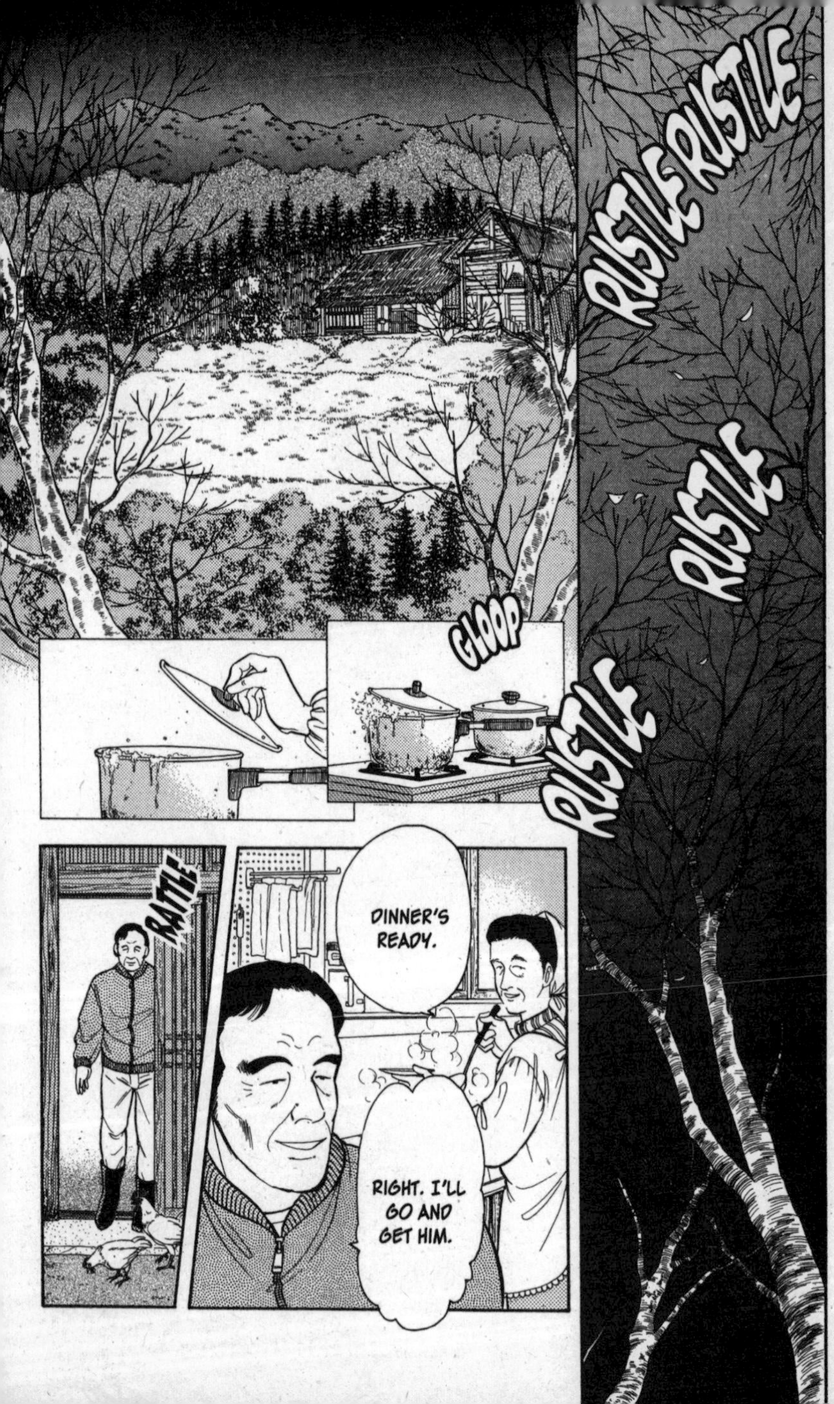
RUSTLE RUSTLE
RUSTLE
RUSTLE
GLOOP
DINNER'S READY.
RIGHT. I'LL GO AND GET HIM.
RATTLE

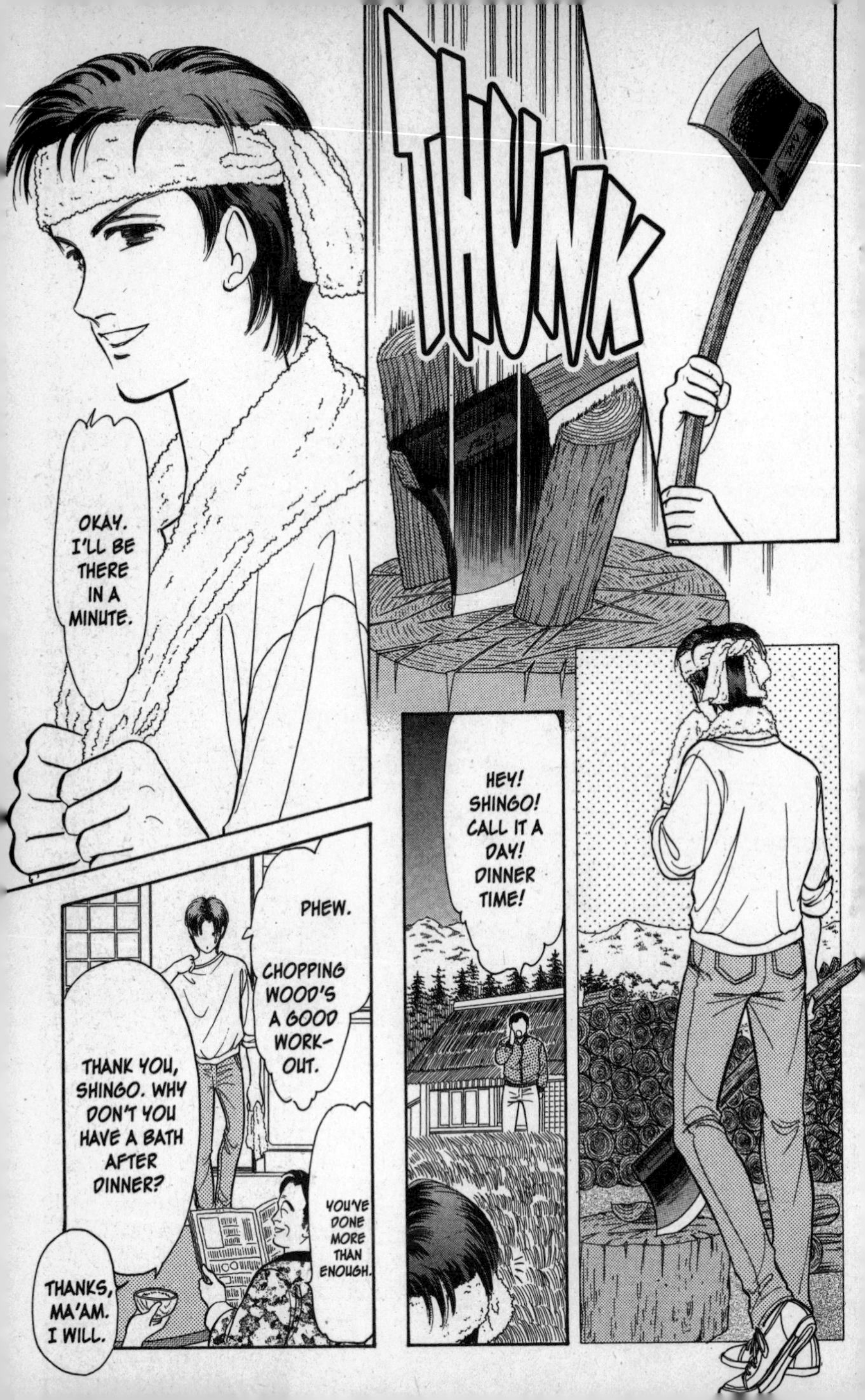
THUNK
HEY! SHINGO! CALL IT A DAY! DINNER TIME!
OKAY. I'LL BE THERE IN A MINUTE.
PHEW.
CHOPPING WOOD'S A GOOD WORK-OUT.
THANK YOU, SHINGO. WHY DON'T YOU HAVE A BATH AFTER DINNER?
YOU'VE DONE MORE THAN ENOUGH.
THANKS, MA'AM. I WILL.

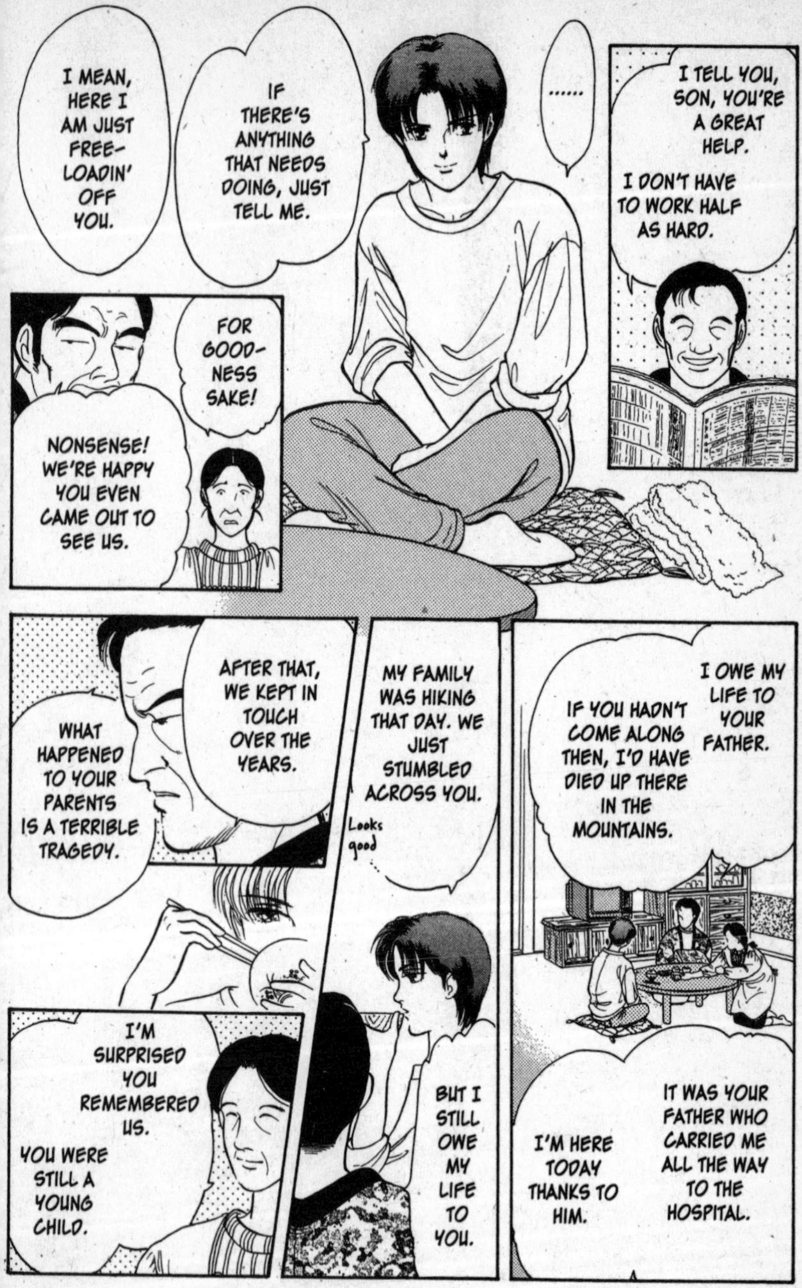

I TELL YOU, SON, YOU'RE A GREAT HELP.
I DON'T HAVE TO WORK HALF AS HARD.
......
IF THERE'S ANYTHING THAT NEEDS DOING, JUST TELL ME.
I MEAN, HERE I AM JUST FREE-LOADIN' OFF YOU.
FOR GOOD-NESS SAKE!
NONSENSE! WE'RE HAPPY YOU EVEN CAME OUT TO SEE US.
I OWE MY LIFE TO YOUR FATHER.
IF YOU HADN'T COME ALONG THEN, I'D HAVE DIED UP THERE IN THE MOUNTAINS.
IT WAS YOUR FATHER WHO CARRIED ME ALL THE WAY TO THE HOSPITAL.
I'M HERE TODAY THANKS TO HIM.
MY FAMILY WAS HIKING THAT DAY. WE JUST STUMBLED ACROSS YOU.
Looks good
BUT I STILL OWE MY LIFE TO YOU.
AFTER THAT, WE KEPT IN TOUCH OVER THE YEARS.
WHAT HAPPENED TO YOUR PARENTS IS A TERRIBLE TRAGEDY.
I'M SURPRISED YOU REMEMBERED US.
YOU WERE STILL A YOUNG CHILD.

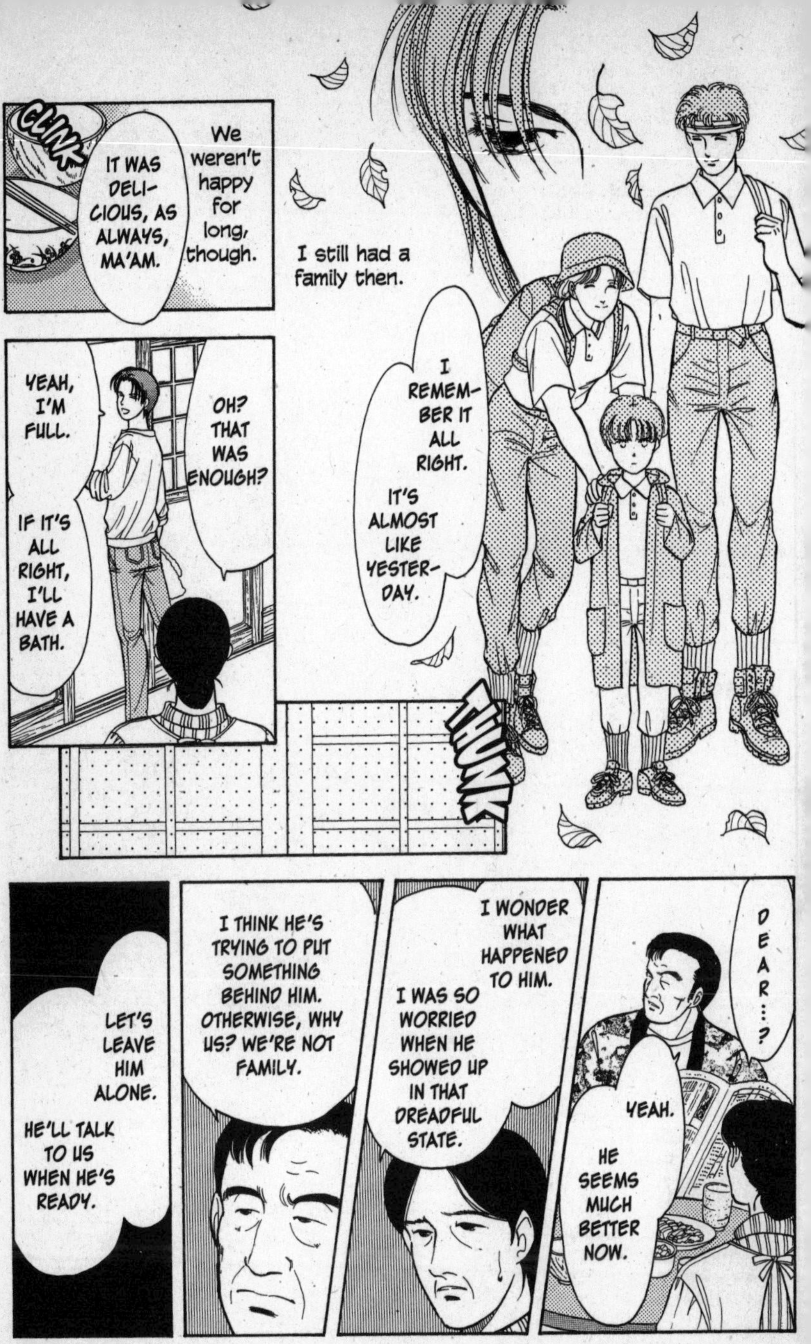
I still had a family then.
I REMEMBER IT ALL RIGHT.
IT'S ALMOST LIKE YESTERDAY.
We weren't happy for long, though.
IT WAS DELICIOUS, AS ALWAYS, MA'AM.
CLINK
OH? THAT WAS ENOUGH?
YEAH, I'M FULL.
IF IT'S ALL RIGHT, I'LL HAVE A BATH.
THUNK
DEAR...?
YEAH.
HE SEEMS MUCH BETTER NOW.
I WONDER WHAT HAPPENED TO HIM.
I WAS SO WORRIED WHEN HE SHOWED UP IN THAT DREADFUL STATE.
I THINK HE'S TRYING TO PUT SOMETHING BEHIND HIM. OTHERWISE, WHY US? WE'RE NOT FAMILY.
LET'S LEAVE HIM ALONE.
HE'LL TALK TO US WHEN HE'S READY.

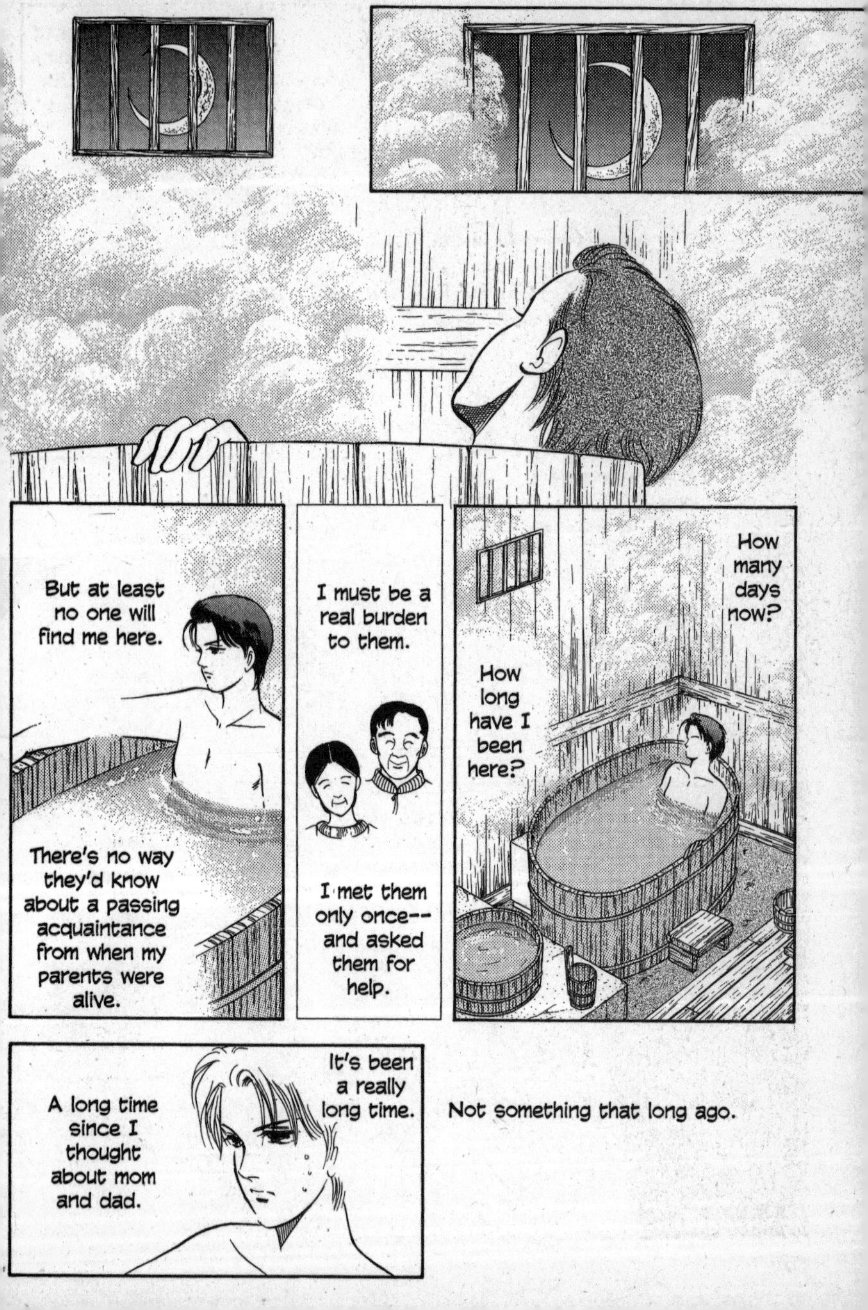
How many days now?
How long have I been here?
I must be a real burden to them.
I met them only once-- and asked them for help.
But at least no one will find me here.
There's no way they'd know about a passing acquaintance from when my parents were alive.
Not something that long ago.
It's been a really long time.
A long time since I thought about mom and dad.

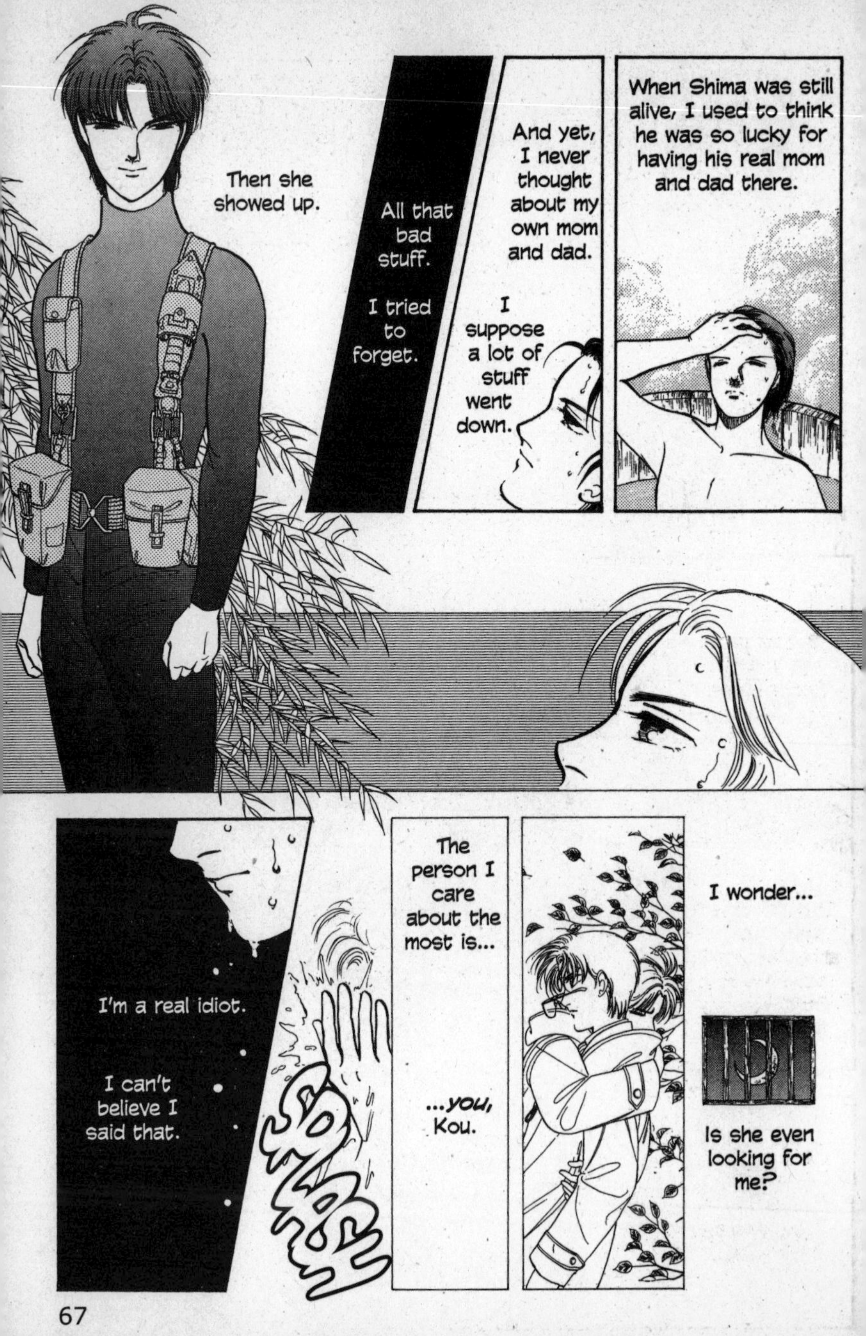
When Shima was still alive, I used to think he was so lucky for having his real mom and dad there.
And yet, I never thought about my own mom and dad.
I suppose a lot of stuff went down.
All that bad stuff.
I tried to forget.
Then she showed up.
I wonder...
Is she even looking for me?
The person I care about the most is...
...you, Kou.
SPLASH
I'm a real idiot.
I can't believe I said that.

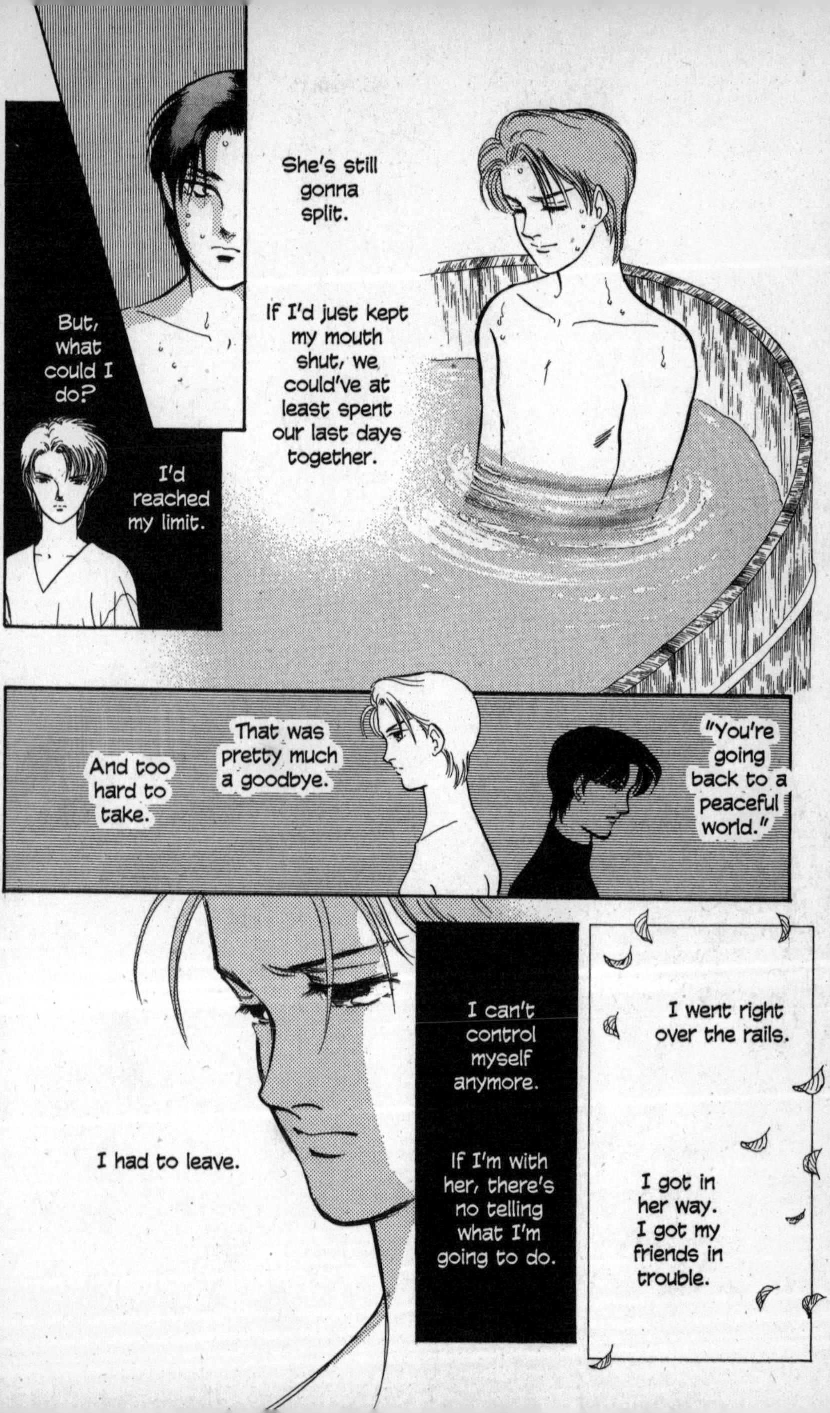
She's still gonna split.
If I'd just kept my mouth shut, we could've at least spent our last days together.
But, what could I do?
I'd reached my limit.
"You're going back to a peaceful world."
That was pretty much a goodbye.
And too hard to take.
I went right over the rails.
I got in her way. I got my friends in trouble.
I can't control myself anymore.
If I'm with her, there's no telling what I'm going to do.
I had to leave.

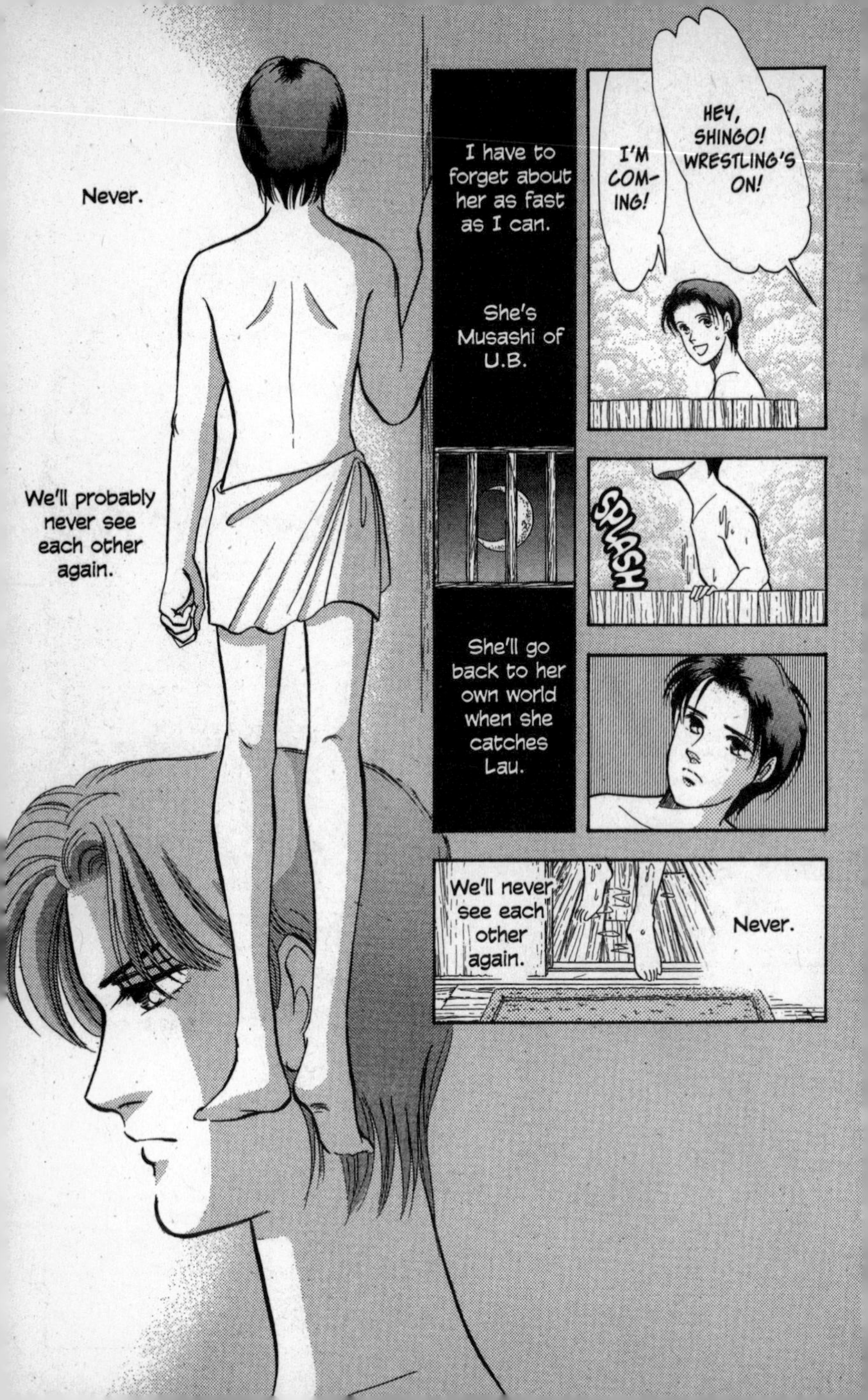
HEY, SHINGO! WRESTLING'S ON!
I'M COMING!
SPLASH
I have to forget about her as fast as I can.
She's Musashi of U.B.
She'll go back to her own world when she catches Lau.
Never.
We'll probably never see each other again.
Never.
We'll never see each other again.

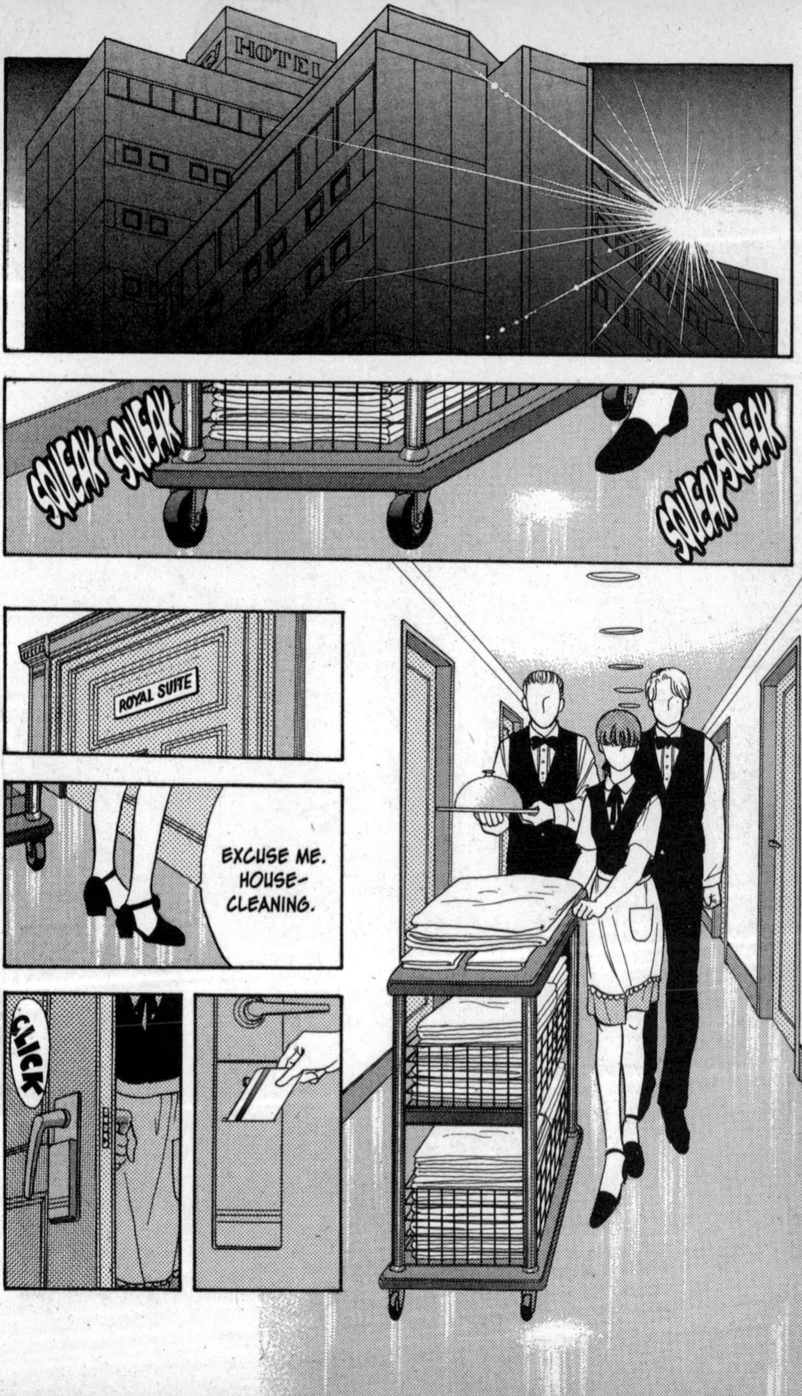
HOTEL
SQUEAKSQUEAK
SQUEAK SQUEAK
ROYAL SUITE
EXCUSE ME. HOUSE-CLEANING.
CLICK

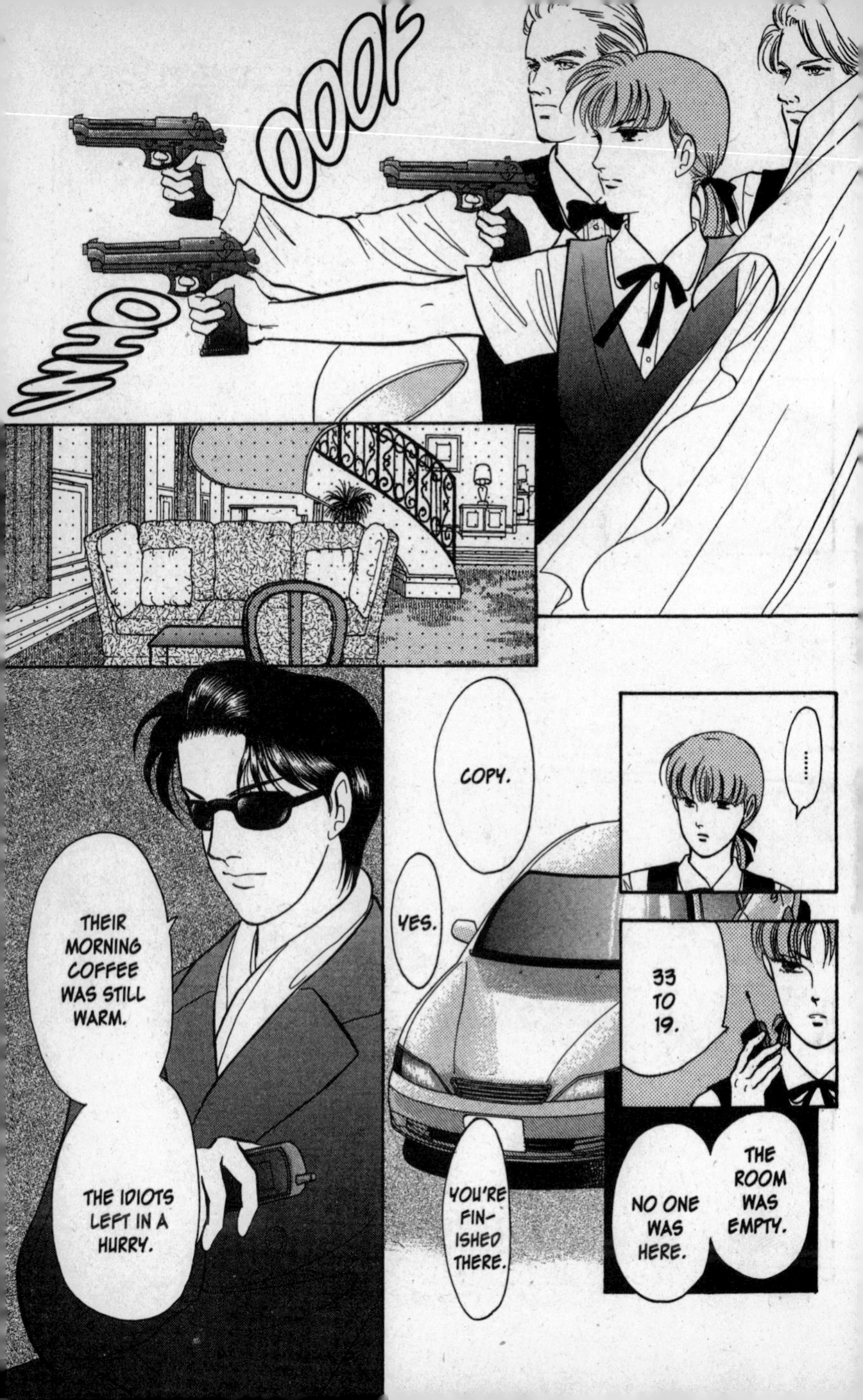
WHOOOOF
......
33 TO 19.
THE ROOM WAS EMPTY.
NO ONE WAS HERE.
COPY.
YES.
YOU'RE FIN-ISHED THERE.
THEIR MORNING COFFEE WAS STILL WARM.
THE IDIOTS LEFT IN A HURRY.

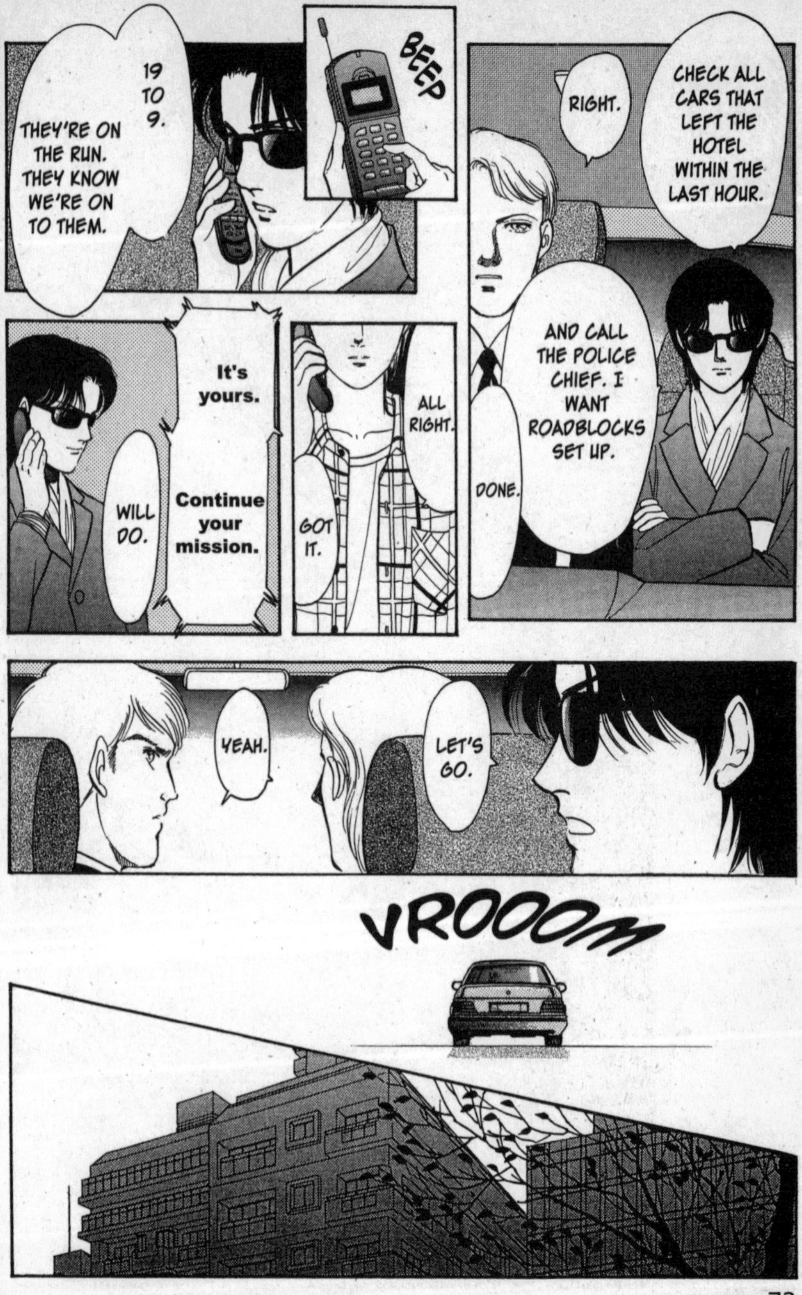
CHECK ALL CARS THAT LEFT THE HOTEL WITHIN THE LAST HOUR.
RIGHT.
AND CALL THE POLICE CHIEF. I WANT ROADBLOCKS SET UP.
DONE.
BEEP
19 TO 9.
THEY'RE ON THE RUN. THEY KNOW WE'RE ON TO THEM.
ALL RIGHT.
GOT IT.
It's yours.
Continue your mission.
WILL DO.
LET'S GO.
YEAH.
VROOOM

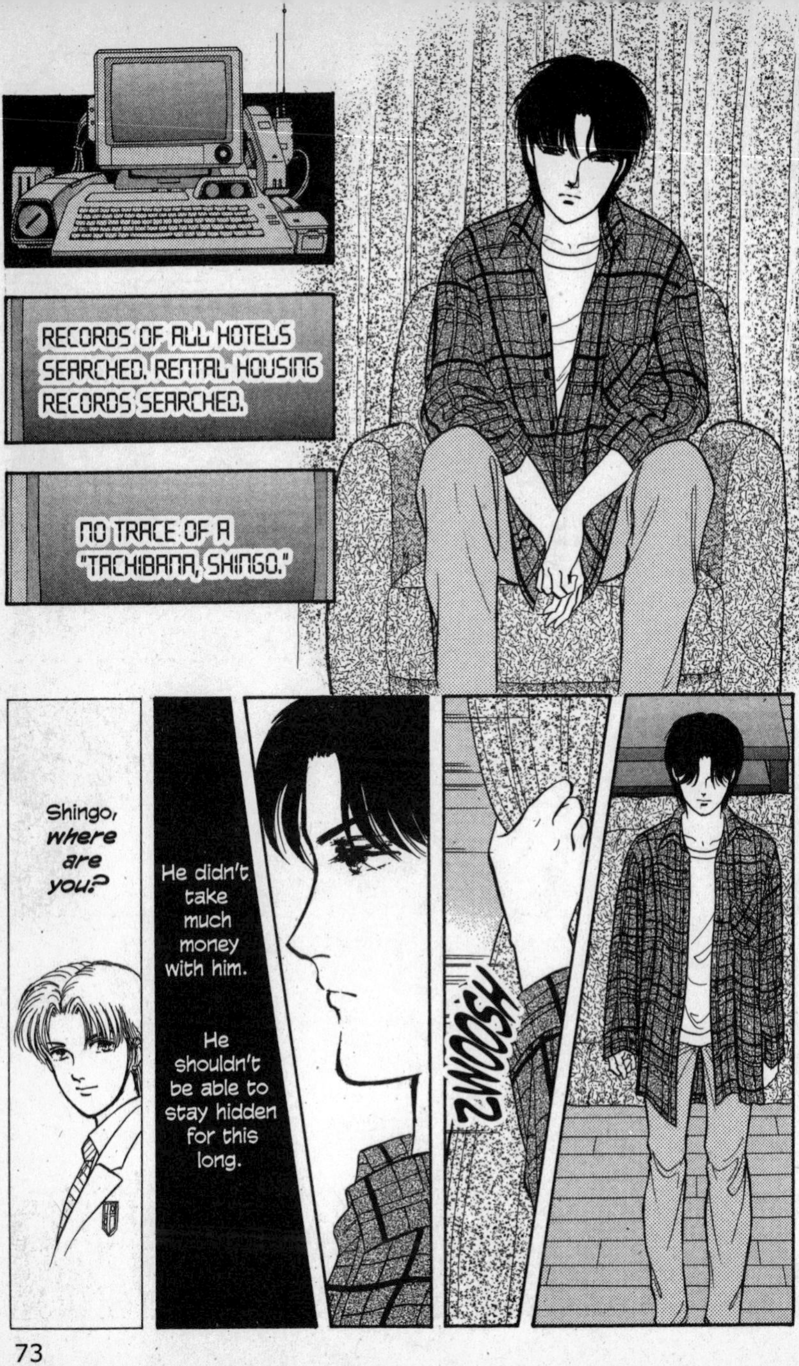
RECORDS OF ALL HOTELS SEARCHED. RENTAL HOUSING RECORDS SEARCHED.
NO TRACE OF A "TACHIBANA, SHINGO."
ZWOOSH
He didn't take much money with him.
He shouldn't be able to stay hidden for this long.
Shingo, where are you?

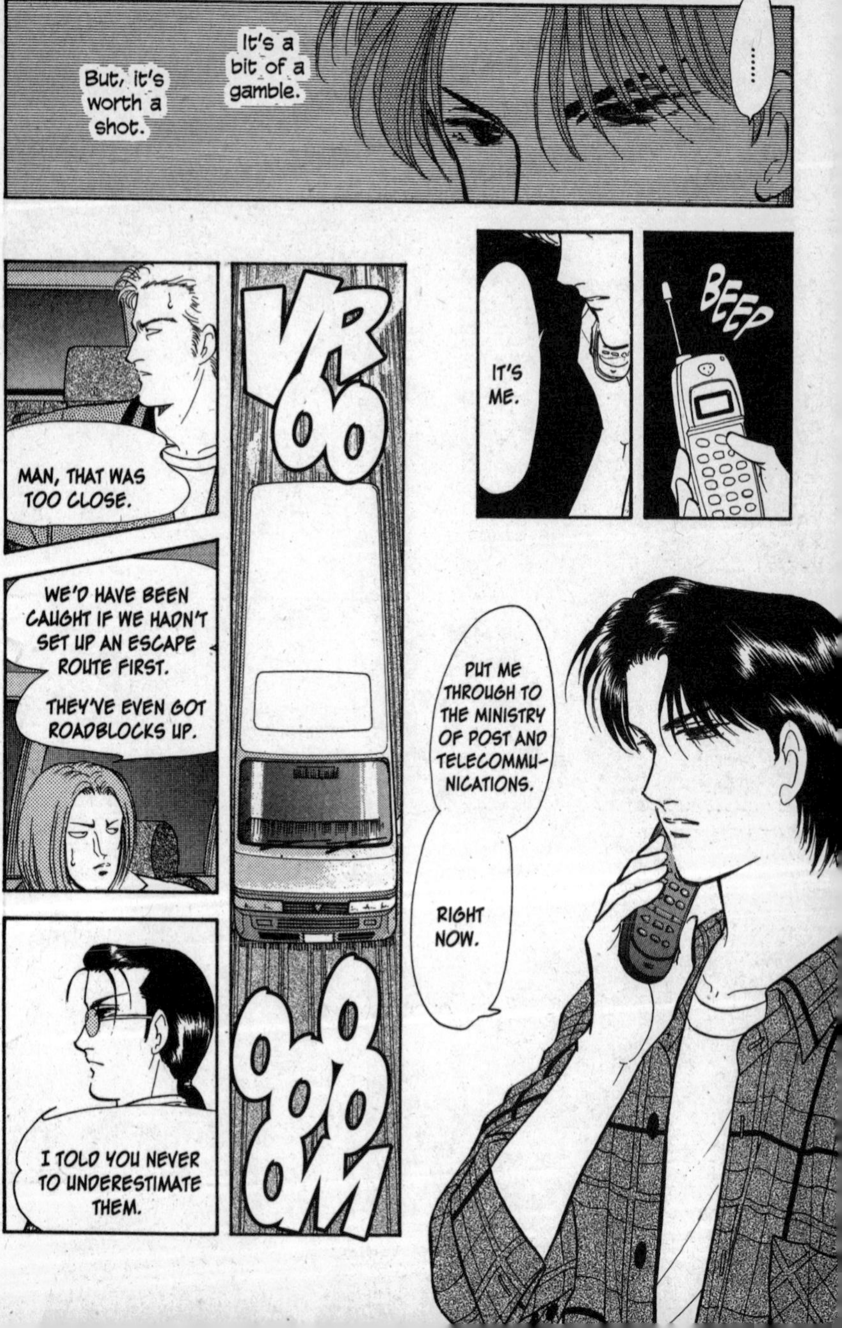
......
It's a bit of a gamble.
But, it's worth a shot.
BEEP
IT'S ME.
PUT ME THROUGH TO THE MINISTRY OF POST AND TELECOMMU-NICATIONS.
RIGHT NOW.
VROOOOOOM
MAN, THAT WAS TOO CLOSE.
WE'D HAVE BEEN CAUGHT IF WE HADN'T SET UP AN ESCAPE ROUTE FIRST.
THEY'VE EVEN GOT ROADBLOCKS UP.
I TOLD YOU NEVER TO UNDERESTIMATE THEM.

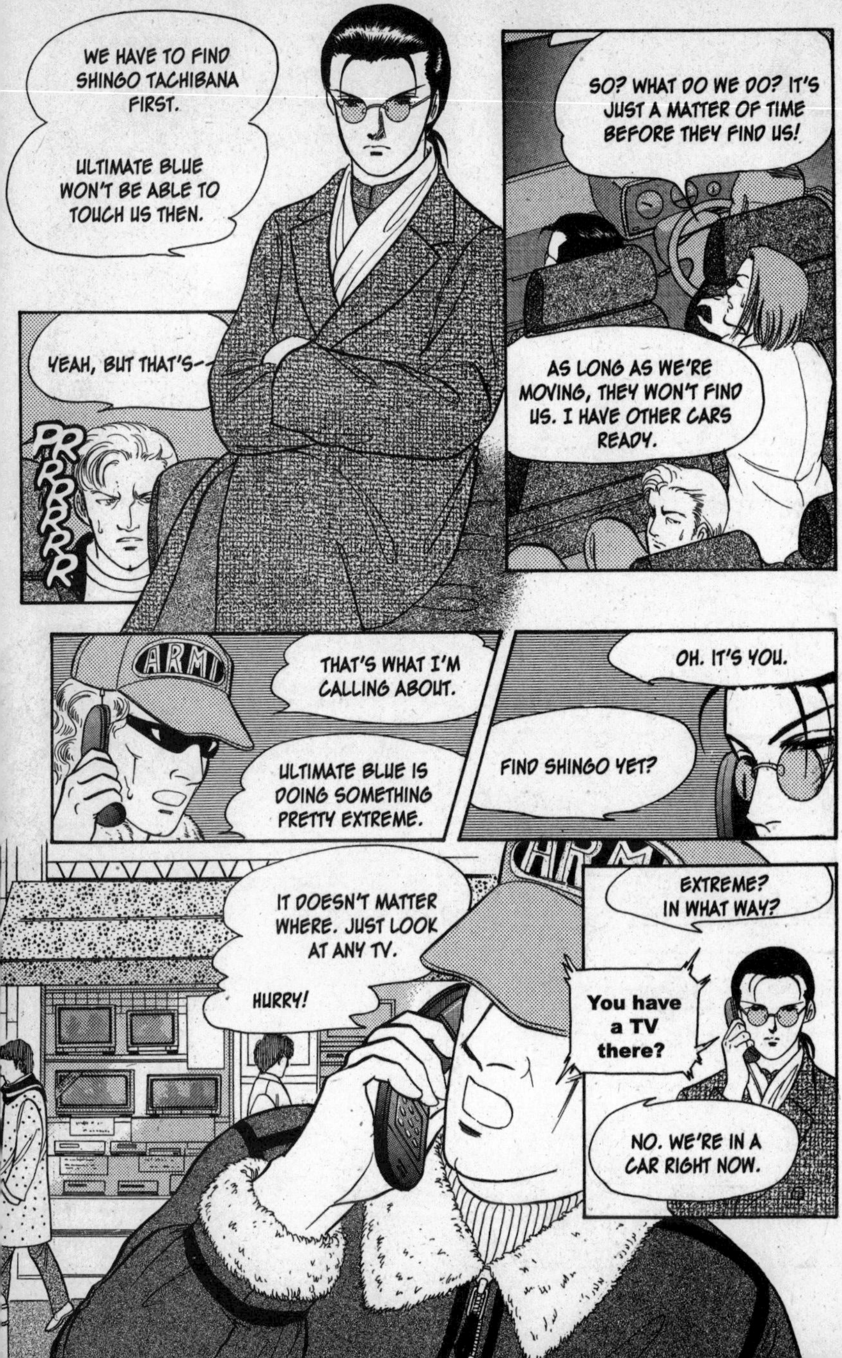
SO? WHAT DO WE DO? IT'S JUST A MATTER OF TIME BEFORE THEY FIND US!
AS LONG AS WE'RE MOVING, THEY WON'T FIND US. I HAVE OTHER CARS READY.
WE HAVE TO FIND SHINGO TACHIBANA FIRST.
ULTIMATE BLUE WON'T BE ABLE TO TOUCH US THEN.
YEAH, BUT THAT'S--
PRRRRRR
OH. IT'S YOU.
FIND SHINGO YET?
ARMI
THAT'S WHAT I'M CALLING ABOUT.
ULTIMATE BLUE IS DOING SOMETHING PRETTY EXTREME.
EXTREME? IN WHAT WAY?
IT DOESN'T MATTER WHERE. JUST LOOK AT ANY TV.
HURRY!
You have a TV there?
NO. WE'RE IN A CAR RIGHT NOW.

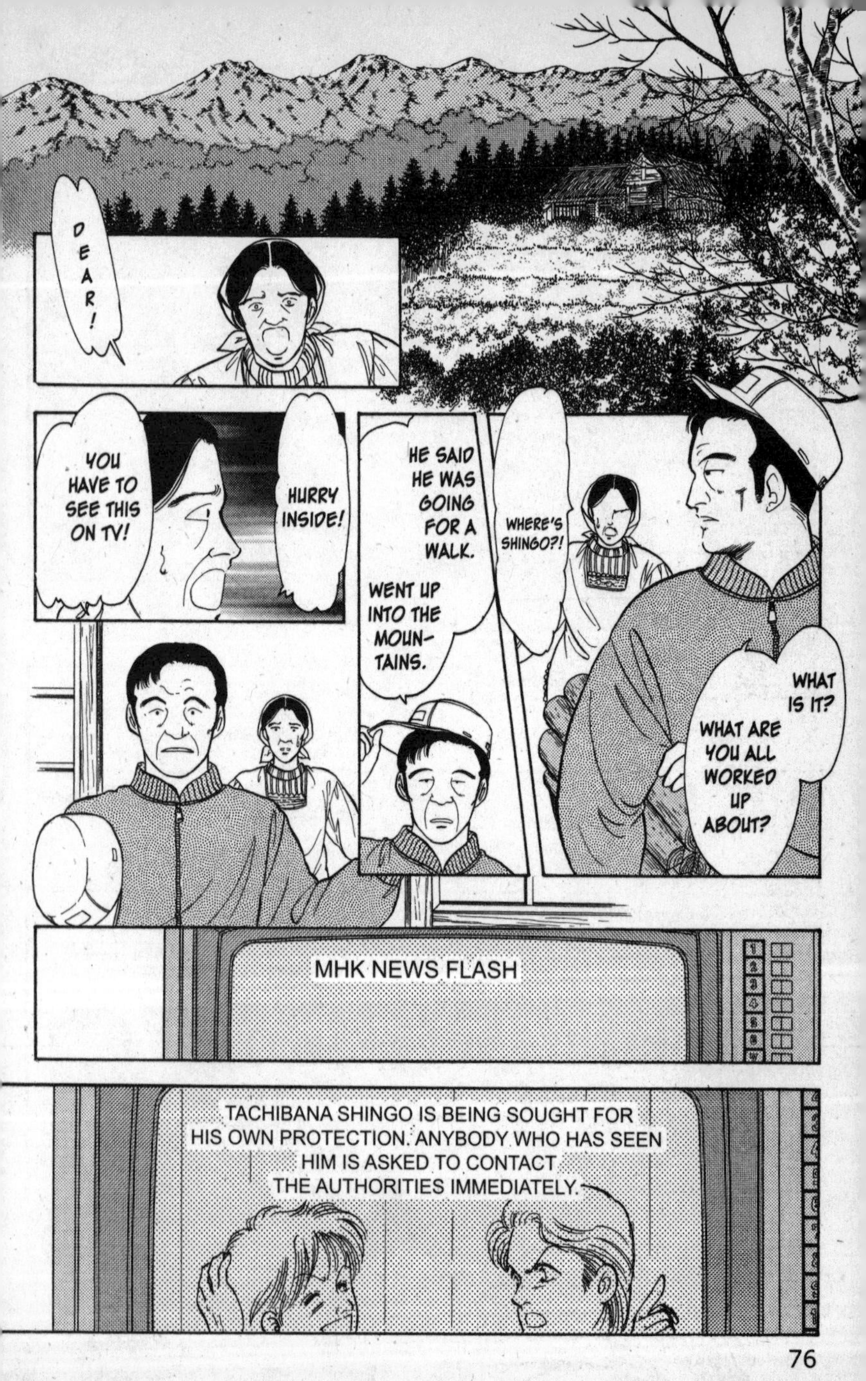
DEAR!
WHERE'S SHINGO?!
WHAT IS IT?
WHAT ARE YOU ALL WORKED UP ABOUT?
HE SAID HE WAS GOING FOR A WALK.
WENT UP INTO THE MOUN-TAINS.
HURRY INSIDE!
YOU HAVE TO SEE THIS ON TV!
MHK NEWS FLASH
TACHIBANA SHINGO IS BEING SOUGHT FOR HIS OWN PROTECTION. ANYBODY WHO HAS SEEN HIM IS ASKED TO CONTACT THE AUTHORITIES IMMEDIATELY.

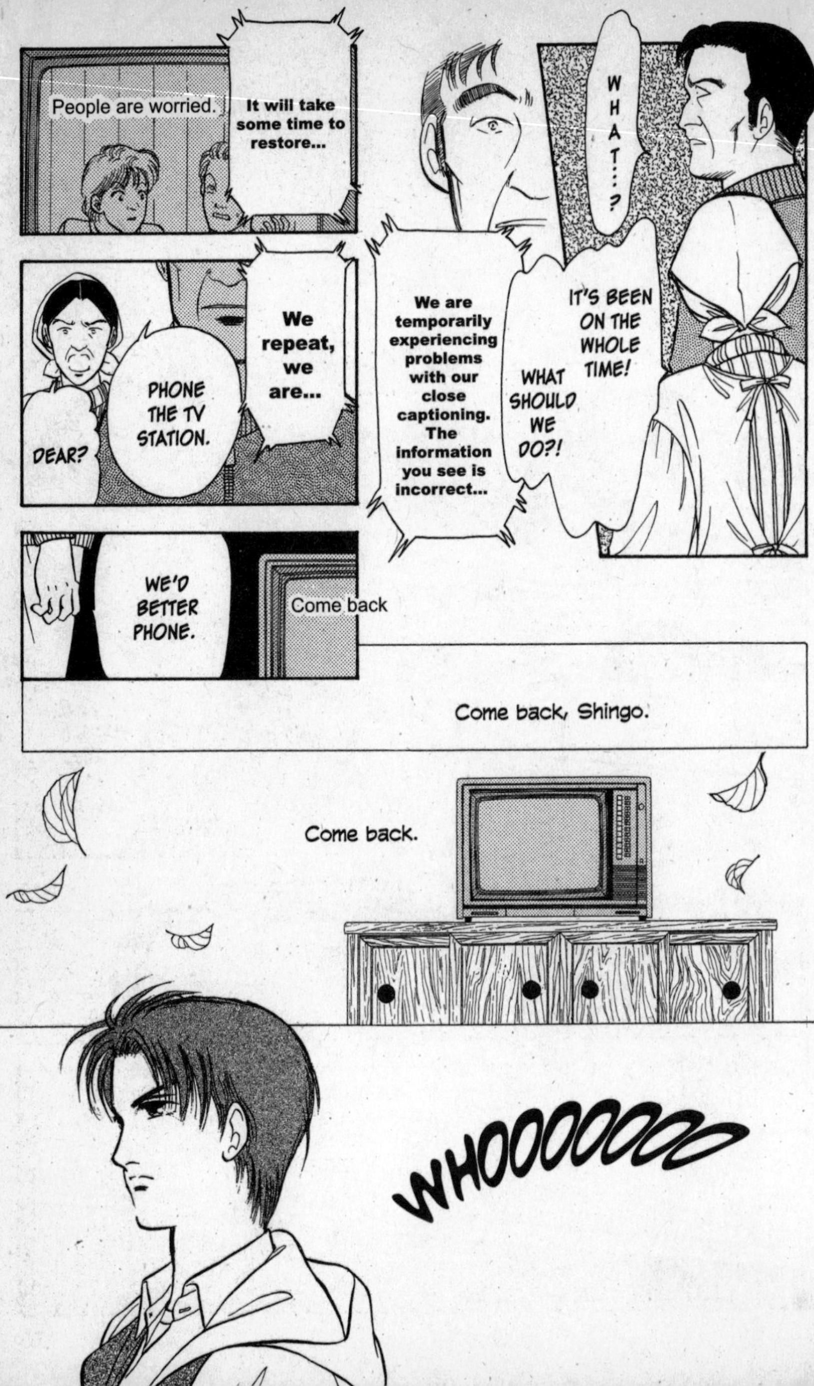
WHAT...?
IT'S BEEN ON THE WHOLE TIME!
WHAT SHOULD WE DO?!
It will take some time to restore...
People are worried.
We are temporarily experiencing problems with our close captioning. The information you see is incorrect...
We repeat, we are...
PHONE THE TV STATION.
DEAR?
Come back
WE'D BETTER PHONE.
Come back, Shingo.
Come back.
WHOOOOOOO

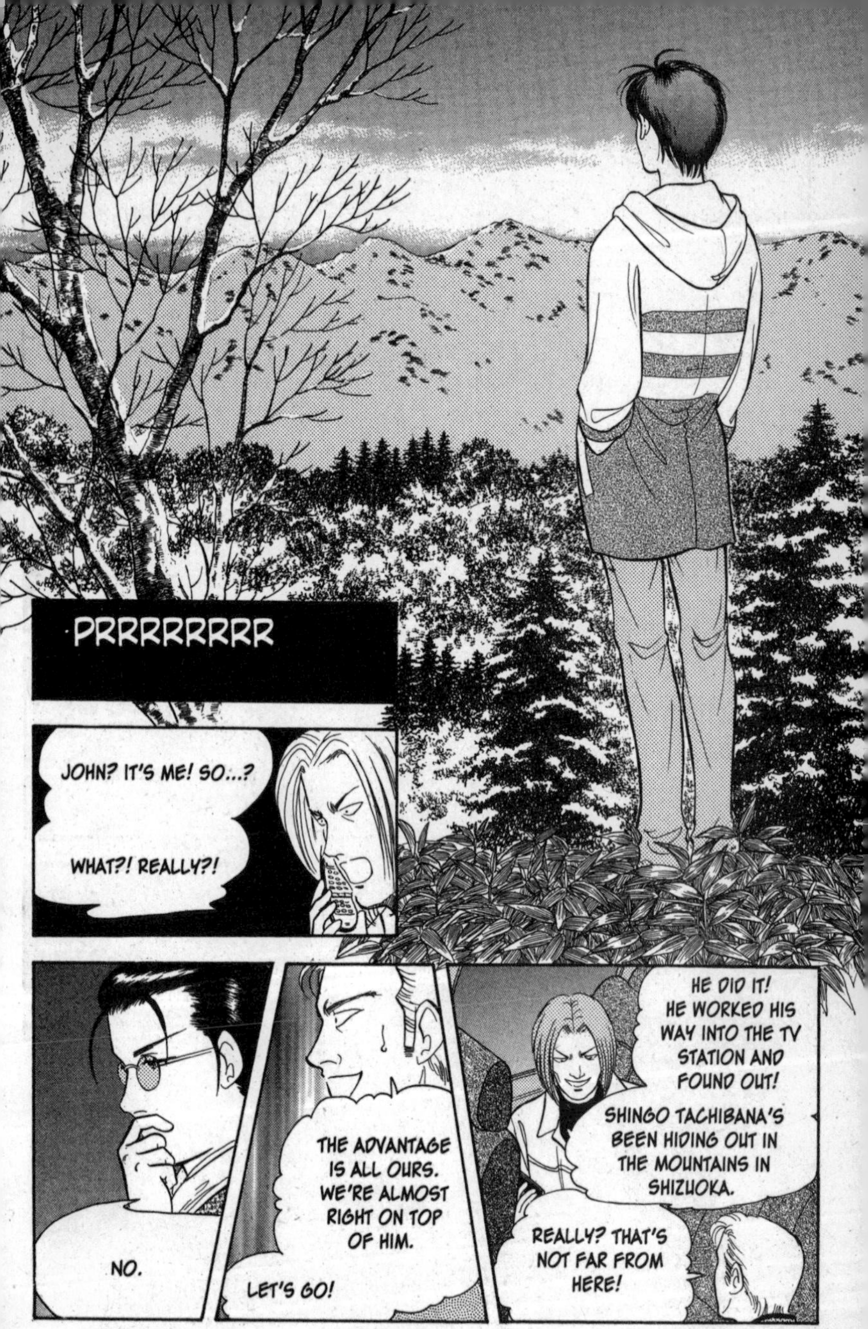
PRRRRRRRR
JOHN? IT'S ME! SO...?
WHAT?! REALLY?!
HE DID IT! HE WORKED HIS WAY INTO THE TV STATION AND FOUND OUT!
SHINGO TACHIBANA'S BEEN HIDING OUT IN THE MOUNTAINS IN SHIZUOKA.
REALLY? THAT'S NOT FAR FROM HERE!
THE ADVANTAGE IS ALL OURS. WE'RE ALMOST RIGHT ON TOP OF HIM.
LET'S GO!
NO.

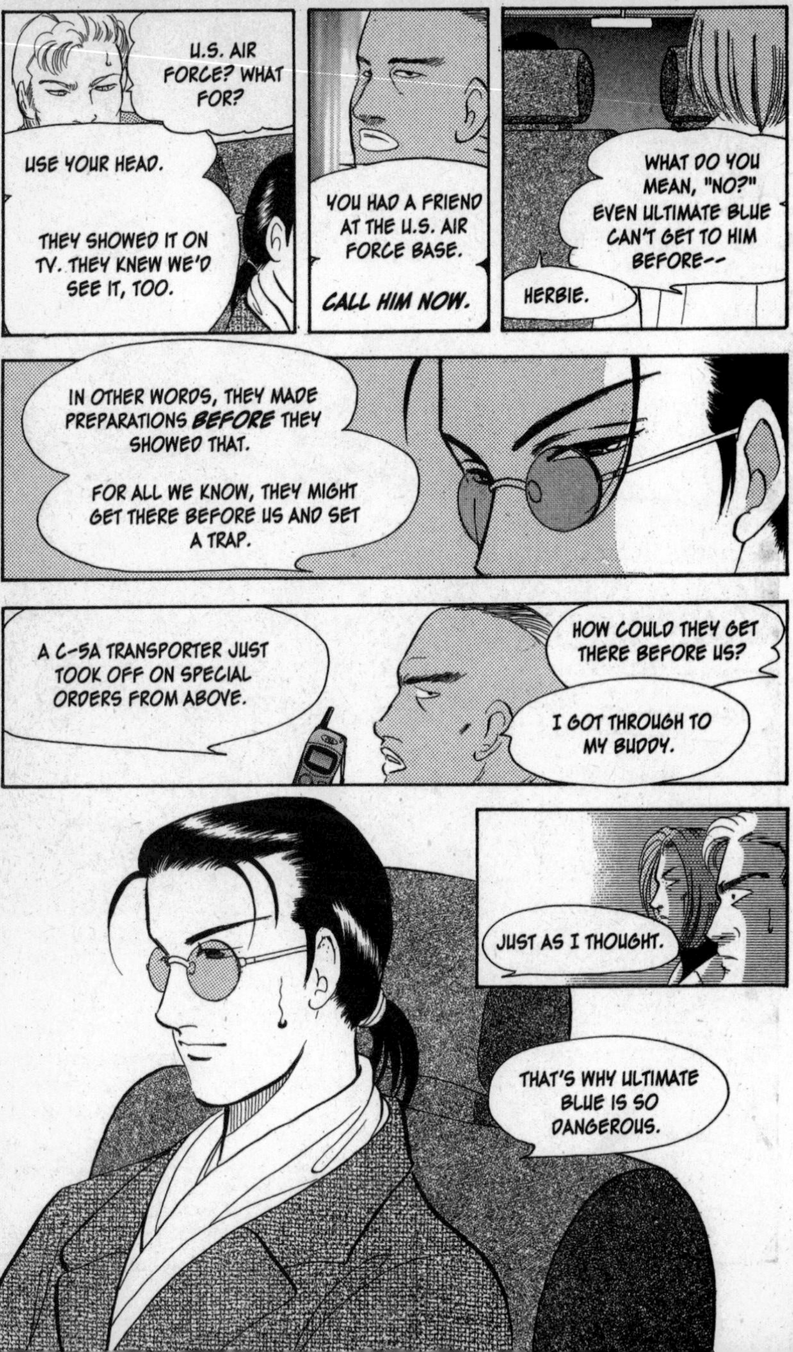
WHAT DO YOU MEAN, "NO?" EVEN ULTIMATE BLUE CAN'T GET TO HIM BEFORE--
HERBIE.
YOU HAD A FRIEND AT THE U.S. AIR FORCE BASE.
CALL HIM NOW.
U.S. AIR FORCE? WHAT FOR?
USE YOUR HEAD.
THEY SHOWED IT ON TV. THEY KNEW WE'D SEE IT, TOO.
IN OTHER WORDS, THEY MADE PREPARATIONS BEFORE THEY SHOWED THAT.
FOR ALL WE KNOW, THEY MIGHT GET THERE BEFORE US AND SET A TRAP.
HOW COULD THEY GET THERE BEFORE US?
I GOT THROUGH TO MY BUDDY.
A C-5A TRANSPORTER JUST TOOK OFF ON SPECIAL ORDERS FROM ABOVE.
JUST AS I THOUGHT.
THAT'S WHY ULTIMATE BLUE IS SO DANGEROUS.

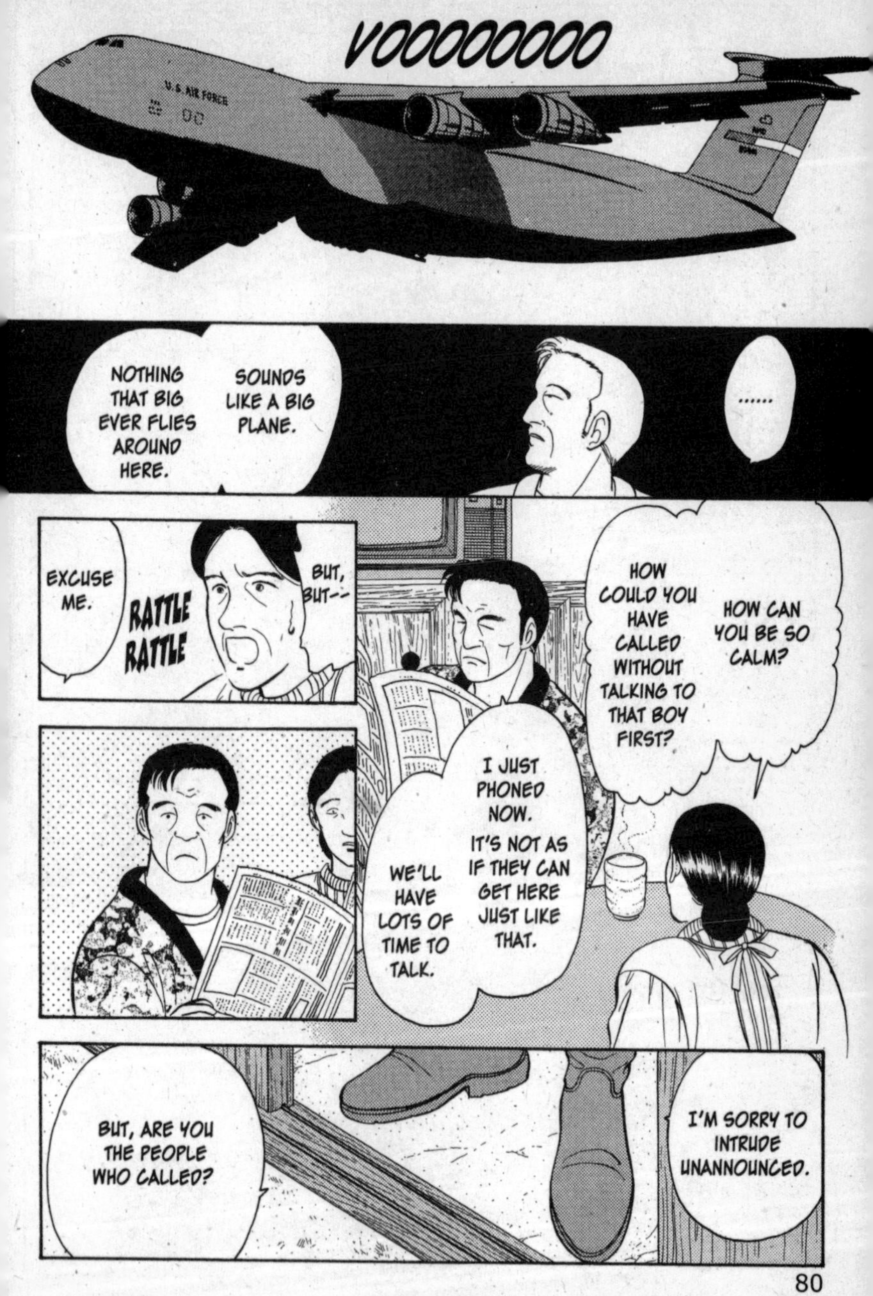
VOOOOOOOO
U.S. AIR FORCE
......
SOUNDS LIKE A BIG PLANE.
NOTHING THAT BIG EVER FLIES AROUND HERE.
HOW CAN YOU BE SO CALM?
HOW COULD YOU HAVE CALLED WITHOUT TALKING TO THAT BOY FIRST?
I JUST PHONED NOW.
IT'S NOT AS IF THEY CAN GET HERE JUST LIKE THAT.
WE'LL HAVE LOTS OF TIME TO TALK.
BUT, BUT--
RATTLE RATTLE
EXCUSE ME.
I'M SORRY TO INTRUDE UNANNOUNCED.
BUT, ARE YOU THE PEOPLE WHO CALLED?

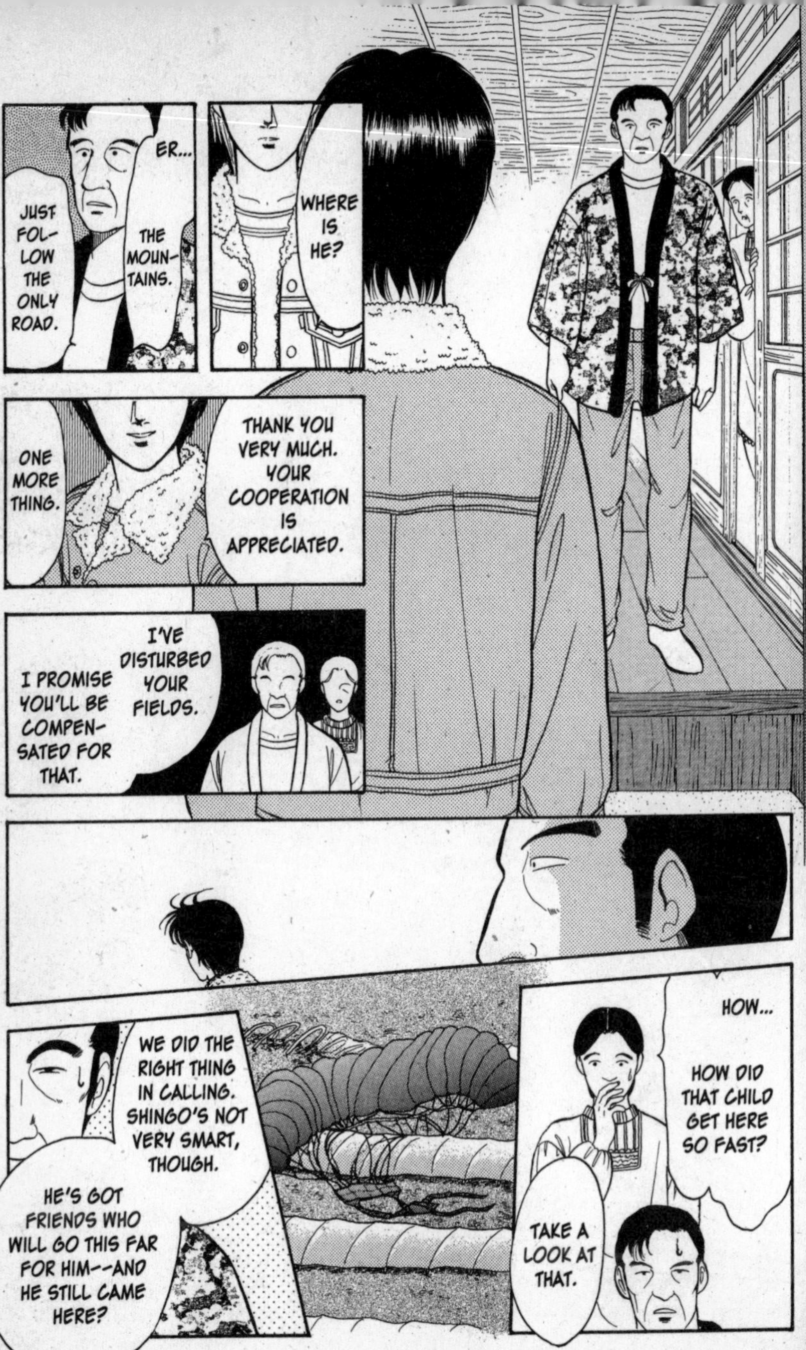
WHERE IS HE?
ER...
THE MOUNTAINS.
JUST FOLLOW THE ONLY ROAD.
THANK YOU VERY MUCH. YOUR COOPERATION IS APPRECIATED.
ONE MORE THING.
I'VE DISTURBED YOUR FIELDS.
I PROMISE YOU'LL BE COMPENSATED FOR THAT.
HOW...
HOW DID THAT CHILD GET HERE SO FAST?
TAKE A LOOK AT THAT.
WE DID THE RIGHT THING IN CALLING. SHINGO'S NOT VERY SMART, THOUGH.
HE'S GOT FRIENDS WHO WILL GO THIS FAR FOR HIM--AND HE STILL CAME HERE?

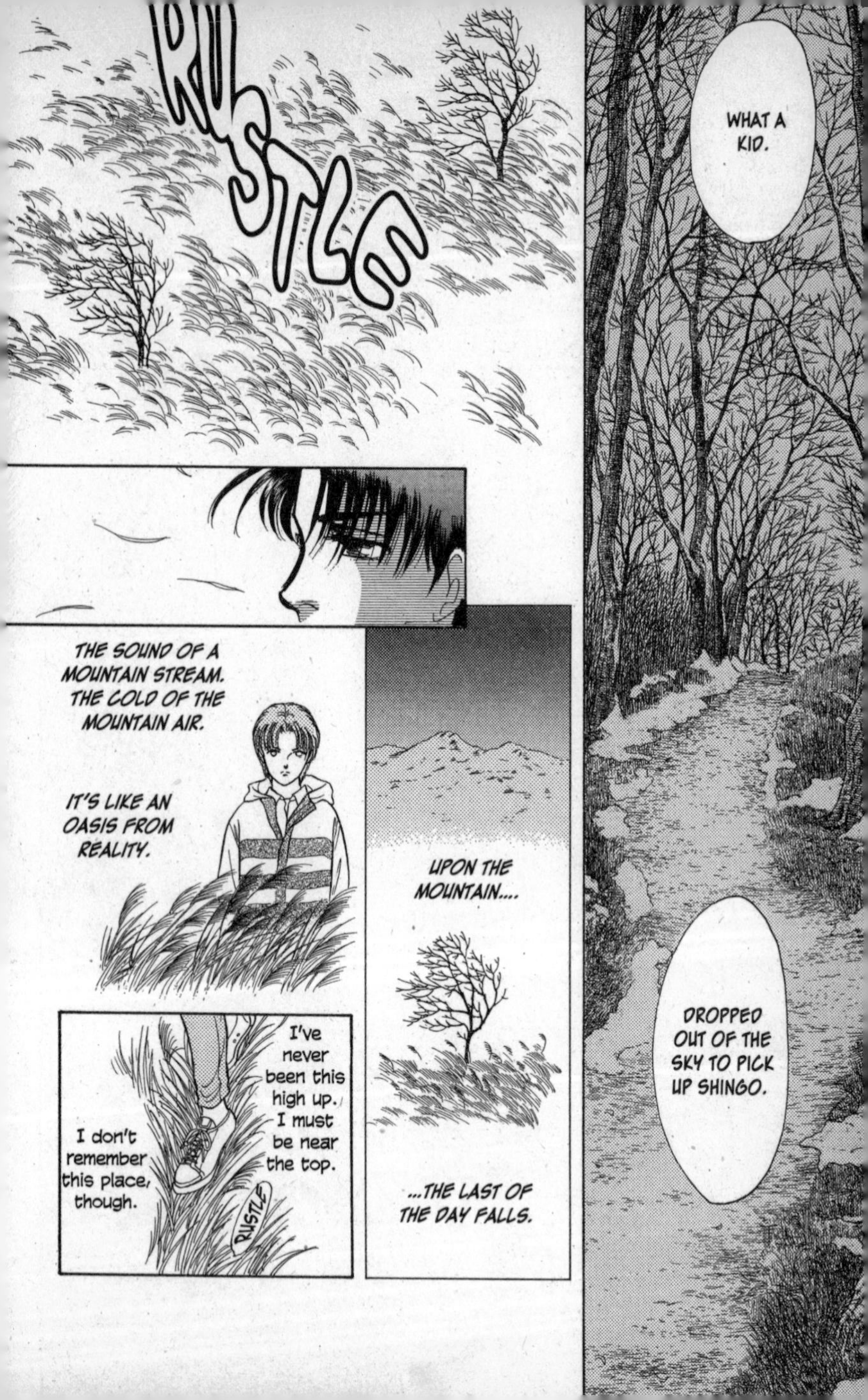
WHAT A KID.
DROPPED OUT OF THE SKY TO PICK UP SHINGO.
RUSTLE
UPON THE MOUNTAIN....
...THE LAST OF THE DAY FALLS.
THE SOUND OF A MOUNTAIN STREAM. THE COLD OF THE MOUNTAIN AIR.
IT'S LIKE AN OASIS FROM REALITY.
I've never been this high up. I must be near the top.
I don't remember this place, though.
RUSTLE

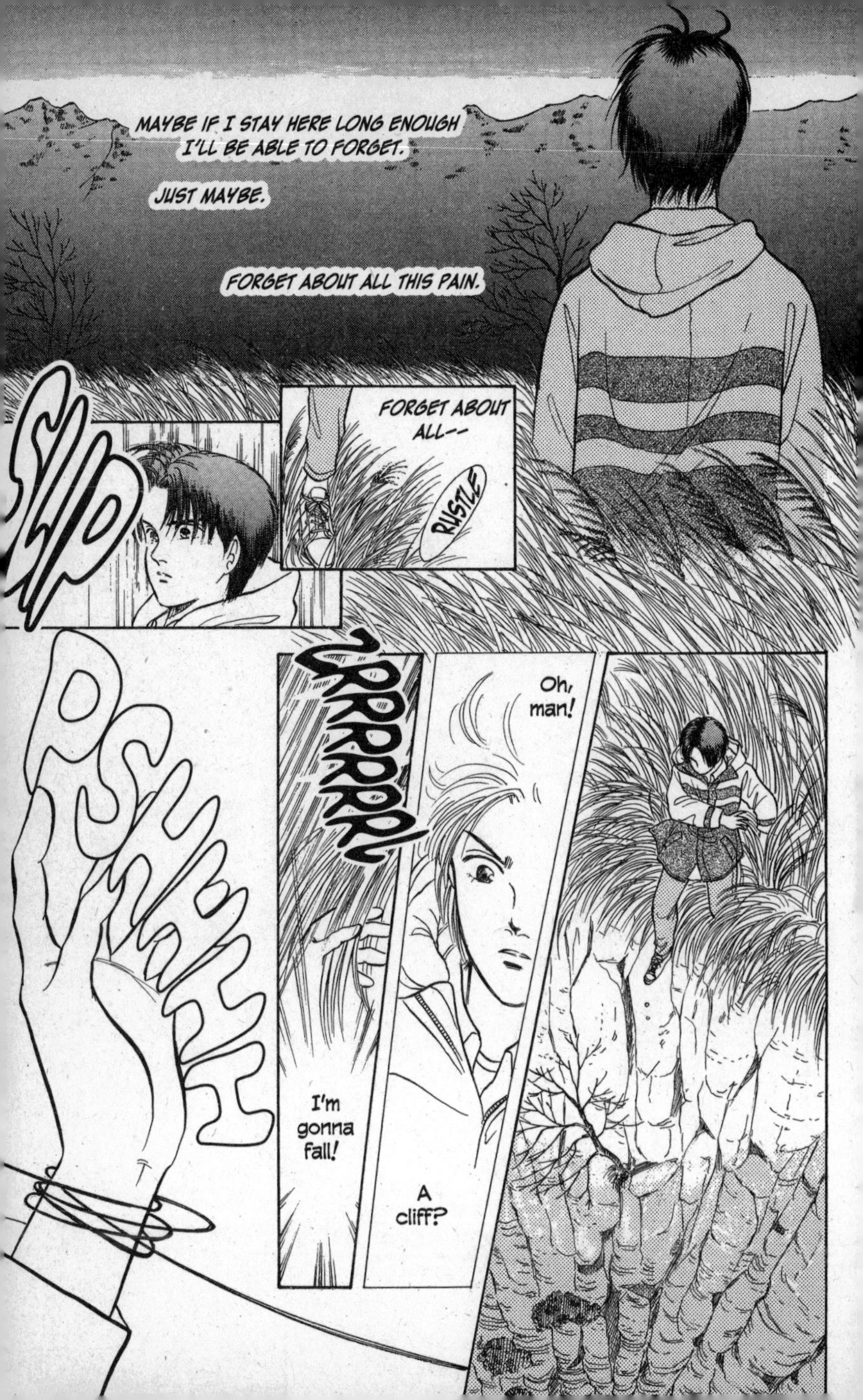
MAYBE IF I STAY HERE LONG ENOUGH I'LL BE ABLE TO FORGET.
JUST MAYBE.
FORGET ABOUT ALL THIS PAIN.
FORGET ABOUT ALL--
RUSTLE
SLIP
Oh, man!
A cliff?
URRRRRRL
I'm gonna fall!
PSHWAH

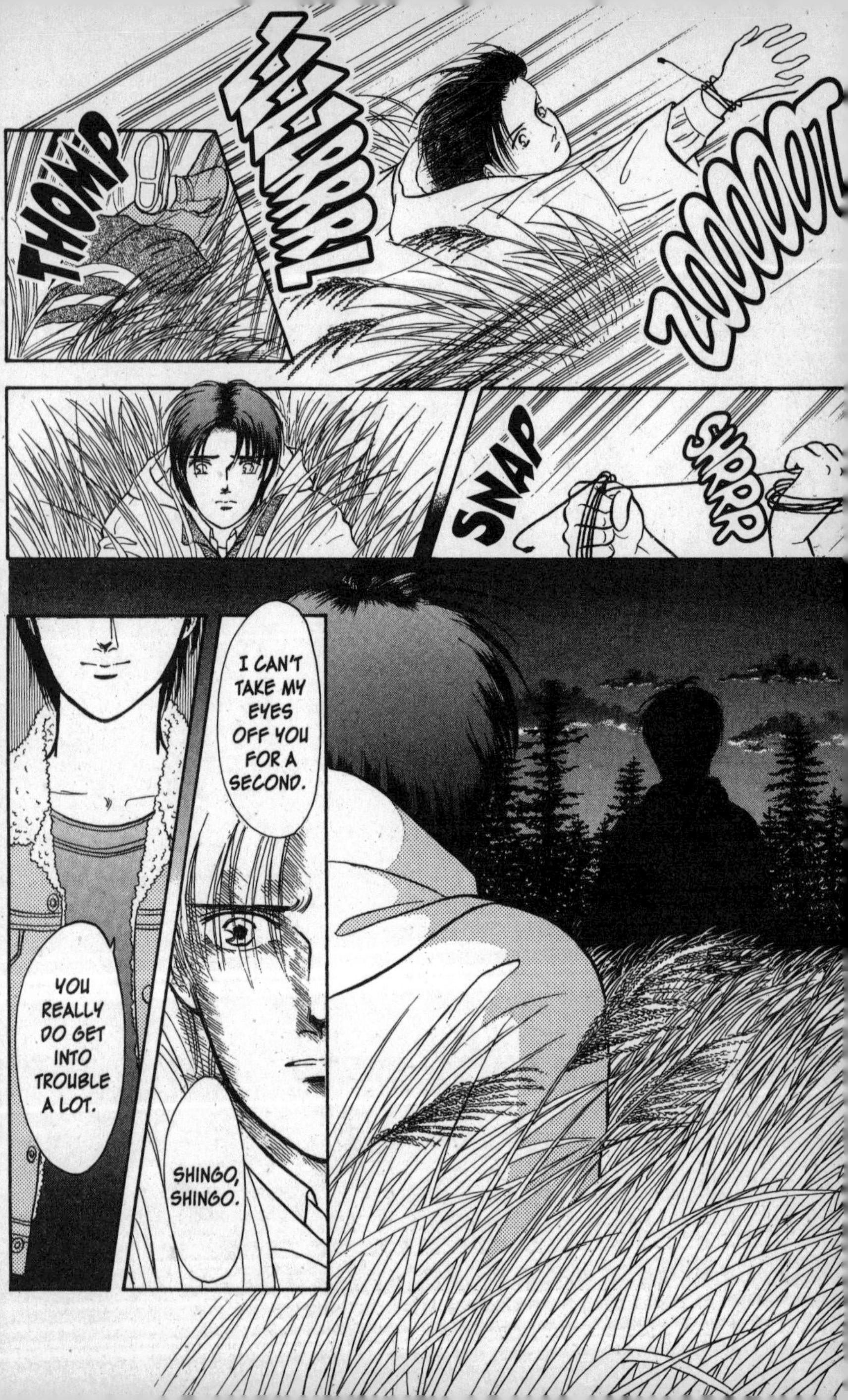
ZOOOOOT
THOMP
SHRRR
SNAP
I CAN'T TAKE MY EYES OFF YOU FOR A SECOND.
SHINGO, SHINGO.
YOU REALLY DO GET INTO TROUBLE A LOT.

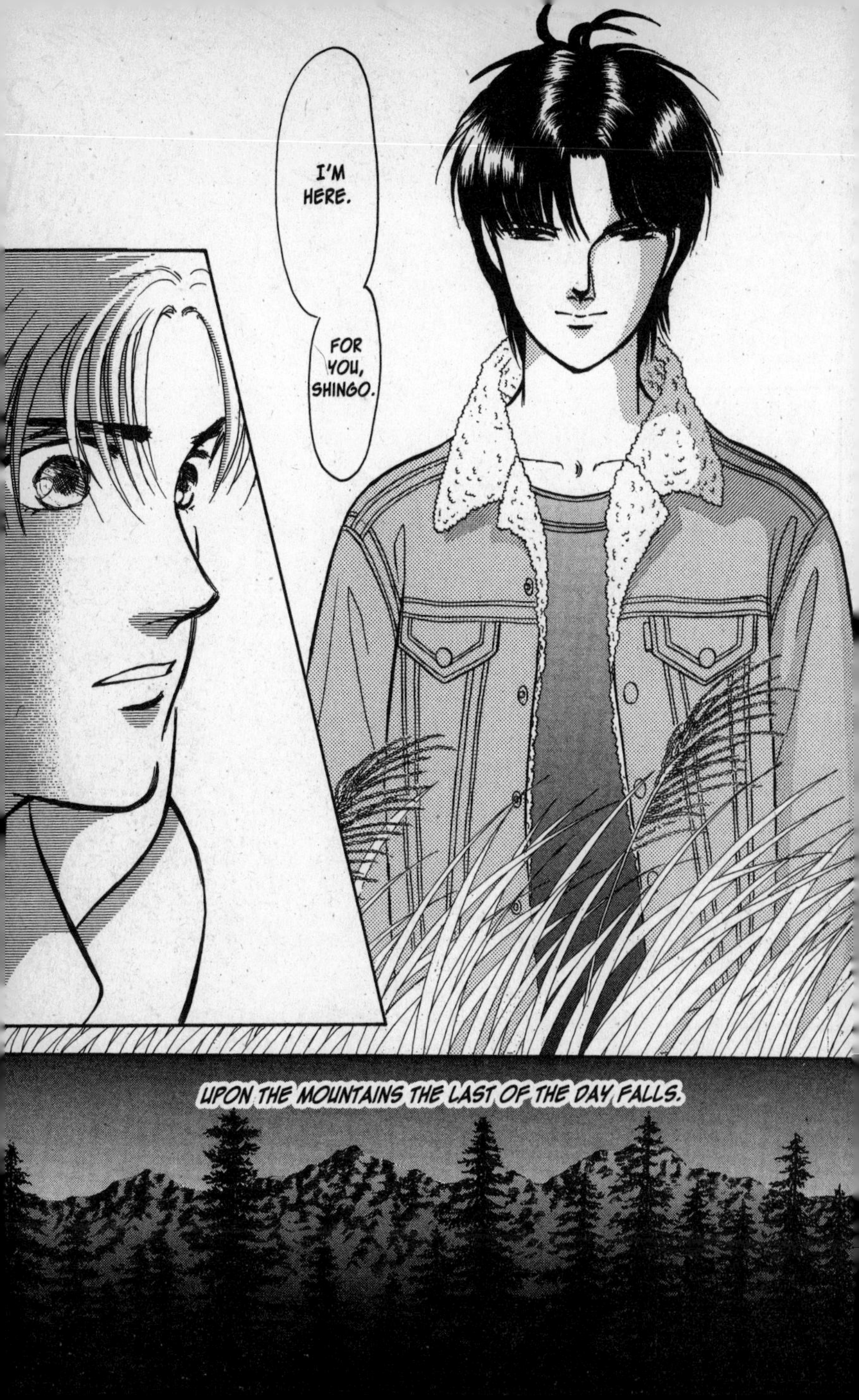
I'M HERE.
FOR YOU, SHINGO.
UPON THE MOUNTAINS THE LAST OF THE DAY FALLS.

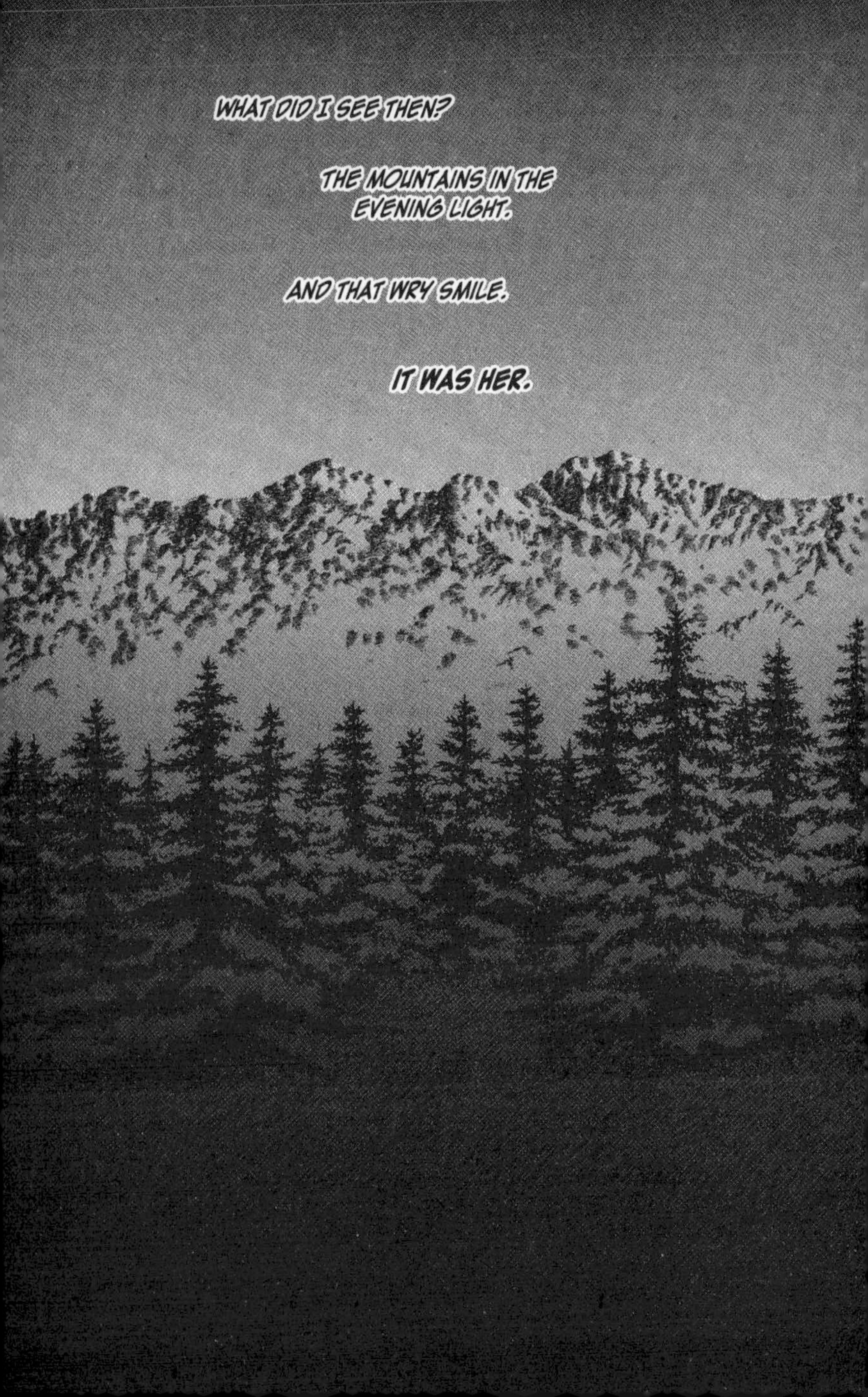
WHAT DID I SEE THEN?
THE MOUNTAINS IN THE EVENING LIGHT.
AND THAT WRY SMILE.
IT WAS HER.

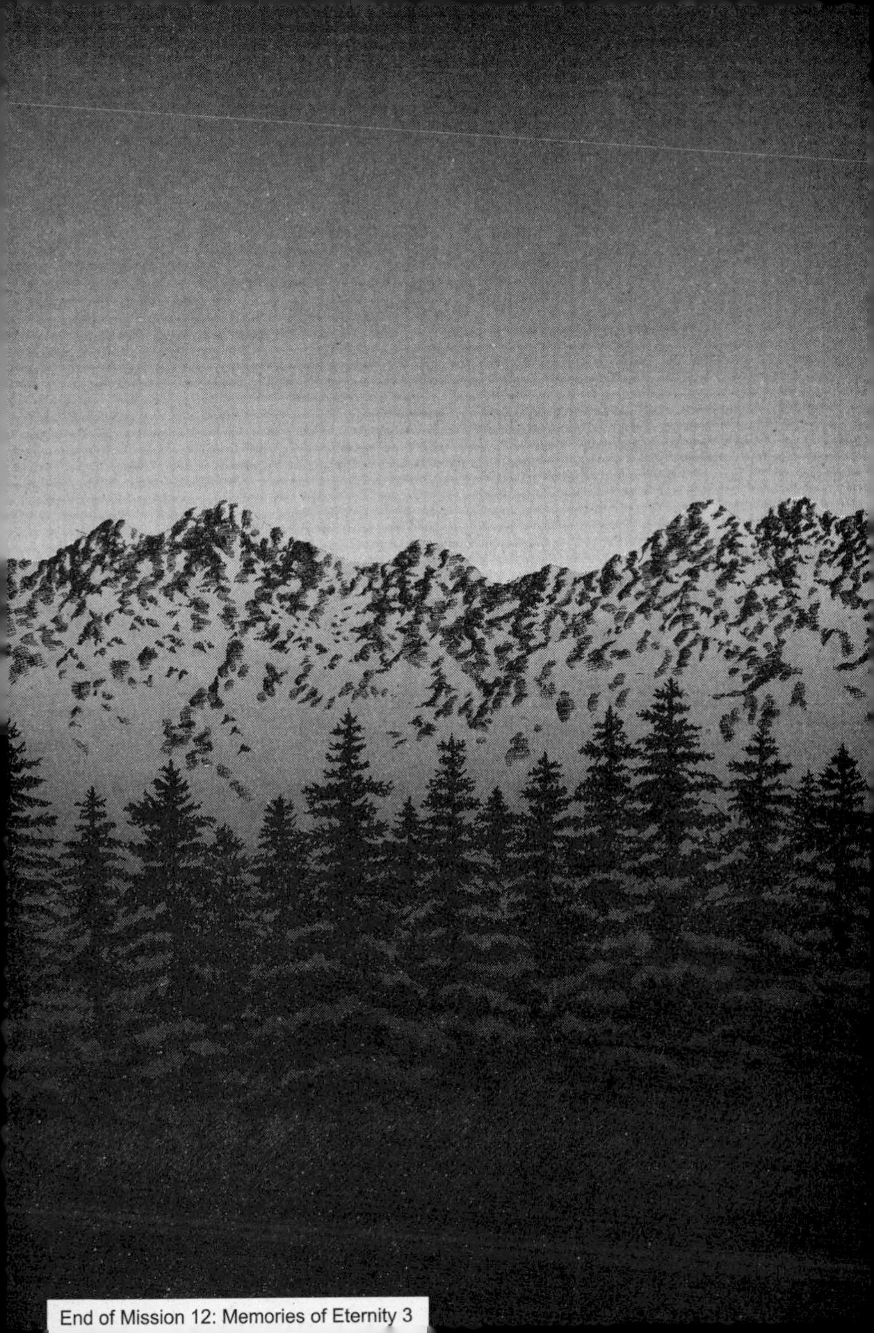
End of Mission 12: Memories of Eternity 3

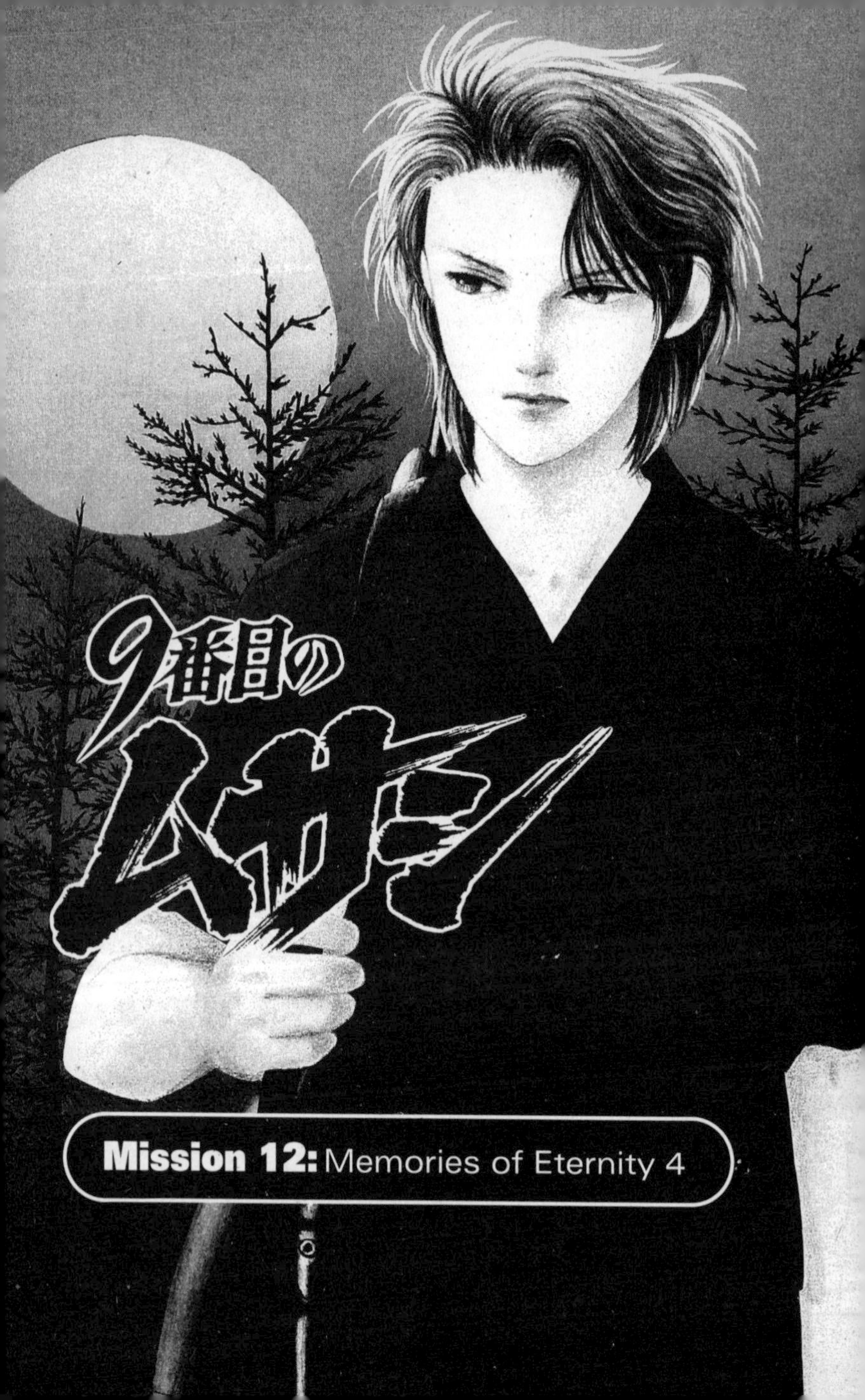
9番目のムサシ
Mission 12: Memories of Eternity 4

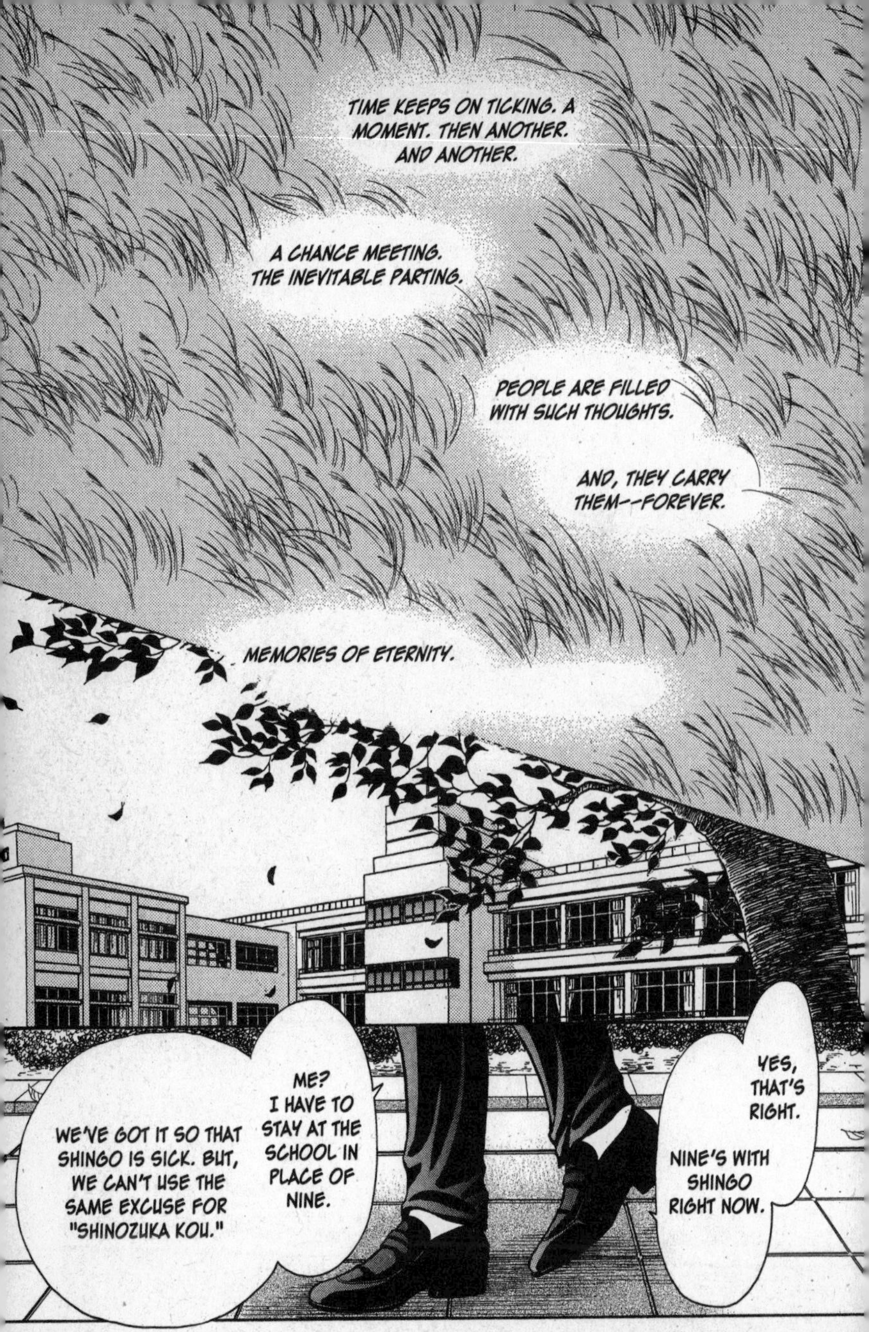
TIME KEEPS ON TICKING. A MOMENT. THEN ANOTHER. AND ANOTHER.
A CHANCE MEETING. THE INEVITABLE PARTING.
PEOPLE ARE FILLED WITH SUCH THOUGHTS.
AND, THEY CARRY THEM--FOREVER.
MEMORIES OF ETERNITY.
YES, THAT'S RIGHT.
NINE'S WITH SHINGO RIGHT NOW.
ME? I HAVE TO STAY AT THE SCHOOL IN PLACE OF NINE.
WE'VE GOT IT SO THAT SHINGO IS SICK. BUT, WE CAN'T USE THE SAME EXCUSE FOR "SHINOZUKA KOU."

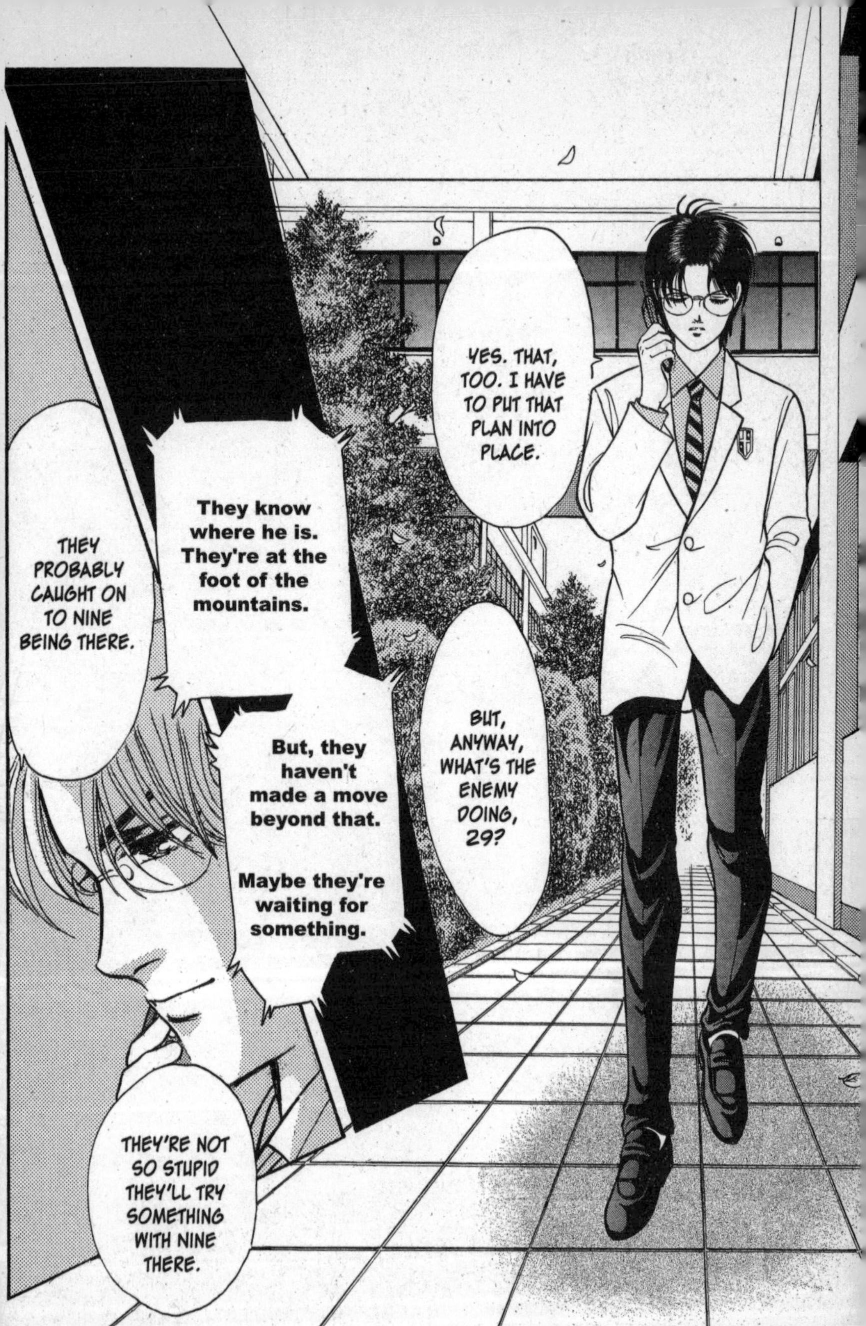
YES. THAT, TOO. I HAVE TO PUT THAT PLAN INTO PLACE.
BUT, ANYWAY, WHAT'S THE ENEMY DOING, 29?
They know where he is. They're at the foot of the mountains.
But, they haven't made a move beyond that.
Maybe they're waiting for something.
THEY PROBABLY CAUGHT ON TO NINE BEING THERE.
THEY'RE NOT SO STUPID THEY'LL TRY SOMETHING WITH NINE THERE.

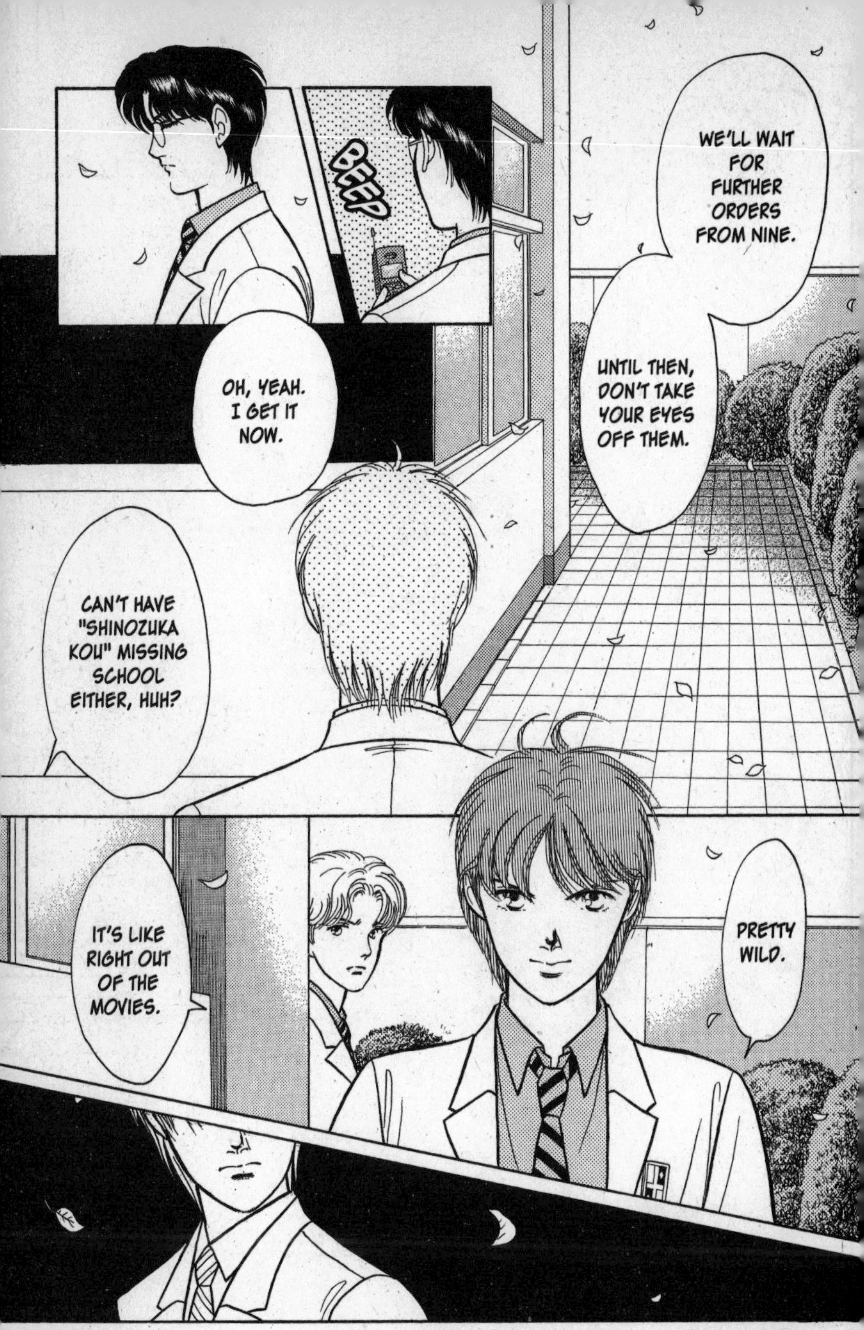
WE'LL WAIT FOR FURTHER ORDERS FROM NINE.
UNTIL THEN, DON'T TAKE YOUR EYES OFF THEM.
BEEP
OH, YEAH. I GET IT NOW.
CAN'T HAVE "SHINOZUKA KOU" MISSING SCHOOL EITHER, HUH?
PRETTY WILD.
IT'S LIKE RIGHT OUT OF THE MOVIES.

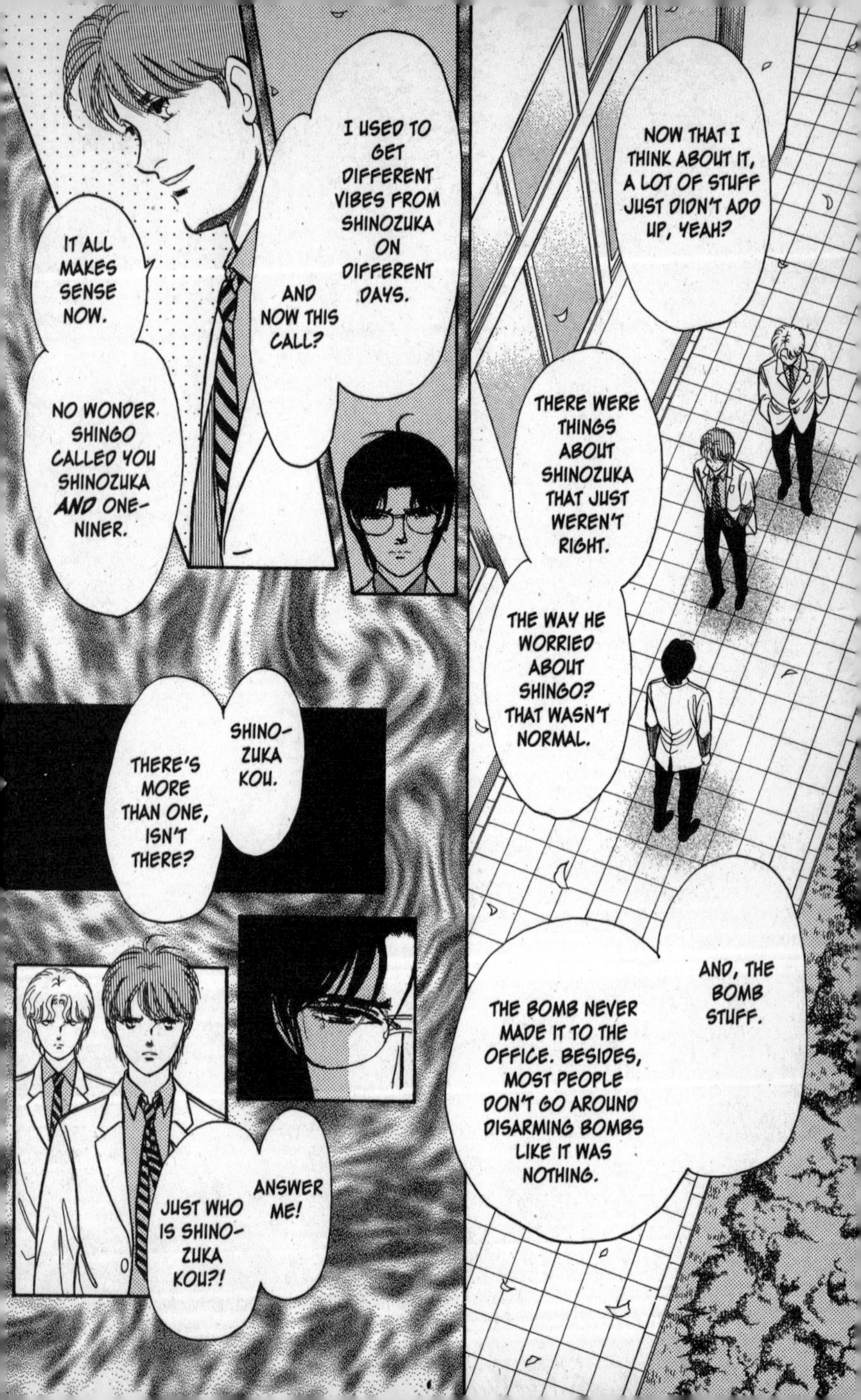
NOW THAT I THINK ABOUT IT, A LOT OF STUFF JUST DIDN'T ADD UP, YEAH?
THERE WERE THINGS ABOUT SHINOZUKA THAT JUST WEREN'T RIGHT.
THE WAY HE WORRIED ABOUT SHINGO? THAT WASN'T NORMAL.
AND, THE BOMB STUFF.
THE BOMB NEVER MADE IT TO THE OFFICE. BESIDES, MOST PEOPLE DON'T GO AROUND DISARMING BOMBS LIKE IT WAS NOTHING.
I USED TO GET DIFFERENT VIBES FROM SHINOZUKA ON DIFFERENT DAYS.
AND NOW THIS CALL?
IT ALL MAKES SENSE NOW.
NO WONDER SHINGO CALLED YOU SHINOZUKA *AND* ONE-NINER.
SHINO-ZUKA KOU.
THERE'S MORE THAN ONE, ISN'T THERE?
ANSWER ME!
JUST WHO IS SHINO-ZUKA KOU?!

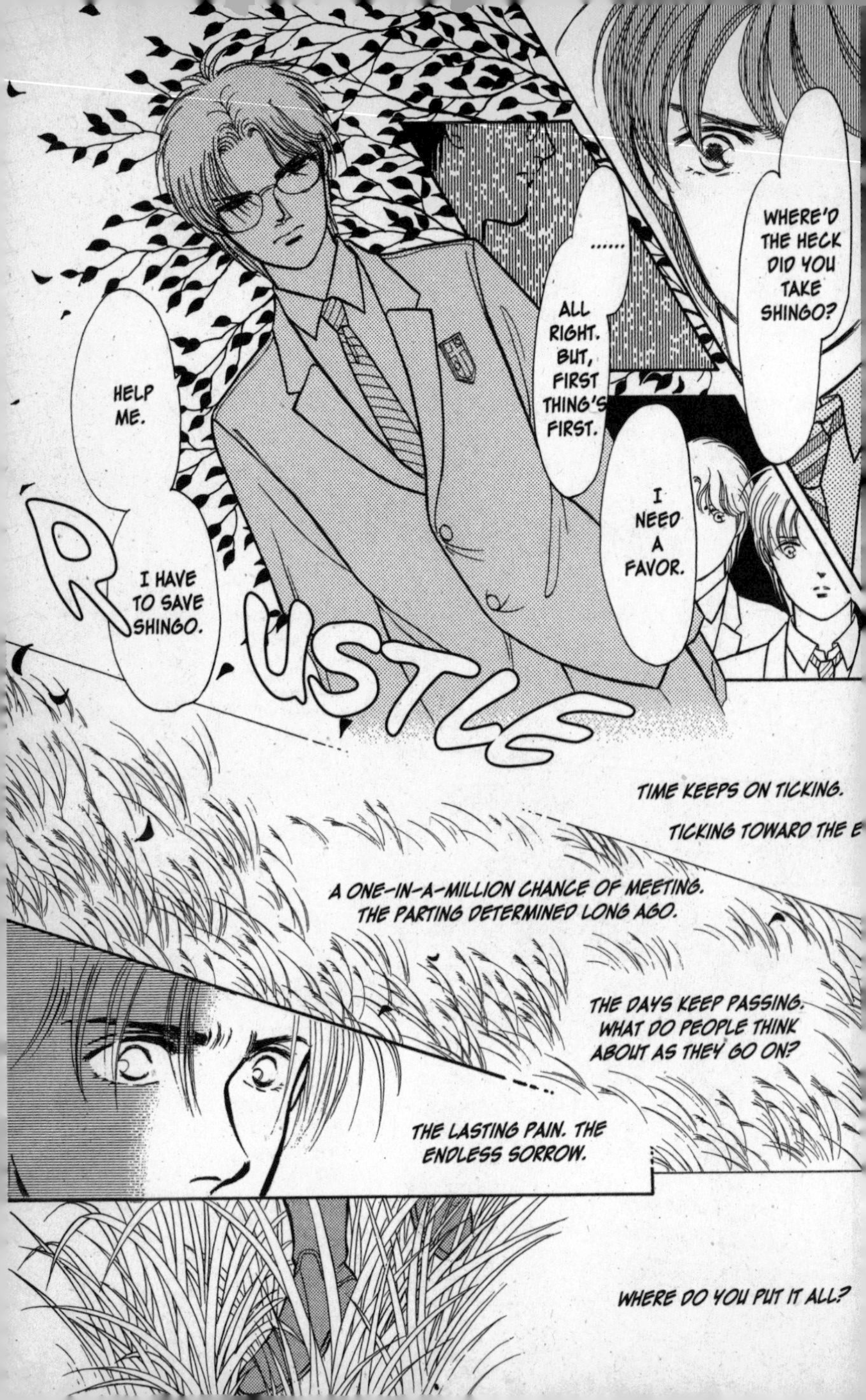
WHERE'D THE HECK DID YOU TAKE SHINGO?
......
ALL RIGHT. BUT, FIRST THING'S FIRST.
I NEED A FAVOR.
HELP ME.
I HAVE TO SAVE SHINGO.
RUSTLE
TIME KEEPS ON TICKING.
TICKING TOWARD THE E
A ONE-IN-A-MILLION CHANCE OF MEETING. THE PARTING DETERMINED LONG AGO.
THE DAYS KEEP PASSING. WHAT DO PEOPLE THINK ABOUT AS THEY GO ON?
THE LASTING PAIN. THE ENDLESS SORROW.
WHERE DO YOU PUT IT ALL?

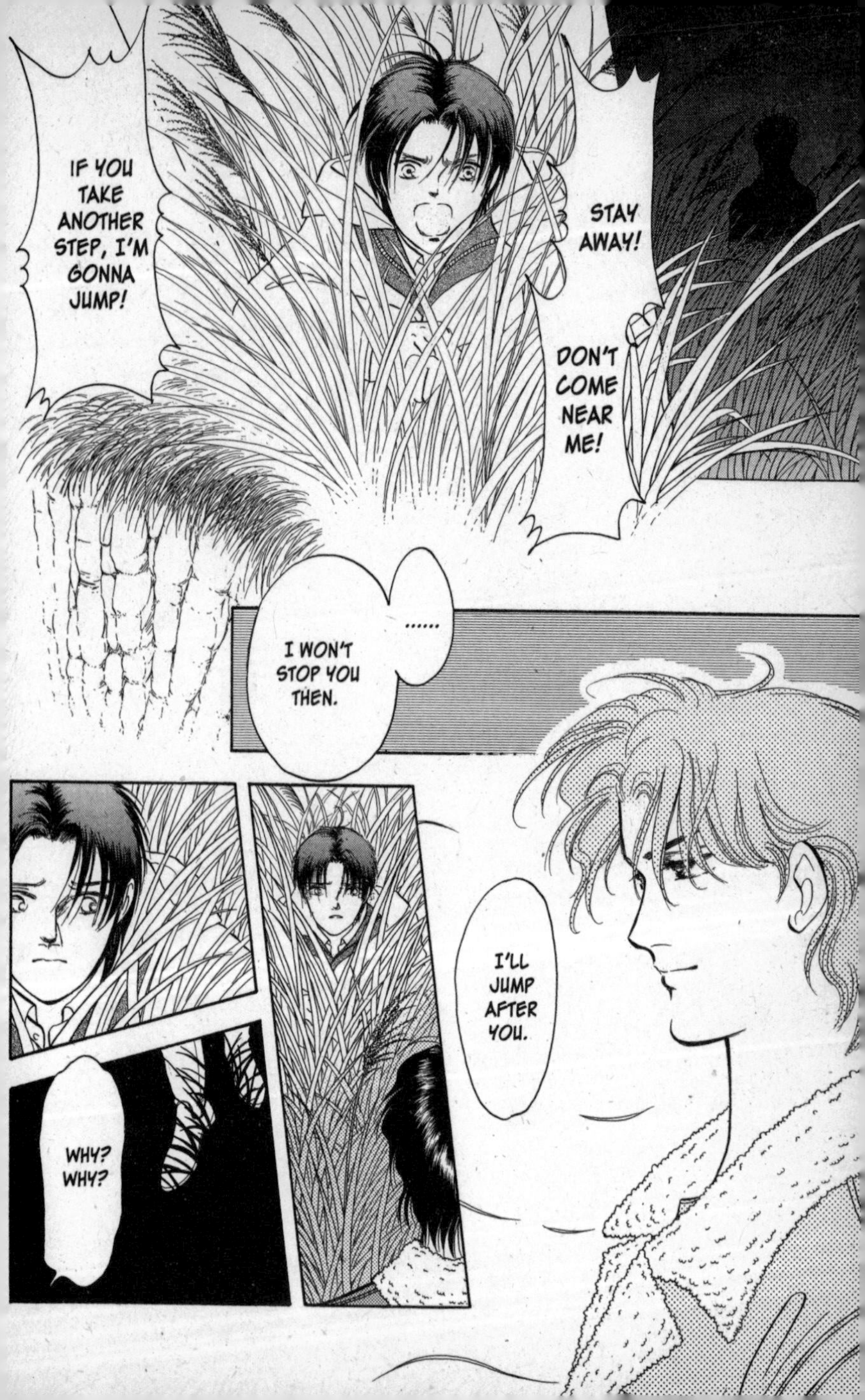
STAY AWAY!
DON'T COME NEAR ME!
IF YOU TAKE ANOTHER STEP, I'M GONNA JUMP!
......
I WON'T STOP YOU THEN.
I'LL JUMP AFTER YOU.
WHY? WHY?

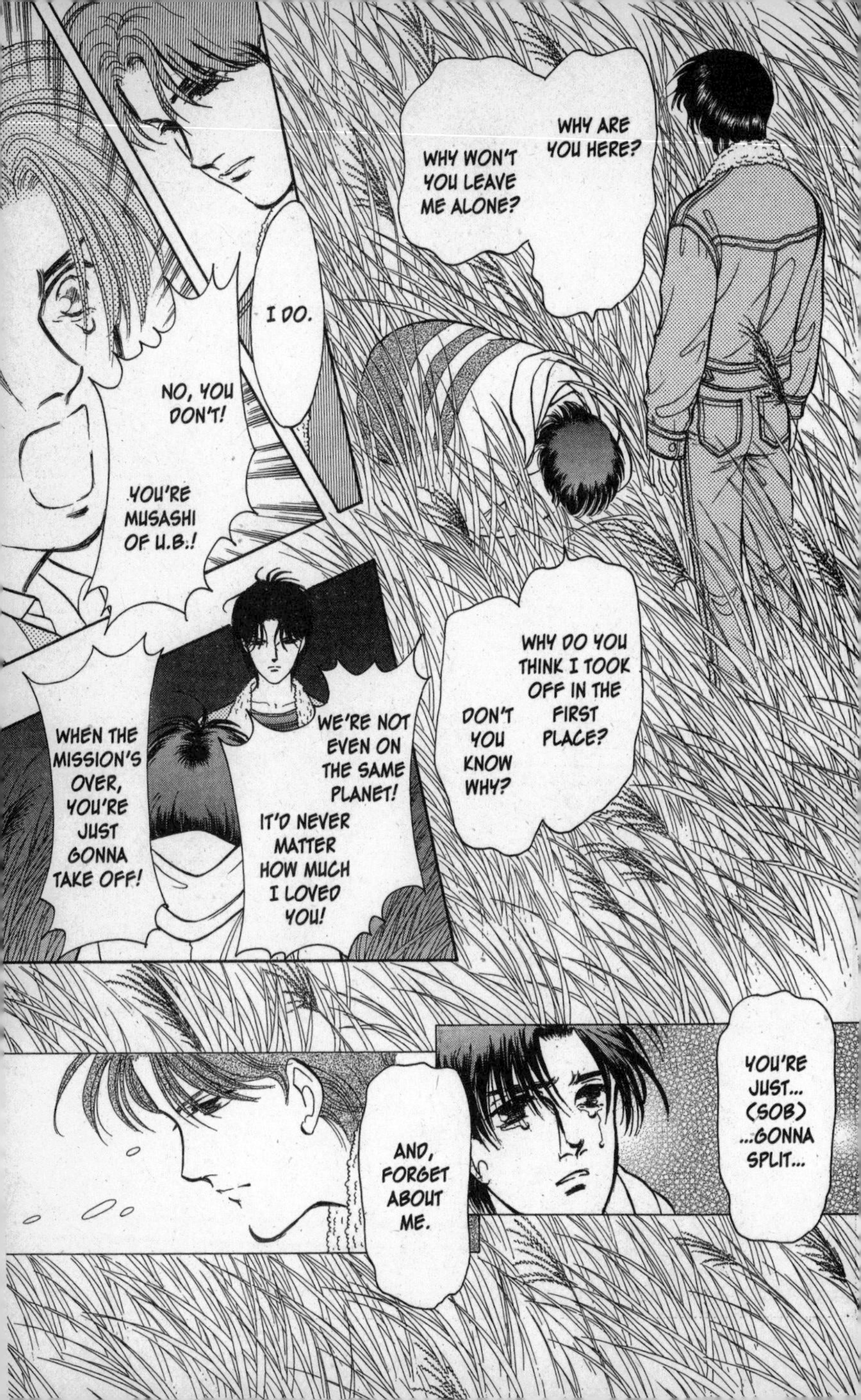
WHY ARE YOU HERE?
WHY WON'T YOU LEAVE ME ALONE?
WHY DO YOU THINK I TOOK OFF IN THE FIRST PLACE?
DON'T YOU KNOW WHY?
I DO.
NO, YOU DON'T!
YOU'RE MUSASHI OF U.B.!
WE'RE NOT EVEN ON THE SAME PLANET!
IT'D NEVER MATTER HOW MUCH I LOVED YOU!
WHEN THE MISSION'S OVER, YOU'RE JUST GONNA TAKE OFF!
YOU'RE JUST... (SOB) ...GONNA SPLIT...
AND, FORGET ABOUT ME.

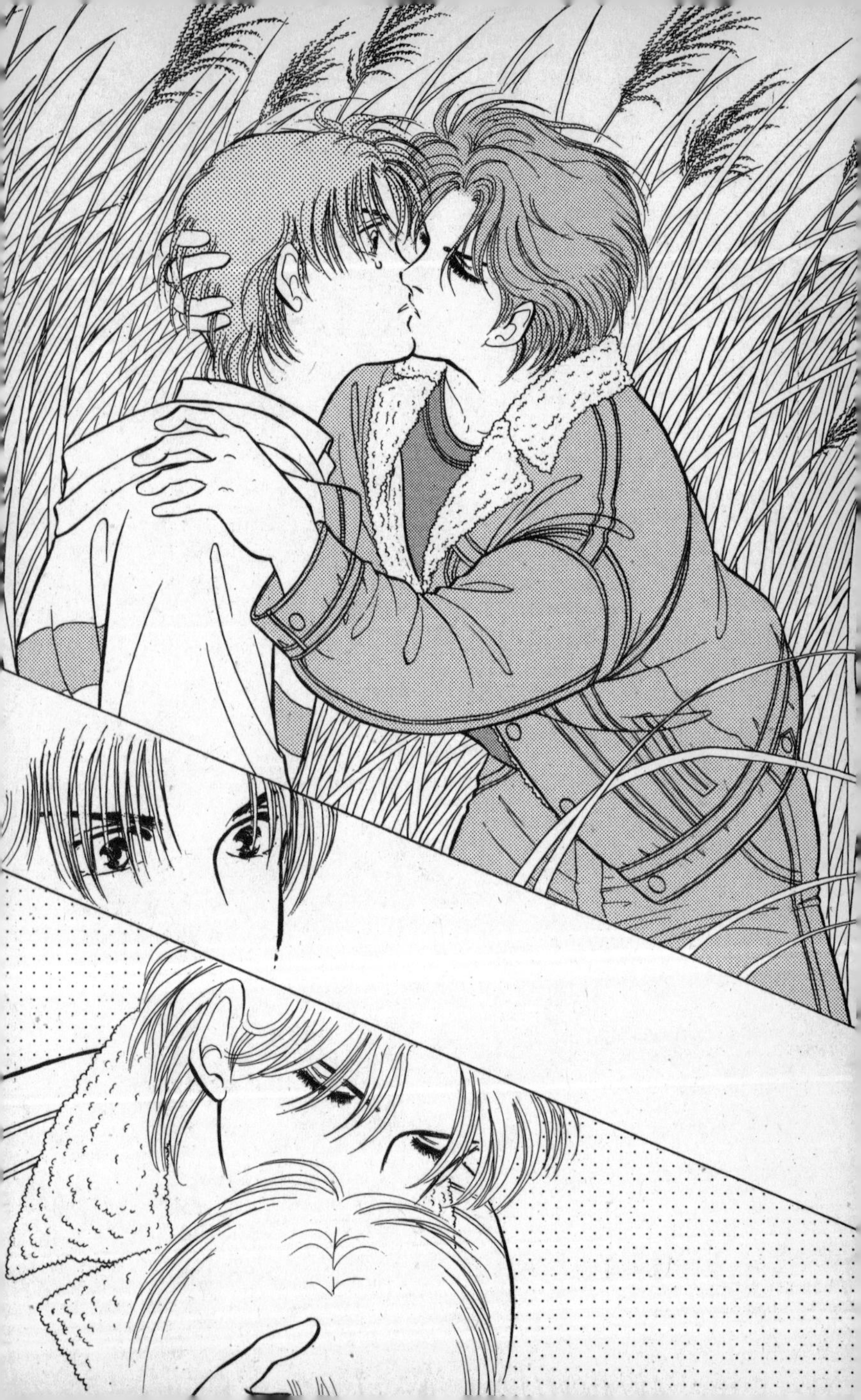

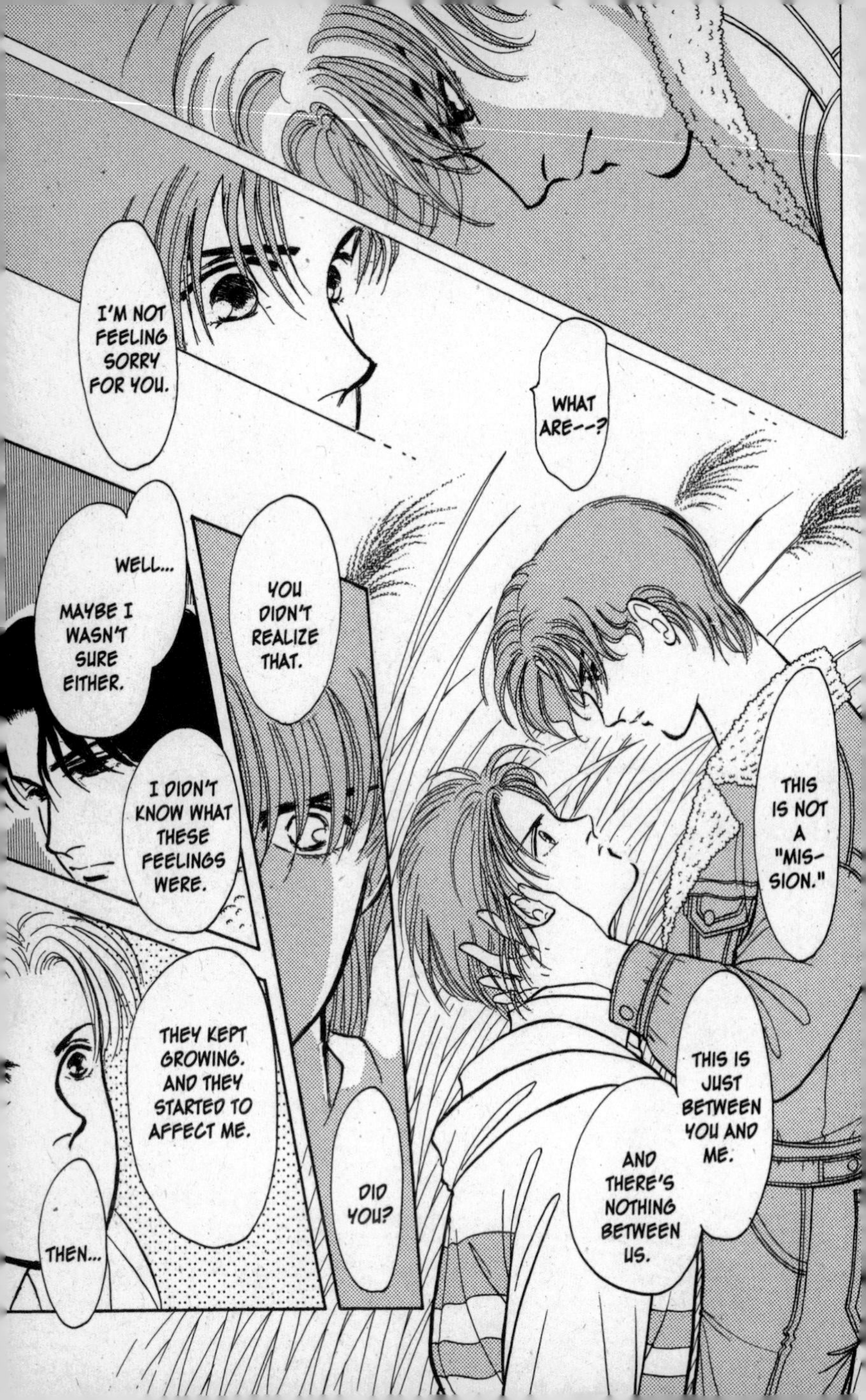
I'M NOT FEELING SORRY FOR YOU.
WHAT ARE--?
THIS IS NOT A "MIS-SION."
THIS IS JUST BETWEEN YOU AND ME.
AND THERE'S NOTHING BETWEEN US.
YOU DIDN'T REALIZE THAT.
DID YOU?
WELL...
MAYBE I WASN'T SURE EITHER.
I DIDN'T KNOW WHAT THESE FEELINGS WERE.
THEY KEPT GROWING. AND THEY STARTED TO AFFECT ME.
THEN...

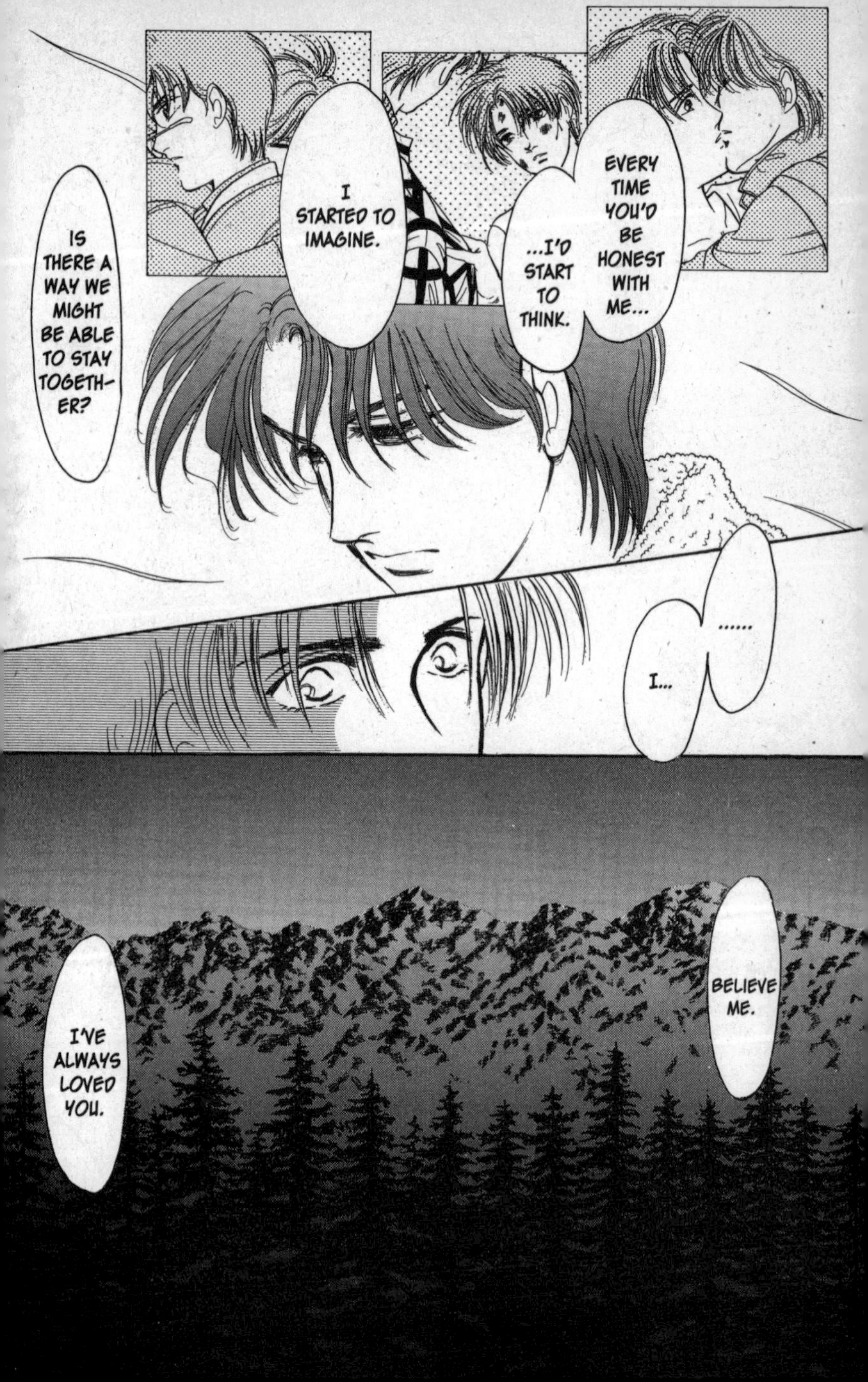
EVERY TIME YOU'D BE HONEST WITH ME...
...I'D START TO THINK.
I STARTED TO IMAGINE.
IS THERE A WAY WE MIGHT BE ABLE TO STAY TOGETH-ER?
......
I...
BELIEVE ME.
I'VE ALWAYS LOVED YOU.

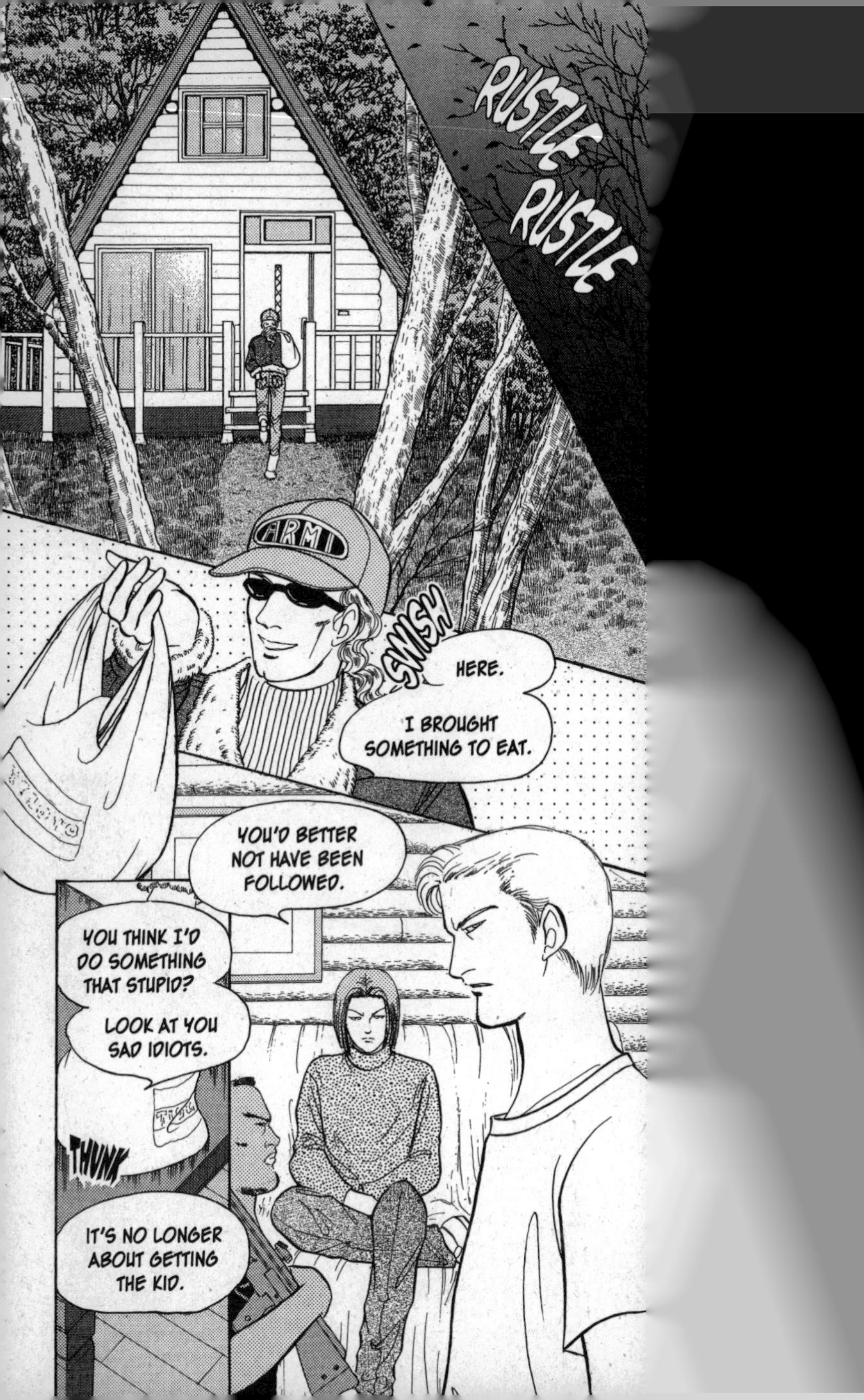
RUSTLE RUSTLE
ARMI
SWISH
HERE.
I BROUGHT SOMETHING TO EAT.
YOU'D BETTER NOT HAVE BEEN FOLLOWED.
YOU THINK I'D DO SOMETHING THAT STUPID?
LOOK AT YOU SAD IDIOTS.
THUNK
IT'S NO LONGER ABOUT GETTING THE KID.

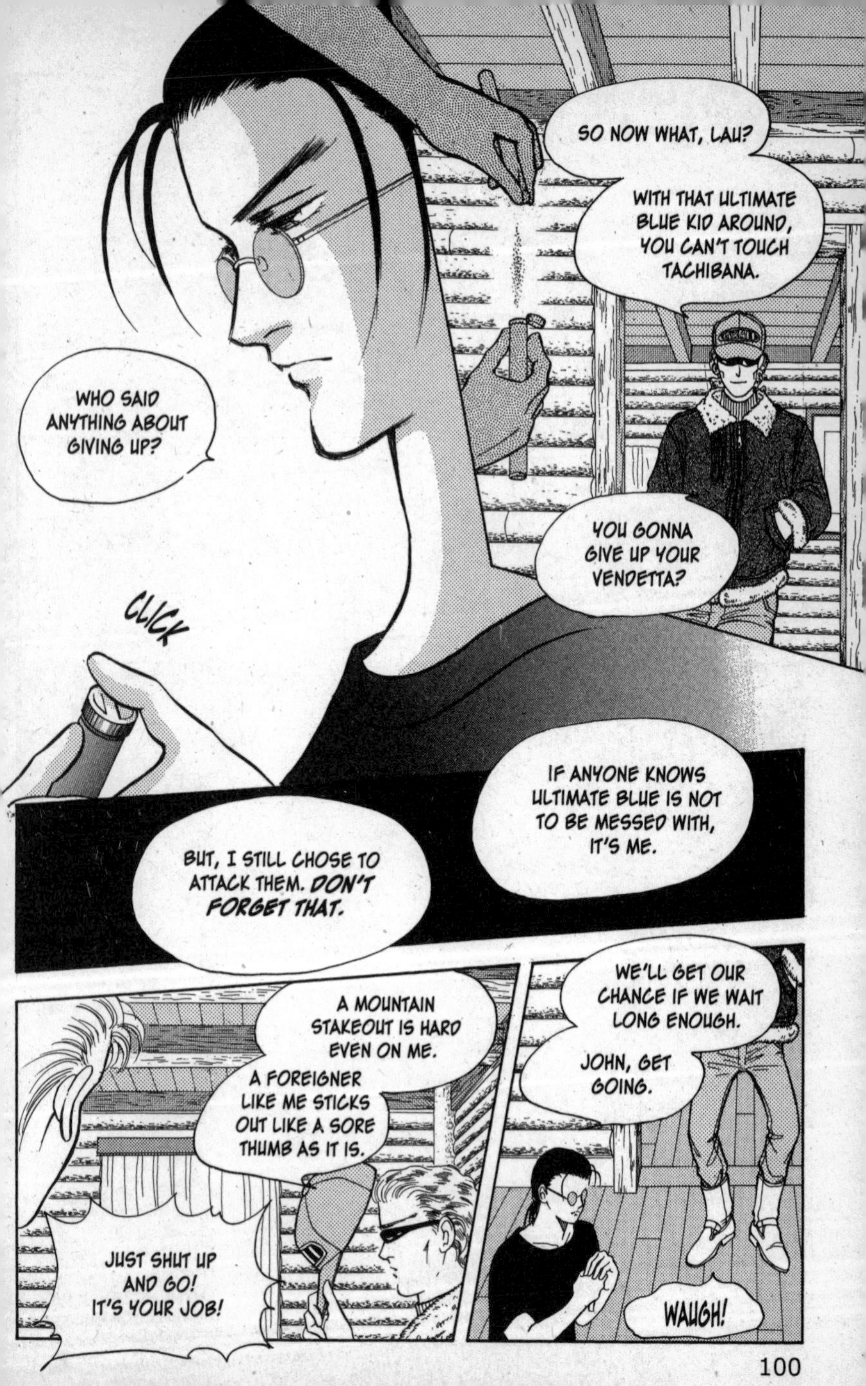
SO NOW WHAT, LAU?
WITH THAT ULTIMATE BLUE KID AROUND, YOU CAN'T TOUCH TACHIBANA.
YOU GONNA GIVE UP YOUR VENDETTA?
WHO SAID ANYTHING ABOUT GIVING UP?
CLICK
IF ANYONE KNOWS ULTIMATE BLUE IS NOT TO BE MESSED WITH, IT'S ME.
BUT, I STILL CHOSE TO ATTACK THEM. *DON'T FORGET THAT.*
WE'LL GET OUR CHANCE IF WE WAIT LONG ENOUGH.
JOHN, GET GOING.
WAUGH!
A MOUNTAIN STAKEOUT IS HARD EVEN ON ME.
A FOREIGNER LIKE ME STICKS OUT LIKE A SORE THUMB AS IT IS.
JUST SHUT UP AND GO! IT'S YOUR JOB!

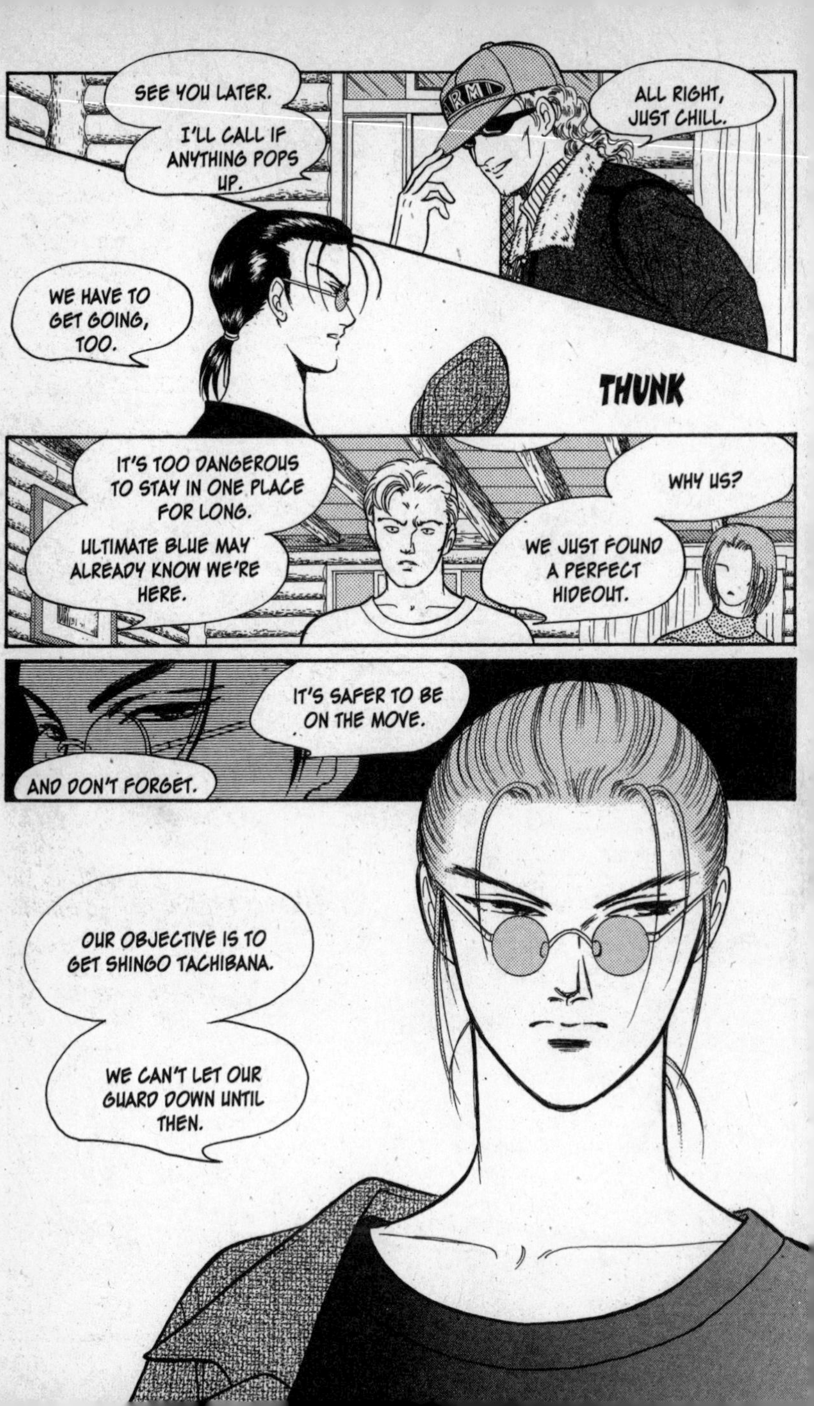
ALL RIGHT, JUST CHILL.
SEE YOU LATER.
I'LL CALL IF ANYTHING POPS UP.
WE HAVE TO GET GOING, TOO.
THUNK
WHY US?
WE JUST FOUND A PERFECT HIDEOUT.
IT'S TOO DANGEROUS TO STAY IN ONE PLACE FOR LONG.
ULTIMATE BLUE MAY ALREADY KNOW WE'RE HERE.
IT'S SAFER TO BE ON THE MOVE.
AND DON'T FORGET.
OUR OBJECTIVE IS TO GET SHINGO TACHIBANA.
WE CAN'T LET OUR GUARD DOWN UNTIL THEN.

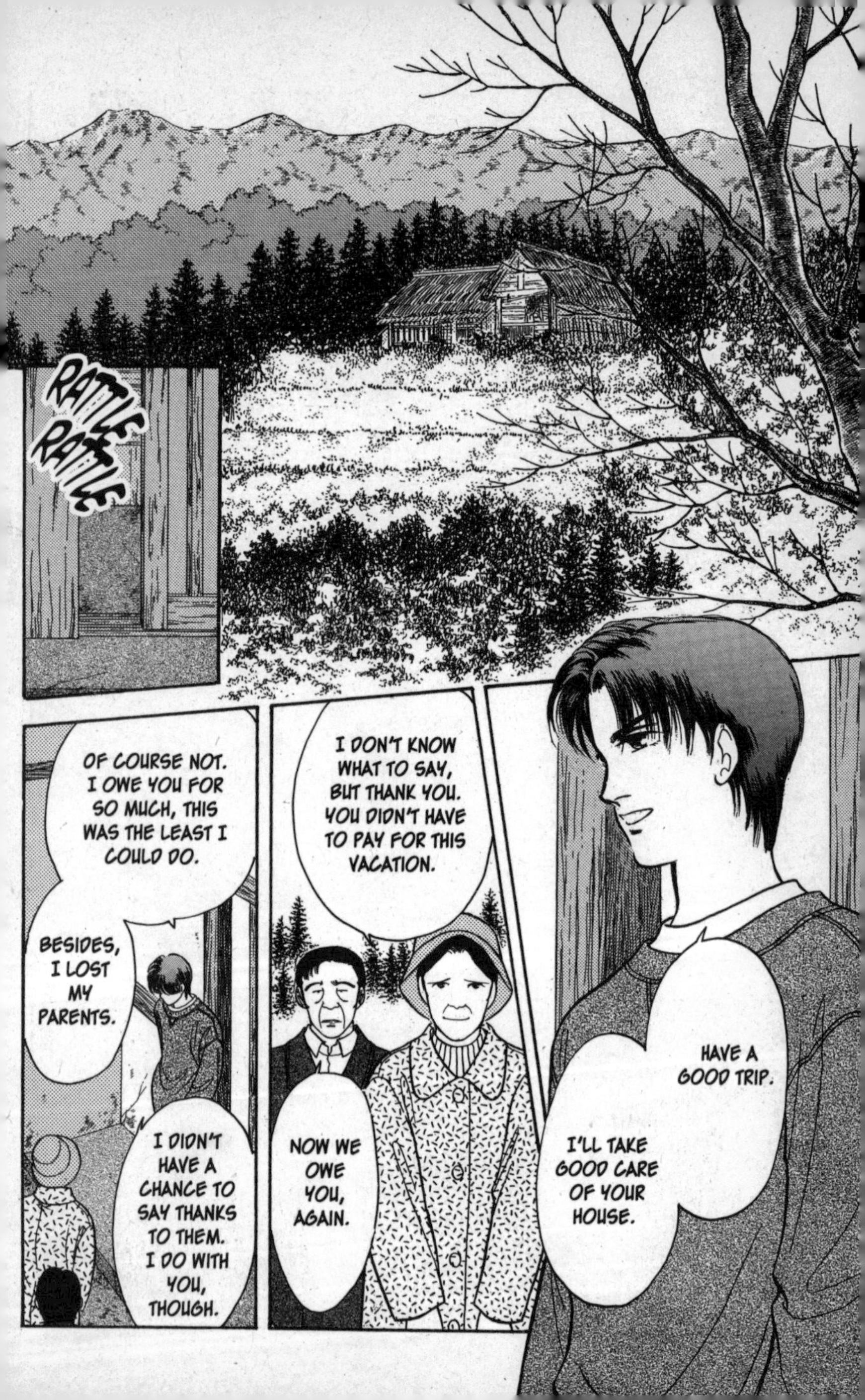
RATTLE RATTLE
HAVE A GOOD TRIP.
I'LL TAKE GOOD CARE OF YOUR HOUSE.
I DON'T KNOW WHAT TO SAY, BUT THANK YOU. YOU DIDN'T HAVE TO PAY FOR THIS VACATION.
NOW WE OWE YOU, AGAIN.
OF COURSE NOT. I OWE YOU FOR SO MUCH, THIS WAS THE LEAST I COULD DO.
BESIDES, I LOST MY PARENTS.
I DIDN'T HAVE A CHANCE TO SAY THANKS TO THEM. I DO WITH YOU, THOUGH.

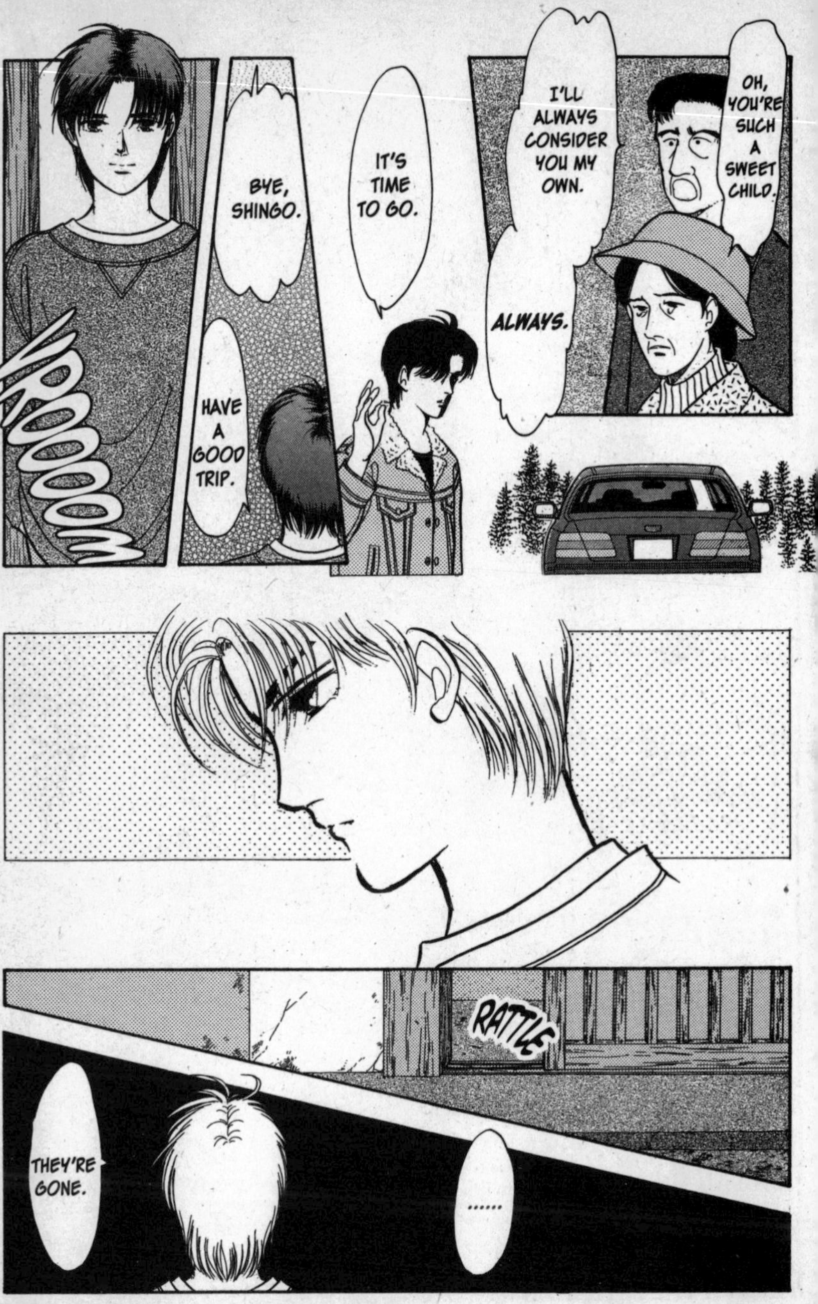

OH, YOU'RE SUCH A SWEET CHILD.
I'LL ALWAYS CONSIDER YOU MY OWN.
ALWAYS.
IT'S TIME TO GO.
BYE, SHINGO.
HAVE A GOOD TRIP.
VROOOOOM
RATTLE
......
THEY'RE GONE.

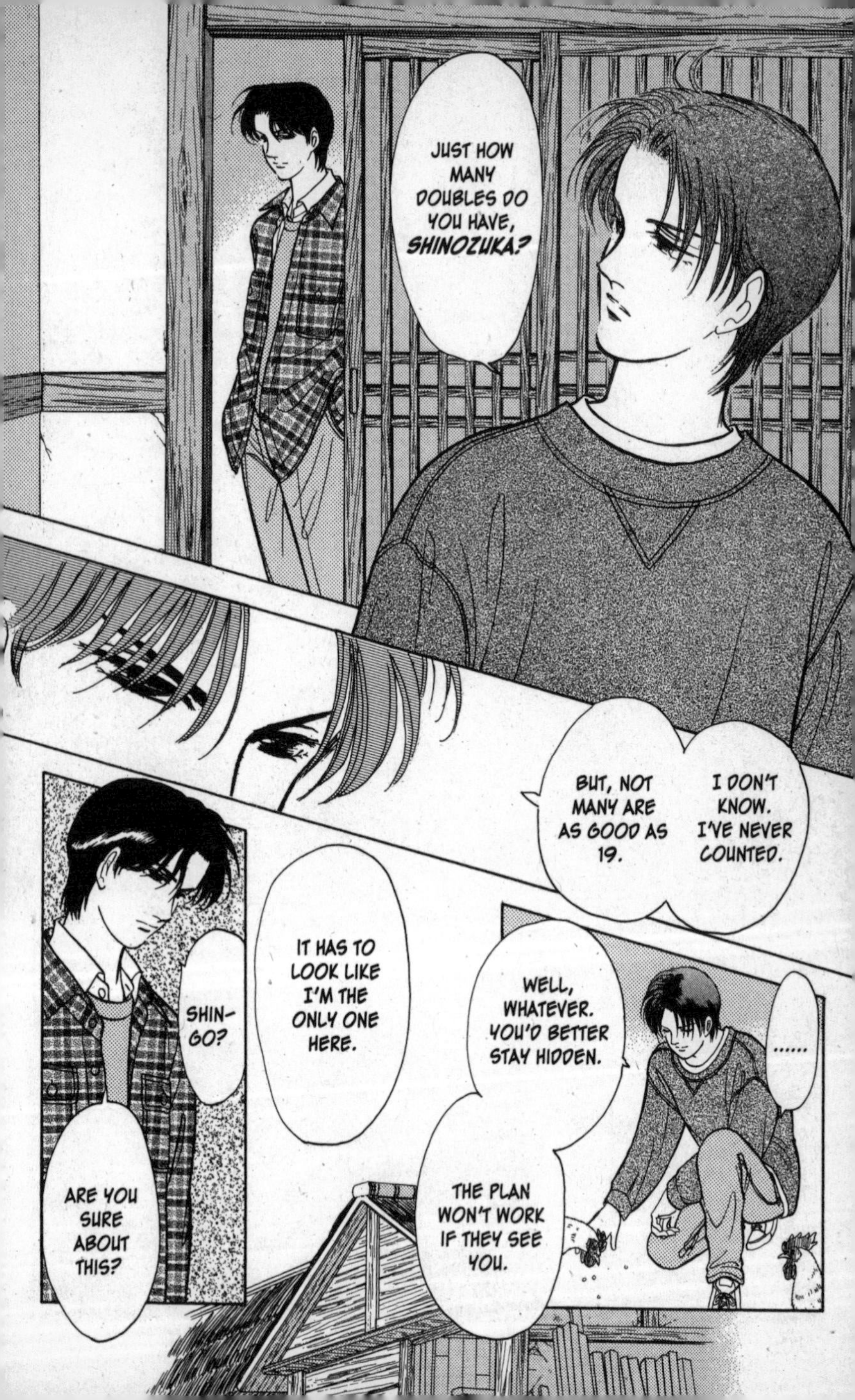
JUST HOW MANY DOUBLES DO YOU HAVE, SHINOZUKA?
I DON'T KNOW. I'VE NEVER COUNTED.
BUT, NOT MANY ARE AS GOOD AS 19.
......
WELL, WHATEVER. YOU'D BETTER STAY HIDDEN.
THE PLAN WON'T WORK IF THEY SEE YOU.
IT HAS TO LOOK LIKE I'M THE ONLY ONE HERE.
SHIN-GO?
ARE YOU SURE ABOUT THIS?

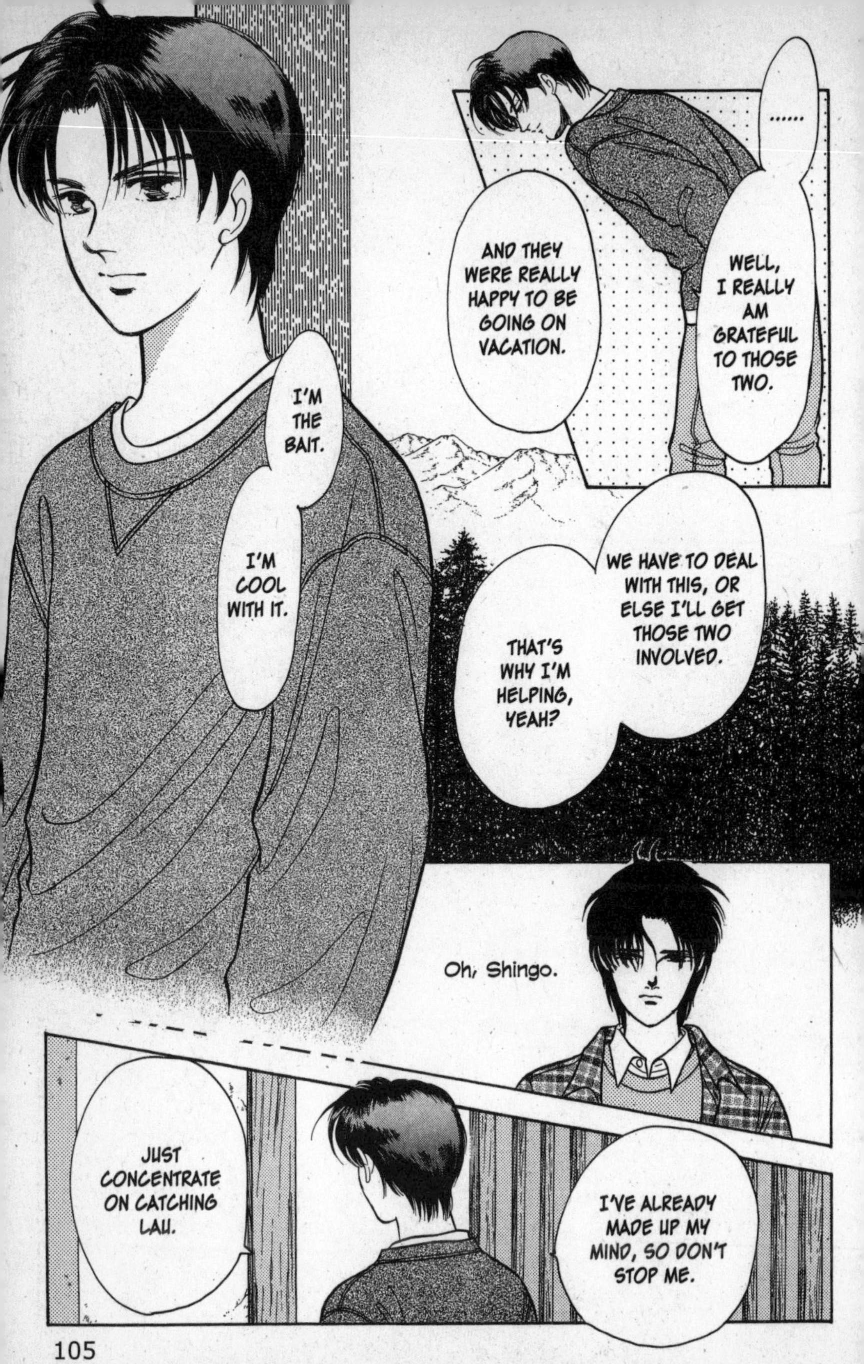
......
WELL, I REALLY AM GRATEFUL TO THOSE TWO.
AND THEY WERE REALLY HAPPY TO BE GOING ON VACATION.
WE HAVE TO DEAL WITH THIS, OR ELSE I'LL GET THOSE TWO INVOLVED.
THAT'S WHY I'M HELPING, YEAH?
Oh, Shingo.
I'M THE BAIT.
I'M COOL WITH IT.
I'VE ALREADY MADE UP MY MIND, SO DON'T STOP ME.
JUST CONCENTRATE ON CATCHING LAU.

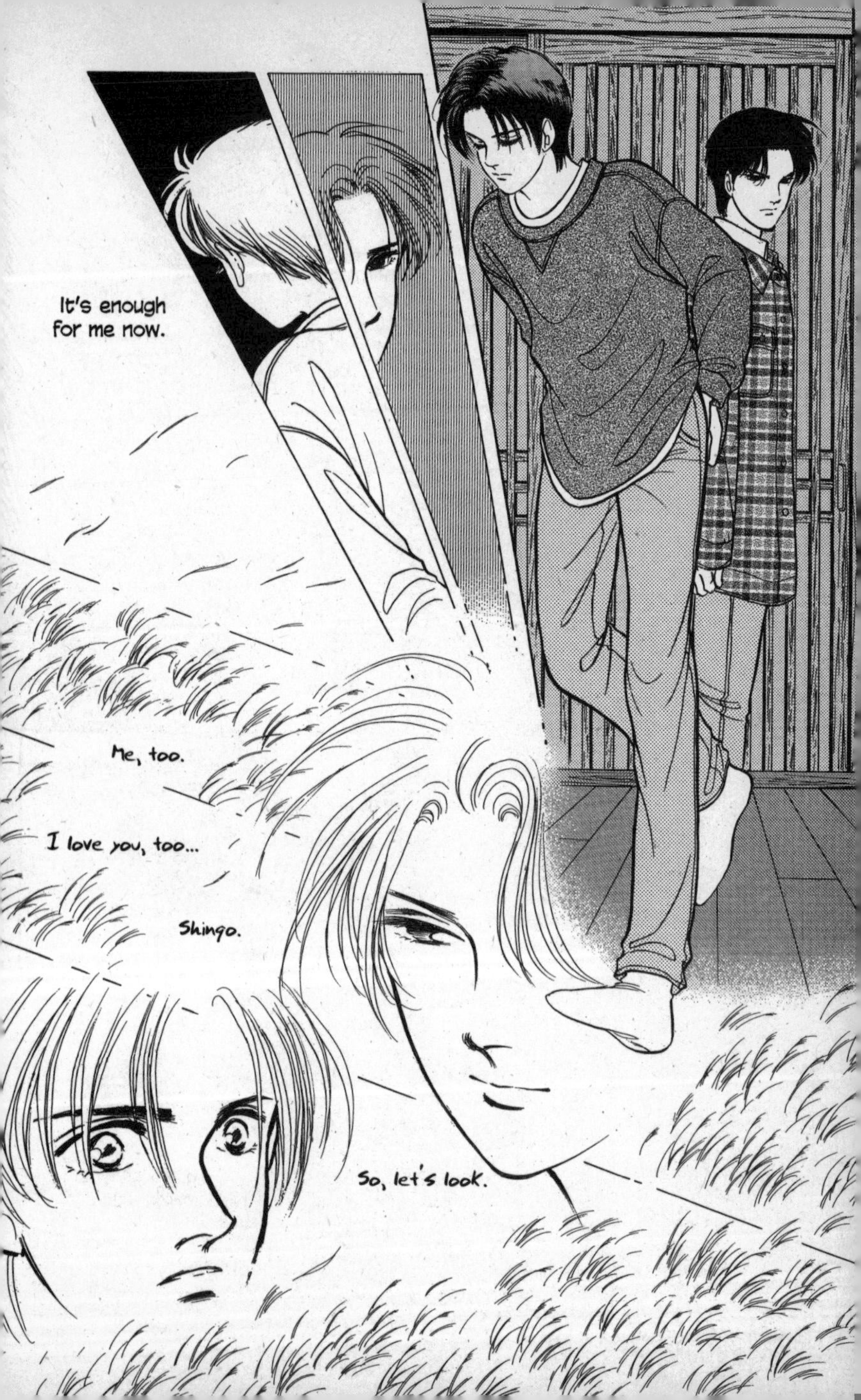
It's enough for me now.
Me, too.
I love you, too...
Shingo.
So, let's look.

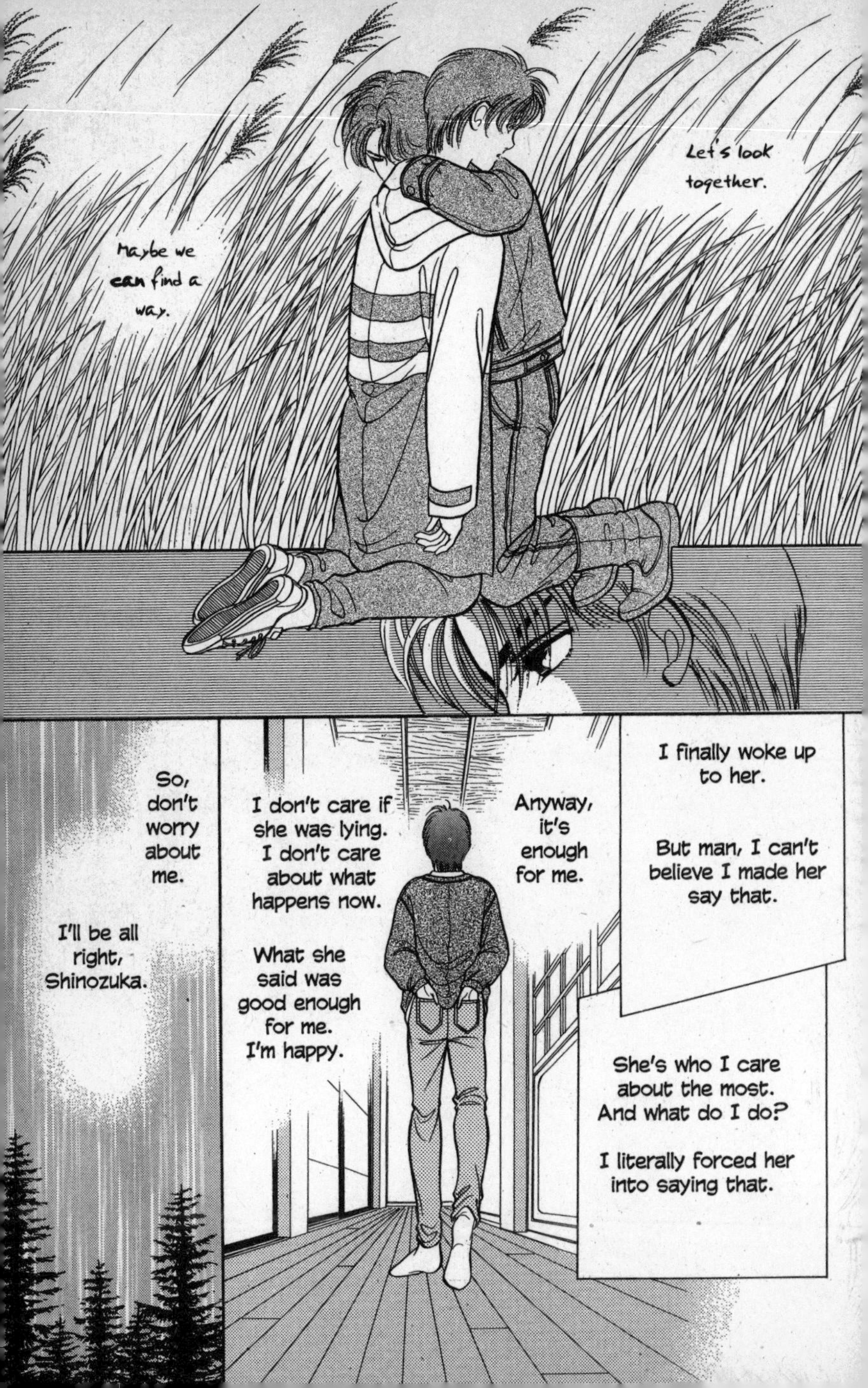
Let's look together.
Maybe we can find a way.
I finally woke up to her.
But man, I can't believe I made her say that.
She's who I care about the most. And what do I do?
I literally forced her into saying that.
Anyway, it's enough for me.
I don't care if she was lying. I don't care about what happens now.
What she said was good enough for me. I'm happy.
So, don't worry about me.
I'll be all right, Shinozuka.

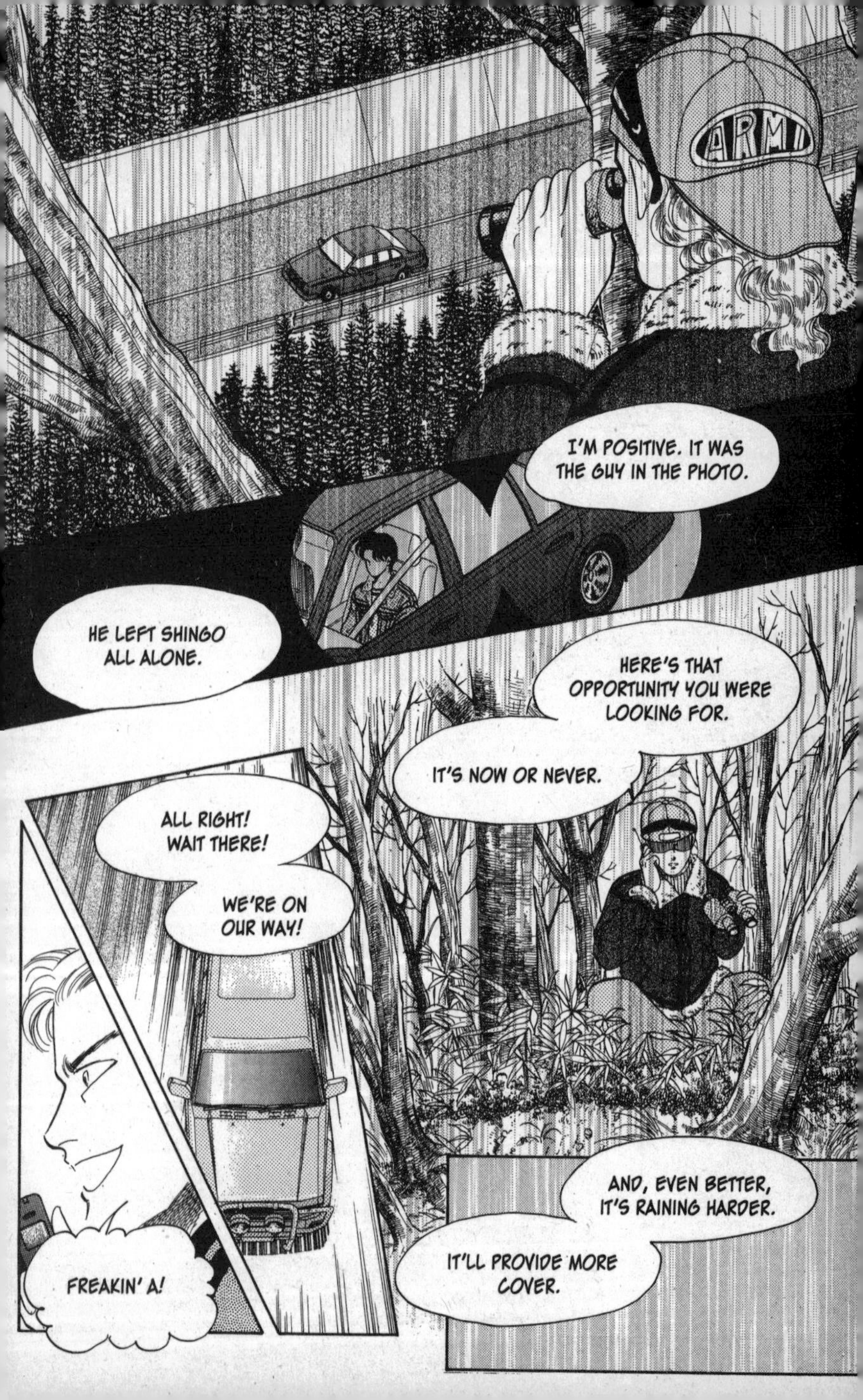
I'M POSITIVE. IT WAS THE GUY IN THE PHOTO.
HE LEFT SHINGO ALL ALONE.
HERE'S THAT OPPORTUNITY YOU WERE LOOKING FOR.
IT'S NOW OR NEVER.
ALL RIGHT! WAIT THERE!
WE'RE ON OUR WAY!
AND, EVEN BETTER, IT'S RAINING HARDER.
IT'LL PROVIDE MORE COVER.
FREAKIN' A!

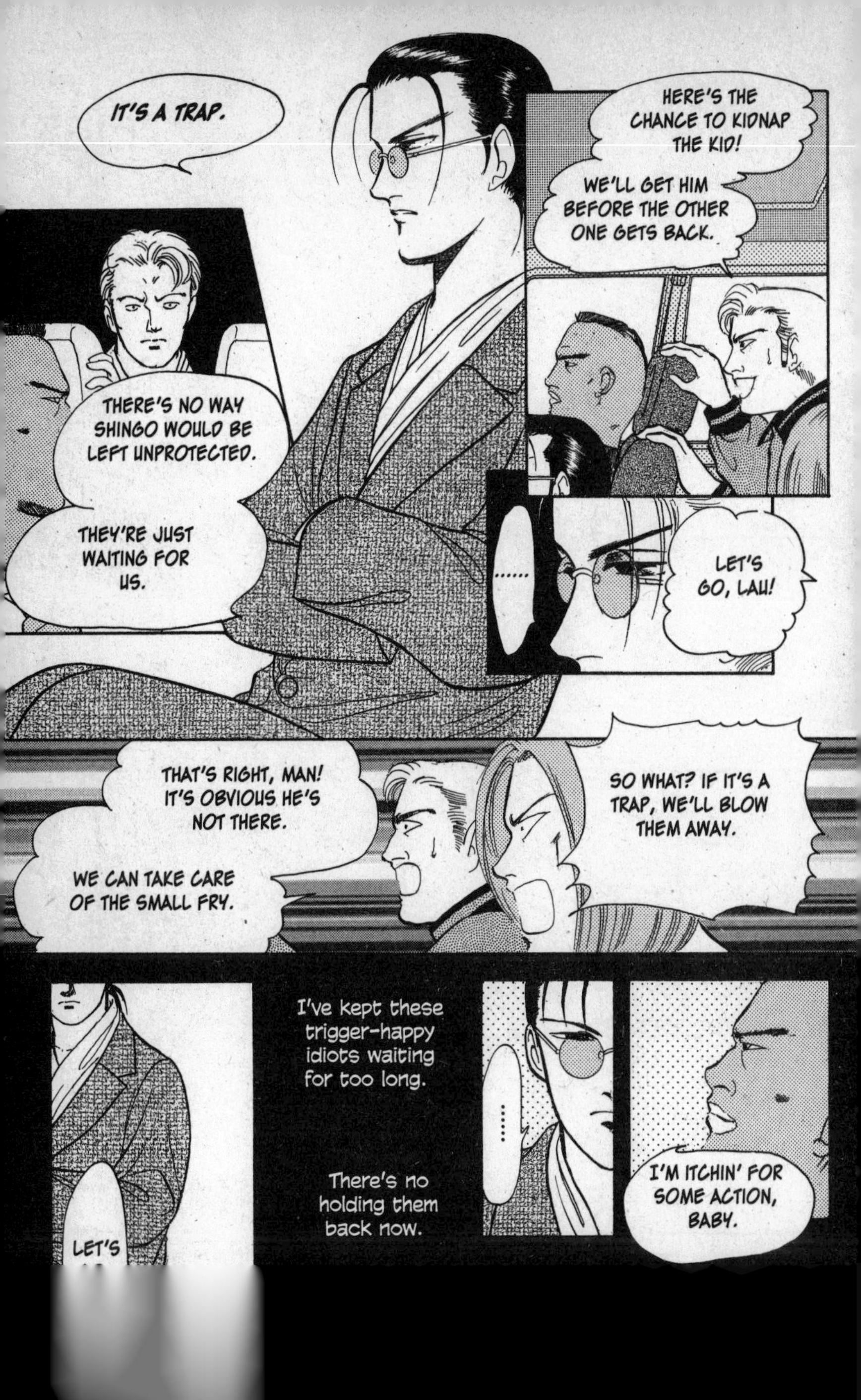
HERE'S THE CHANCE TO KIDNAP THE KID!
WE'LL GET HIM BEFORE THE OTHER ONE GETS BACK.
LET'S GO, LAU!
......
IT'S A TRAP.
THERE'S NO WAY SHINGO WOULD BE LEFT UNPROTECTED.
THEY'RE JUST WAITING FOR US.
SO WHAT? IF IT'S A TRAP, WE'LL BLOW THEM AWAY.
THAT'S RIGHT, MAN! IT'S OBVIOUS HE'S NOT THERE.
WE CAN TAKE CARE OF THE SMALL FRY.
I'M ITCHIN' FOR SOME ACTION, BABY.
......
I've kept these trigger-happy idiots waiting for too long.
There's no holding them back now.
LET'S

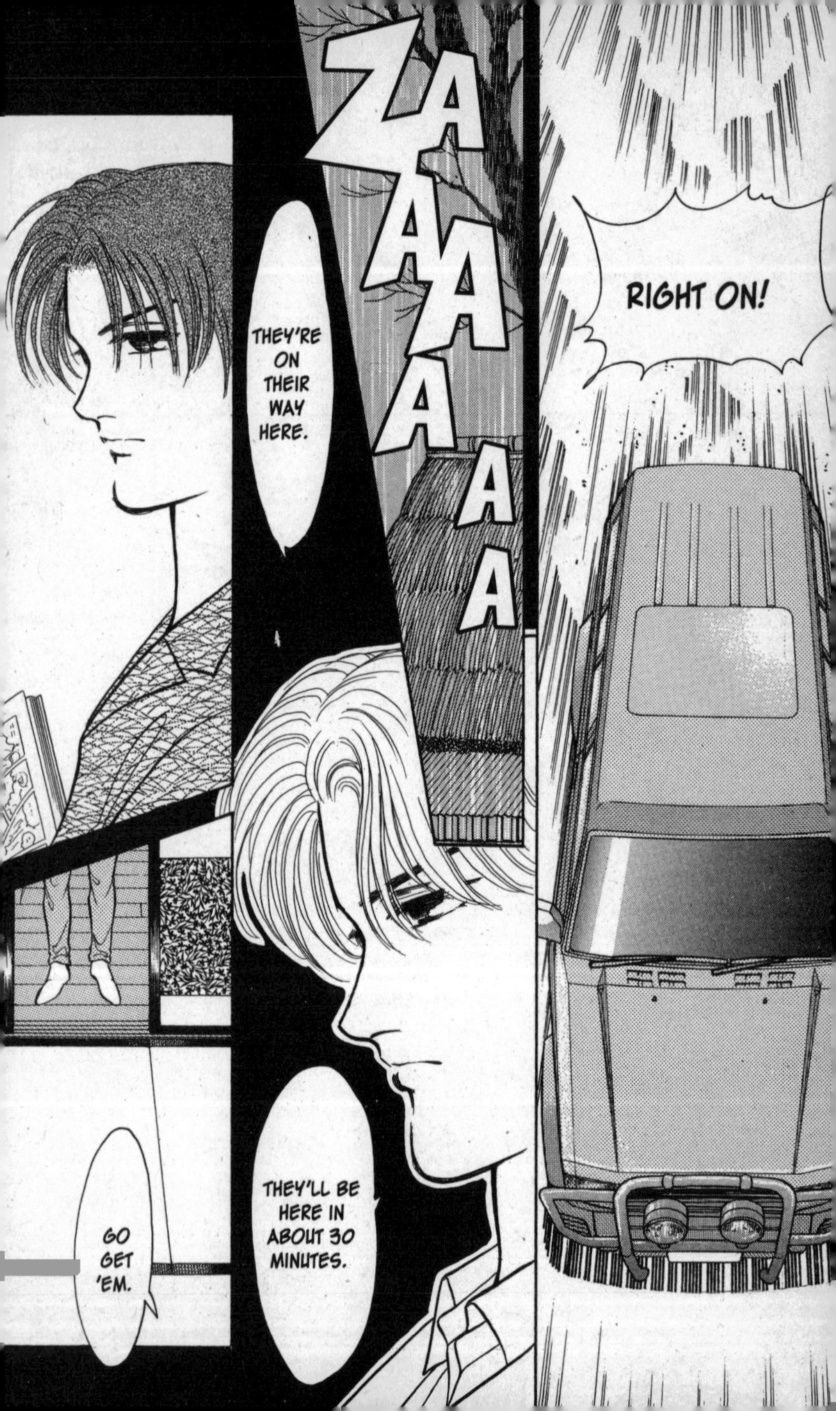
RIGHT ON!
ZAAAAAAA
THEY'RE ON THEIR WAY HERE.
THEY'LL BE HERE IN ABOUT 30 MINUTES.
GO GET 'EM.

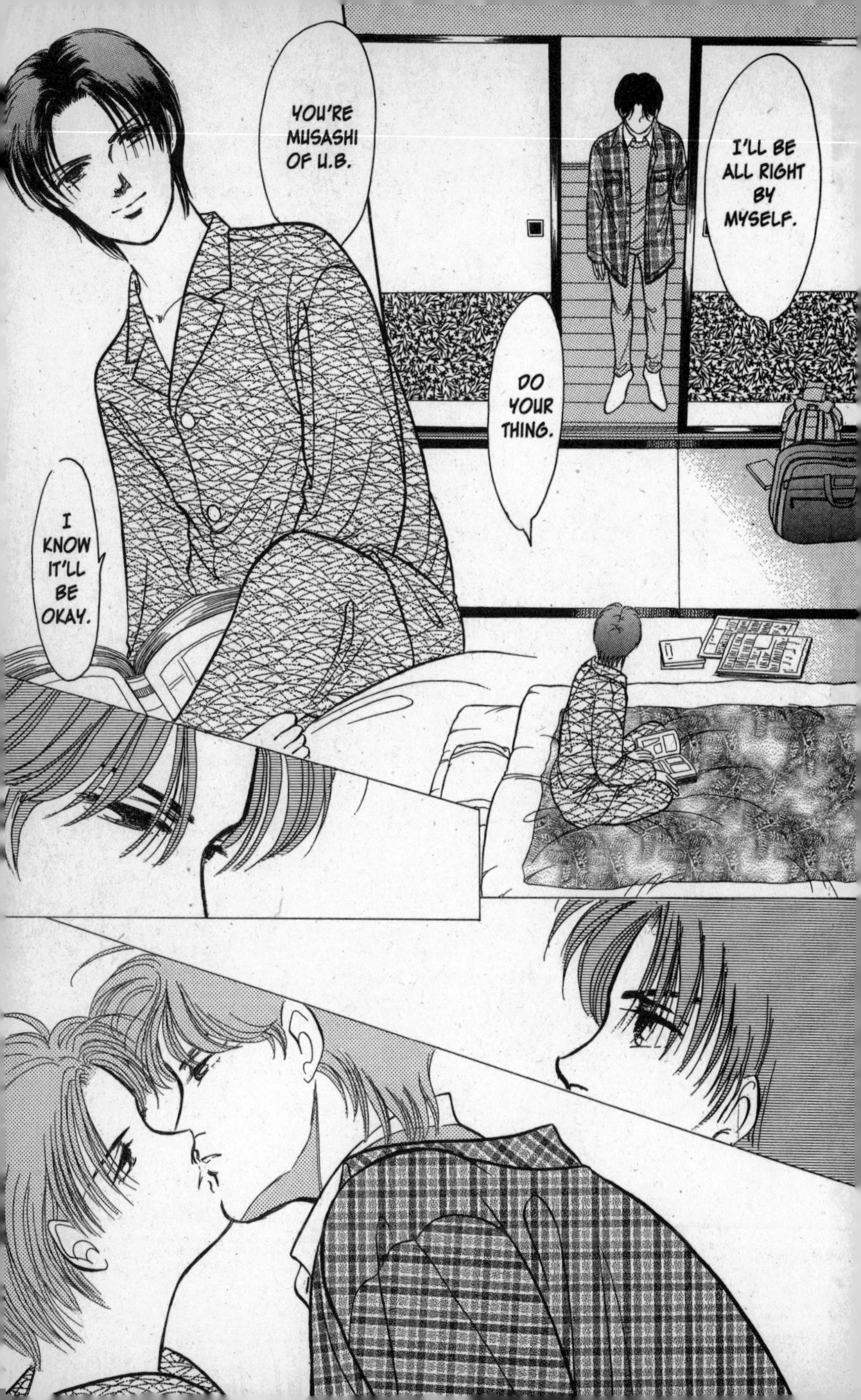
I'LL BE ALL RIGHT BY MYSELF.
DO YOUR THING.
YOU'RE MUSASHI OF U.B.
I KNOW IT'LL BE OKAY.

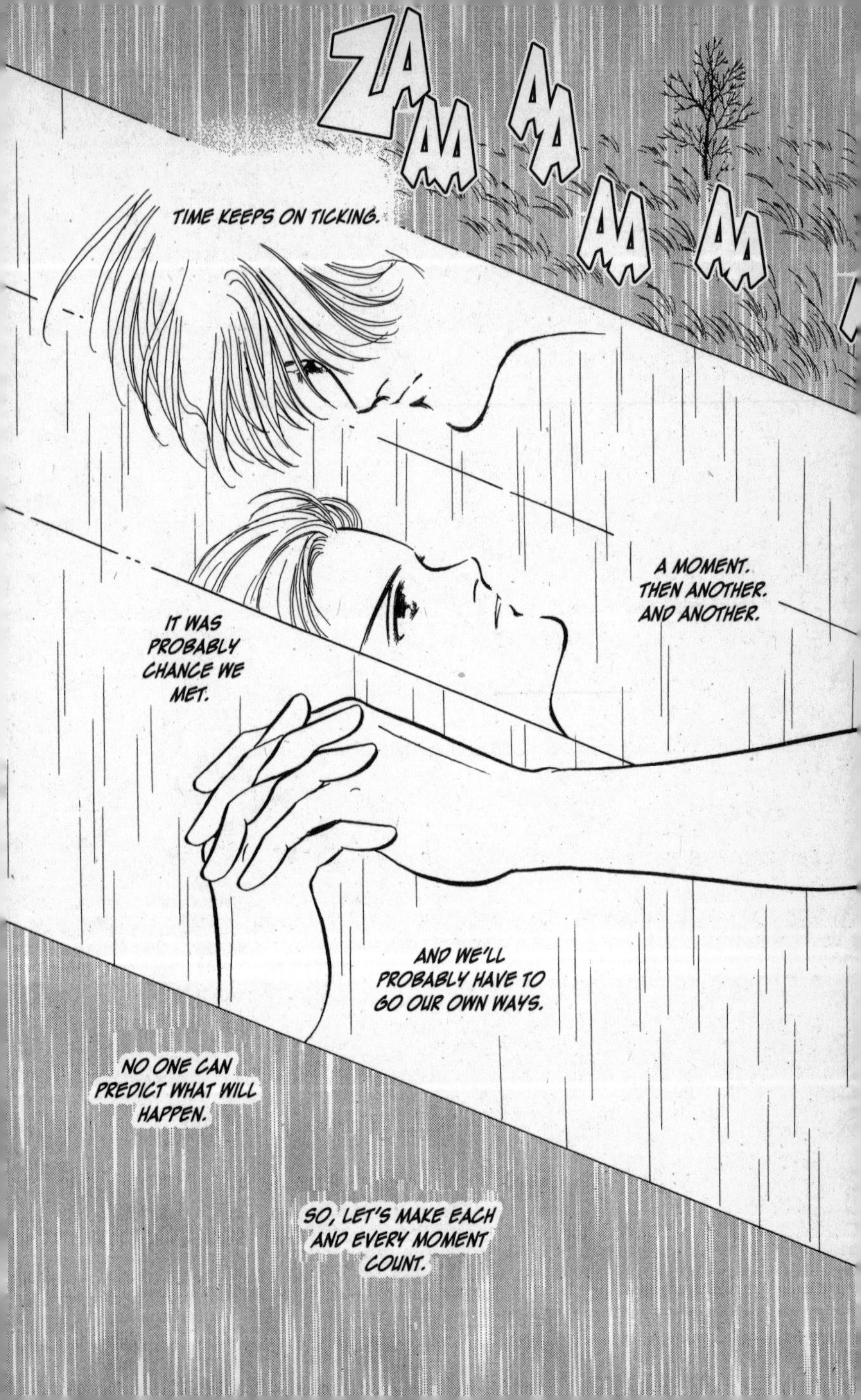

ZAAAAAAAAA
TIME KEEPS ON TICKING.
A MOMENT. THEN ANOTHER. AND ANOTHER.
IT WAS PROBABLY CHANCE WE MET.
AND WE'LL PROBABLY HAVE TO GO OUR OWN WAYS.
NO ONE CAN PREDICT WHAT WILL HAPPEN.
SO, LET'S MAKE EACH AND EVERY MOMENT COUNT.

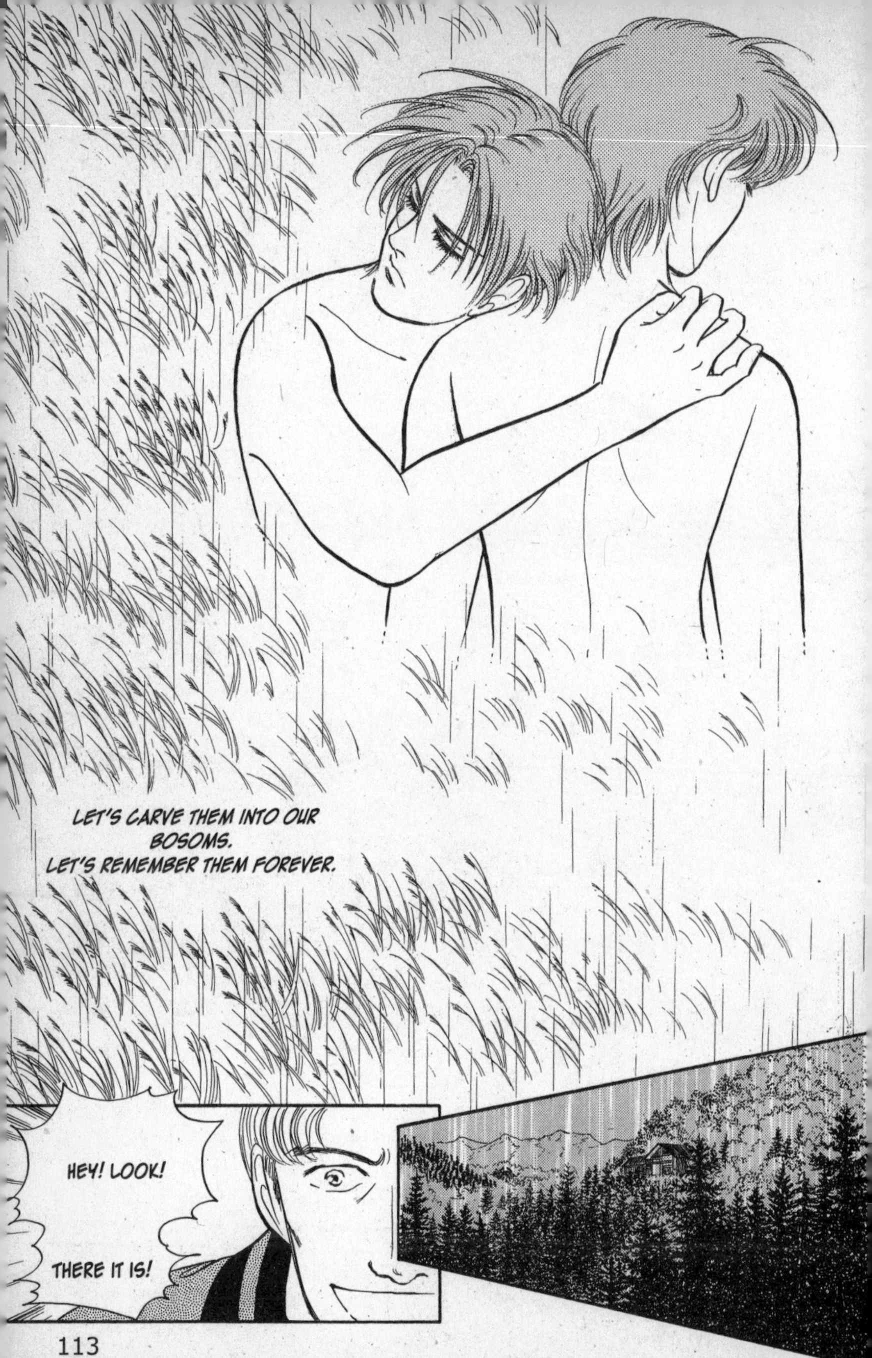
LET'S CARVE THEM INTO OUR BOSOMS.
LET'S REMEMBER THEM FOREVER.
HEY! LOOK!
THERE IT IS!

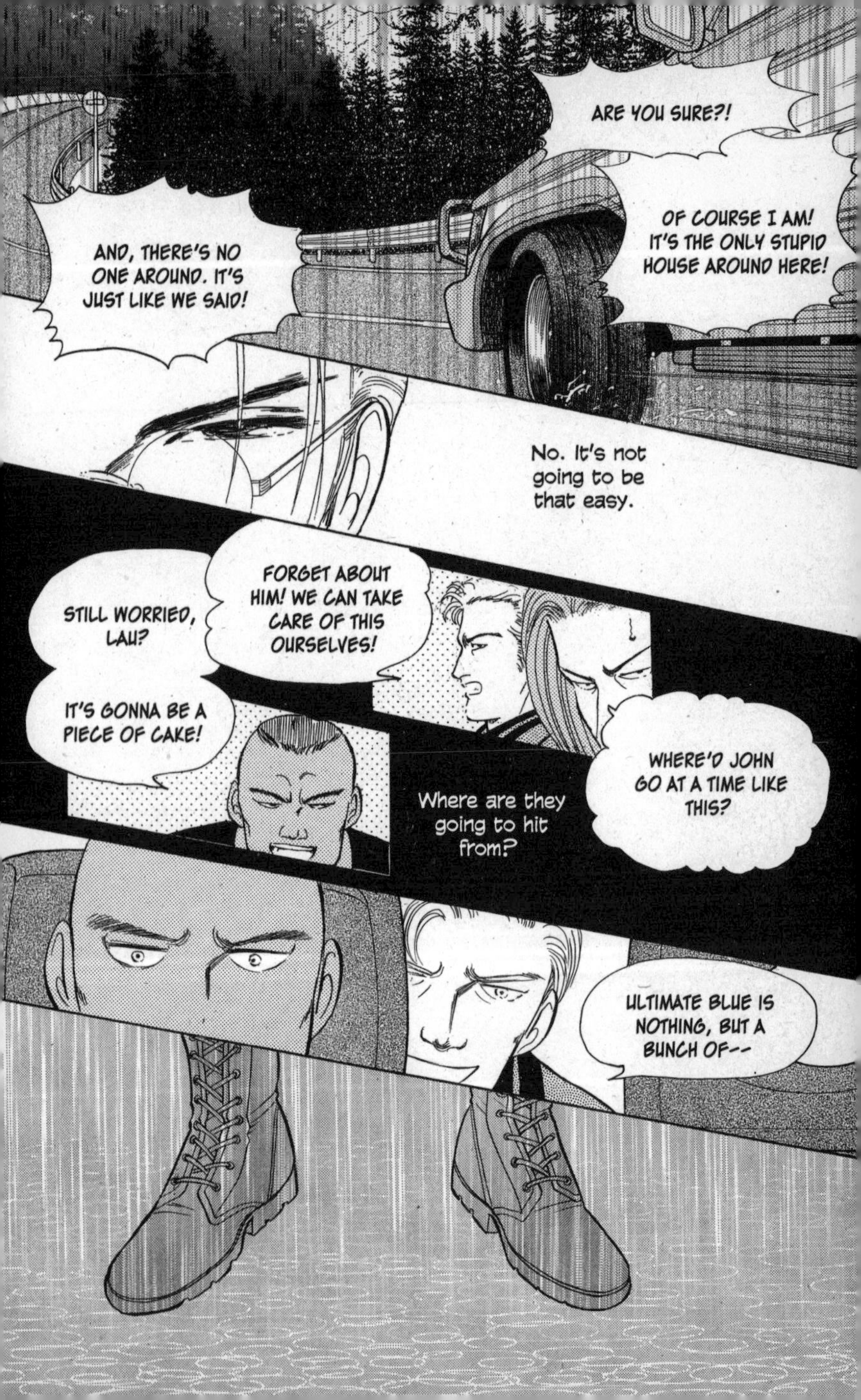
ARE YOU SURE?!
OF COURSE I AM! IT'S THE ONLY STUPID HOUSE AROUND HERE!
AND, THERE'S NO ONE AROUND. IT'S JUST LIKE WE SAID!
No. It's not going to be that easy.
WHERE'D JOHN GO AT A TIME LIKE THIS?
FORGET ABOUT HIM! WE CAN TAKE CARE OF THIS OURSELVES!
STILL WORRIED, LAU?
IT'S GONNA BE A PIECE OF CAKE!
Where are they going to hit from?
ULTIMATE BLUE IS NOTHING, BUT A BUNCH OF--

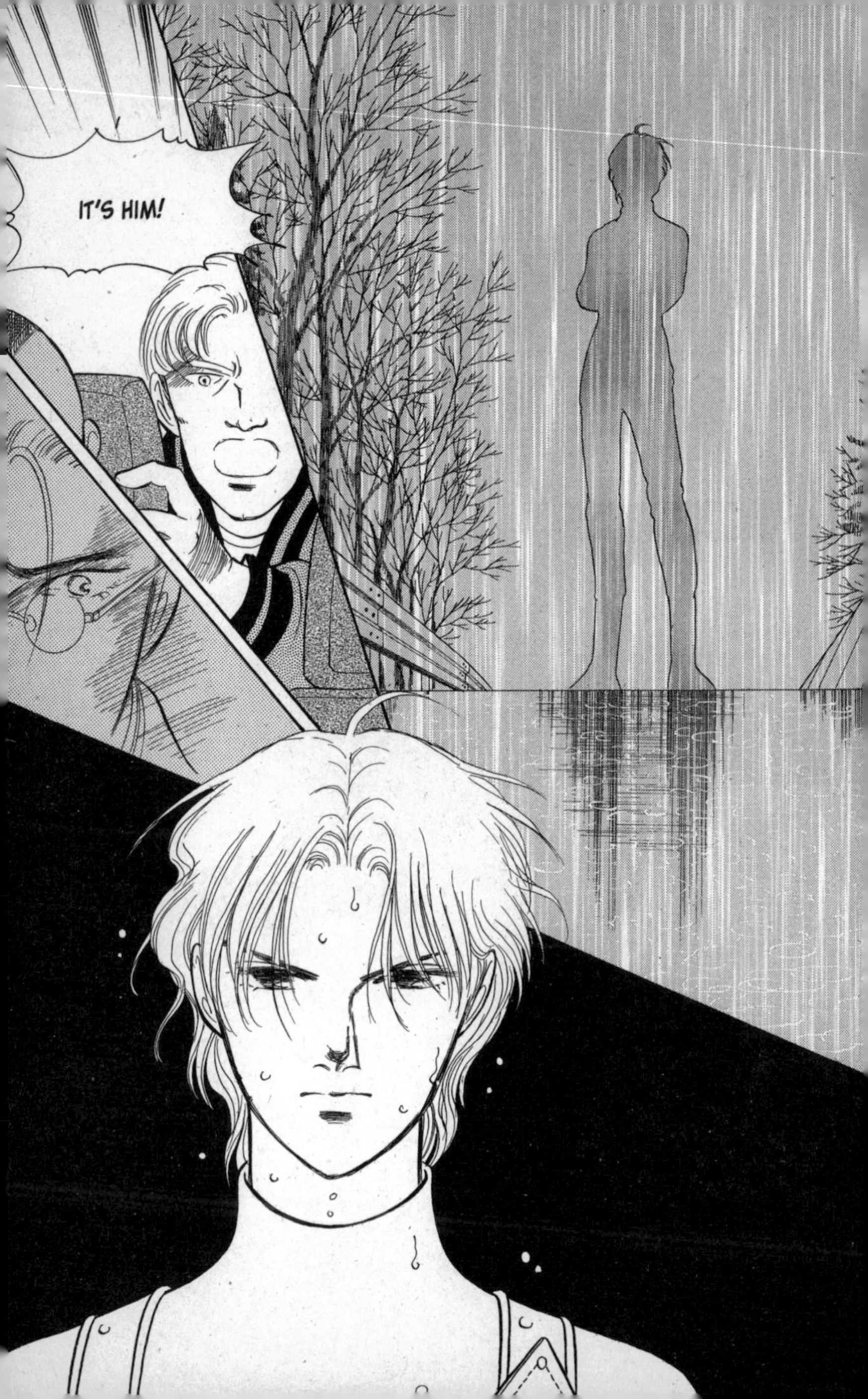
IT'S HIM!

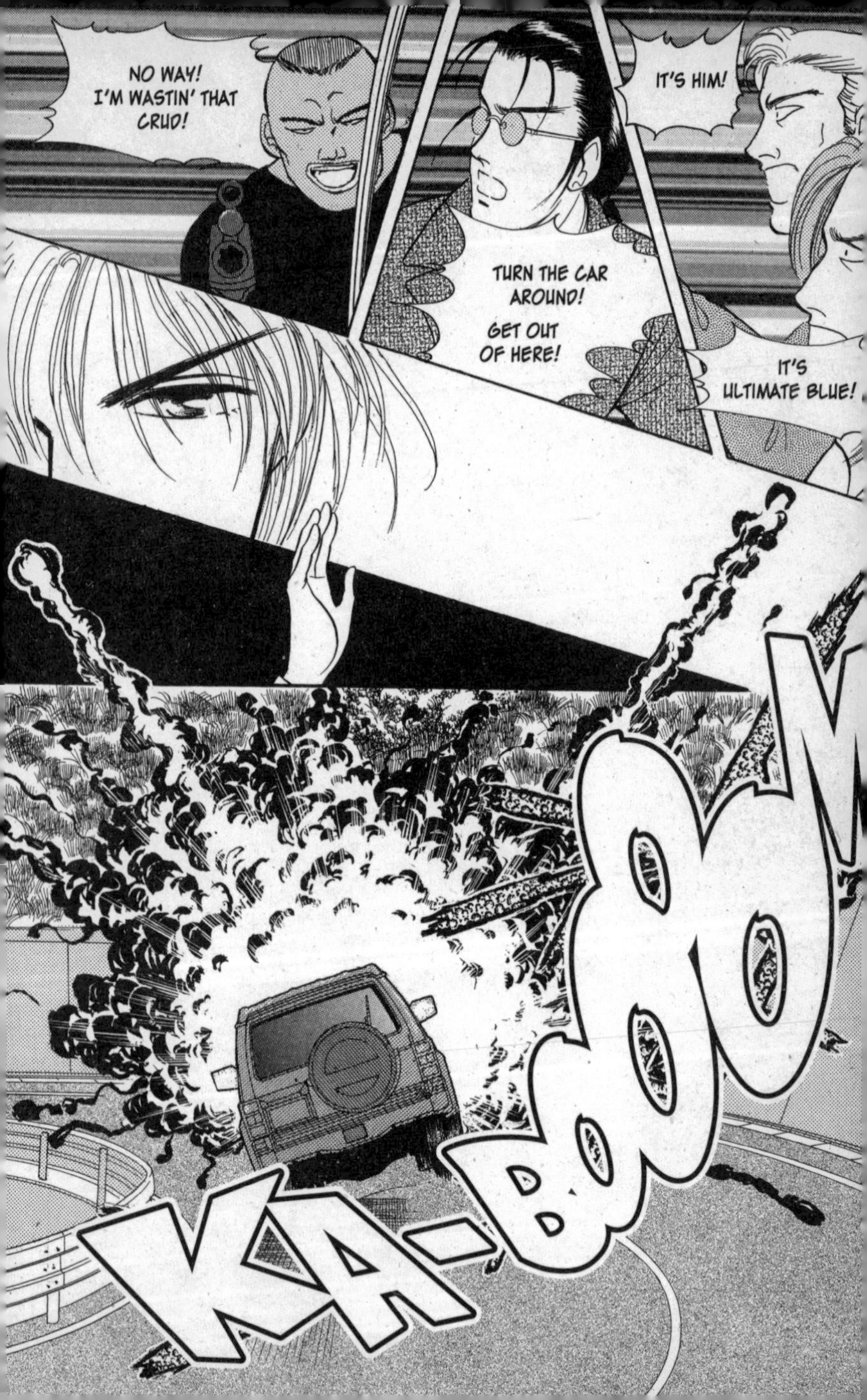
IT'S HIM!
IT'S ULTIMATE BLUE!
TURN THE CAR AROUND!
GET OUT OF HERE!
NO WAY! I'M WASTIN' THAT CRUD!
KA-BOOM

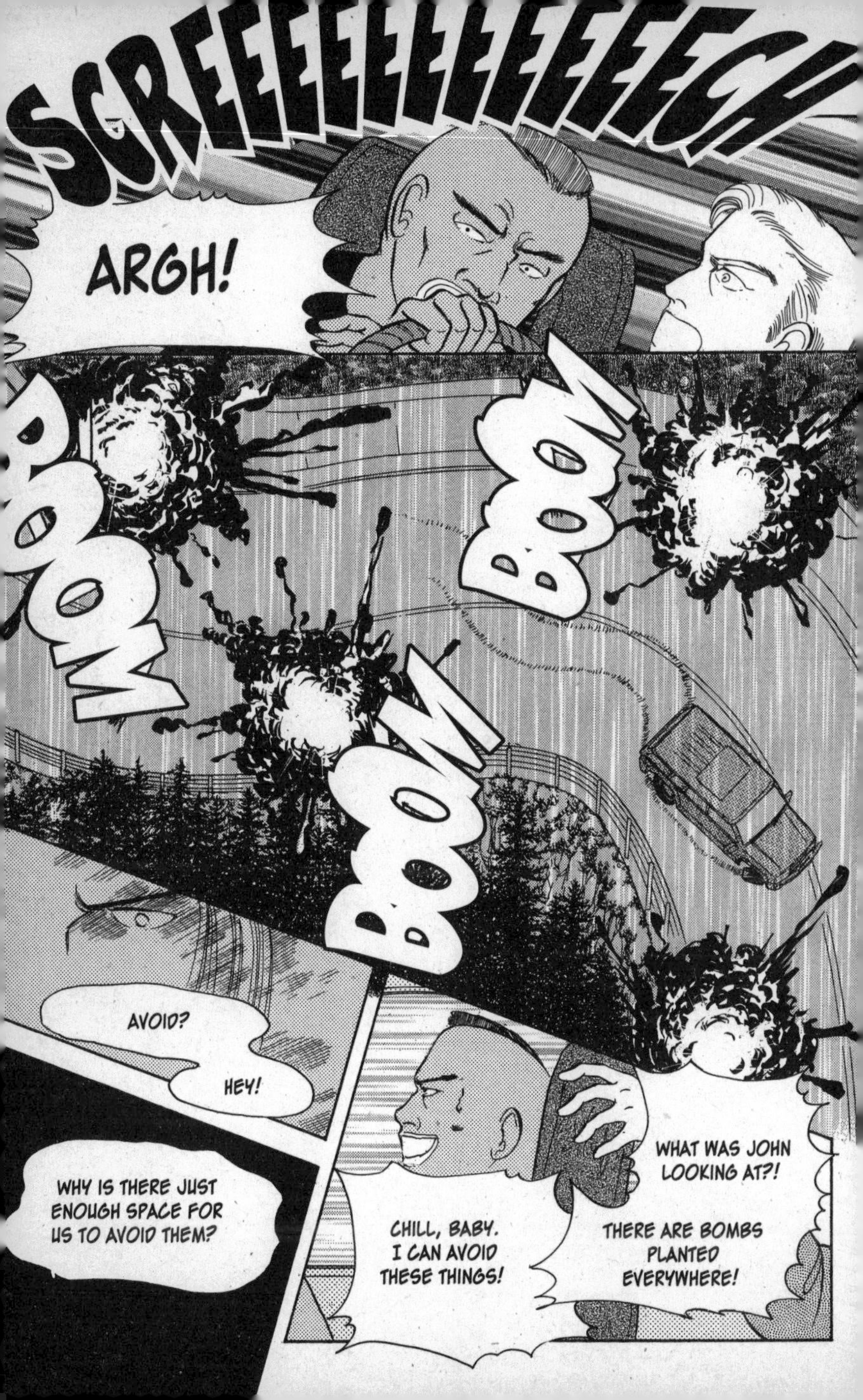
SCREEEEEEEEEEECH!
ARGH!
BOOM
BOOM
BOOM
WHAT WAS JOHN LOOKING AT?!
THERE ARE BOMBS PLANTED EVERYWHERE!
CHILL, BABY. I CAN AVOID THESE THINGS!
AVOID?
HEY!
WHY IS THERE JUST ENOUGH SPACE FOR US TO AVOID THEM?

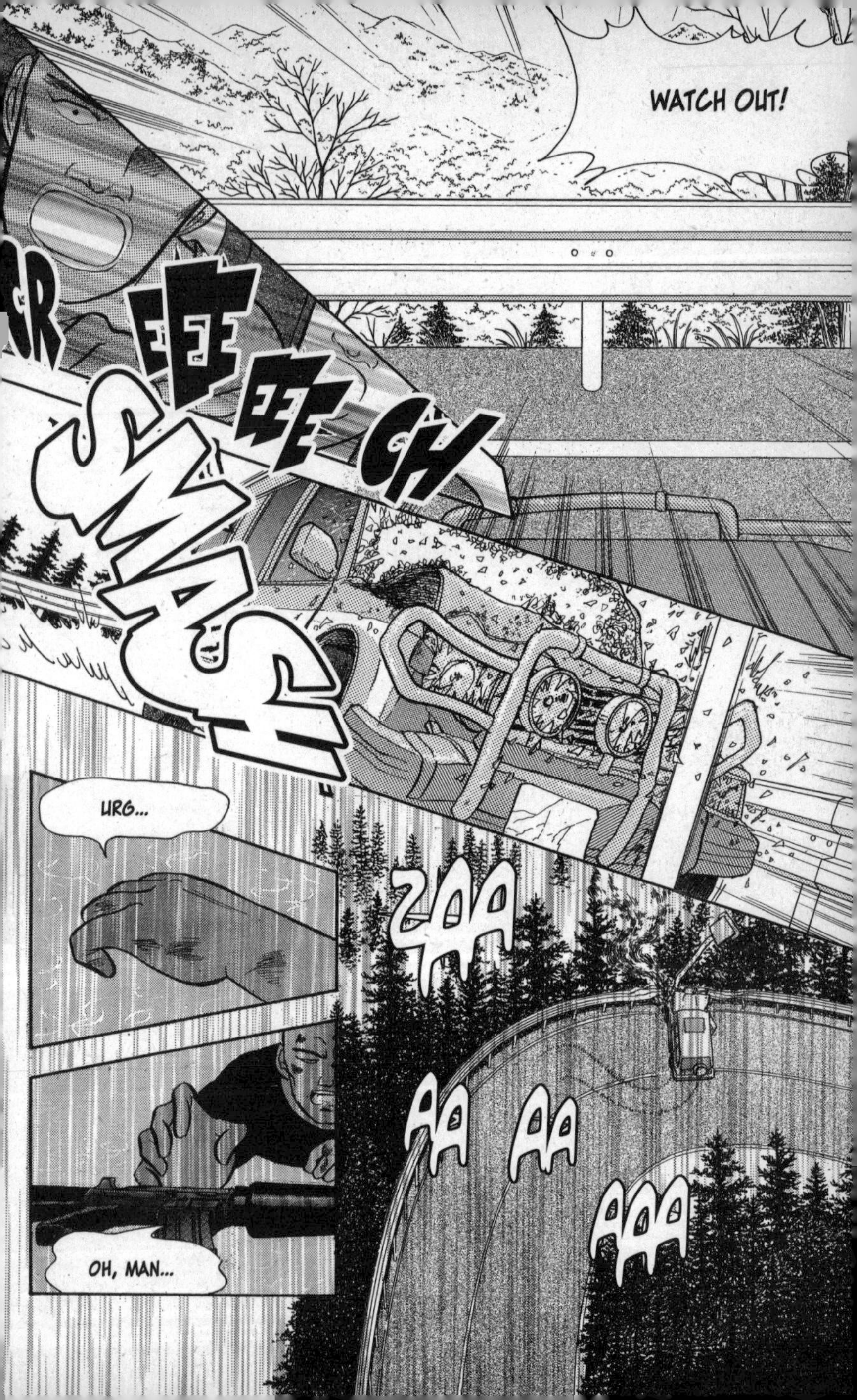
WATCH OUT!
GREEEEEECH
SMASH!
ZAA AA AA AAA
URG...
OH, MAN...

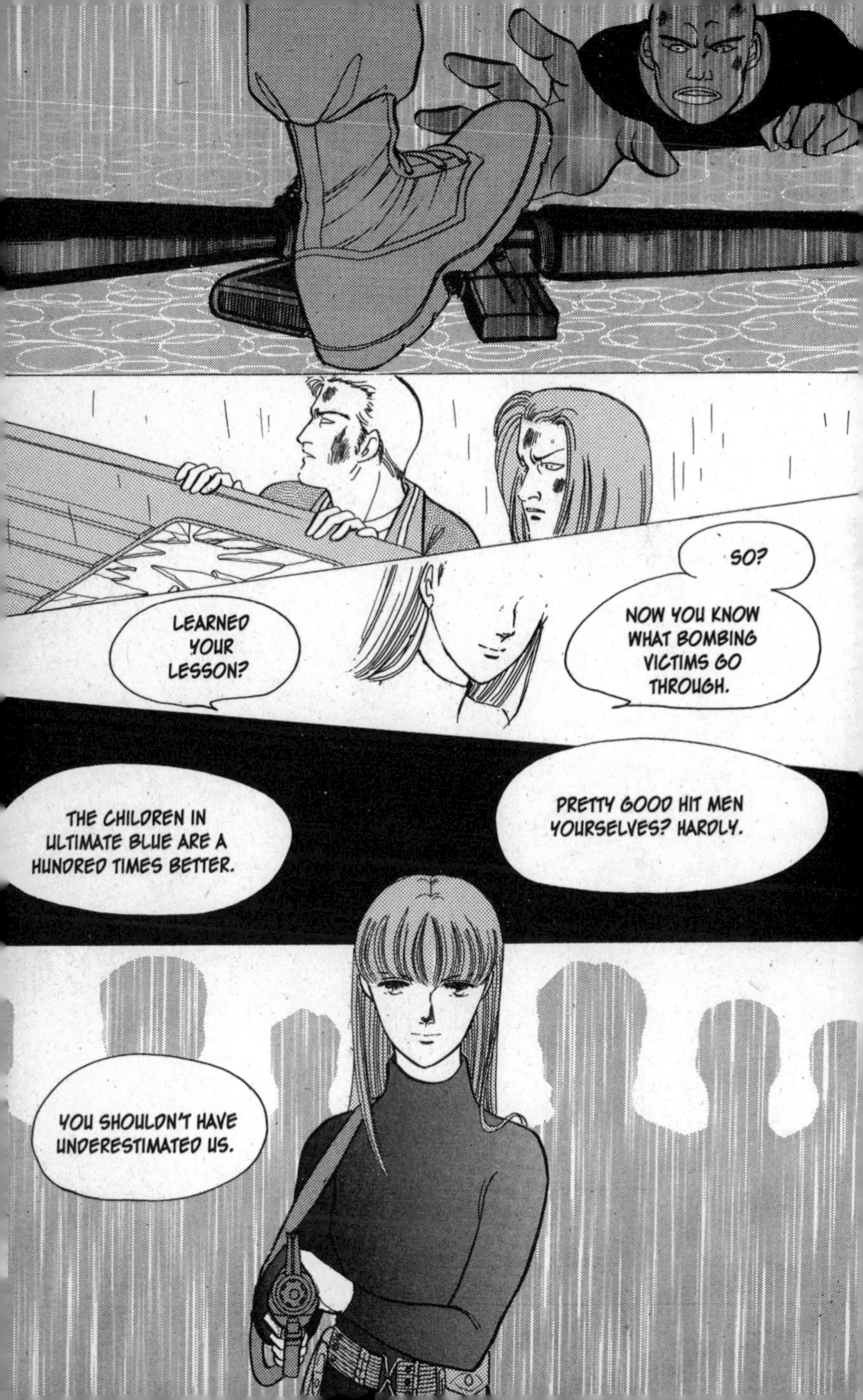
SO? NOW YOU KNOW WHAT BOMBING VICTIMS GO THROUGH.
LEARNED YOUR LESSON?
PRETTY GOOD HIT MEN YOURSELVES? HARDLY.
THE CHILDREN IN ULTIMATE BLUE ARE A HUNDRED TIMES BETTER.
YOU SHOULDN'T HAVE UNDERESTIMATED US.

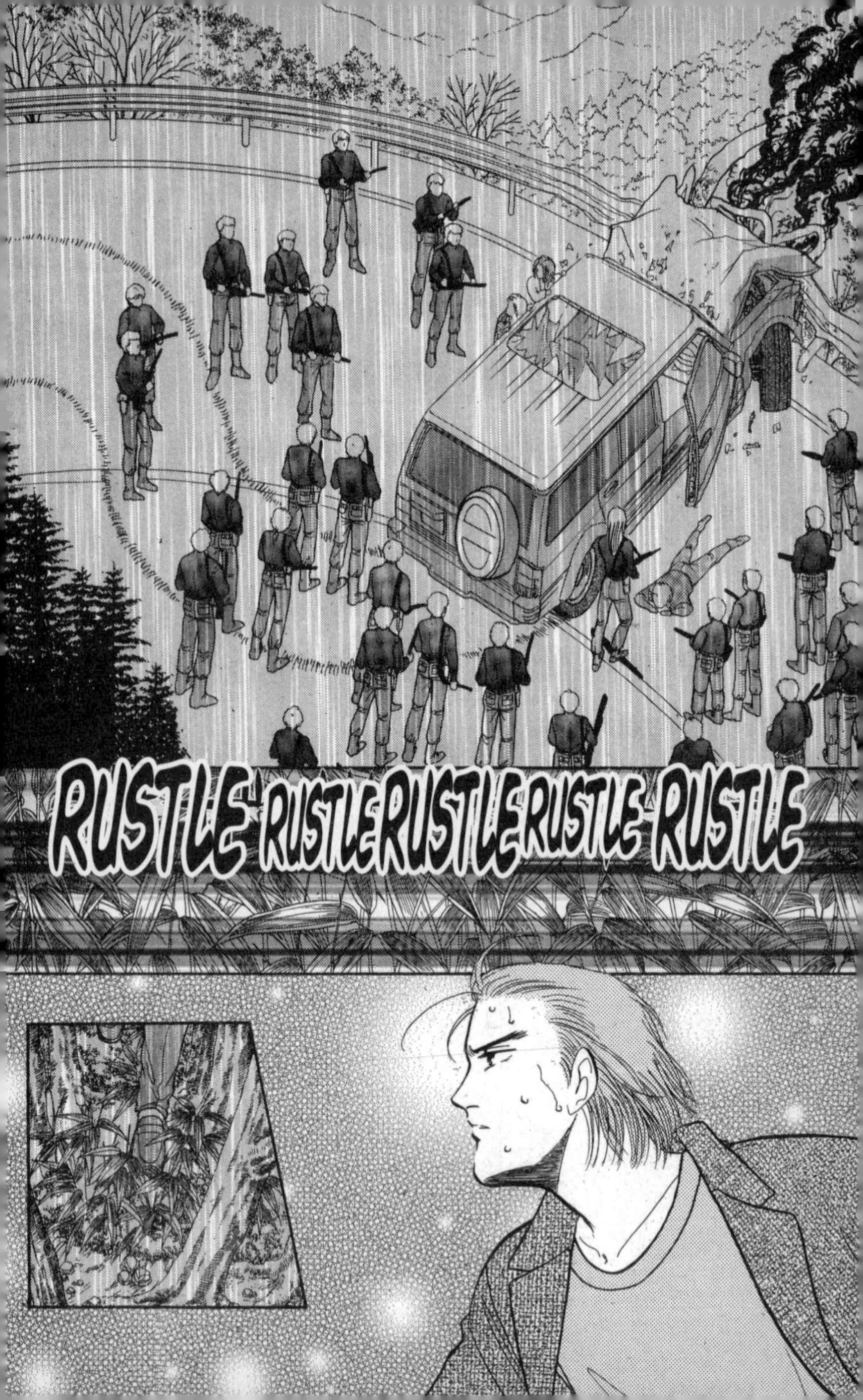
RUSTLE RUSTLE RUSTLE RUSTLE RUSTLE

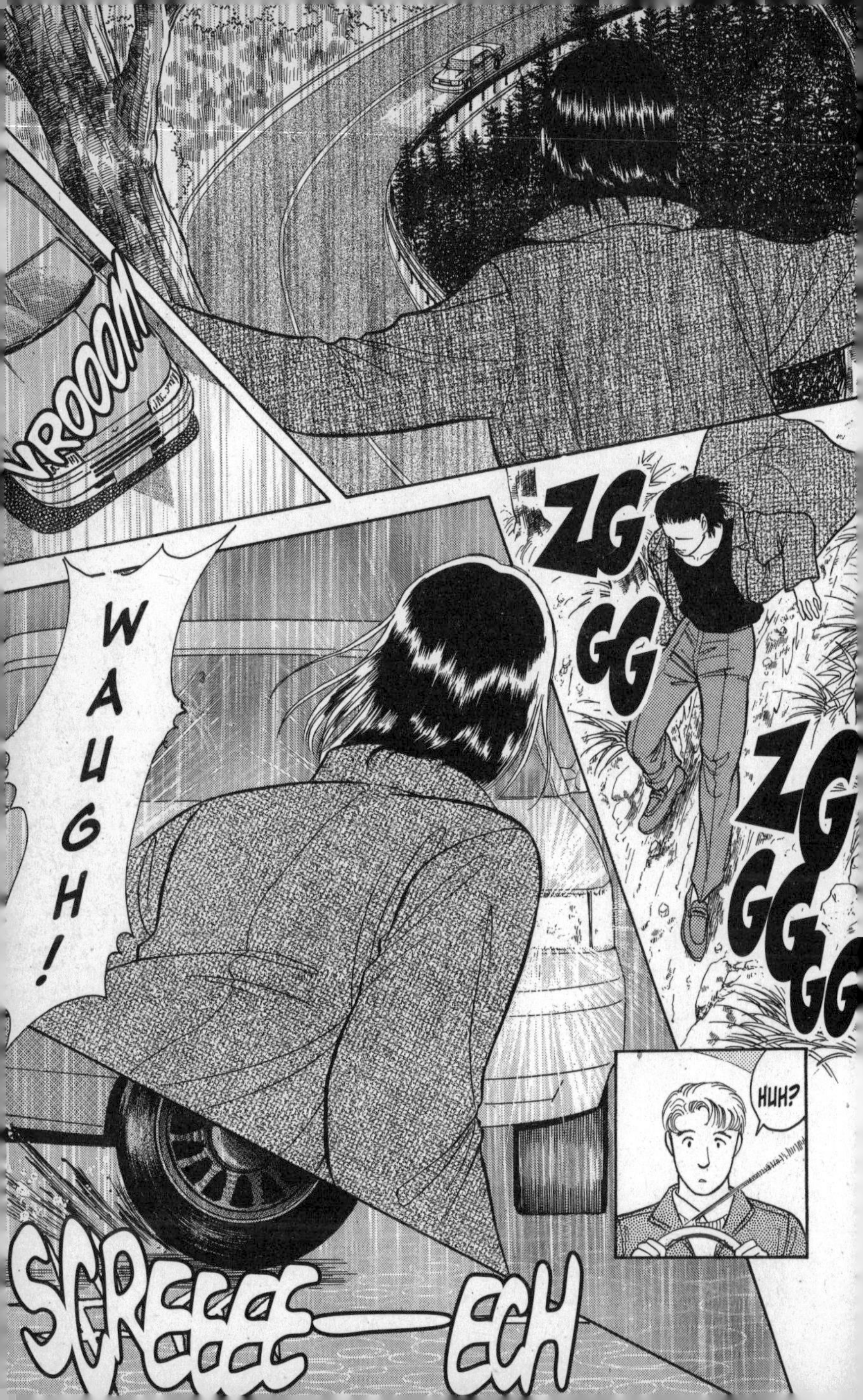
VROOOM
ZGGG
ZGGGGG
WAUGH!
HUH?
SCREEEE—ECH

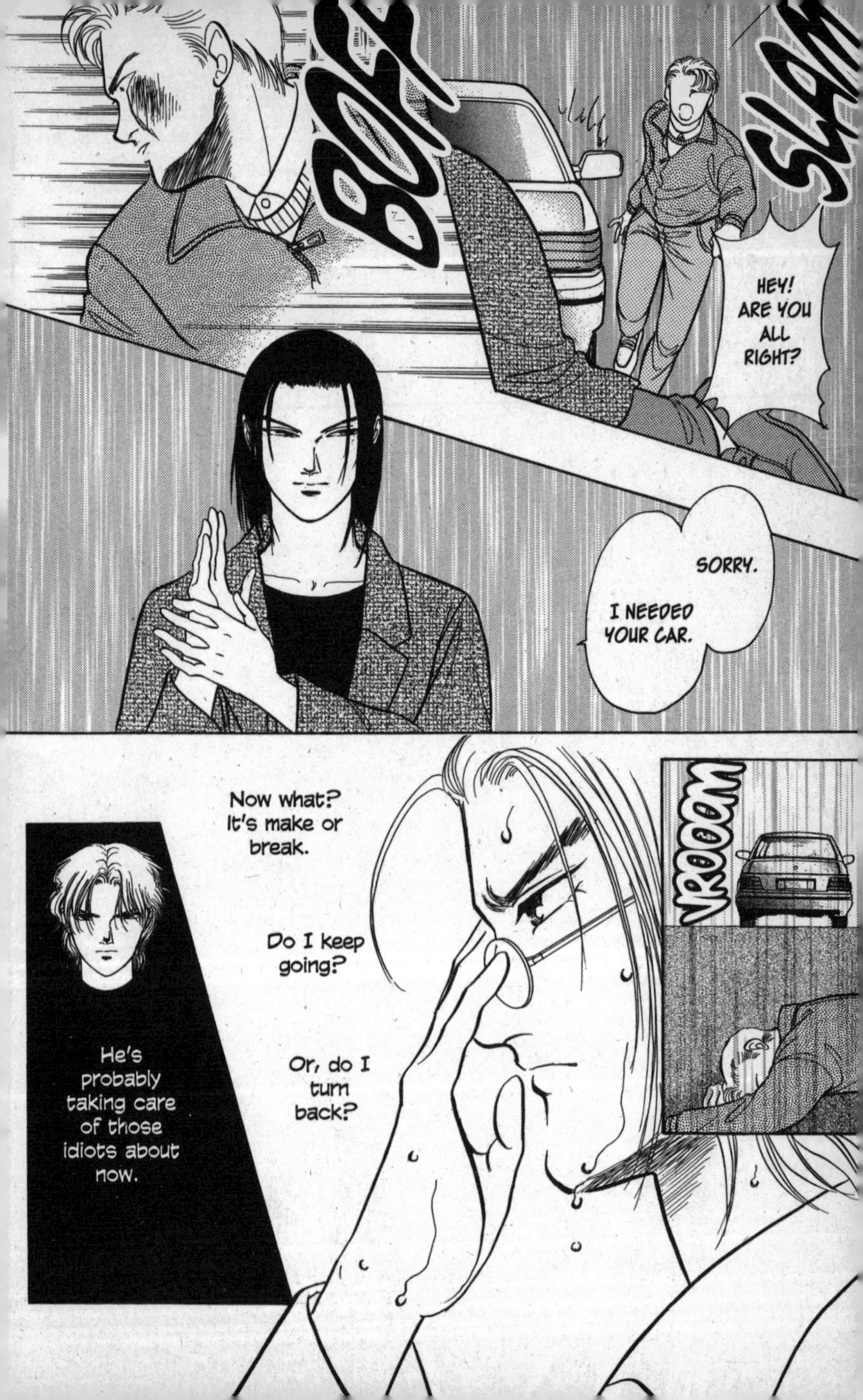
SLAM
BOOF
HEY! ARE YOU ALL RIGHT?
SORRY.
I NEEDED YOUR CAR.
VROOOM
Now what? It's make or break.
Do I keep going?
Or, do I turn back?
He's probably taking care of those idiots about now.

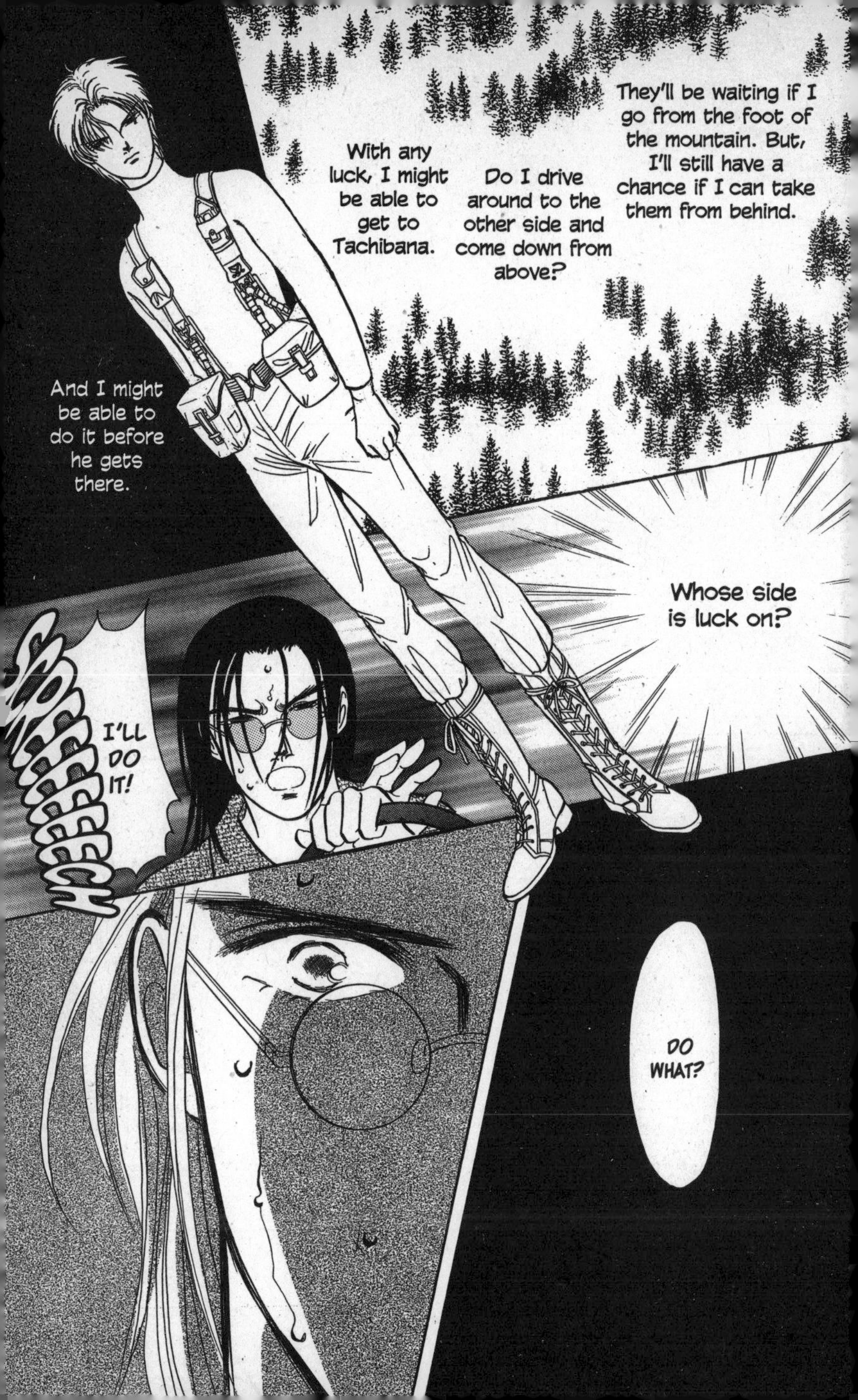
They'll be waiting if I go from the foot of the mountain. But, I'll still have a chance if I can take them from behind.
Do I drive around to the other side and come down from above?
With any luck, I might be able to get to Tachibana.
And I might be able to do it before he gets there.
Whose side is luck on?
I'LL DO IT!
SCREEEEECH
DO WHAT?

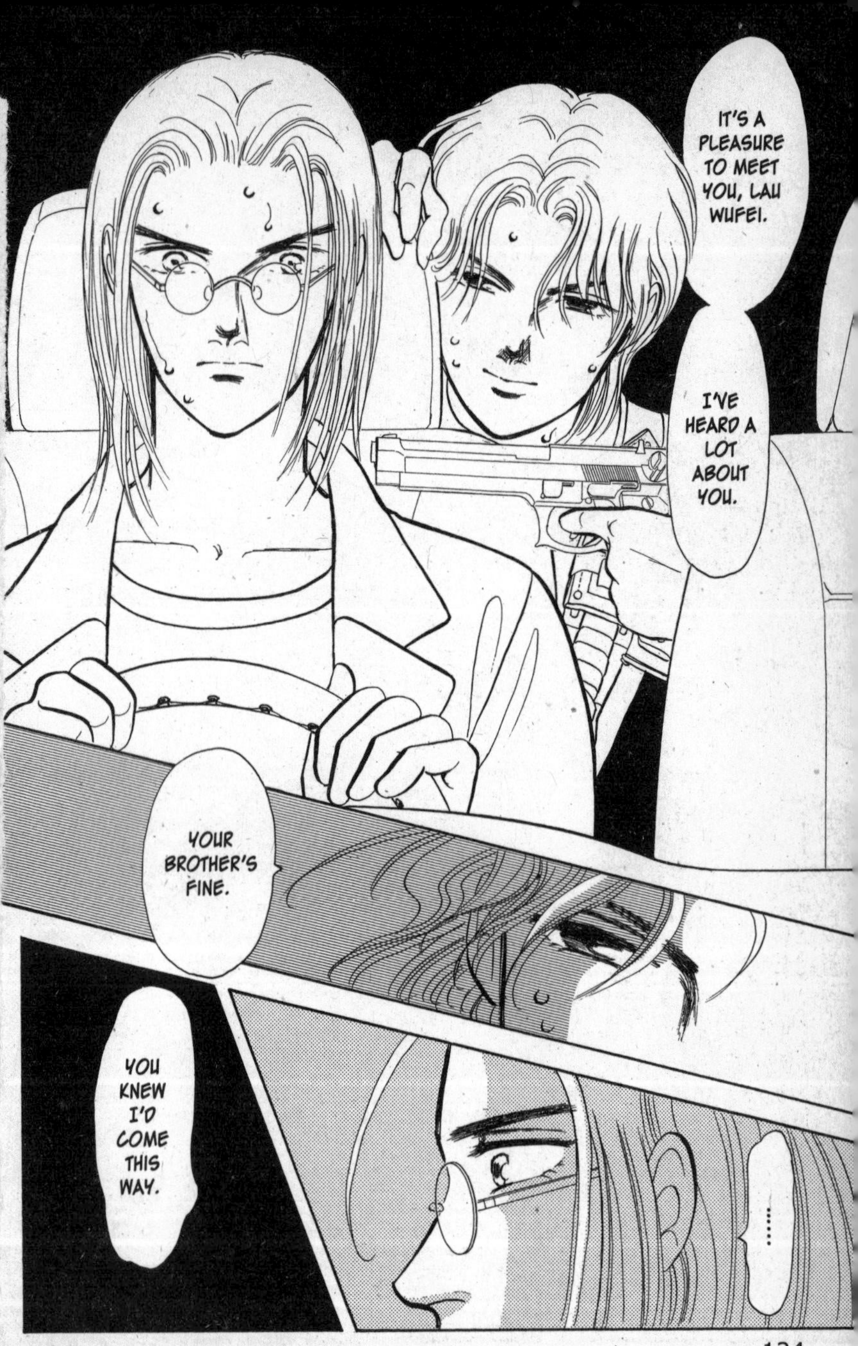
IT'S A PLEASURE TO MEET YOU, LAU WUFEI.
I'VE HEARD A LOT ABOUT YOU.
YOUR BROTHER'S FINE.
......
YOU KNEW I'D COME THIS WAY.

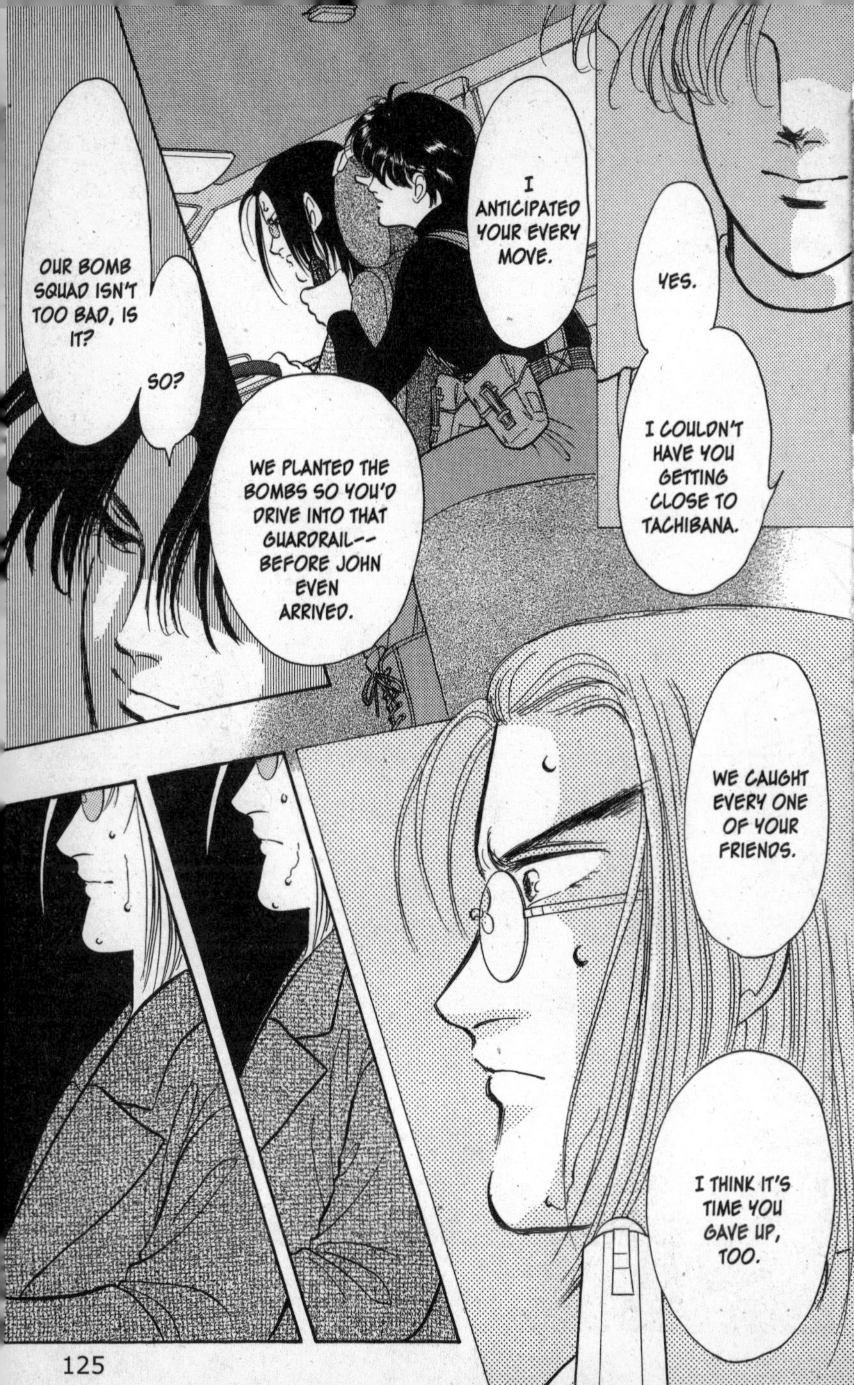
YES.
I COULDN'T HAVE YOU GETTING CLOSE TO TACHIBANA.
I ANTICIPATED YOUR EVERY MOVE.
OUR BOMB SQUAD ISN'T TOO BAD, IS IT?
SO?
WE PLANTED THE BOMBS SO YOU'D DRIVE INTO THAT GUARDRAIL-- BEFORE JOHN EVEN ARRIVED.
WE CAUGHT EVERY ONE OF YOUR FRIENDS.
I THINK IT'S TIME YOU GAVE UP, TOO.

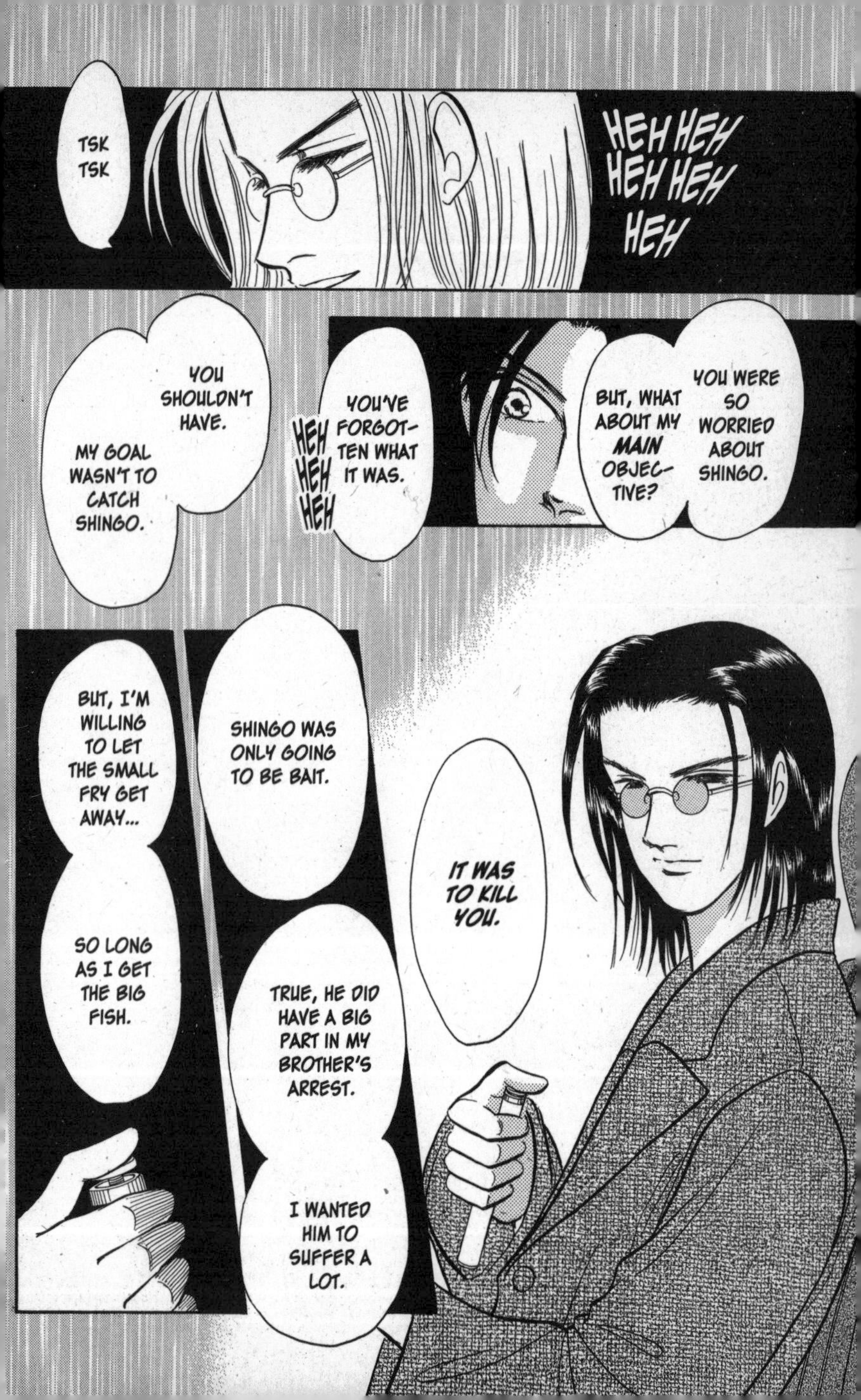
HEH HEH HEH HEH HEH
TSK TSK
YOU WERE SO WORRIED ABOUT SHINGO.
BUT, WHAT ABOUT MY *MAIN* OBJEC-TIVE?
YOU'VE FORGOT-TEN WHAT IT WAS.
HEH HEH HEH
YOU SHOULDN'T HAVE.
MY GOAL WASN'T TO CATCH SHINGO.
IT WAS TO KILL YOU.
SHINGO WAS ONLY GOING TO BE BAIT.
TRUE, HE DID HAVE A BIG PART IN MY BROTHER'S ARREST.
I WANTED HIM TO SUFFER A LOT.
BUT, I'M WILLING TO LET THE SMALL FRY GET AWAY...
SO LONG AS I GET THE BIG FISH.

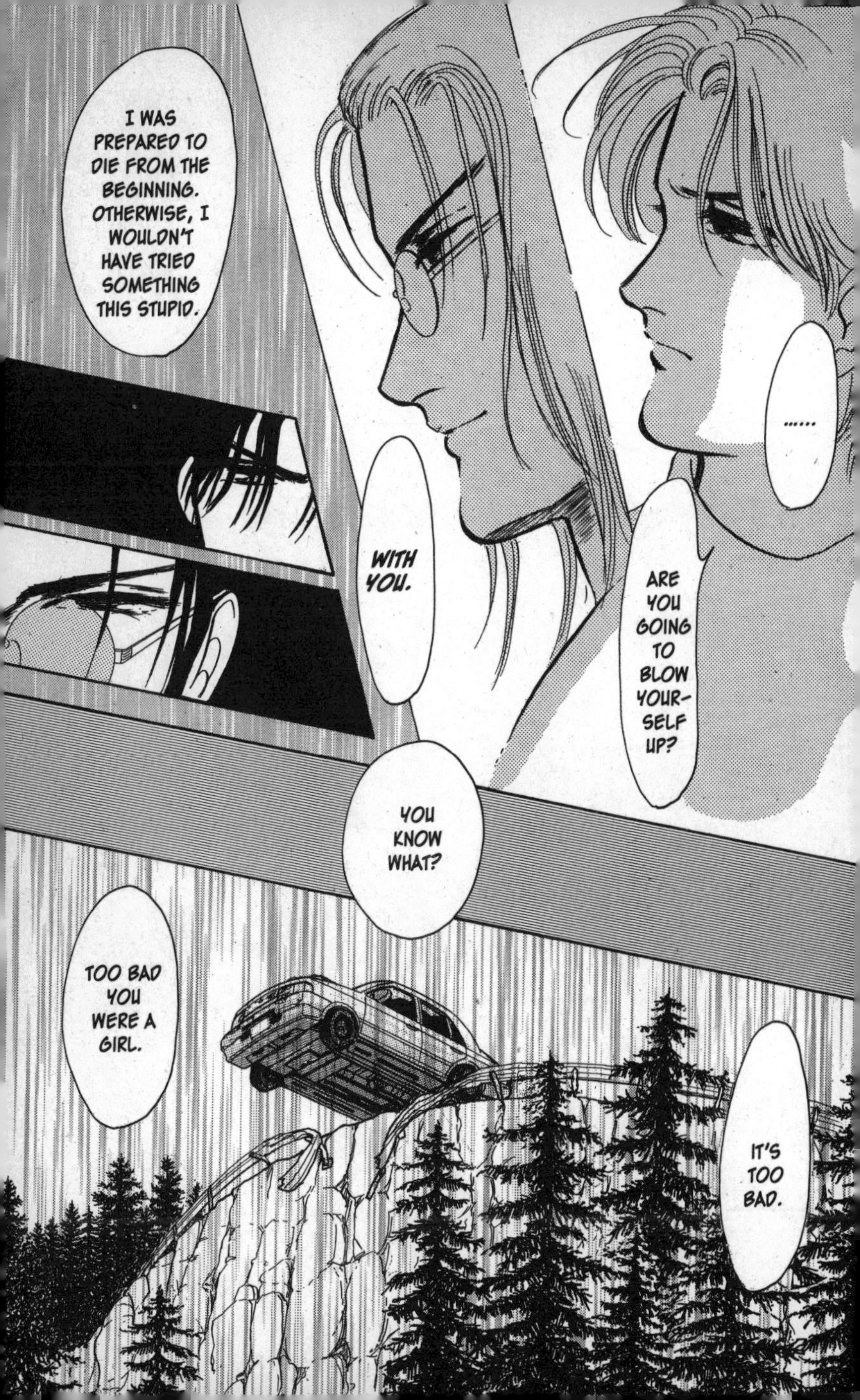
......
ARE YOU GOING TO BLOW YOUR-SELF UP?
WITH YOU.
I WAS PREPARED TO DIE FROM THE BEGINNING. OTHERWISE, I WOULDN'T HAVE TRIED SOMETHING THIS STUPID.
YOU KNOW WHAT?
IT'S TOO BAD.
TOO BAD YOU WERE A GIRL.

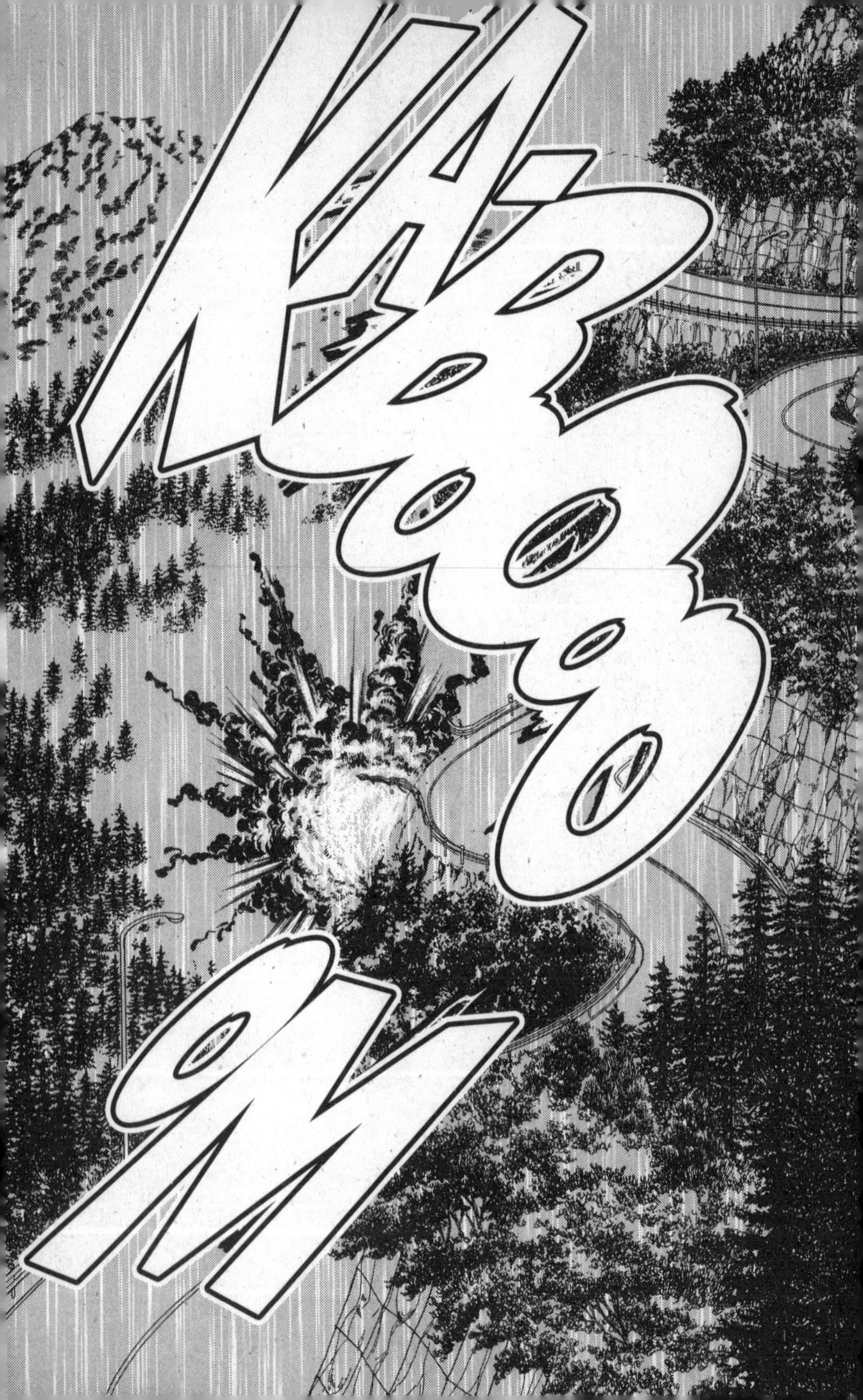

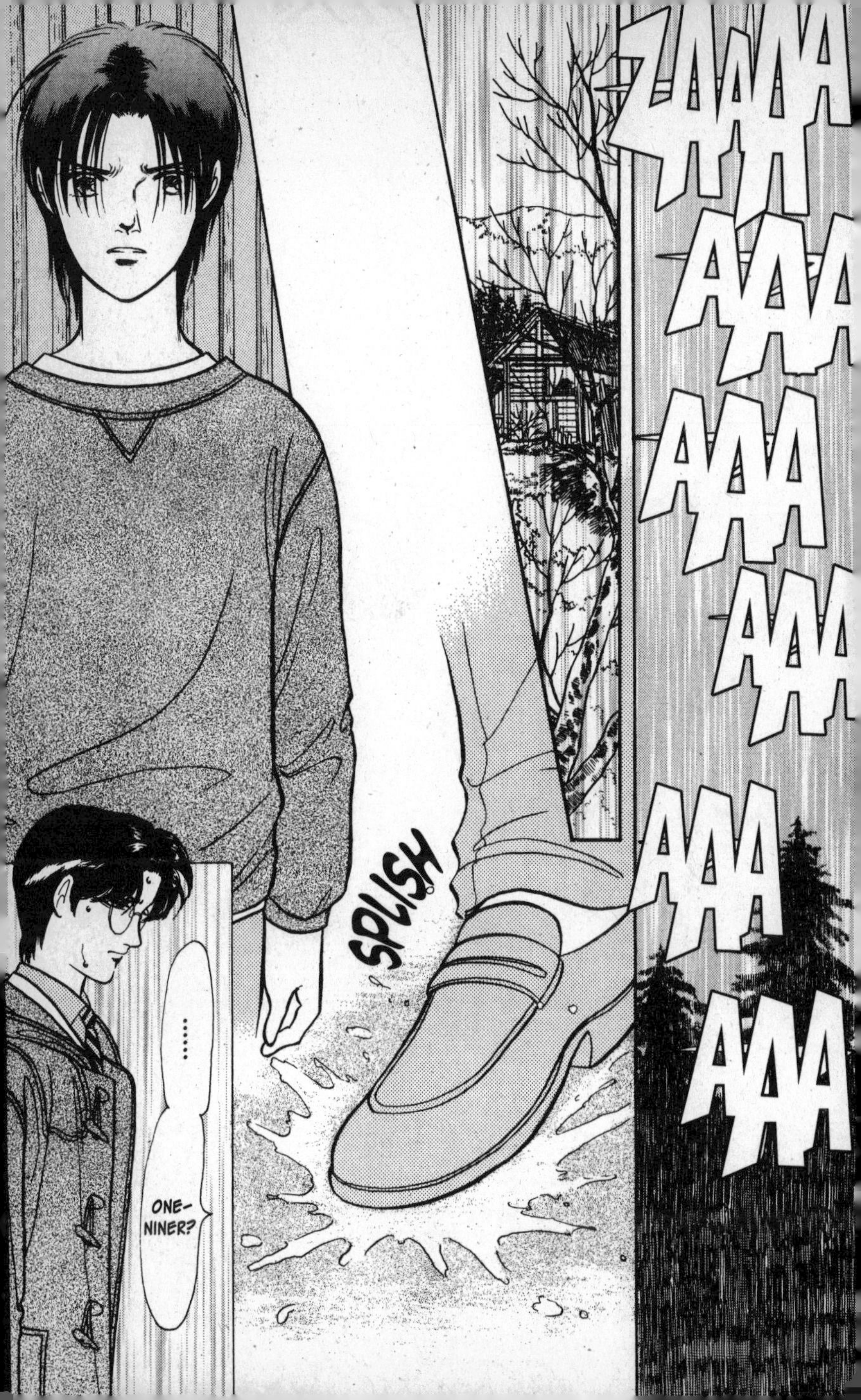
ZAAAAAAAAAAAAAAAAAAA
SPLISH
......
ONE-NINER?

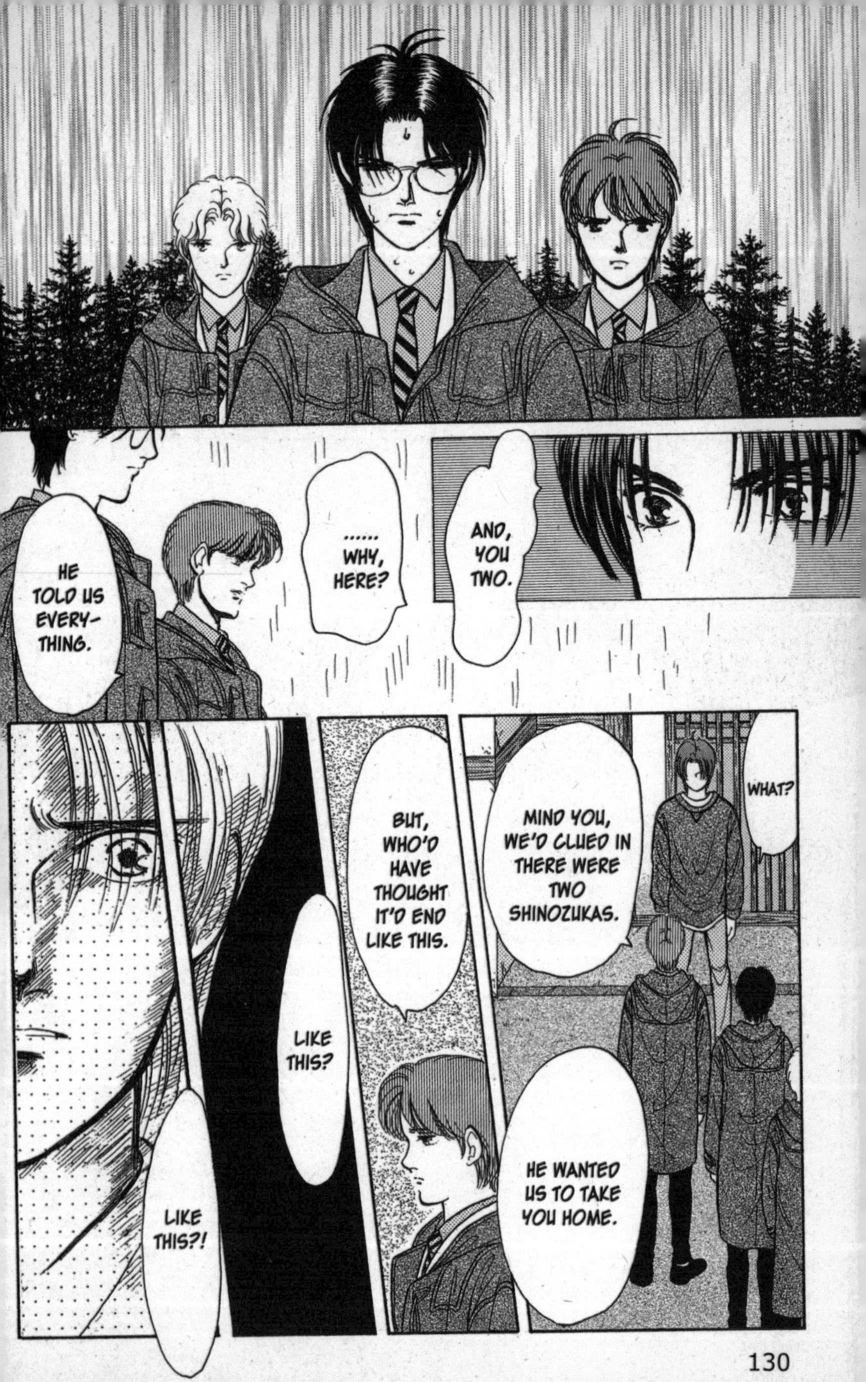
AND, YOU TWO.
...... WHY, HERE?
HE TOLD US EVERY-THING.
WHAT?
MIND YOU, WE'D CLUED IN THERE WERE TWO SHINOZUKAS.
HE WANTED US TO TAKE YOU HOME.
BUT, WHO'D HAVE THOUGHT IT'D END LIKE THIS.
LIKE THIS?
LIKE THIS?!

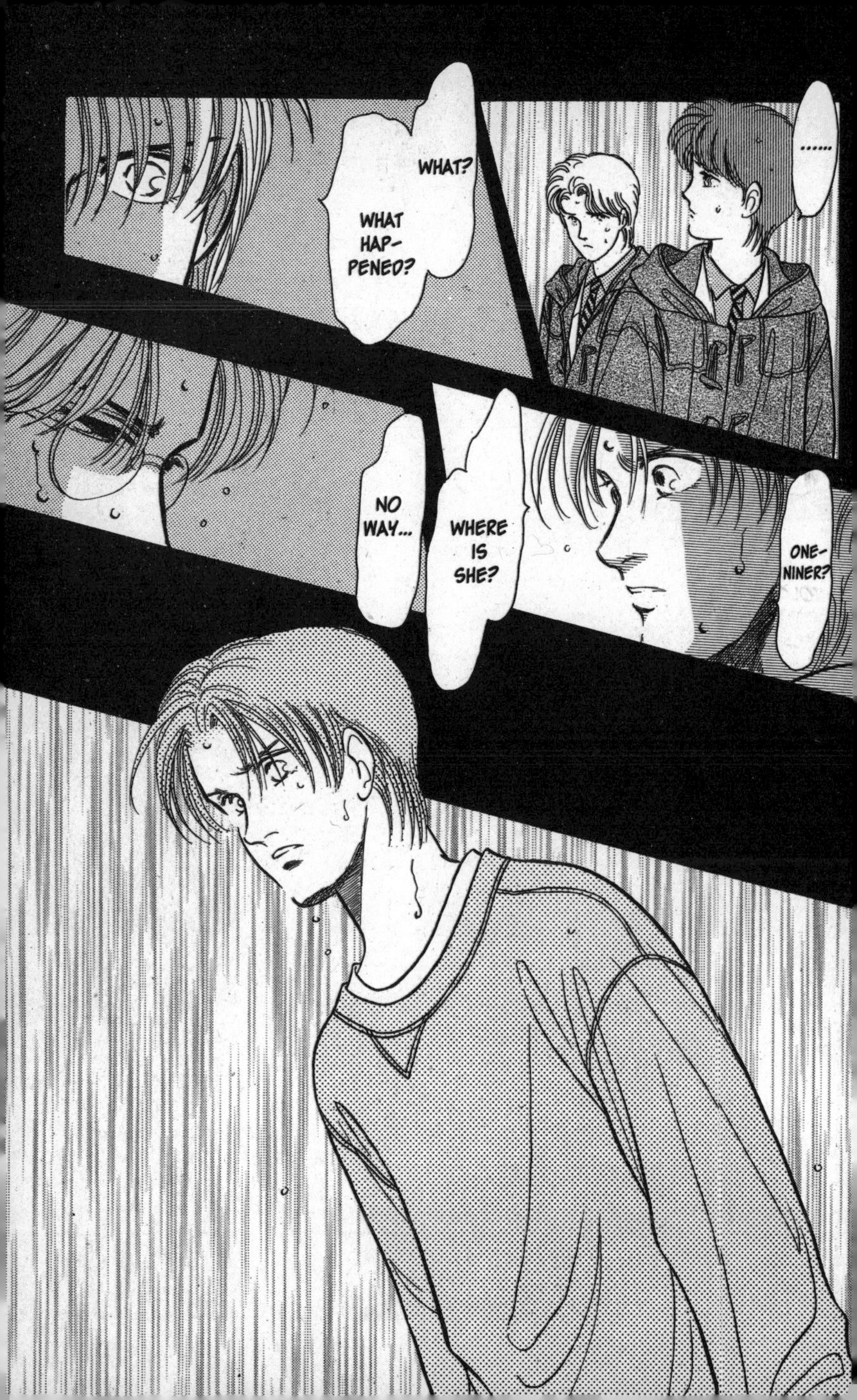
......
WHAT?
WHAT HAP-PENED?
ONE-NINER?
WHERE IS SHE?
NO WAY...

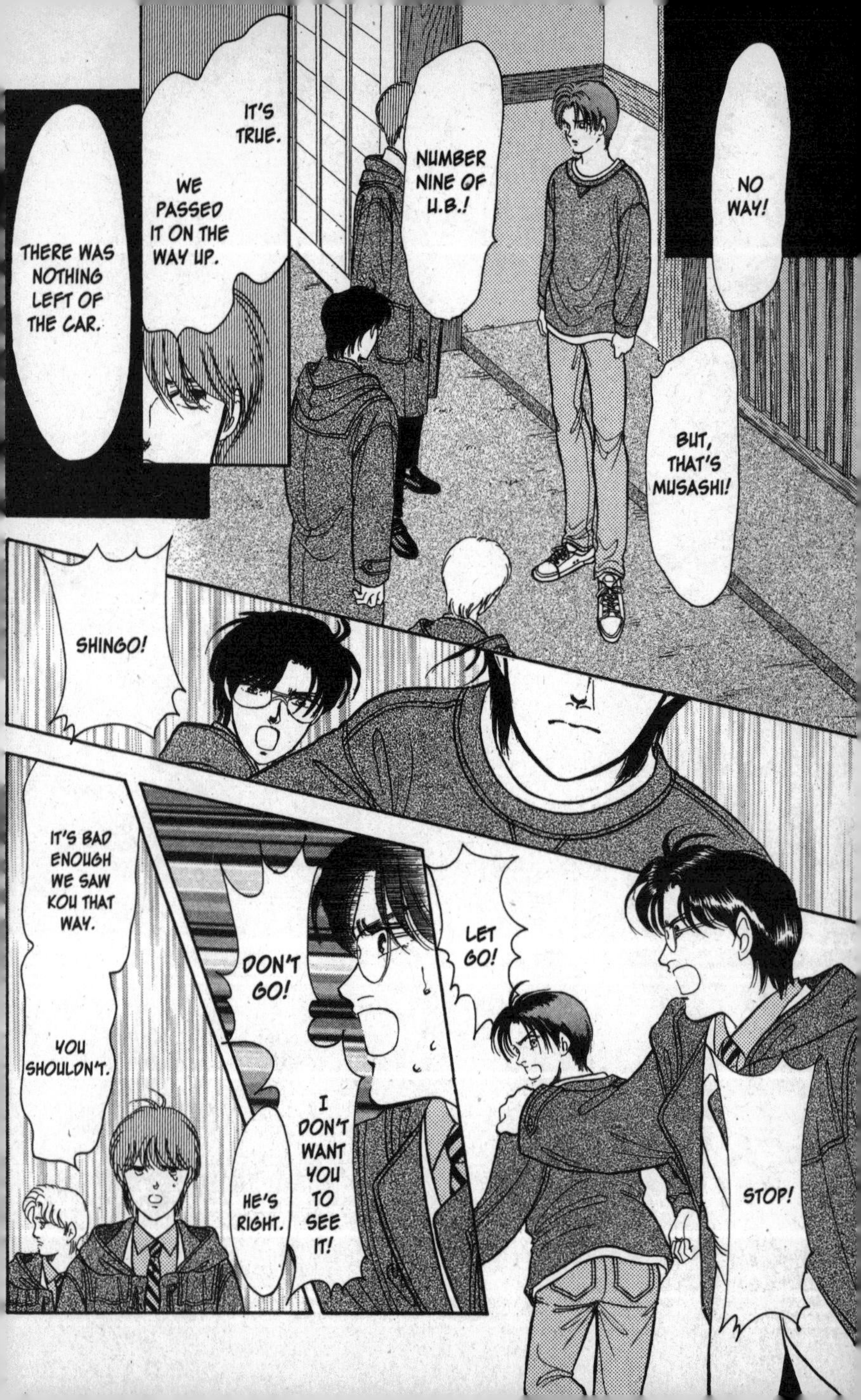
NO WAY!
BUT, THAT'S MUSASHI!
NUMBER NINE OF U.B.!
IT'S TRUE.
WE PASSED IT ON THE WAY UP.
THERE WAS NOTHING LEFT OF THE CAR.
SHINGO!
STOP!
LET GO!
I DON'T WANT YOU TO SEE IT!
DON'T GO!
HE'S RIGHT.
IT'S BAD ENOUGH WE SAW KOU THAT WAY.
YOU SHOULDN'T.

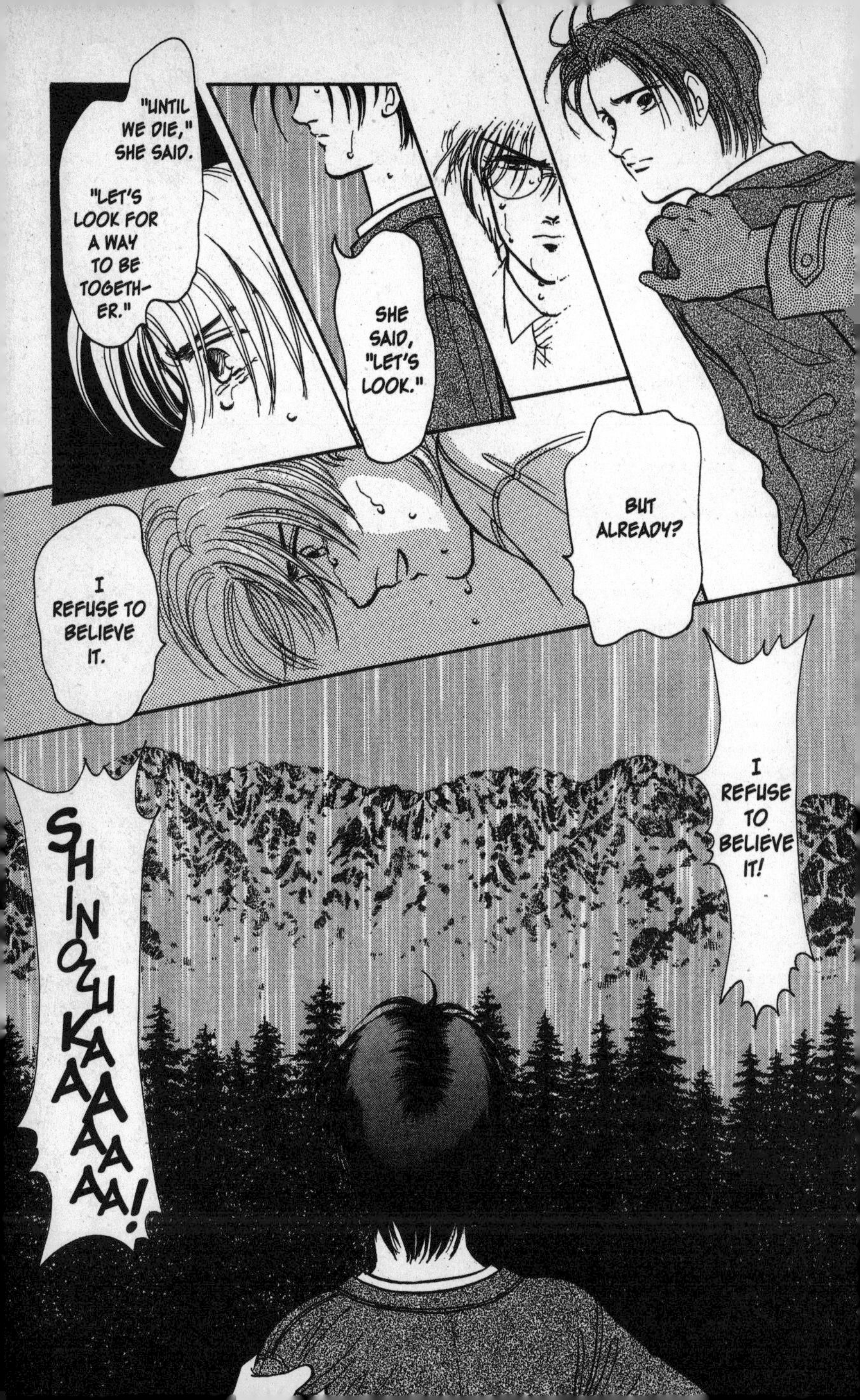
"UNTIL WE DIE," SHE SAID.
"LET'S LOOK FOR A WAY TO BE TOGETH-ER."
SHE SAID, "LET'S LOOK."
BUT ALREADY?
I REFUSE TO BELIEVE IT.
I REFUSE TO BELIEVE IT!
SHINOZUKAAAAAAA!

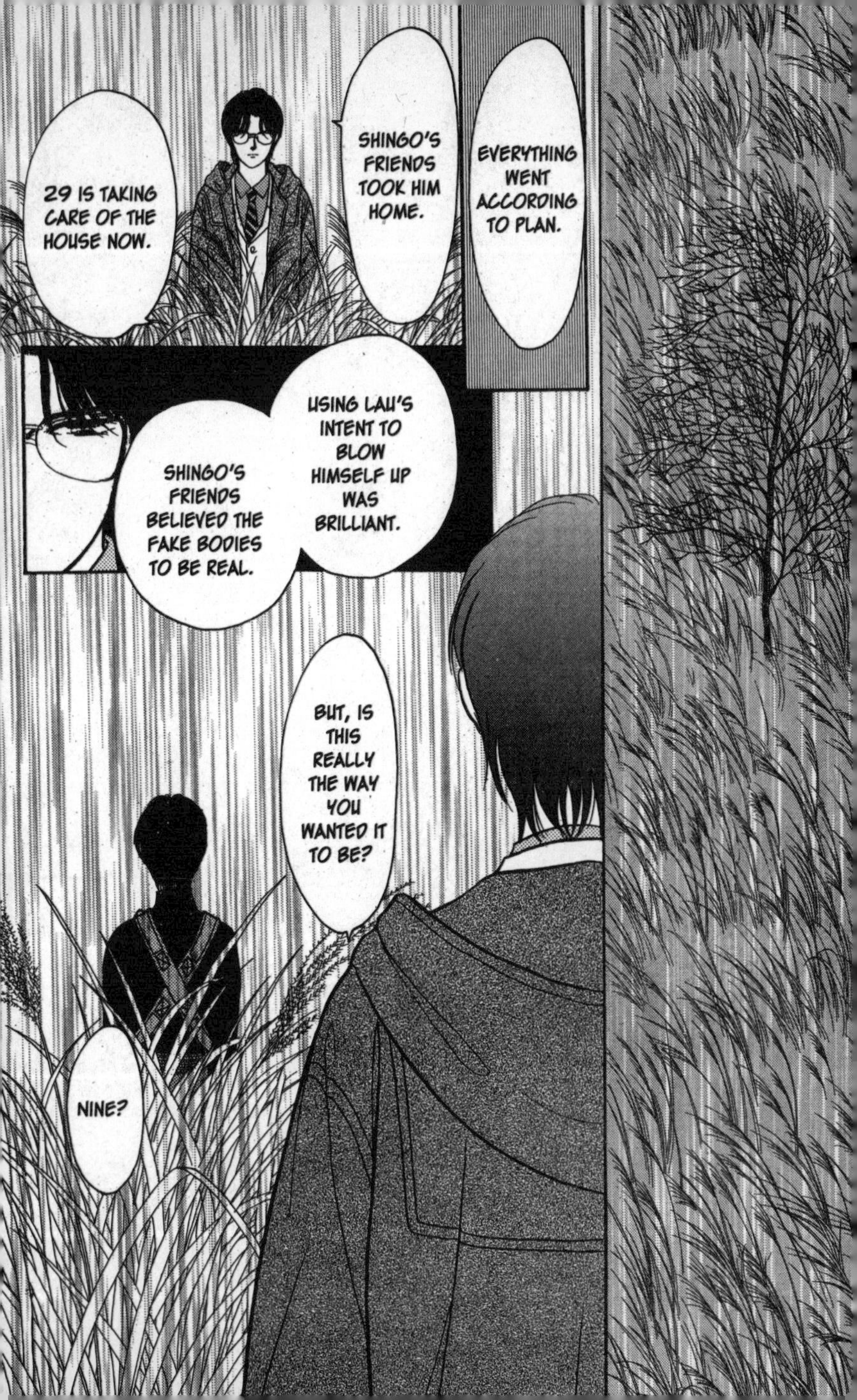
EVERYTHING WENT ACCORDING TO PLAN.
SHINGO'S FRIENDS TOOK HIM HOME.
29 IS TAKING CARE OF THE HOUSE NOW.
USING LAU'S INTENT TO BLOW HIMSELF UP WAS BRILLIANT.
SHINGO'S FRIENDS BELIEVED THE FAKE BODIES TO BE REAL.
BUT, IS THIS REALLY THE WAY YOU WANTED IT TO BE?
NINE?

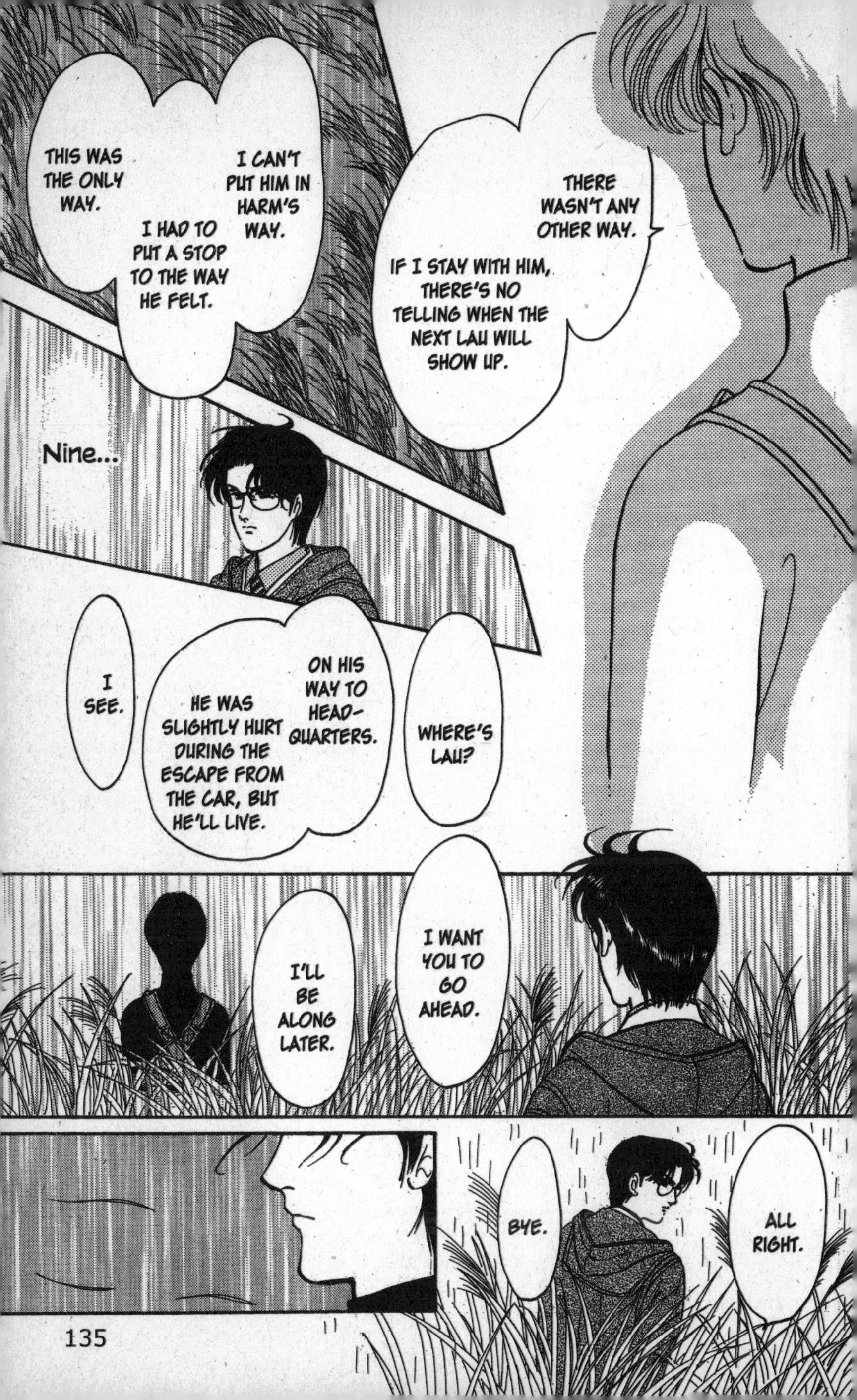
THERE WASN'T ANY OTHER WAY.
IF I STAY WITH HIM, THERE'S NO TELLING WHEN THE NEXT LAU WILL SHOW UP.
I CAN'T PUT HIM IN HARM'S WAY.
THIS WAS THE ONLY WAY.
I HAD TO PUT A STOP TO THE WAY HE FELT.
Nine...
WHERE'S LAU?
ON HIS WAY TO HEAD-QUARTERS.
HE WAS SLIGHTLY HURT DURING THE ESCAPE FROM THE CAR, BUT HE'LL LIVE.
I SEE.
I WANT YOU TO GO AHEAD.
I'LL BE ALONG LATER.
ALL RIGHT.
BYE.

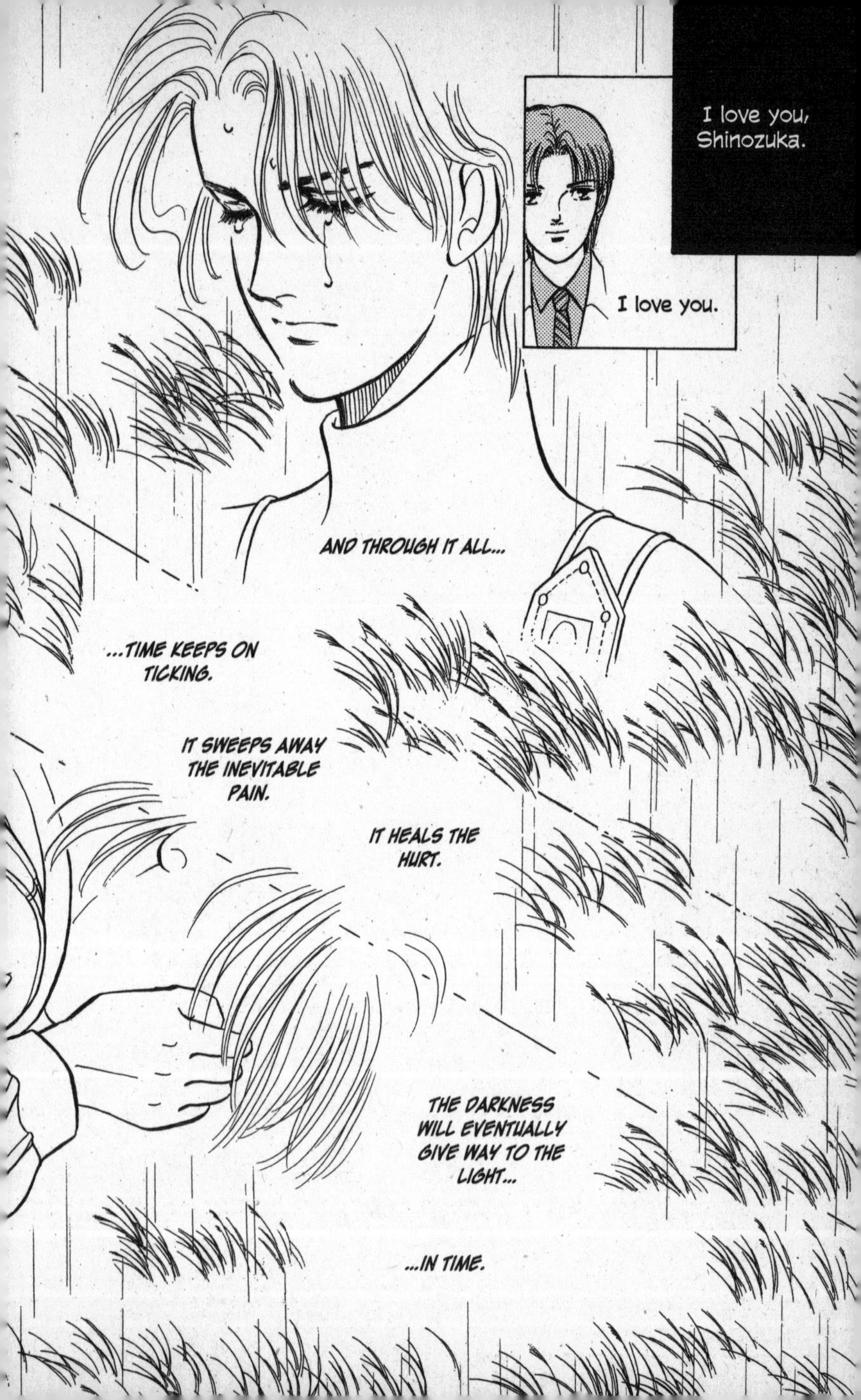
I love you, Shinozuka.
I love you.
AND THROUGH IT ALL...
...TIME KEEPS ON TICKING.
IT SWEEPS AWAY THE INEVITABLE PAIN.
IT HEALS THE HURT.
THE DARKNESS WILL EVENTUALLY GIVE WAY TO THE LIGHT...
...IN TIME.

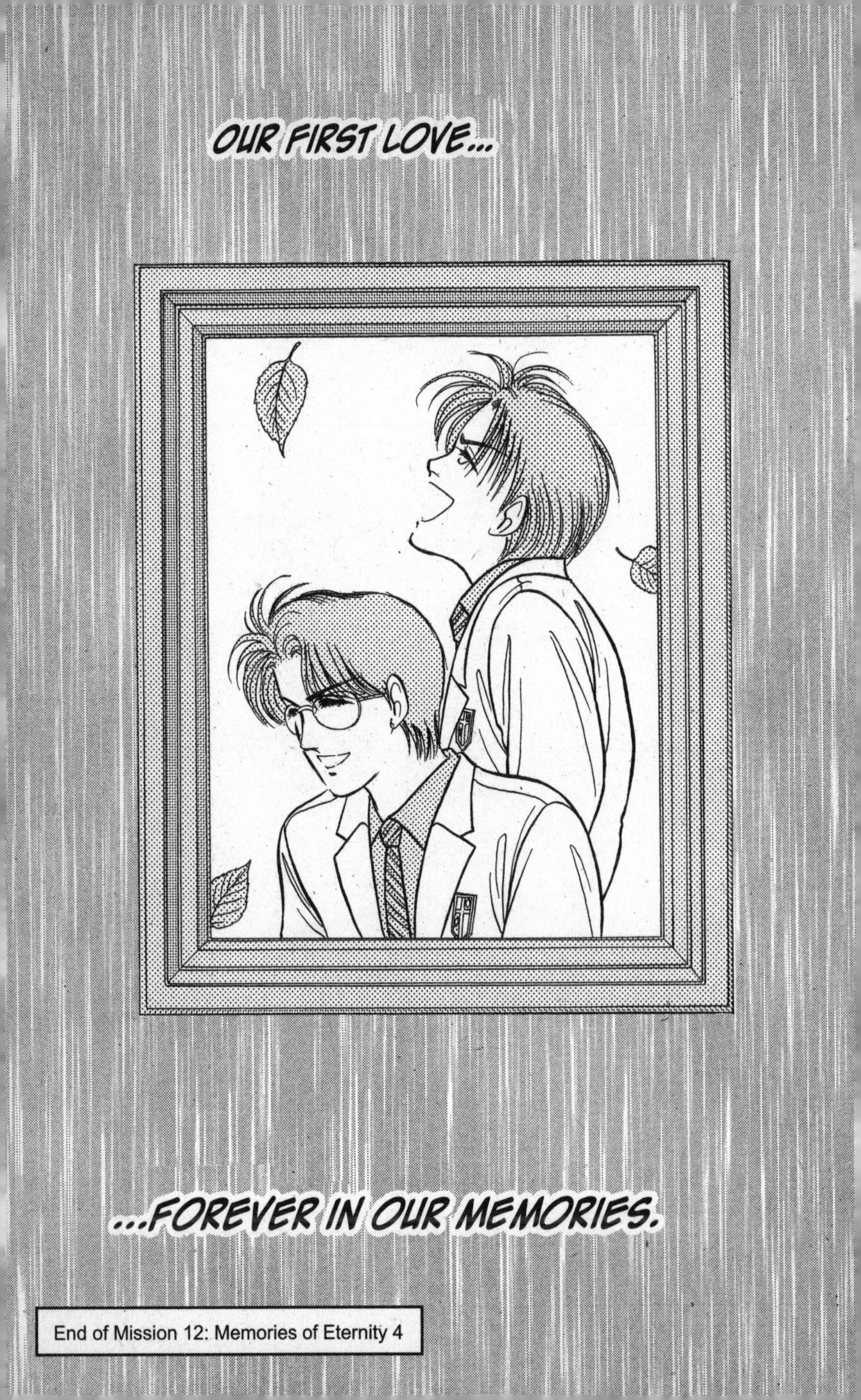
OUR FIRST LOVE...
...FOREVER IN OUR MEMORIES.
End of Mission 12: Memories of Eternity 4

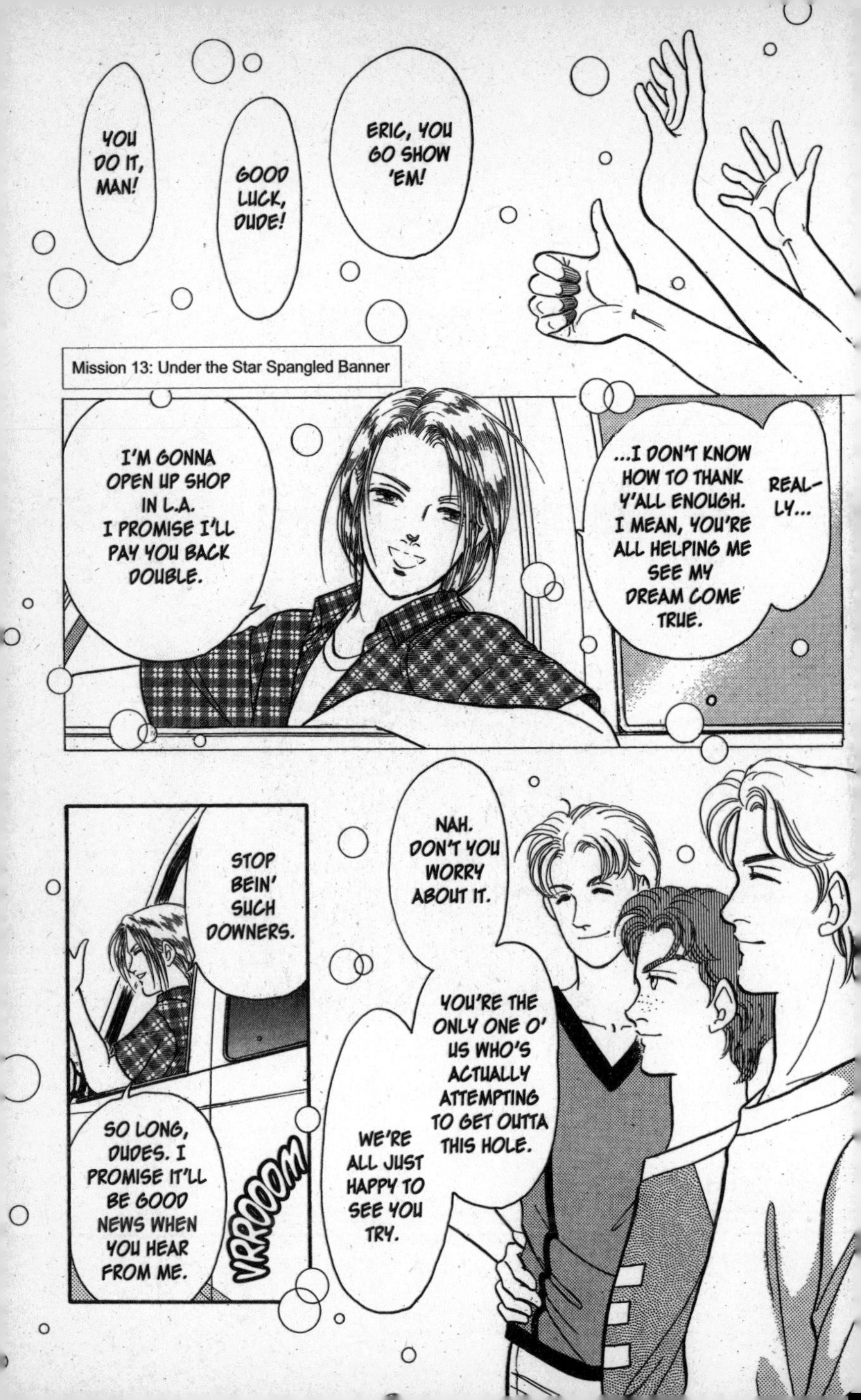
ERIC, YOU GO SHOW 'EM!
GOOD LUCK, DUDE!
YOU DO IT, MAN!
Mission 13: Under the Star Spangled Banner
...I DON'T KNOW HOW TO THANK Y'ALL ENOUGH. I MEAN, YOU'RE ALL HELPING ME SEE MY DREAM COME TRUE.
REAL-LY...
I'M GONNA OPEN UP SHOP IN L.A. I PROMISE I'LL PAY YOU BACK DOUBLE.
NAH. DON'T YOU WORRY ABOUT IT.
YOU'RE THE ONLY ONE O' US WHO'S ACTUALLY ATTEMPTING TO GET OUTTA THIS HOLE.
WE'RE ALL JUST HAPPY TO SEE YOU TRY.
STOP BEIN' SUCH DOWNERS.
SO LONG, DUDES. I PROMISE IT'LL BE GOOD NEWS WHEN YOU HEAR FROM ME.
VRROOOM

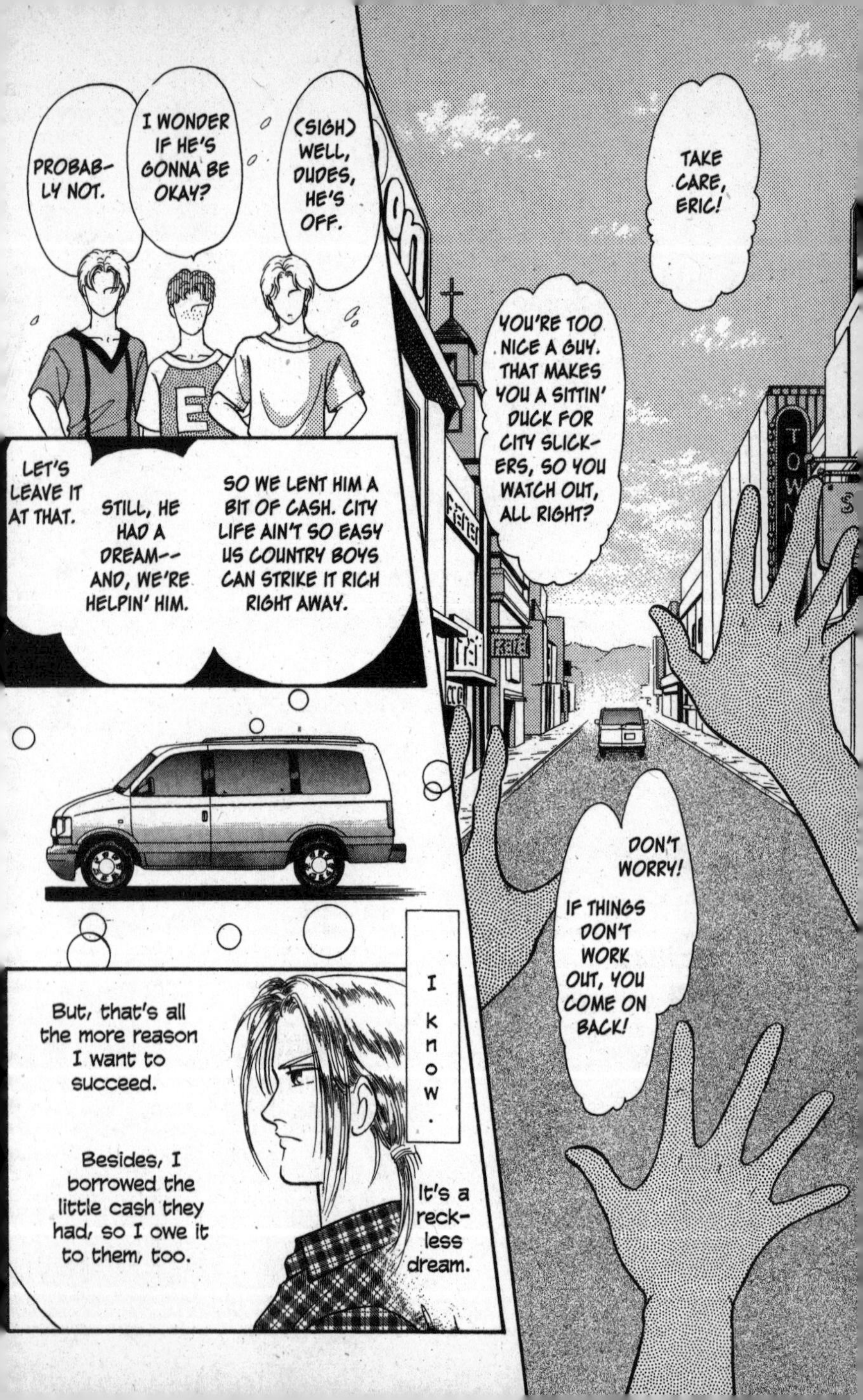
TAKE CARE, ERIC!
YOU'RE TOO NICE A GUY. THAT MAKES YOU A SITTIN' DUCK FOR CITY SLICKERS, SO YOU WATCH OUT, ALL RIGHT?
DON'T WORRY!
IF THINGS DON'T WORK OUT, YOU COME ON BACK!
(SIGH) WELL, DUDES, HE'S OFF.
I WONDER IF HE'S GONNA BE OKAY?
PROBABLY NOT.
SO WE LENT HIM A BIT OF CASH. CITY LIFE AIN'T SO EASY US COUNTRY BOYS CAN STRIKE IT RICH RIGHT AWAY.
STILL, HE HAD A DREAM-- AND, WE'RE HELPIN' HIM.
LET'S LEAVE IT AT THAT.
I know.
It's a reckless dream.
But, that's all the more reason I want to succeed.
Besides, I borrowed the little cash they had, so I owe it to them, too.

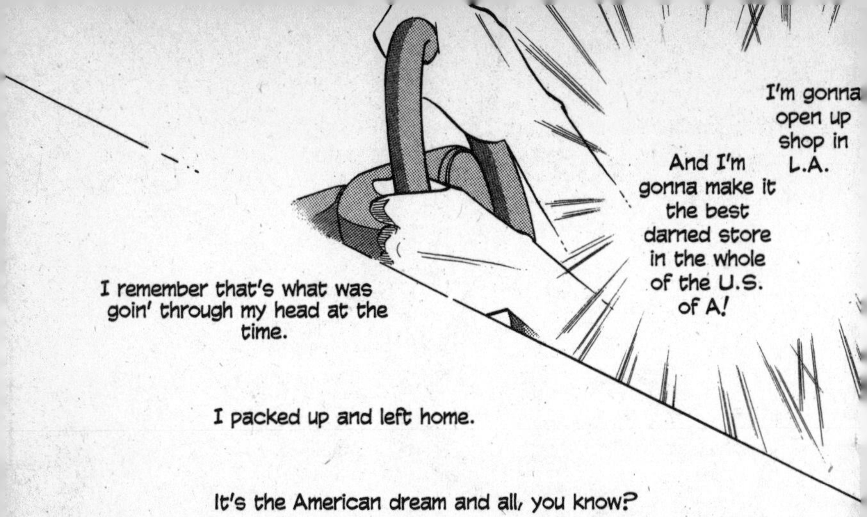
I'm gonna open up shop in L.A.
And I'm gonna make it the best darned store in the whole of the U.S. of A!

I remember that's what was goin' through my head at the time.

I packed up and left home.

It's the American dream and all, you know?

But I didn't know that much.

And I didn't have much experience, either.

I figured there'd be some confusion at first.

But, nothing had prepared me for what was about to go down.

Nothing.

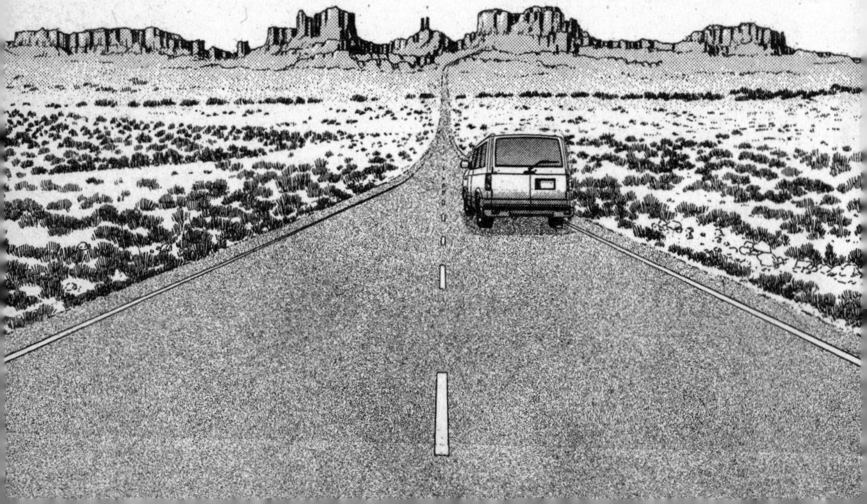

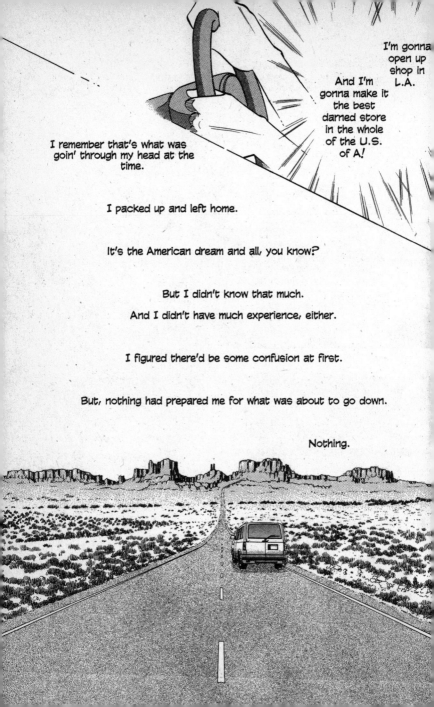

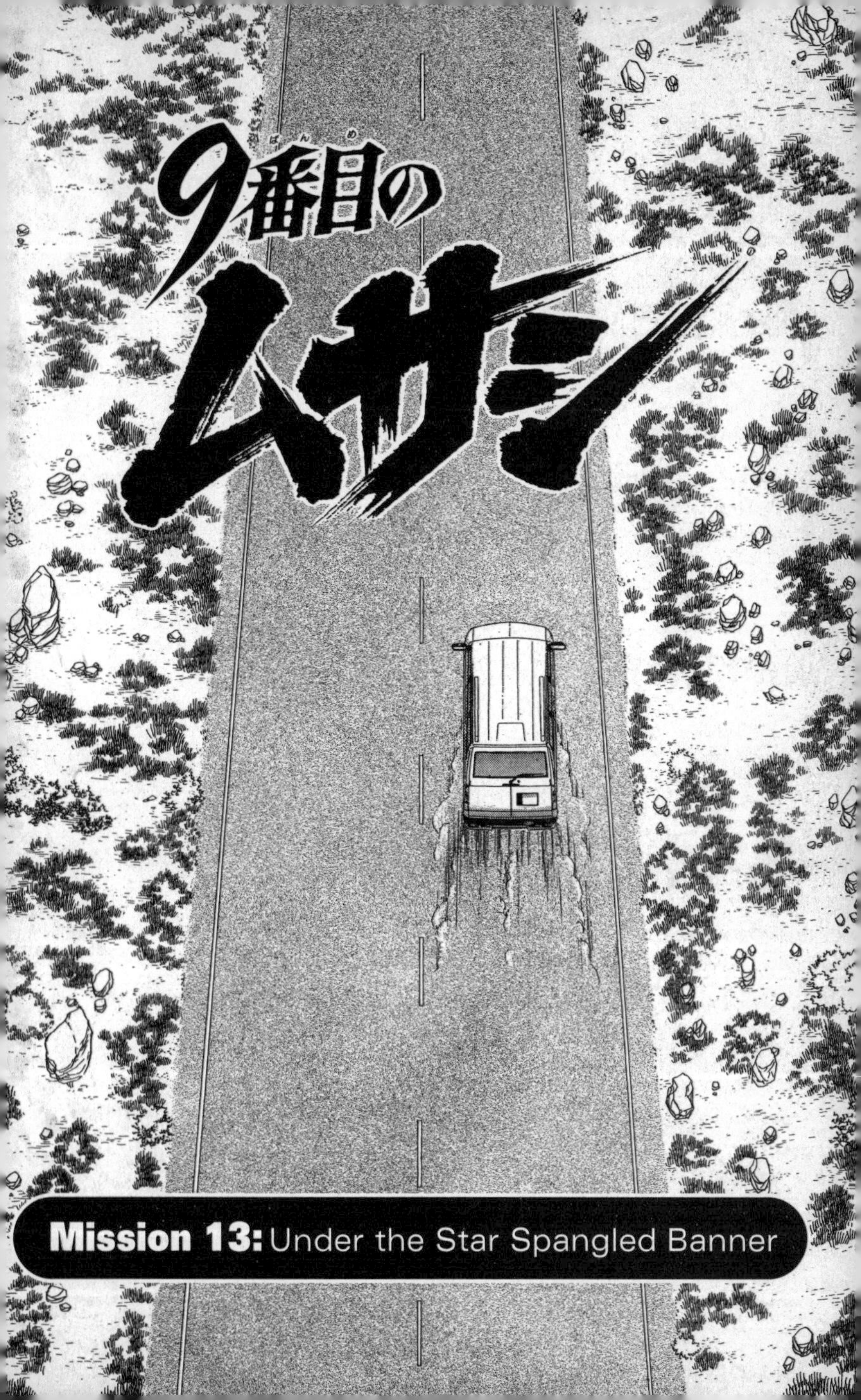
9番目のムサシ
Mission 13: Under the Star Spangled Banner

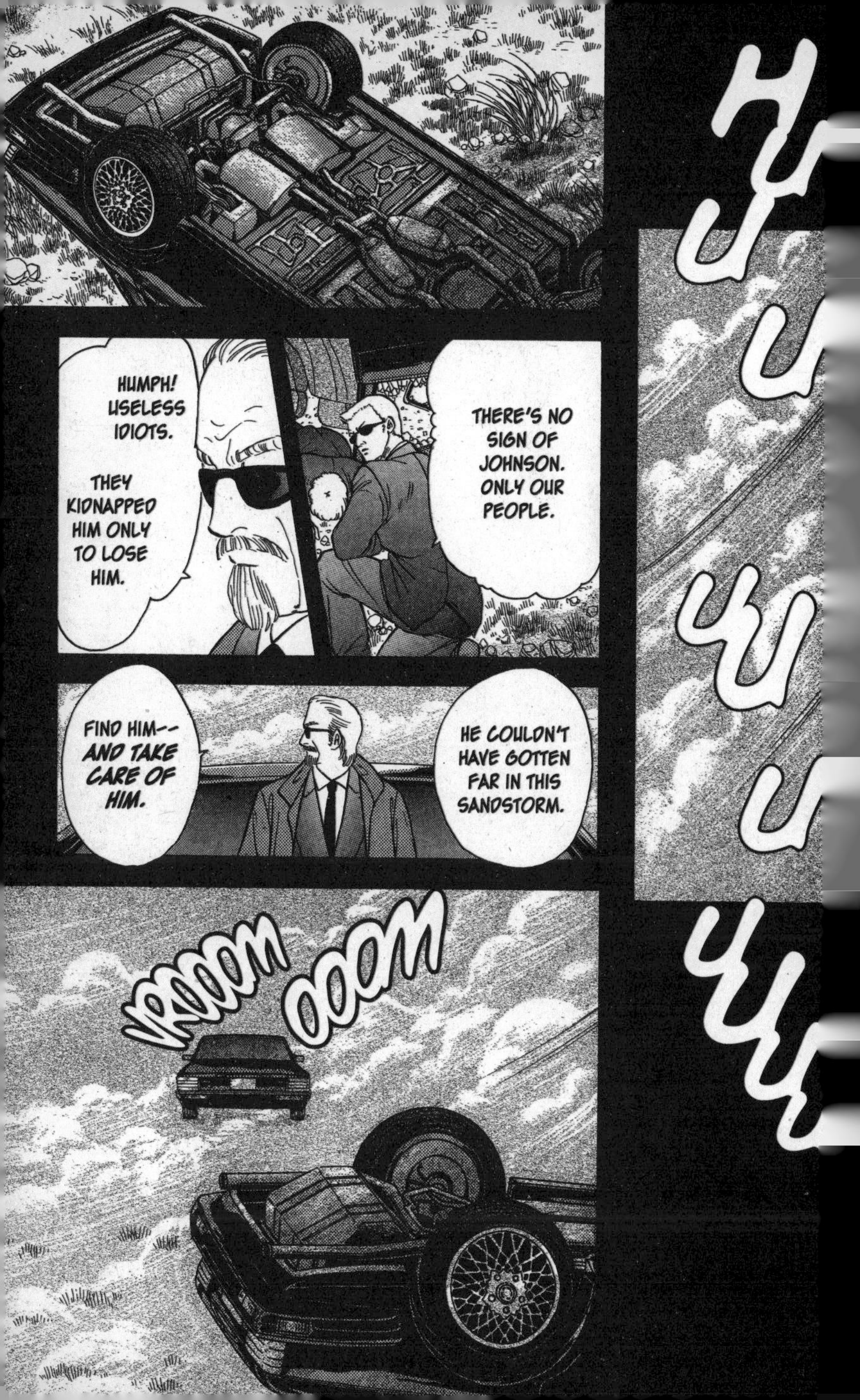
HYUUUUUU
THERE'S NO SIGN OF JOHNSON. ONLY OUR PEOPLE.
HUMPH! USELESS IDIOTS.
THEY KIDNAPPED HIM ONLY TO LOSE HIM.
HE COULDN'T HAVE GOTTEN FAR IN THIS SANDSTORM.
FIND HIM-- AND TAKE CARE OF HIM.
VROOOM OOOM

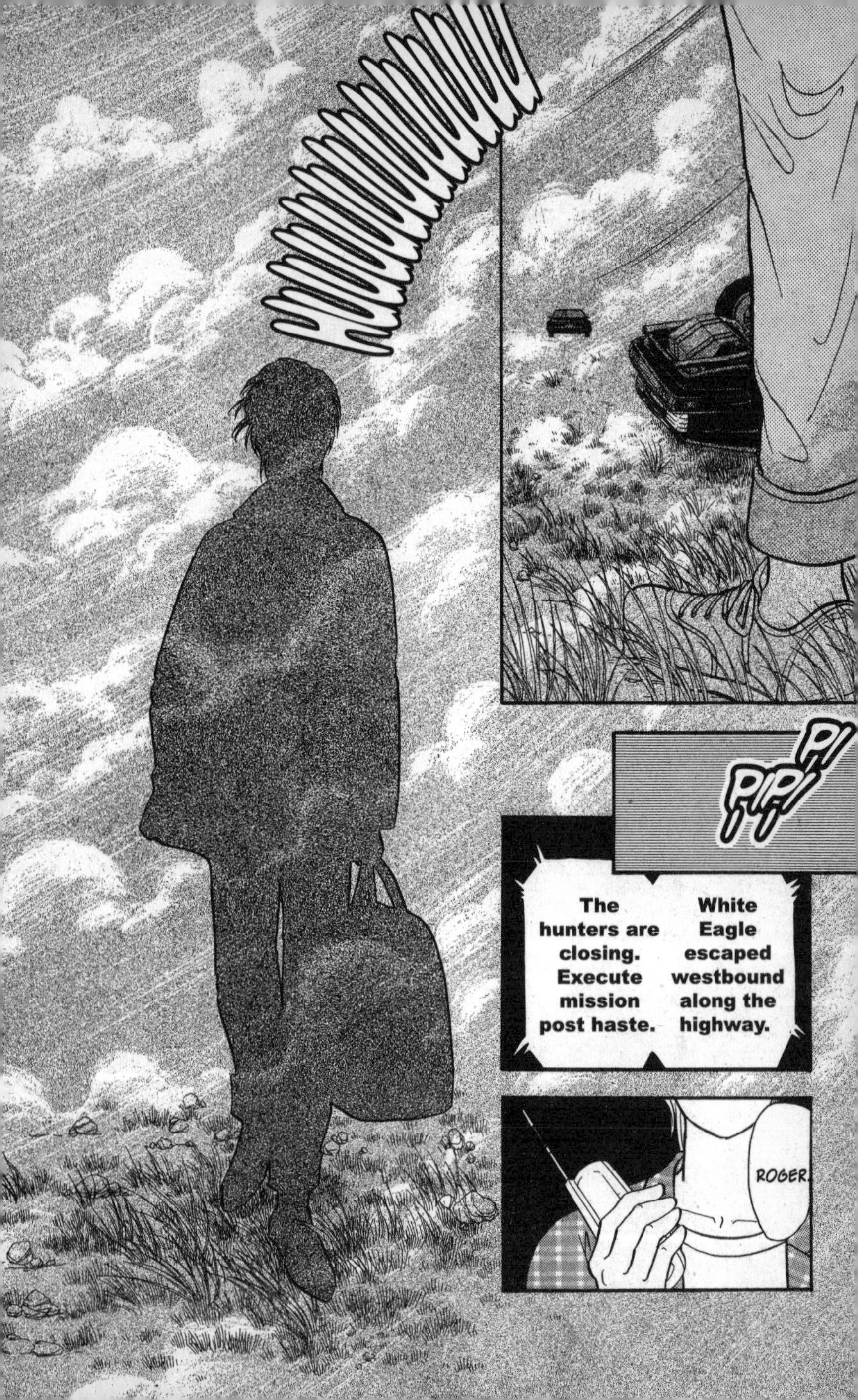
PI PIPI
White Eagle escaped westbound along the highway.
The hunters are closing. Execute mission post haste.
ROGER.

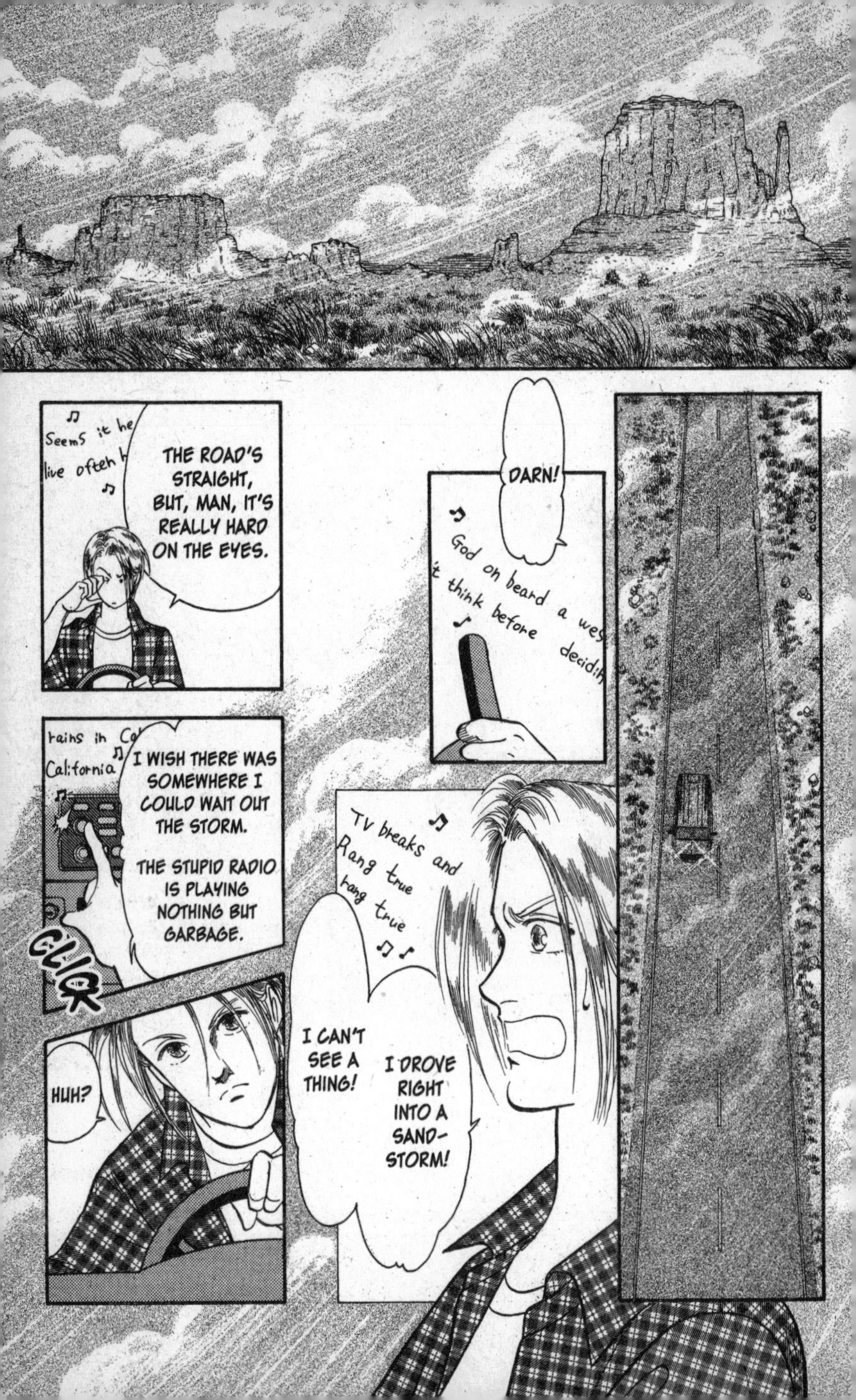
DARN!
God on beard a wes
't think before decidin
Seems it he
live often h
THE ROAD'S STRAIGHT, BUT, MAN, IT'S REALLY HARD ON THE EYES.
TV breaks and
Rang true
rang true
I DROVE RIGHT INTO A SAND-STORM!
I CAN'T SEE A THING!
rains in Ca
California
I WISH THERE WAS SOMEWHERE I COULD WAIT OUT THE STORM.
THE STUPID RADIO IS PLAYING NOTHING BUT GARBAGE.
CLICK
HUH?

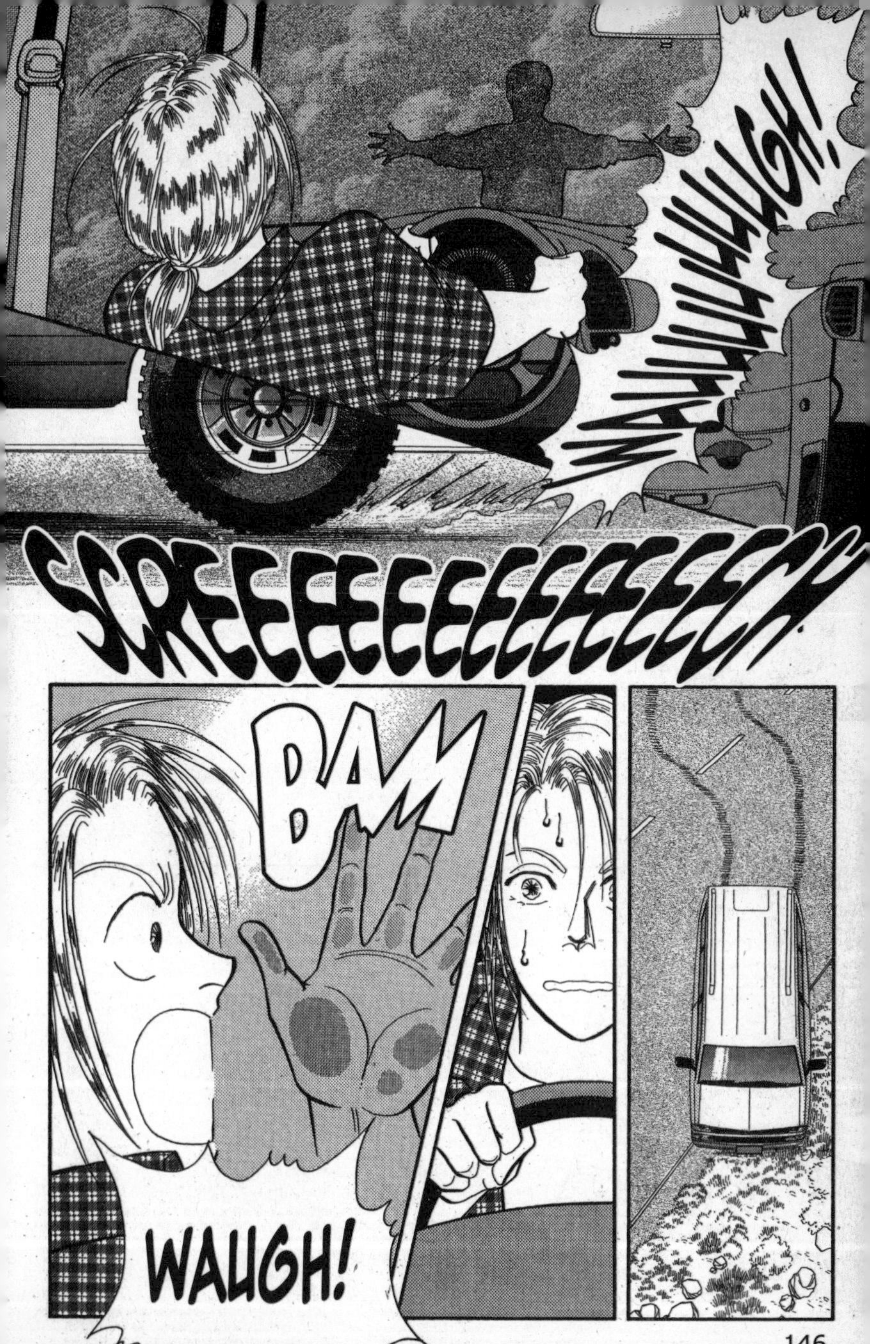

WAHHHHHHUGH!
SCREEEEEEEEEEEEEECH
BAM
WAUGH!

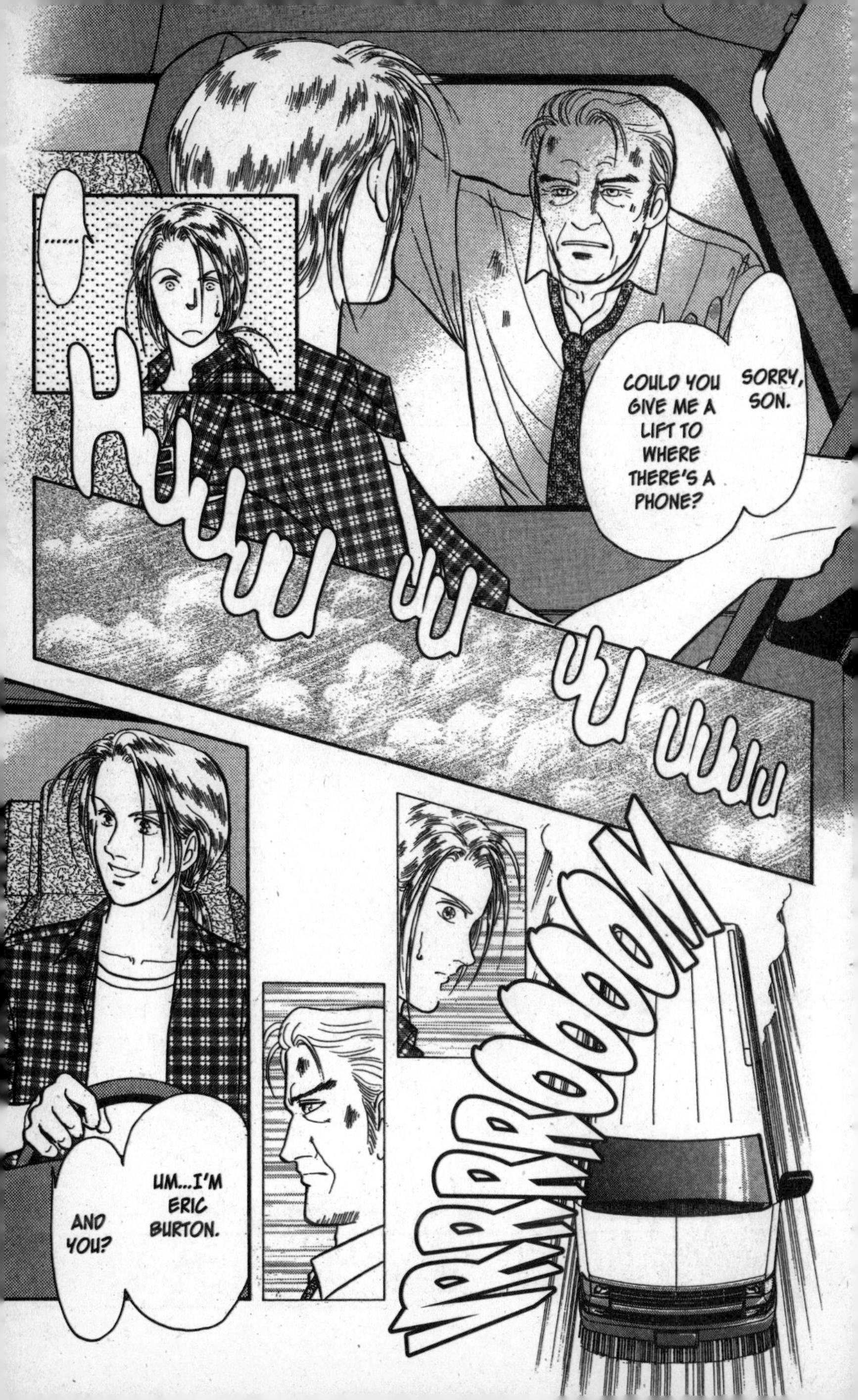
SORRY, SON.
COULD YOU GIVE ME A LIFT TO WHERE THERE'S A PHONE?
......
HUUUU UU UU UUUU
VRRROOOOM
UM...I'M ERIC BURTON.
AND YOU?

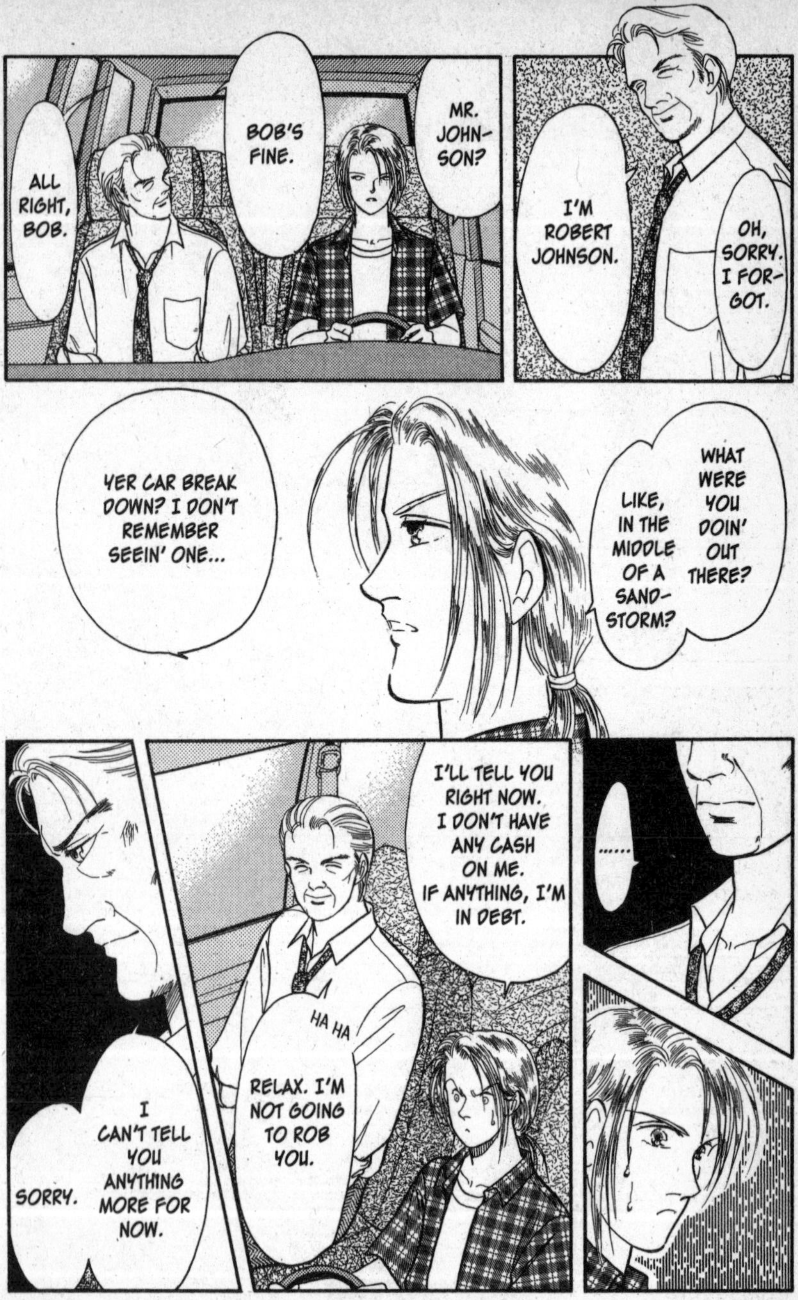
OH, SORRY. I FORGOT.
I'M ROBERT JOHNSON.
MR. JOHNSON?
BOB'S FINE.
ALL RIGHT, BOB.
WHAT WERE YOU DOIN' OUT THERE?
LIKE, IN THE MIDDLE OF A SANDSTORM?
YER CAR BREAK DOWN? I DON'T REMEMBER SEEIN' ONE...
......
I'LL TELL YOU RIGHT NOW. I DON'T HAVE ANY CASH ON ME. IF ANYTHING, I'M IN DEBT.
HA HA
RELAX. I'M NOT GOING TO ROB YOU.
I CAN'T TELL YOU ANYTHING MORE FOR NOW.
SORRY.

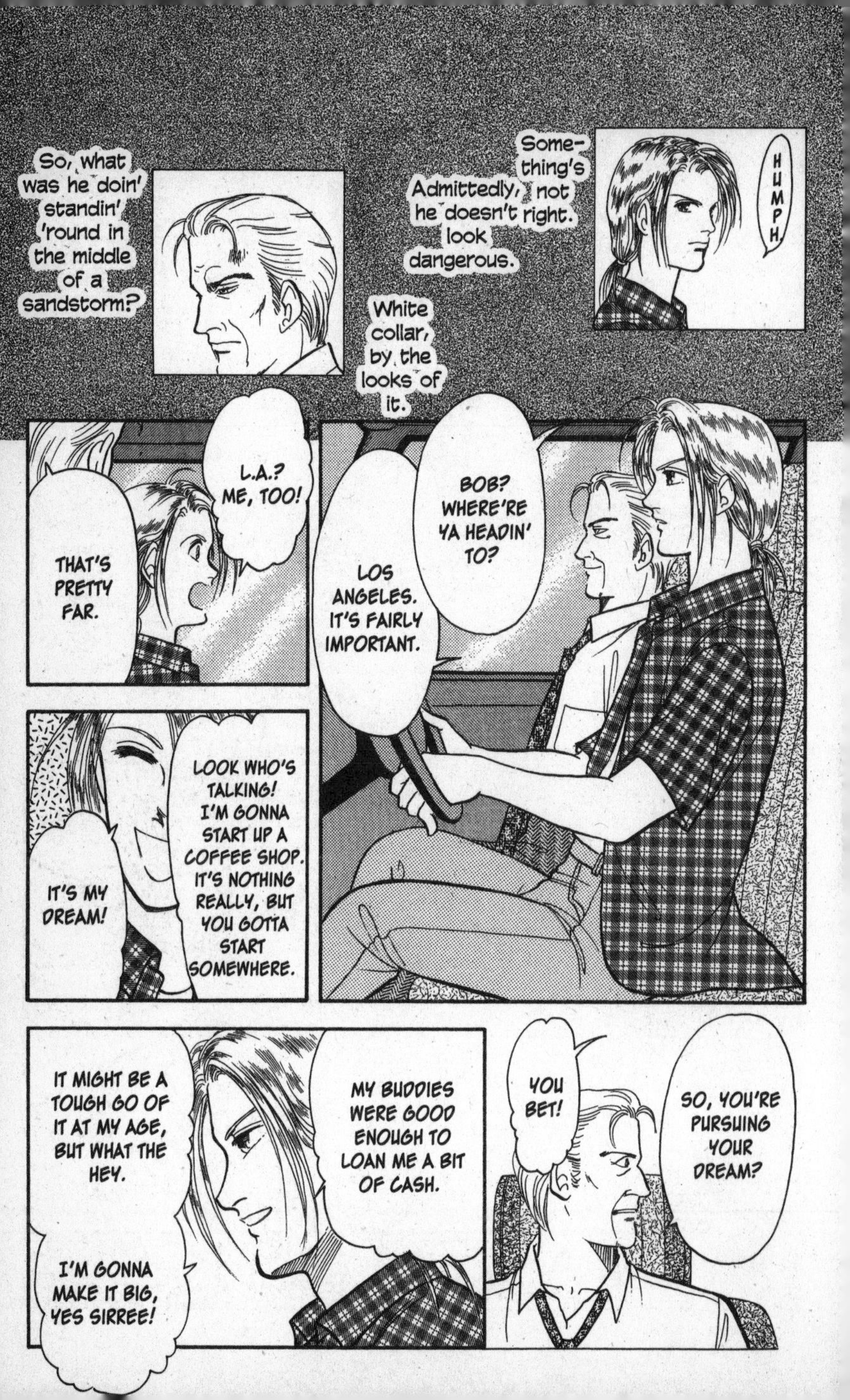
HUMPH
Something's not right.
Admittedly, he doesn't look dangerous.
White collar, by the looks of it.
So, what was he doin' standin' 'round in the middle of a sandstorm?
BOB? WHERE'RE YA HEADIN' TO?
LOS ANGELES. IT'S FAIRLY IMPORTANT.
L.A.? ME, TOO!
THAT'S PRETTY FAR.
LOOK WHO'S TALKING! I'M GONNA START UP A COFFEE SHOP. IT'S NOTHING REALLY, BUT YOU GOTTA START SOMEWHERE.
IT'S MY DREAM!
SO, YOU'RE PURSUING YOUR DREAM?
YOU BET!
MY BUDDIES WERE GOOD ENOUGH TO LOAN ME A BIT OF CASH.
IT MIGHT BE A TOUGH GO OF IT AT MY AGE, BUT WHAT THE HEY.
I'M GONNA MAKE IT BIG, YES SIRREE!

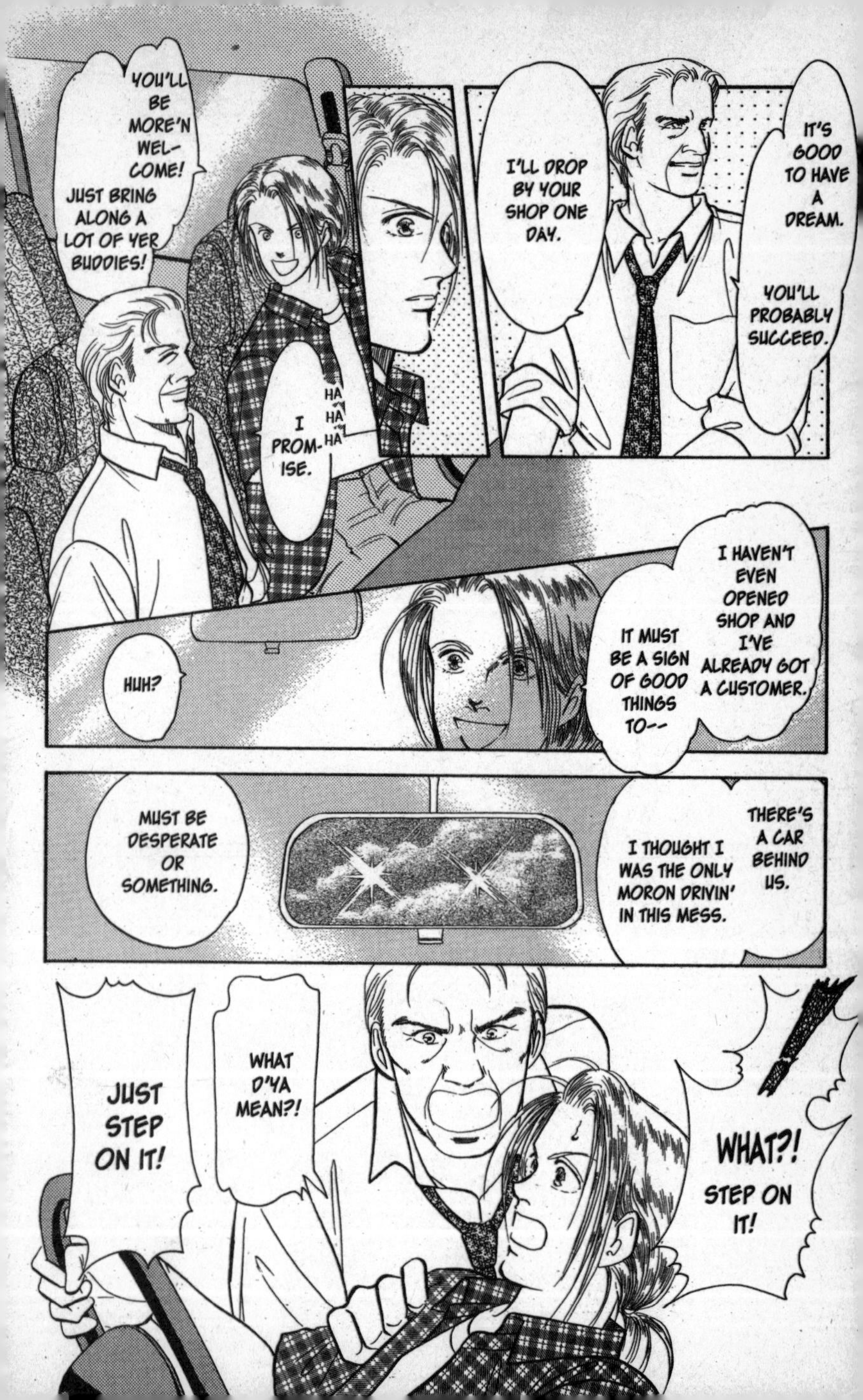
IT'S GOOD TO HAVE A DREAM.
YOU'LL PROBABLY SUCCEED.
I'LL DROP BY YOUR SHOP ONE DAY.
YOU'LL BE MORE'N WEL-COME! JUST BRING ALONG A LOT OF YER BUDDIES!
HA HA HA
I PROM-ISE.
I HAVEN'T EVEN OPENED SHOP AND I'VE ALREADY GOT A CUSTOMER.
IT MUST BE A SIGN OF GOOD THINGS TO--
HUH?
THERE'S A CAR BEHIND US.
I THOUGHT I WAS THE ONLY MORON DRIVIN' IN THIS MESS.
MUST BE DESPERATE OR SOMETHING.
WHAT?!
STEP ON IT!
WHAT D'YA MEAN?!
JUST STEP ON IT!

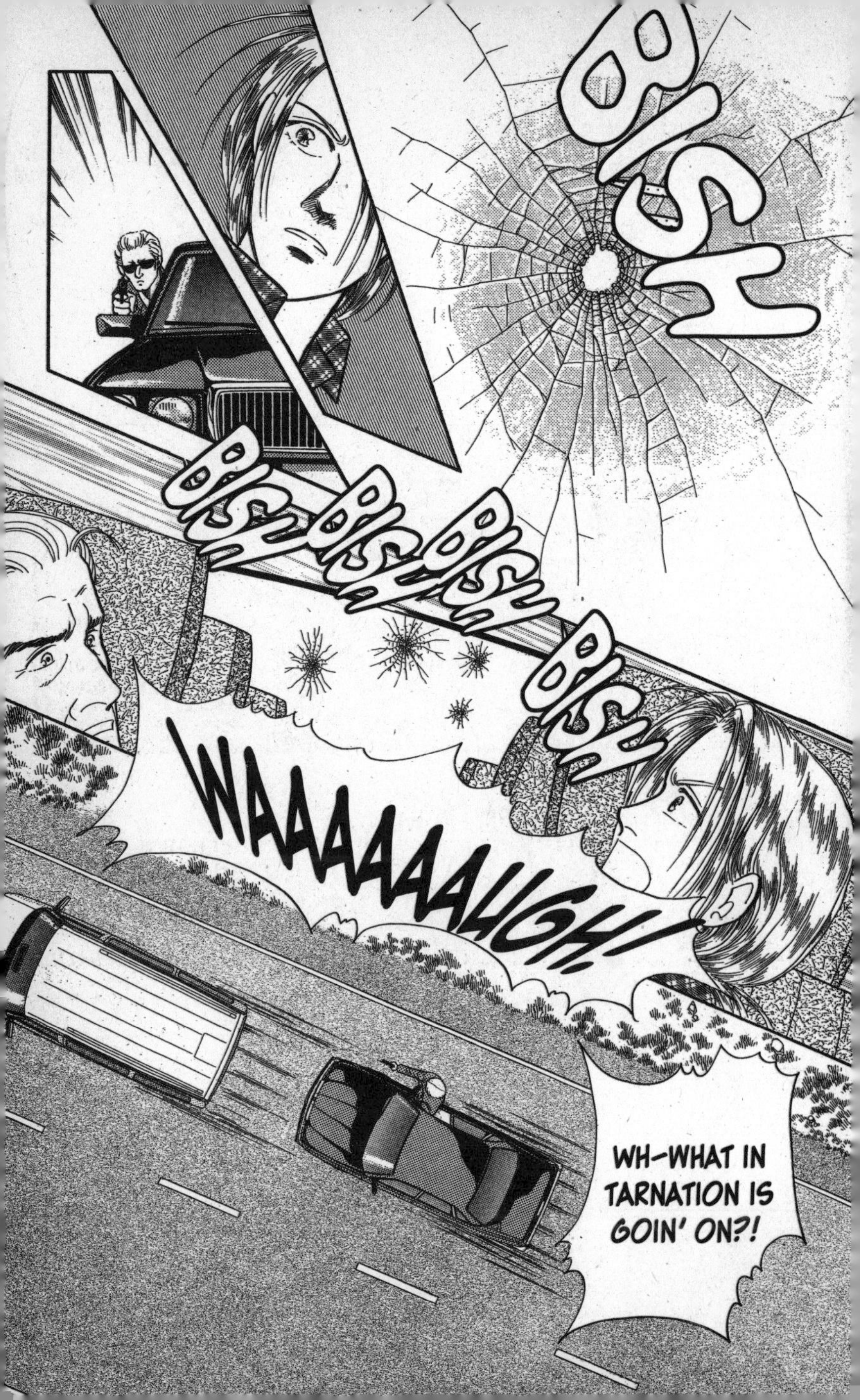
BISH
BISH BISH BISH BISH BISH
WAAAAAAAUGH!!
WH-WHAT IN TARNATION IS GOIN' ON?!

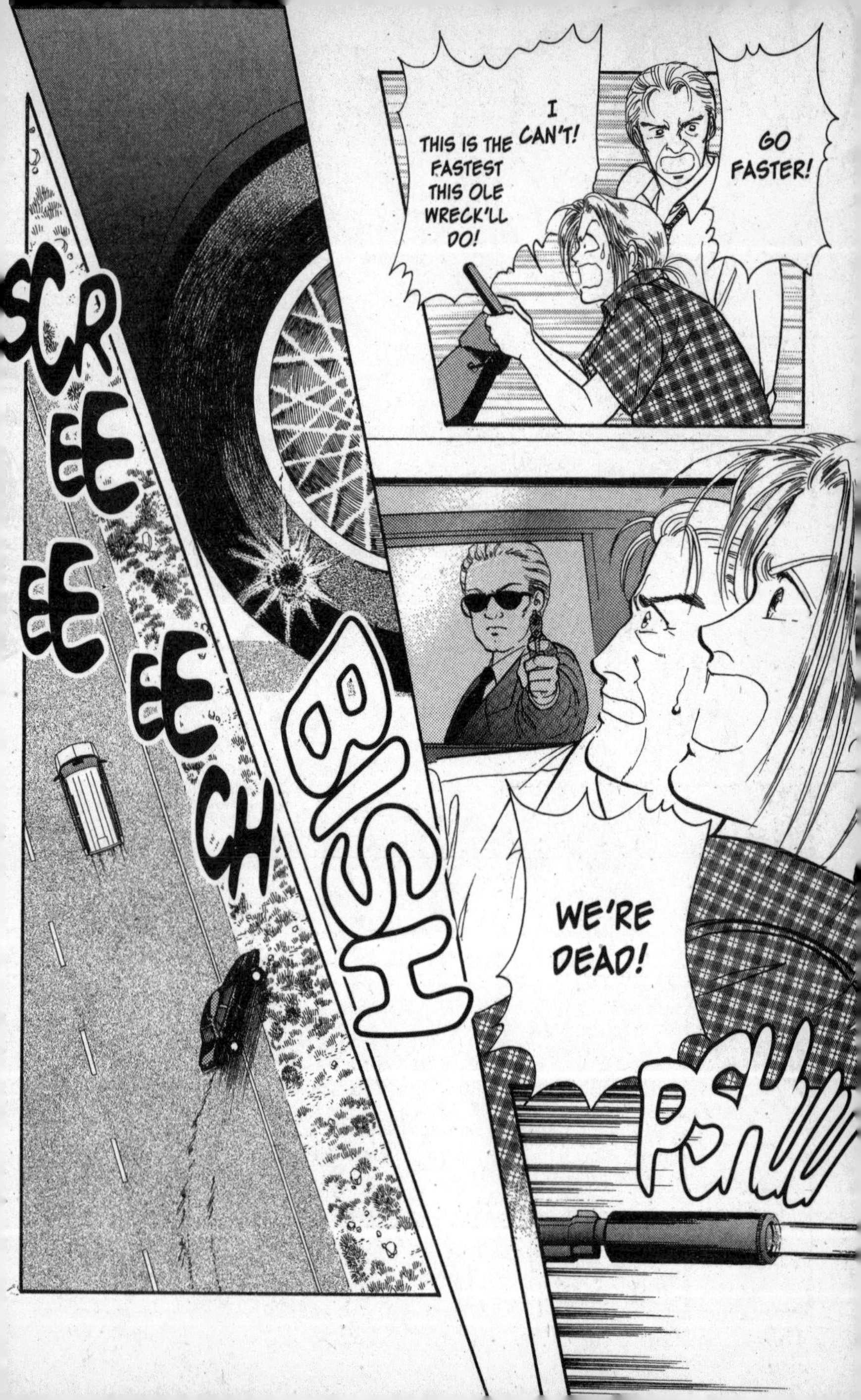
GO FASTER!
I CAN'T!
THIS IS THE FASTEST THIS OLE WRECK'LL DO!
WE'RE DEAD!
PCHU!!
BISH
SCREEEEEECH

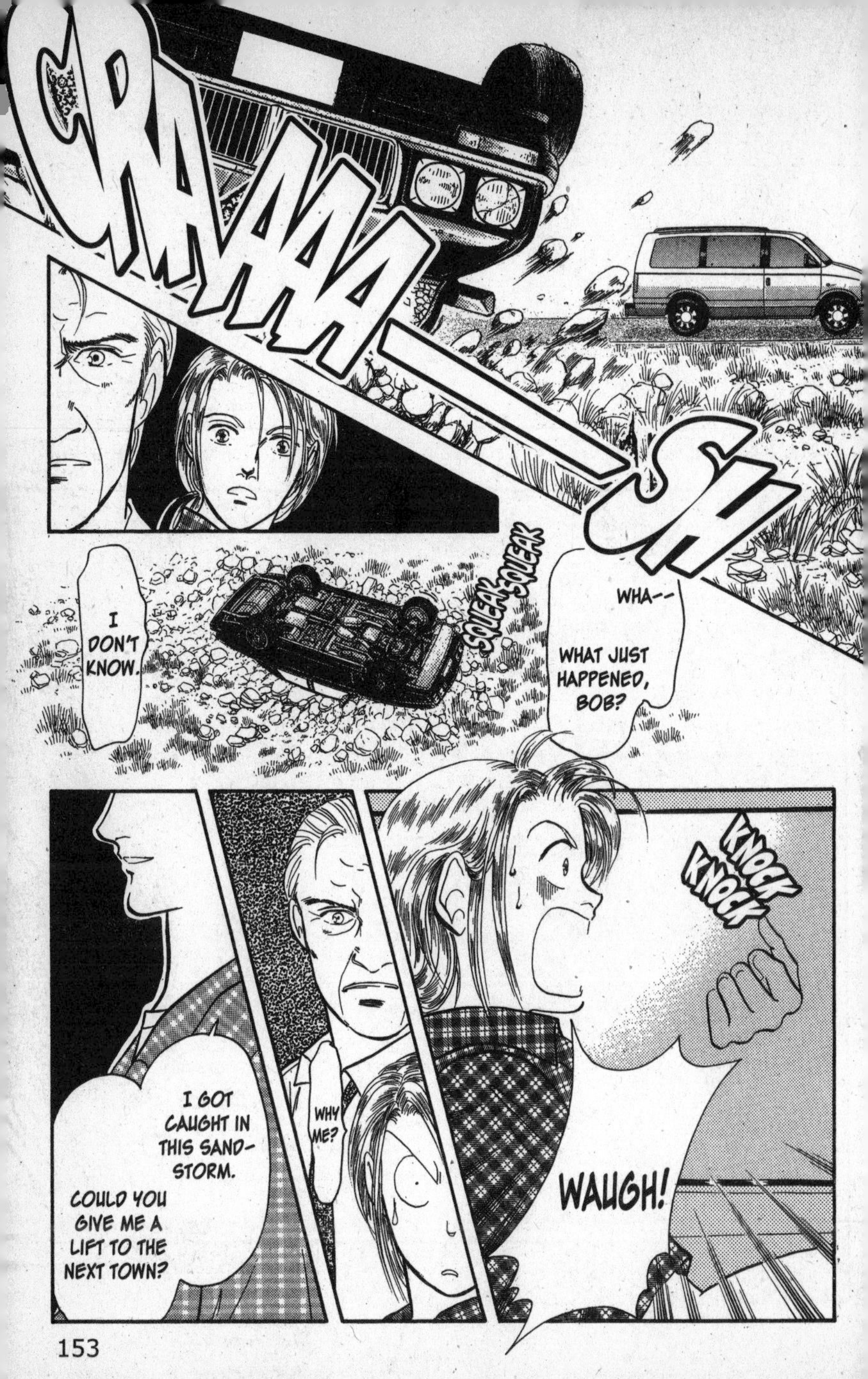
CRAAAASH
WHA-- WHAT JUST HAPPENED, BOB?
SQUEAK-SQUEAK
I DON'T KNOW.
KNOCK KNOCK
WAUGH!
WHY ME?
I GOT CAUGHT IN THIS SAND-STORM.
COULD YOU GIVE ME A LIFT TO THE NEXT TOWN?

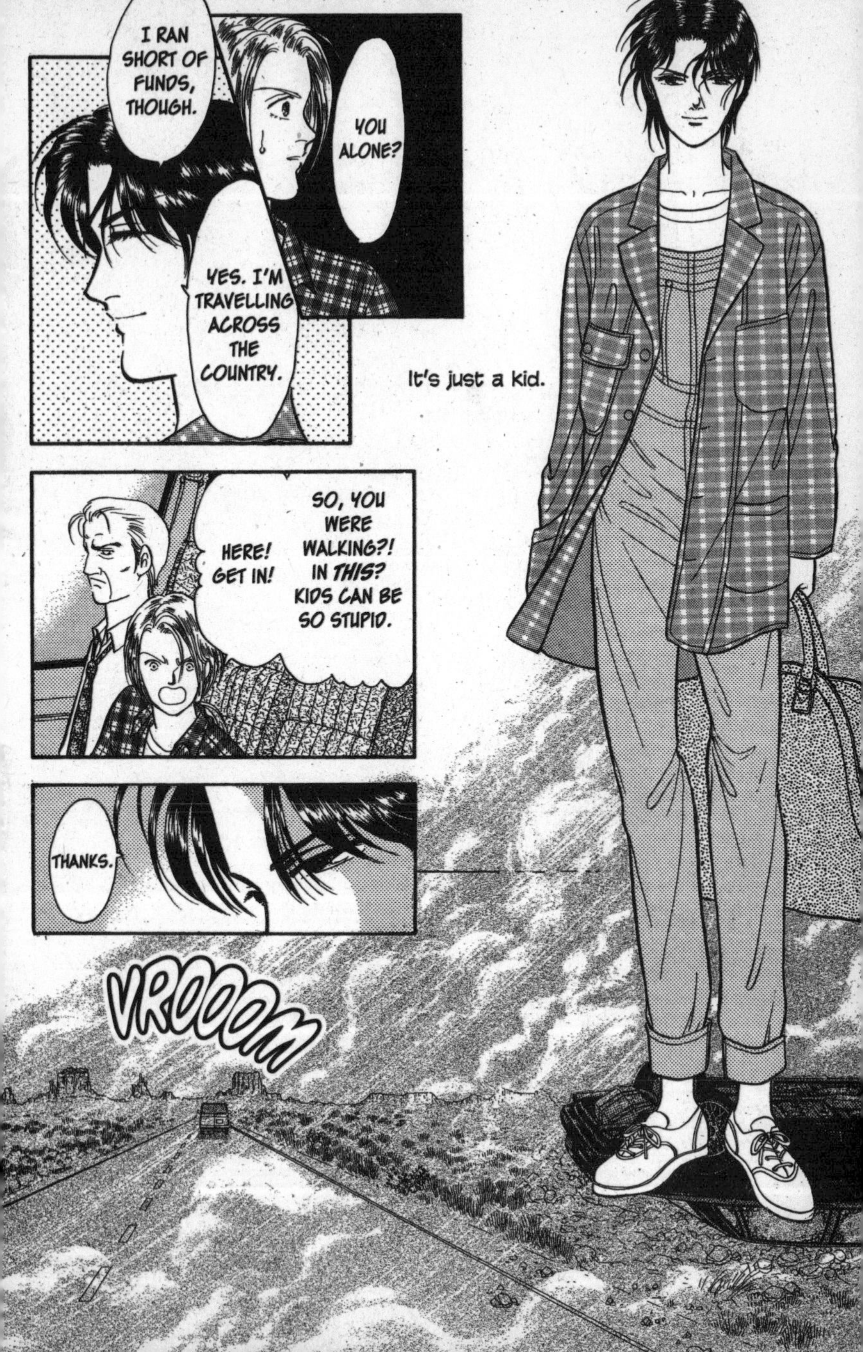
It's just a kid.
YOU ALONE?
YES. I'M TRAVELLING ACROSS THE COUNTRY.
I RAN SHORT OF FUNDS, THOUGH.
SO, YOU WERE WALKING?! IN THIS? KIDS CAN BE SO STUPID.
HERE! GET IN!
THANKS.
VROOOM

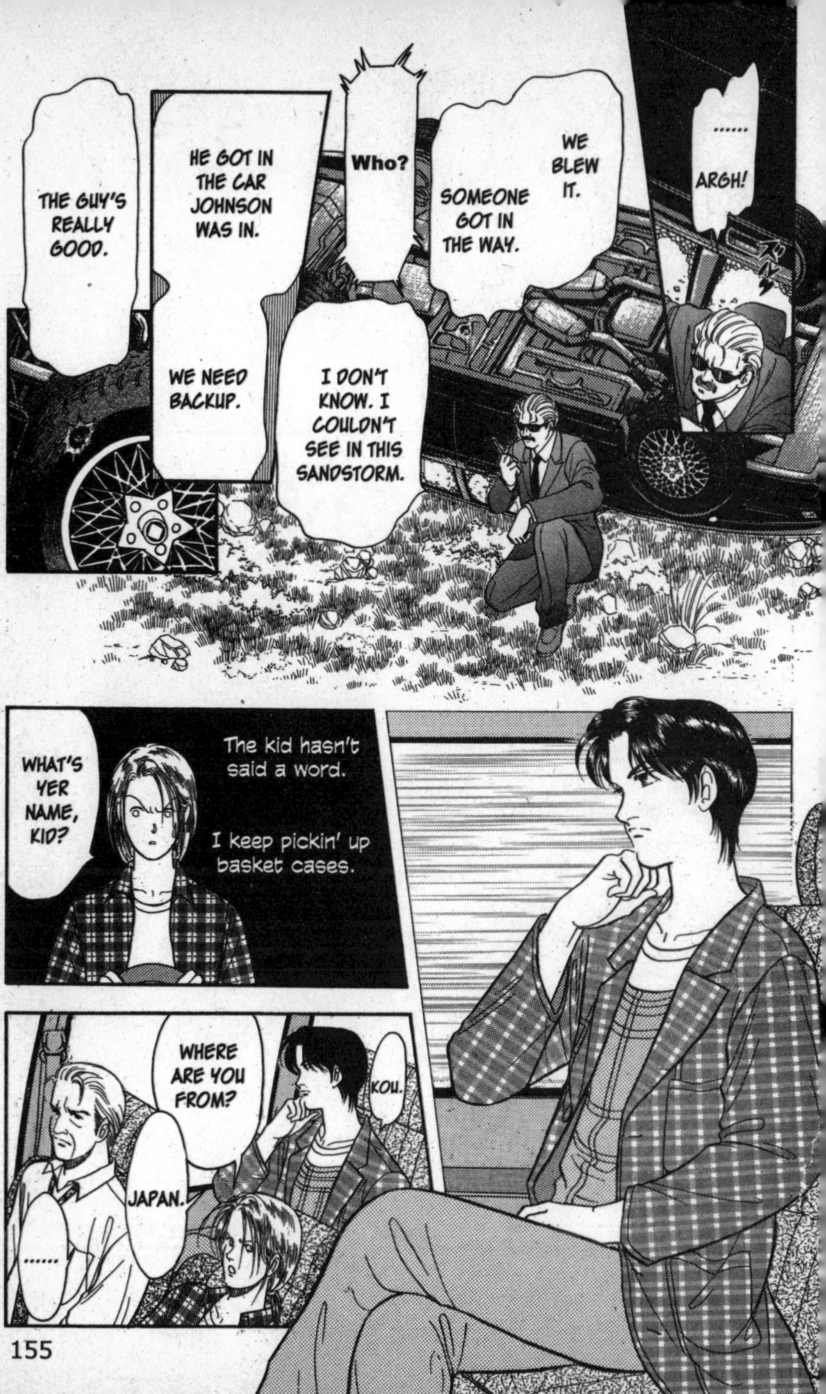

......
ARGH!
WE BLEW IT.
SOMEONE GOT IN THE WAY.
Who?
I DON'T KNOW. I COULDN'T SEE IN THIS SANDSTORM.
HE GOT IN THE CAR JOHNSON WAS IN.
WE NEED BACKUP.
THE GUY'S REALLY GOOD.
The kid hasn't said a word.
I keep pickin' up basket cases.
WHAT'S YER NAME, KID?
KOU.
WHERE ARE YOU FROM?
JAPAN.
......

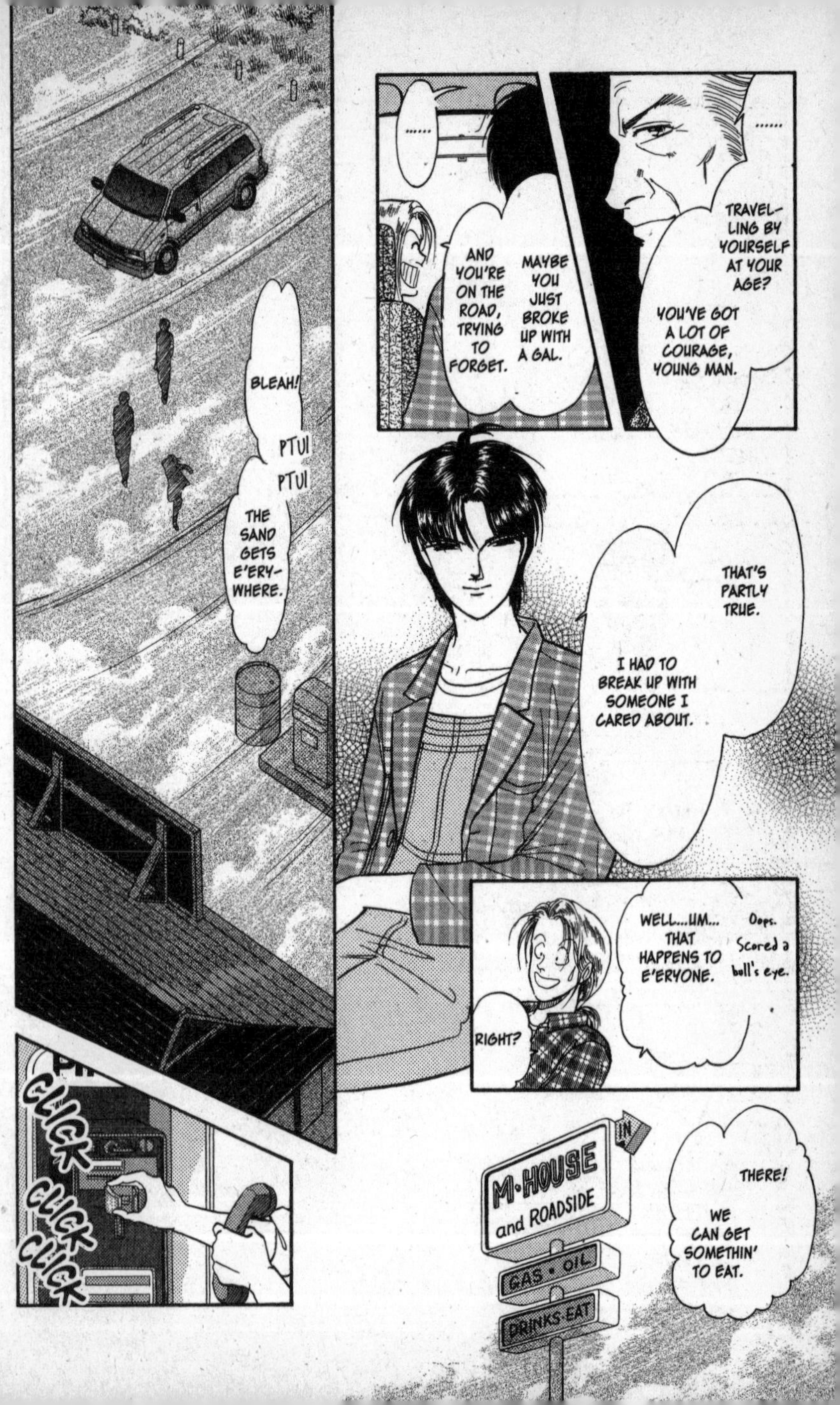
......
TRAVELING BY YOURSELF AT YOUR AGE?
YOU'VE GOT A LOT OF COURAGE, YOUNG MAN.
......
MAYBE YOU JUST BROKE UP WITH A GAL.
AND YOU'RE ON THE ROAD, TRYING TO FORGET.
THAT'S PARTLY TRUE.
I HAD TO BREAK UP WITH SOMEONE I CARED ABOUT.
Oops. Scored a bull's eye.
WELL...UM... THAT HAPPENS TO E'ERYONE.
RIGHT?
THERE!
WE CAN GET SOMETHIN' TO EAT.
IN
M-HOUSE and ROADSIDE
GAS • OIL
DRINKS-EAT
BLEAH!
PTUI
PTUI
THE SAND GETS E'ERYWHERE.
CLICK
CLICK
CLICK

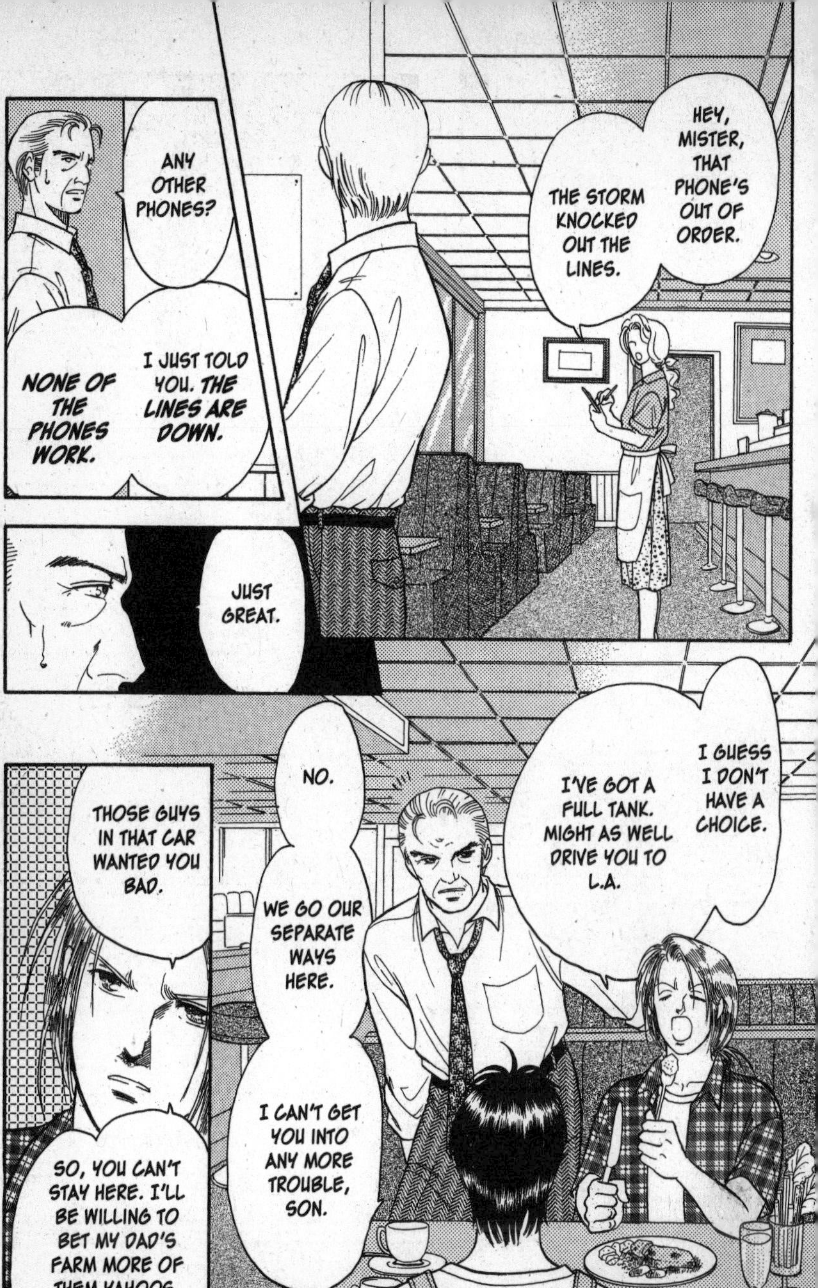
HEY, MISTER, THAT PHONE'S OUT OF ORDER.
THE STORM KNOCKED OUT THE LINES.
ANY OTHER PHONES?
I JUST TOLD YOU. *THE LINES ARE DOWN.*
NONE OF THE PHONES WORK.
JUST GREAT.
I GUESS I DON'T HAVE A CHOICE.
I'VE GOT A FULL TANK. MIGHT AS WELL DRIVE YOU TO L.A.
NO.
WE GO OUR SEPARATE WAYS HERE.
I CAN'T GET YOU INTO ANY MORE TROUBLE, SON.
THOSE GUYS IN THAT CAR WANTED YOU BAD.
SO, YOU CAN'T STAY HERE. I'LL BE WILLING TO BET MY DAD'S FARM MORE OF THEM YAHOOS ARE COMIN'.

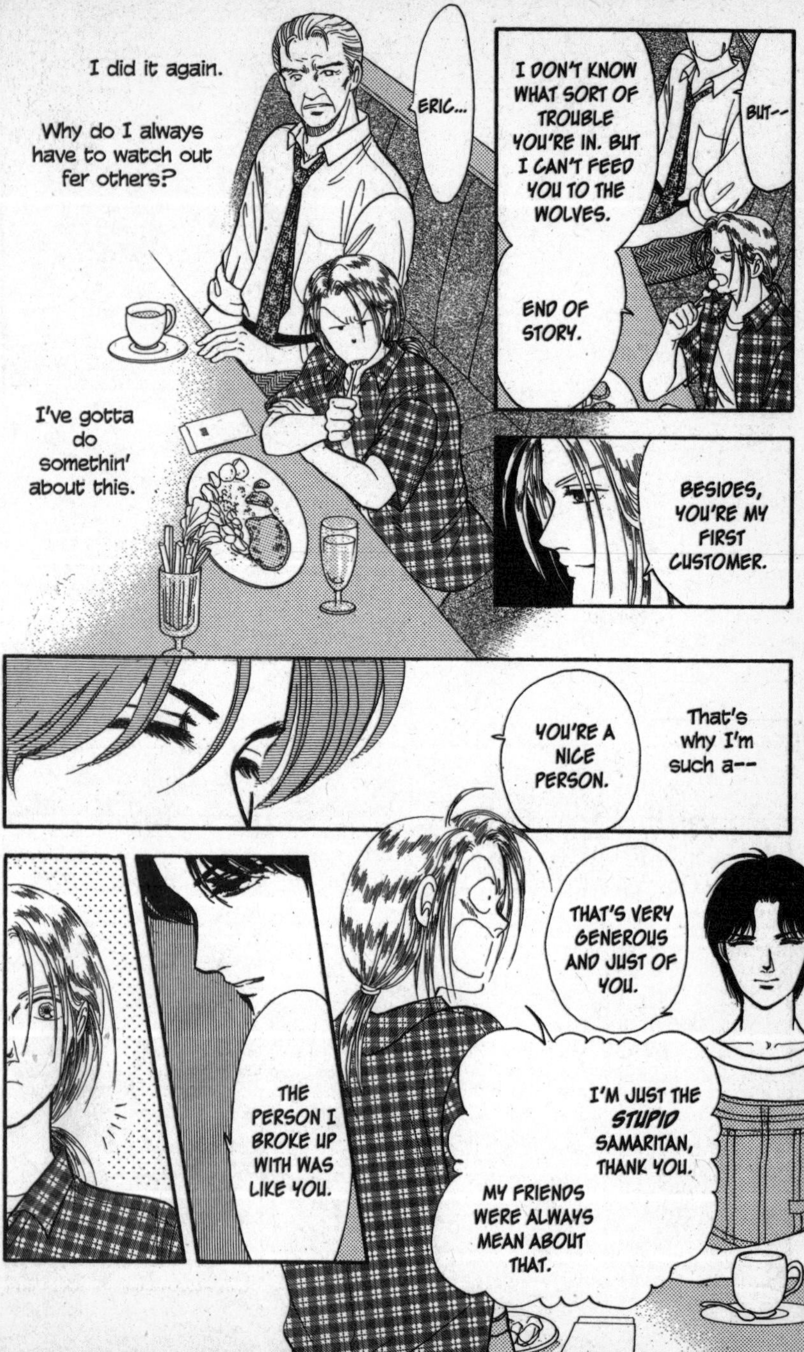
BUT--
I DON'T KNOW WHAT SORT OF TROUBLE YOU'RE IN. BUT I CAN'T FEED YOU TO THE WOLVES.
END OF STORY.
BESIDES, YOU'RE MY FIRST CUSTOMER.
ERIC...
I did it again.
Why do I always have to watch out fer others?
I've gotta do somethin' about this.
That's why I'm such a--
YOU'RE A NICE PERSON.
THAT'S VERY GENEROUS AND JUST OF YOU.
I'M JUST THE STUPID SAMARITAN, THANK YOU.
MY FRIENDS WERE ALWAYS MEAN ABOUT THAT.
THE PERSON I BROKE UP WITH WAS LIKE YOU.

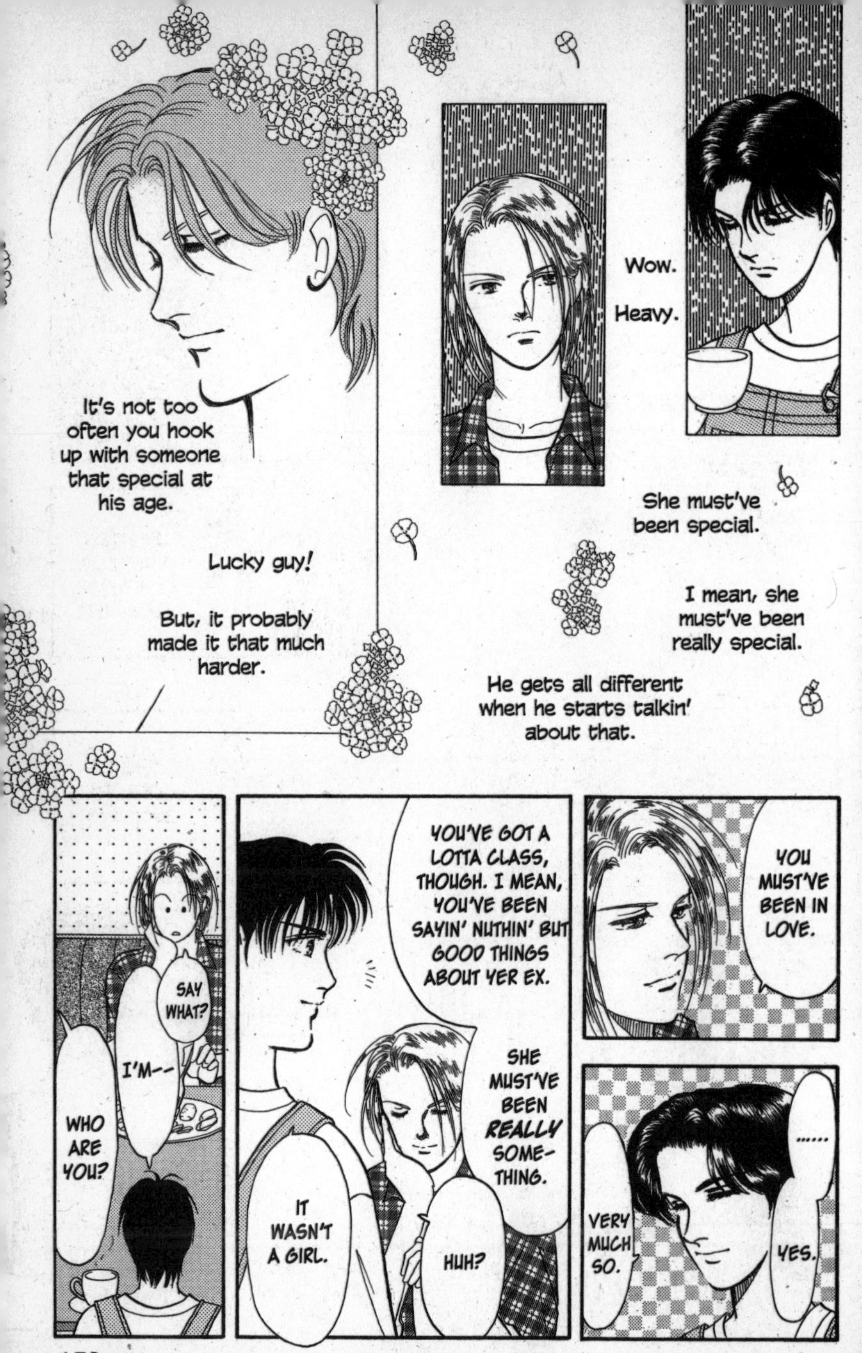
Wow.
Heavy.
She must've been special.
I mean, she must've been really special.
He gets all different when he starts talkin' about that.
It's not too often you hook up with someone that special at his age.
Lucky guy!
But, it probably made it that much harder.
YOU MUST'VE BEEN IN LOVE.
......
YES.
VERY MUCH SO.
YOU'VE GOT A LOTTA CLASS, THOUGH. I MEAN, YOU'VE BEEN SAYIN' NUTHIN' BUT GOOD THINGS ABOUT YER EX.
SHE MUST'VE BEEN REALLY SOME-THING.
HUH?
IT WASN'T A GIRL.
SAY WHAT?
I'M--
WHO ARE YOU?

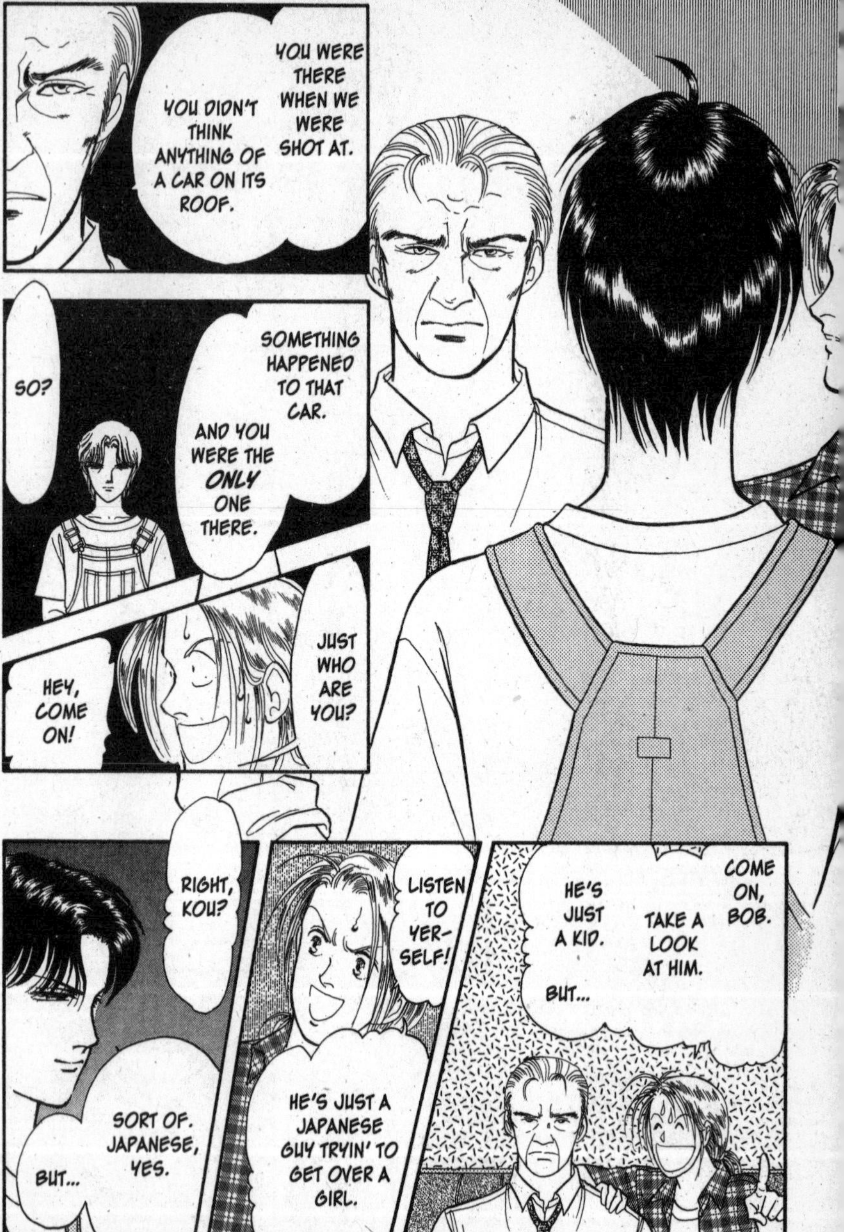
YOU WERE THERE WHEN WE WERE SHOT AT.
YOU DIDN'T THINK ANYTHING OF A CAR ON ITS ROOF.
SOMETHING HAPPENED TO THAT CAR.
AND YOU WERE THE *ONLY* ONE THERE.
SO?
JUST WHO ARE YOU?
HEY, COME ON!
COME ON, BOB.
TAKE A LOOK AT HIM.
HE'S JUST A KID.
BUT...
LISTEN TO YER-SELF!
HE'S JUST A JAPANESE GUY TRYIN' TO GET OVER A GIRL.
RIGHT, KOU?
SORT OF. JAPANESE, YES.
BUT...

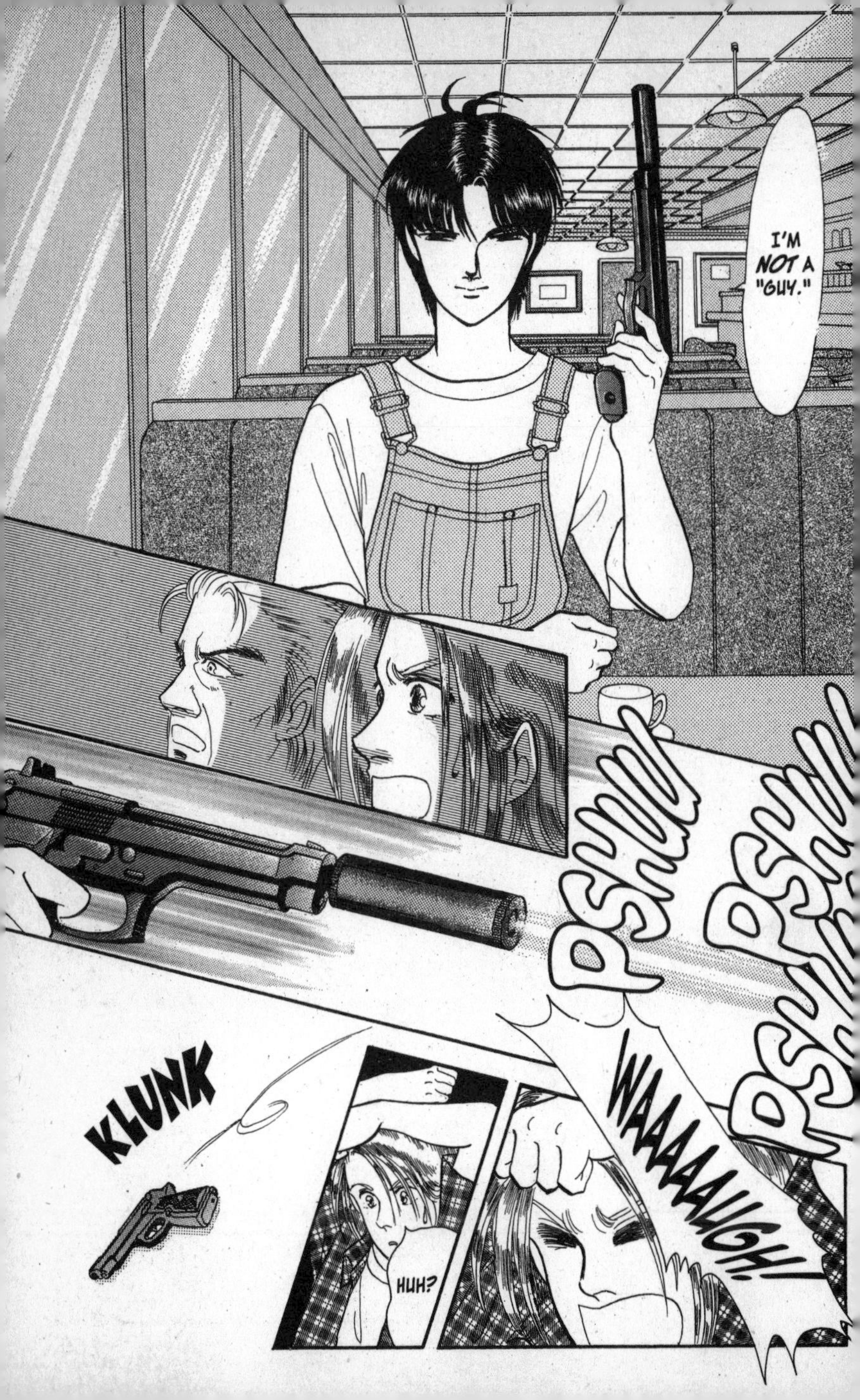
I'M NOT A "GUY."
PSHUT
PSHUT
PSHUT
WAAAAAUGH!!
KLUNK
HUH?

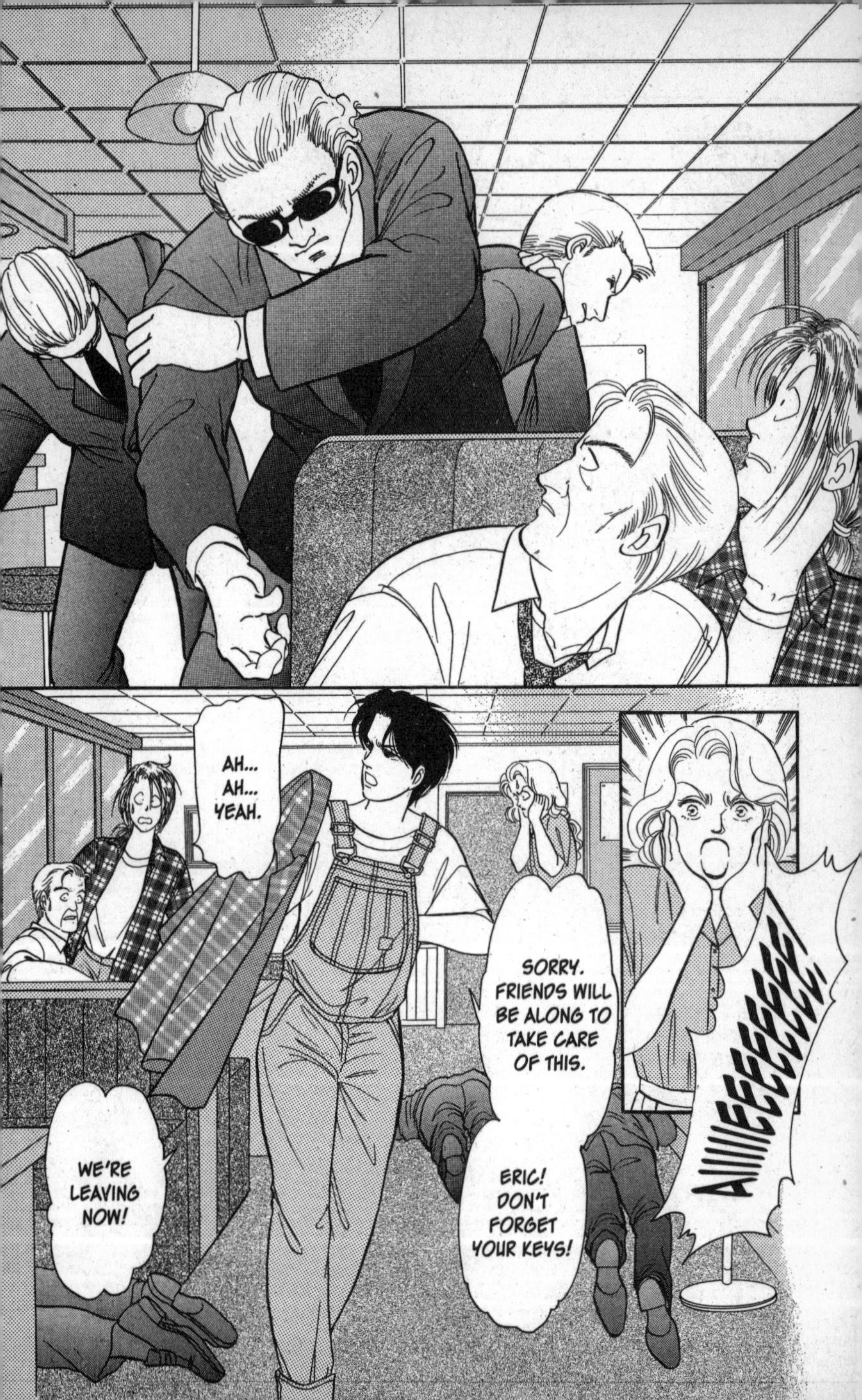
AIIIIIIEEEEEEEE!
SORRY. FRIENDS WILL BE ALONG TO TAKE CARE OF THIS.
ERIC! DON'T FORGET YOUR KEYS!
AH... AH... YEAH.
WE'RE LEAVING NOW!

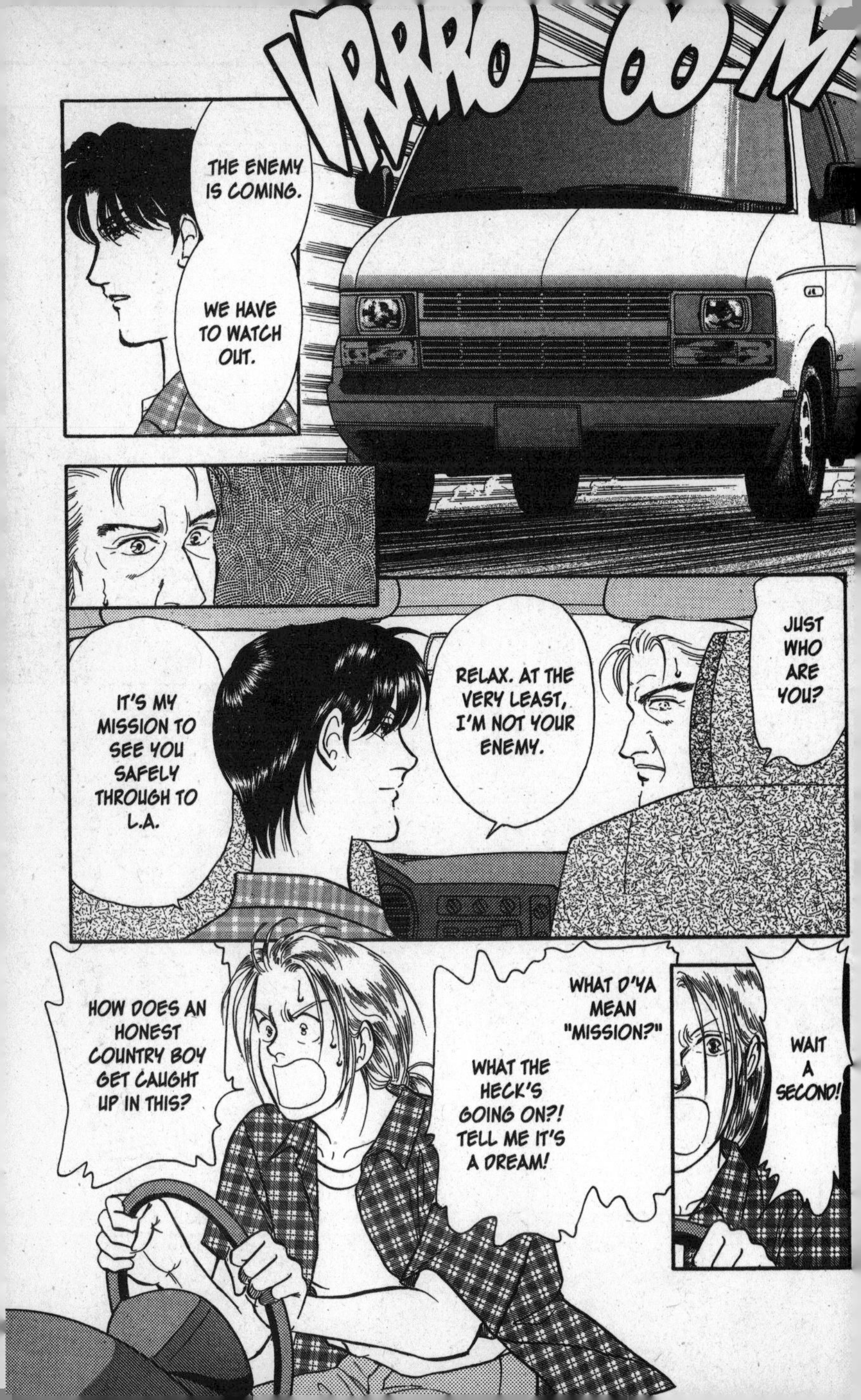
VRRRO OO-M
THE ENEMY IS COMING.
WE HAVE TO WATCH OUT.
JUST WHO ARE YOU?
RELAX. AT THE VERY LEAST, I'M NOT YOUR ENEMY.
IT'S MY MISSION TO SEE YOU SAFELY THROUGH TO L.A.
WAIT A SECOND!
WHAT D'YA MEAN "MISSION?"
WHAT THE HECK'S GOING ON?! TELL ME IT'S A DREAM!
HOW DOES AN HONEST COUNTRY BOY GET CAUGHT UP IN THIS?

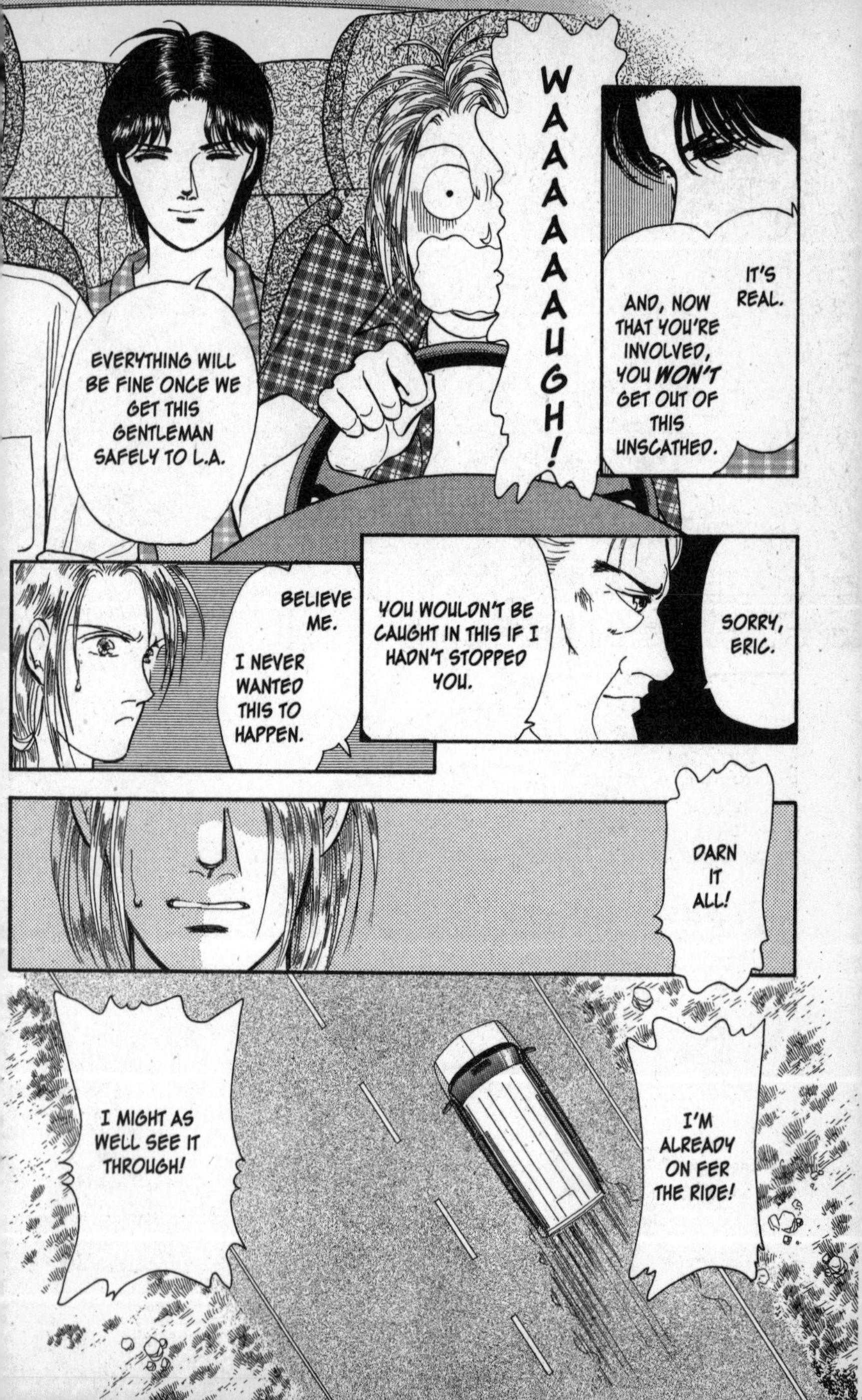
IT'S REAL.
AND, NOW THAT YOU'RE INVOLVED, YOU WON'T GET OUT OF THIS UNSCATHED.
WAAAAAAUGH!
EVERYTHING WILL BE FINE ONCE WE GET THIS GENTLEMAN SAFELY TO L.A.
SORRY, ERIC.
YOU WOULDN'T BE CAUGHT IN THIS IF I HADN'T STOPPED YOU.
BELIEVE ME.
I NEVER WANTED THIS TO HAPPEN.
DARN IT ALL!
I'M ALREADY ON FER THE RIDE!
I MIGHT AS WELL SEE IT THROUGH!

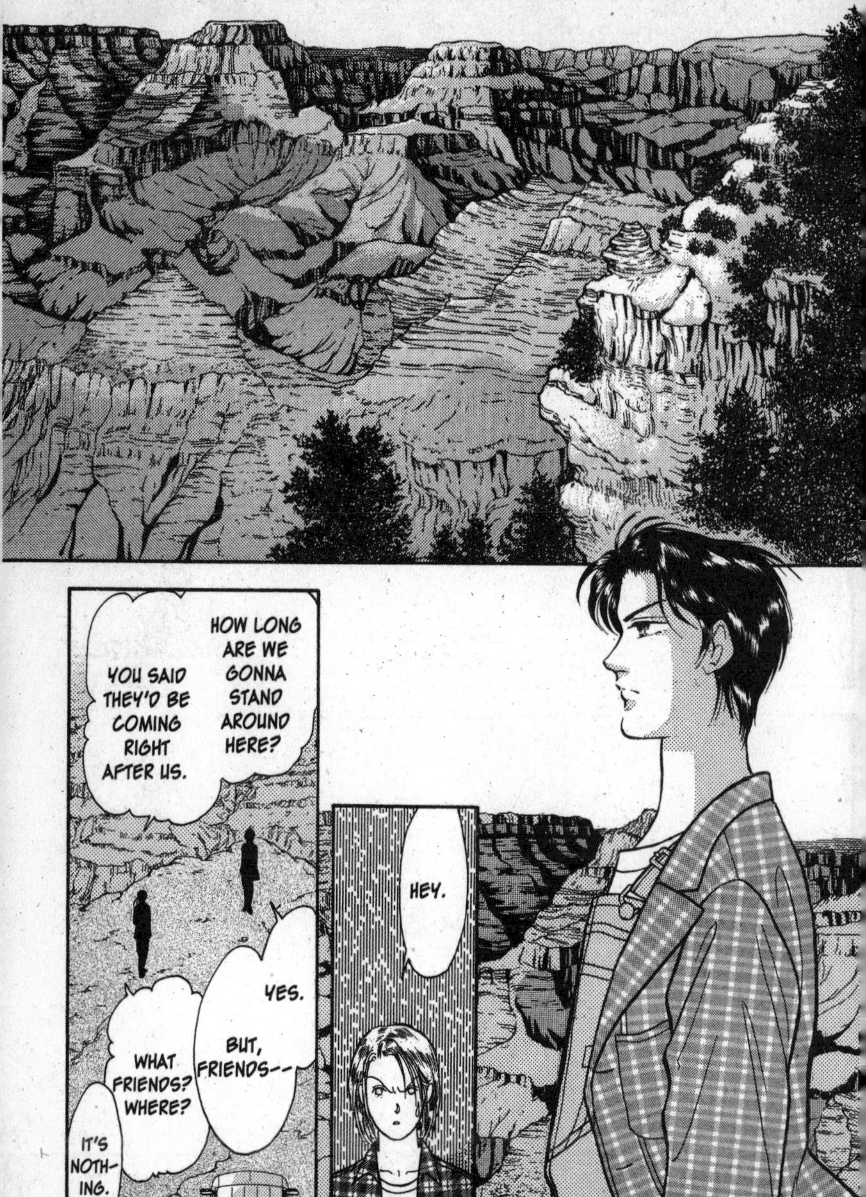
HEY.
HOW LONG ARE WE GONNA STAND AROUND HERE?
YOU SAID THEY'D BE COMING RIGHT AFTER US.
YES.
BUT, FRIENDS--
WHAT FRIENDS? WHERE?
IT'S NOTH-ING.

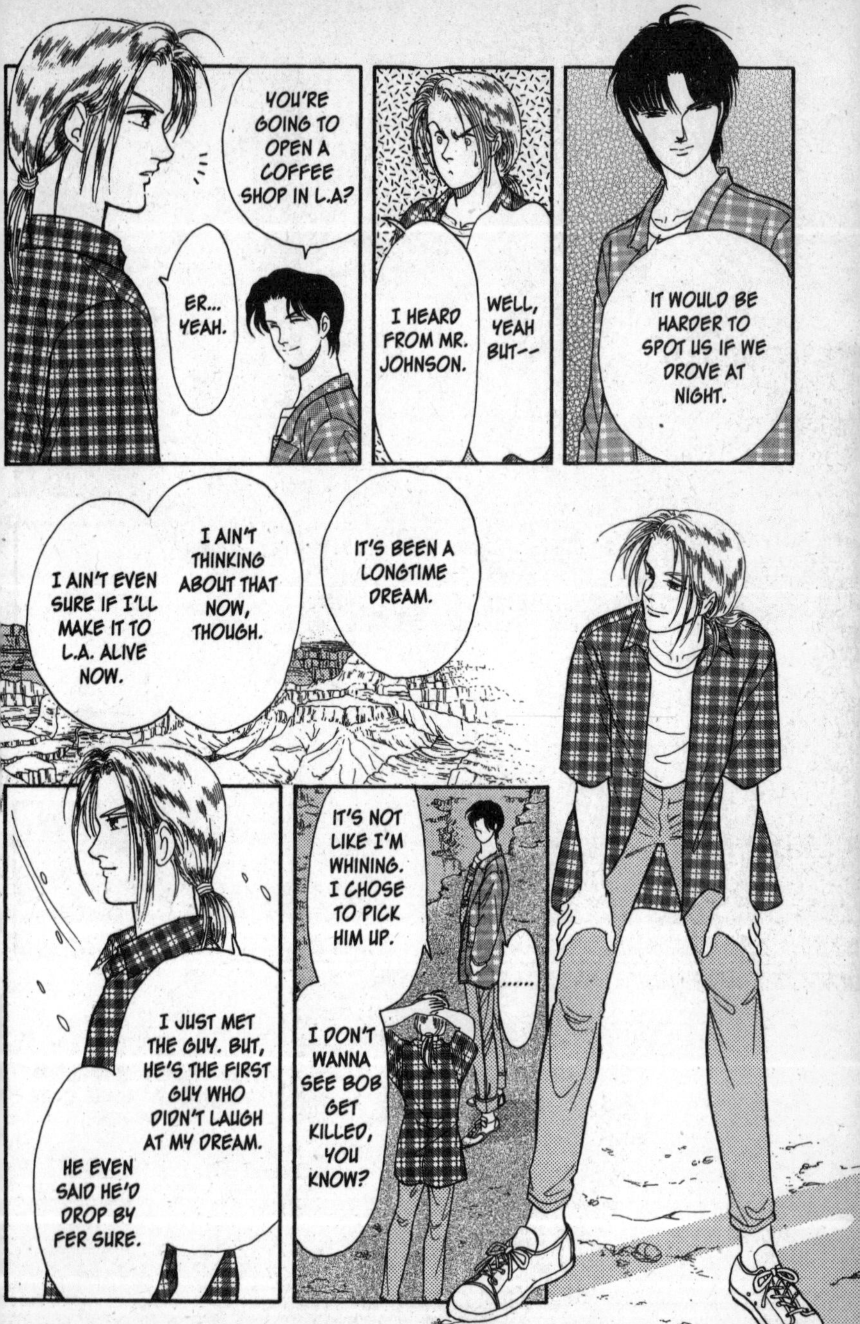
IT WOULD BE HARDER TO SPOT US IF WE DROVE AT NIGHT.
WELL, YEAH BUT--
I HEARD FROM MR. JOHNSON.
YOU'RE GOING TO OPEN A COFFEE SHOP IN L.A?
ER... YEAH.
IT'S BEEN A LONGTIME DREAM.
I AIN'T THINKING ABOUT THAT NOW, THOUGH.
I AIN'T EVEN SURE IF I'LL MAKE IT TO L.A. ALIVE NOW.
IT'S NOT LIKE I'M WHINING. I CHOSE TO PICK HIM UP.
......
I DON'T WANNA SEE BOB GET KILLED, YOU KNOW?
I JUST MET THE GUY. BUT, HE'S THE FIRST GUY WHO DIDN'T LAUGH AT MY DREAM.
HE EVEN SAID HE'D DROP BY FER SURE.

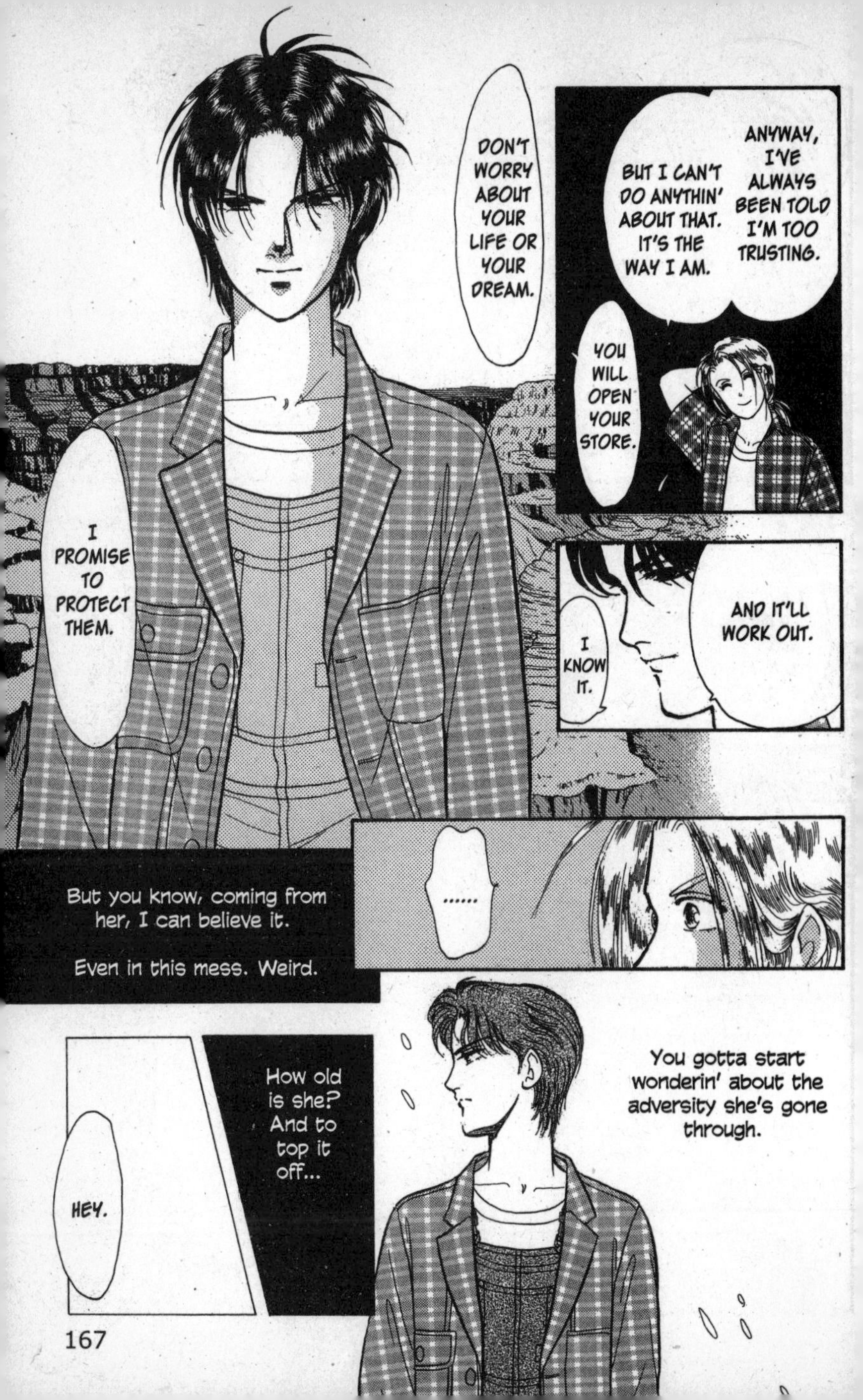
ANYWAY, I'VE ALWAYS BEEN TOLD I'M TOO TRUSTING.
BUT I CAN'T DO ANYTHIN' ABOUT THAT. IT'S THE WAY I AM.
YOU WILL OPEN YOUR STORE.
AND IT'LL WORK OUT.
I KNOW IT.
DON'T WORRY ABOUT YOUR LIFE OR YOUR DREAM.
I PROMISE TO PROTECT THEM.
......
But you know, coming from her, I can believe it.
Even in this mess. Weird.
You gotta start wonderin' about the adversity she's gone through.
How old is she? And to top it off...
HEY.

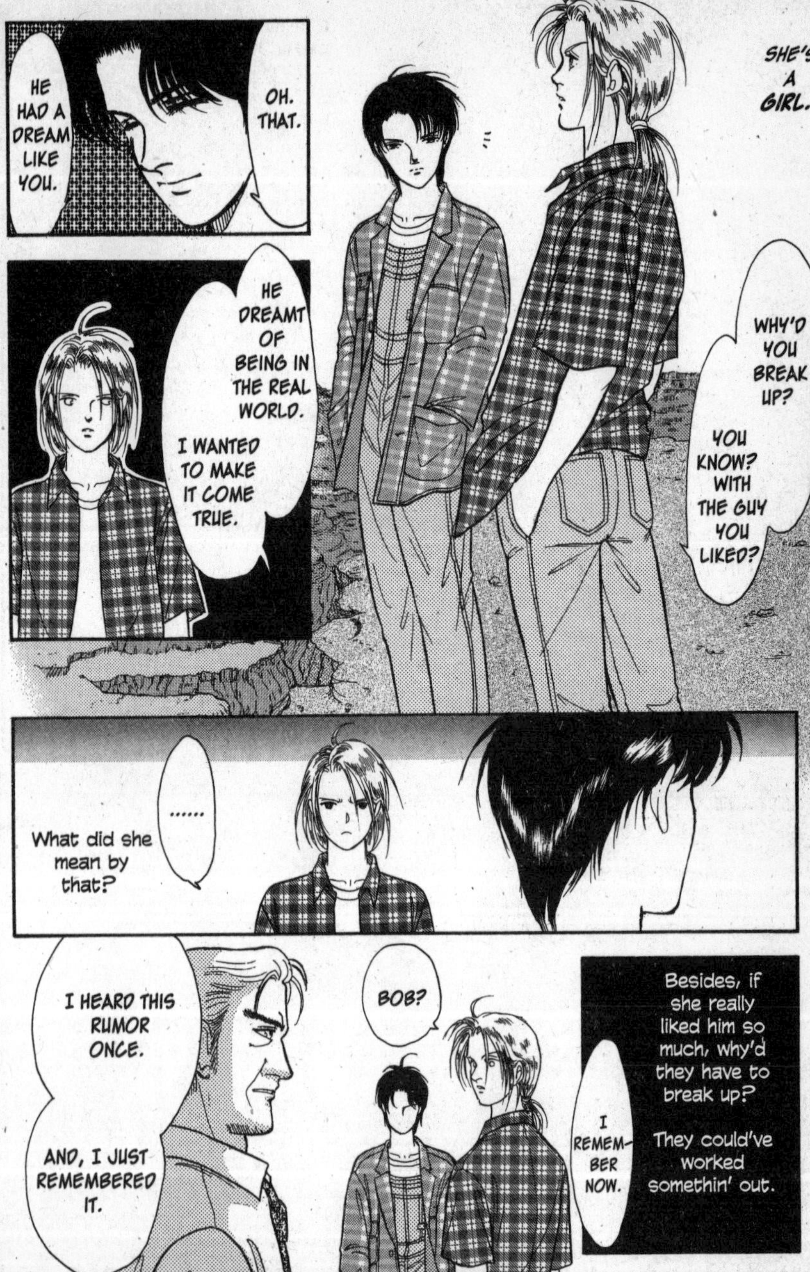
SHE'S A GIRL.
WHY'D YOU BREAK UP?
YOU KNOW? WITH THE GUY YOU LIKED?
OH. THAT.
HE HAD A DREAM LIKE YOU.
HE DREAMT OF BEING IN THE REAL WORLD.
I WANTED TO MAKE IT COME TRUE.
......
What did she mean by that?
Besides, if she really liked him so much, why'd they have to break up?
They could've worked somethin' out.
I REMEM-BER NOW.
BOB?
I HEARD THIS RUMOR ONCE.
AND, I JUST REMEMBERED IT.

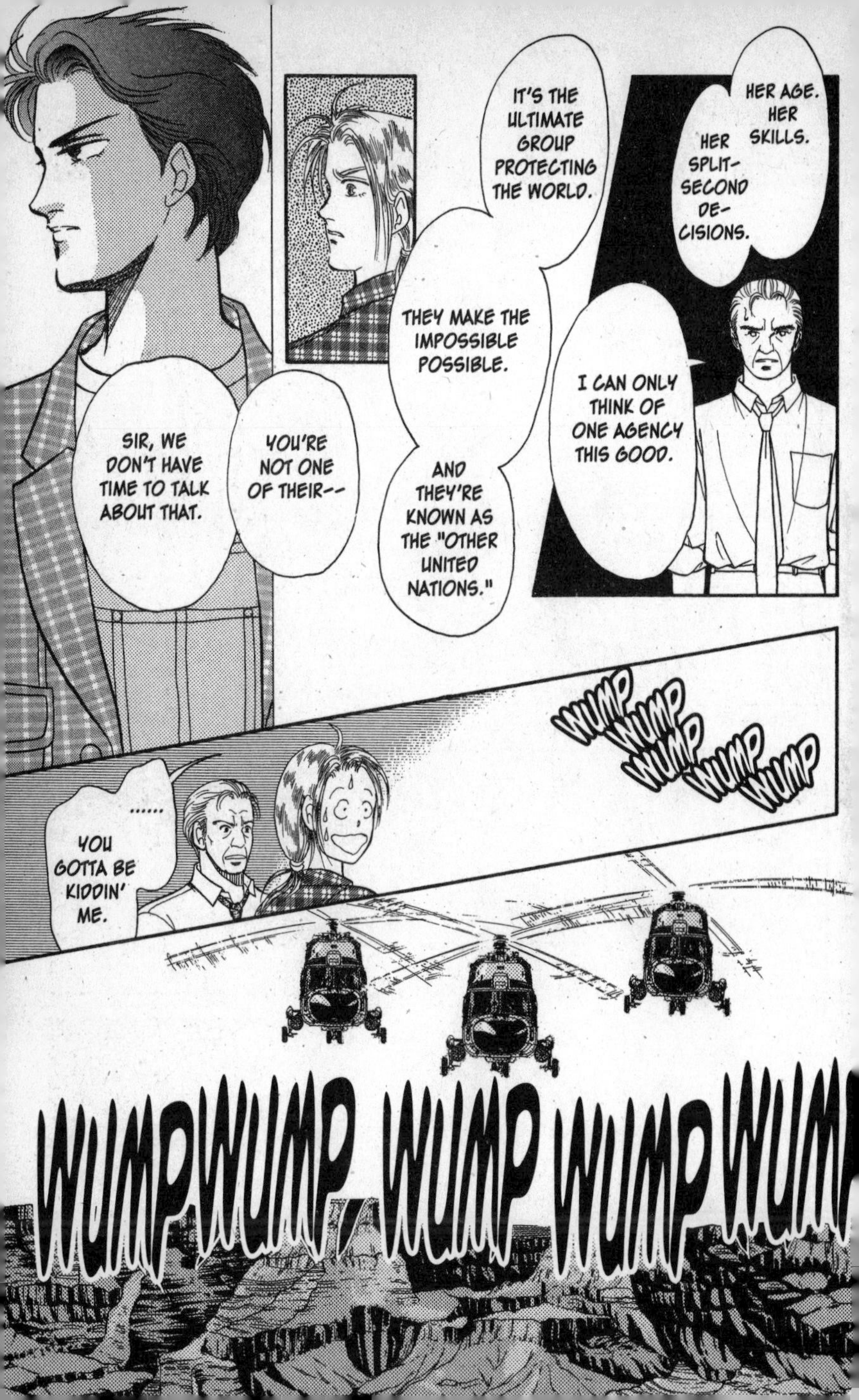
HER AGE. HER SKILLS.
HER SPLIT-SECOND DE-CISIONS.
I CAN ONLY THINK OF ONE AGENCY THIS GOOD.
IT'S THE ULTIMATE GROUP PROTECTING THE WORLD.
THEY MAKE THE IMPOSSIBLE POSSIBLE.
AND THEY'RE KNOWN AS THE "OTHER UNITED NATIONS."
YOU'RE NOT ONE OF THEIR--
SIR, WE DON'T HAVE TIME TO TALK ABOUT THAT.
WUMP WUMP WUMP WUMP WUMP
......
YOU GOTTA BE KIDDIN' ME.
WUMP WUMP WUMP WUMP

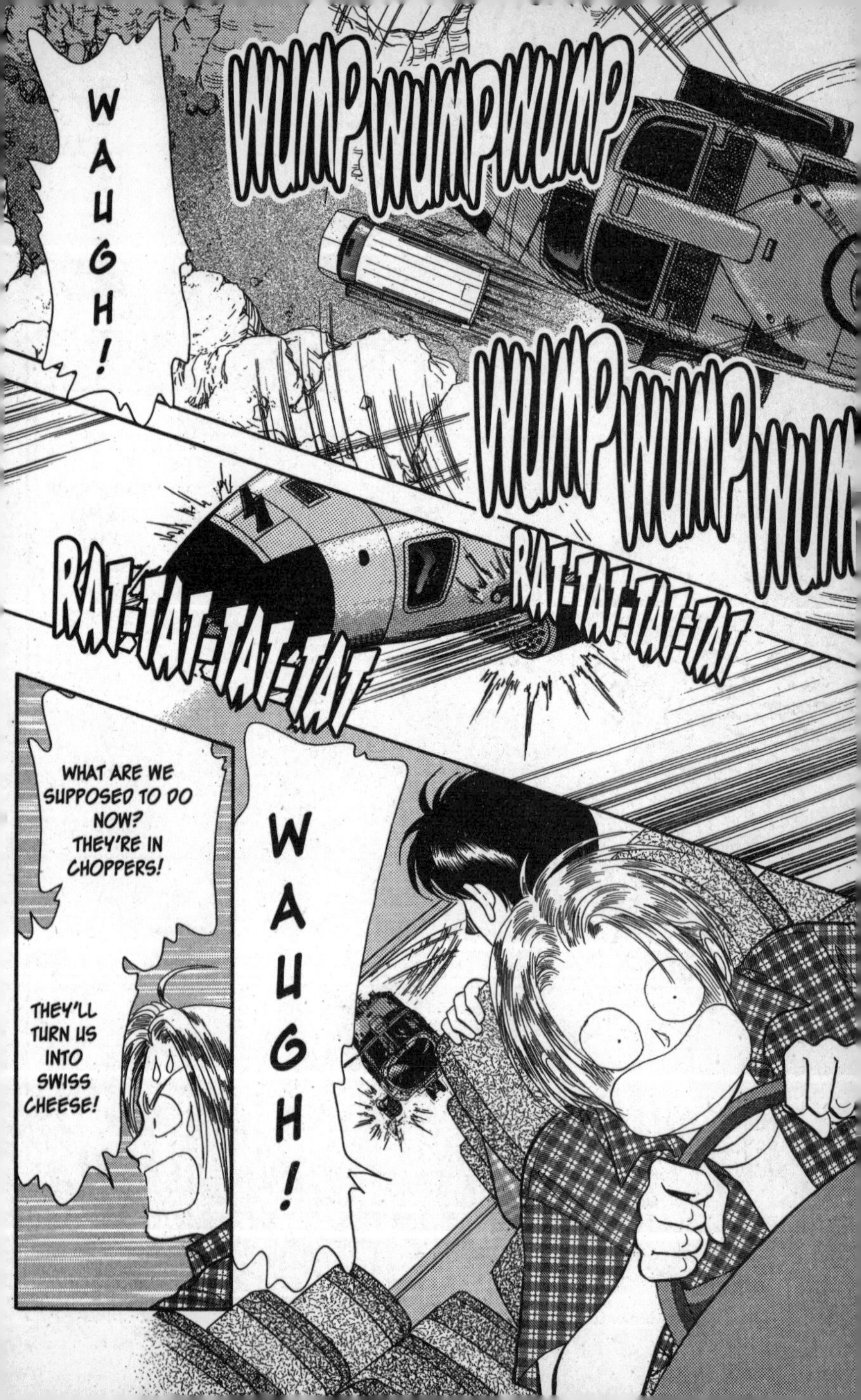
WUMP WUMP WUMP
WAUGH!
WUMP WUMP WUM
RAT-TAT-TAT-TAT
RAT-TAT-TAT-TAT
WAUGH!
WHAT ARE WE SUPPOSED TO DO NOW? THEY'RE IN CHOPPERS!
THEY'LL TURN US INTO SWISS CHEESE!

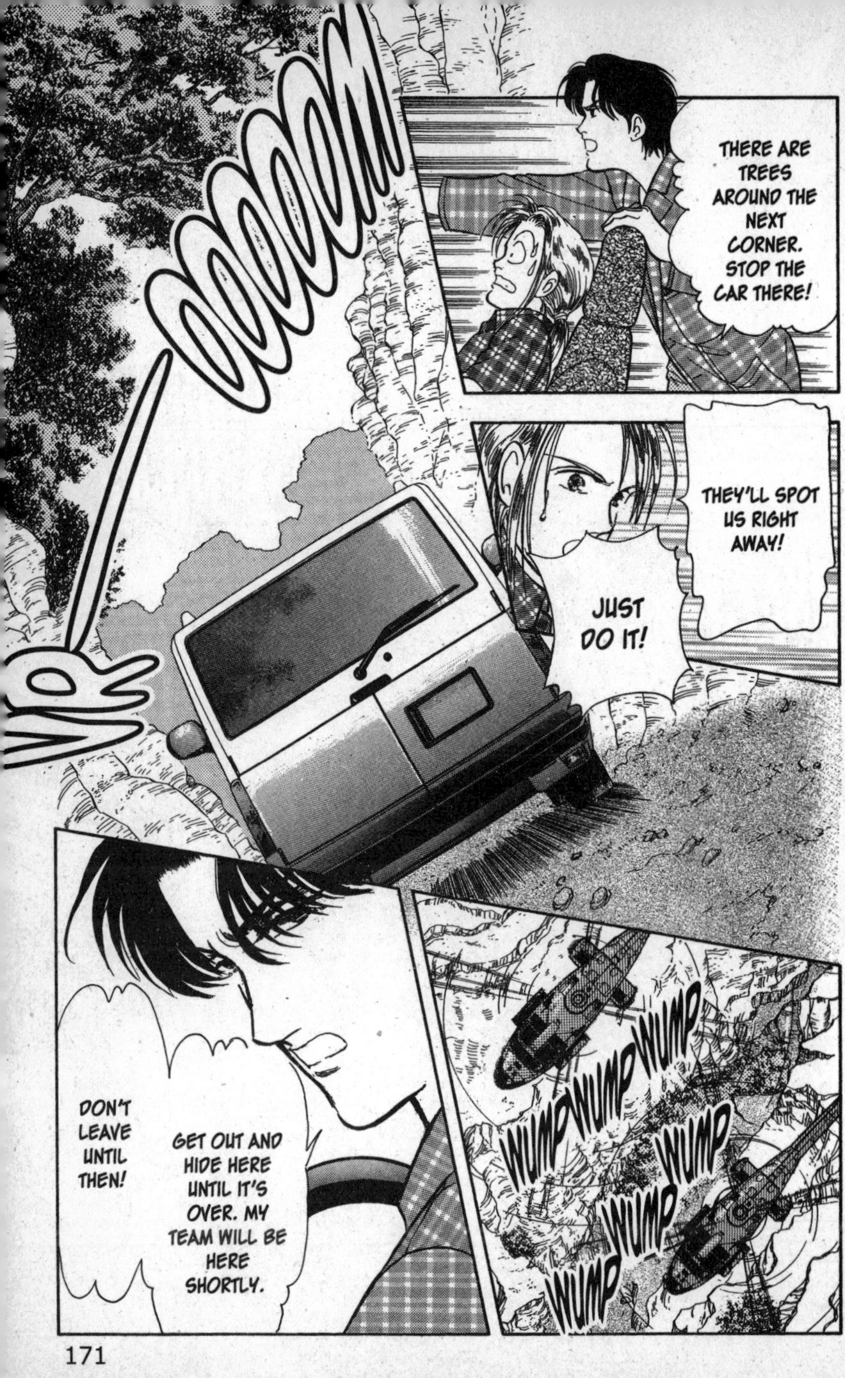

THERE ARE TREES AROUND THE NEXT CORNER. STOP THE CAR THERE!
THEY'LL SPOT US RIGHT AWAY!
JUST DO IT!
VROOOOOOM
WUMP WUMP WUMP
WUMP WUMP WUMP
GET OUT AND HIDE HERE UNTIL IT'S OVER. MY TEAM WILL BE HERE SHORTLY.
DON'T LEAVE UNTIL THEN!

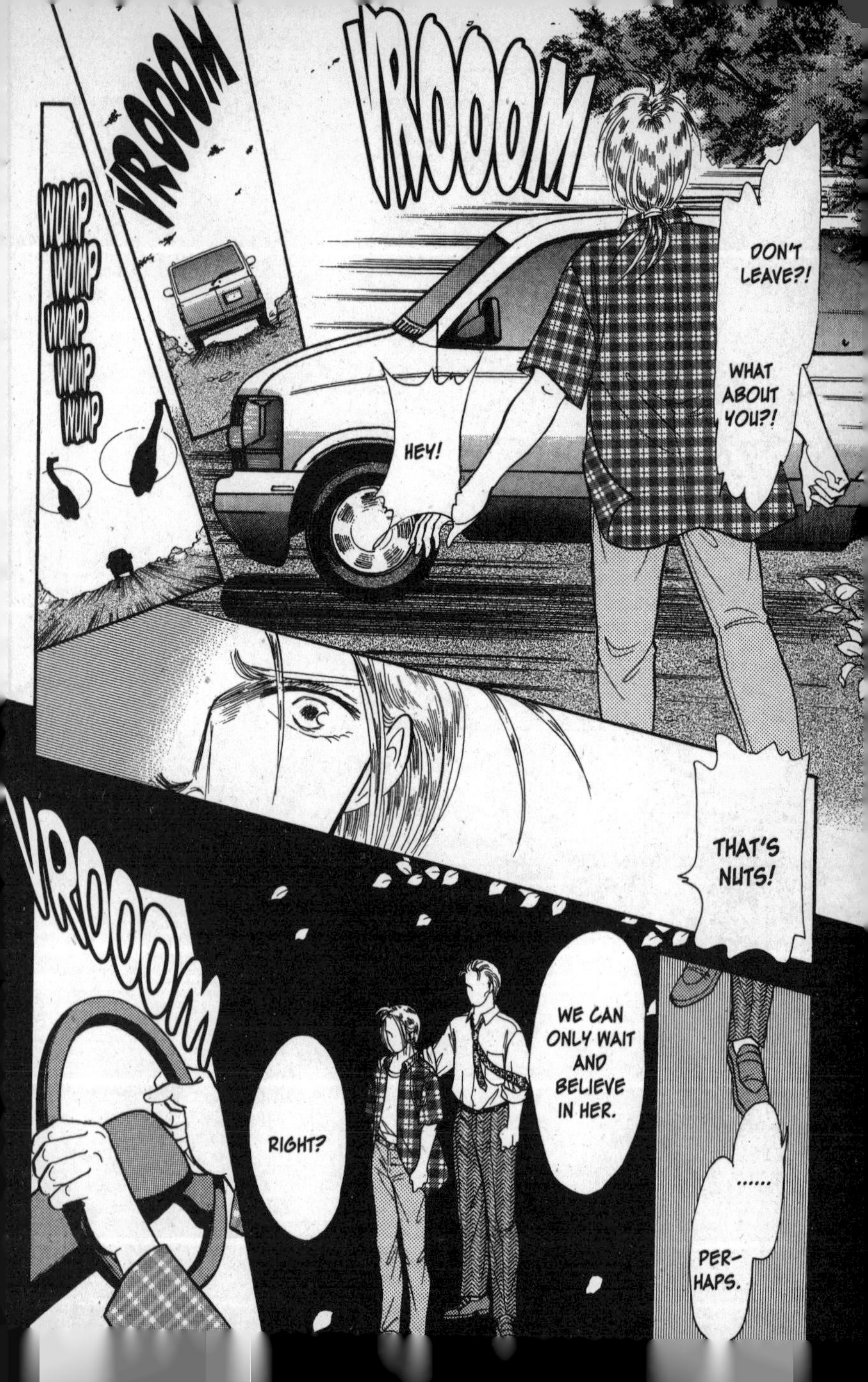
VROOOM
DON'T LEAVE?!
WHAT ABOUT YOU?!
HEY!
VROOOM
WUMP WUMP WUMP WUMP WUMP
THAT'S NUTS!
......
PER-HAPS.
WE CAN ONLY WAIT AND BELIEVE IN HER.
RIGHT?
VROOOM

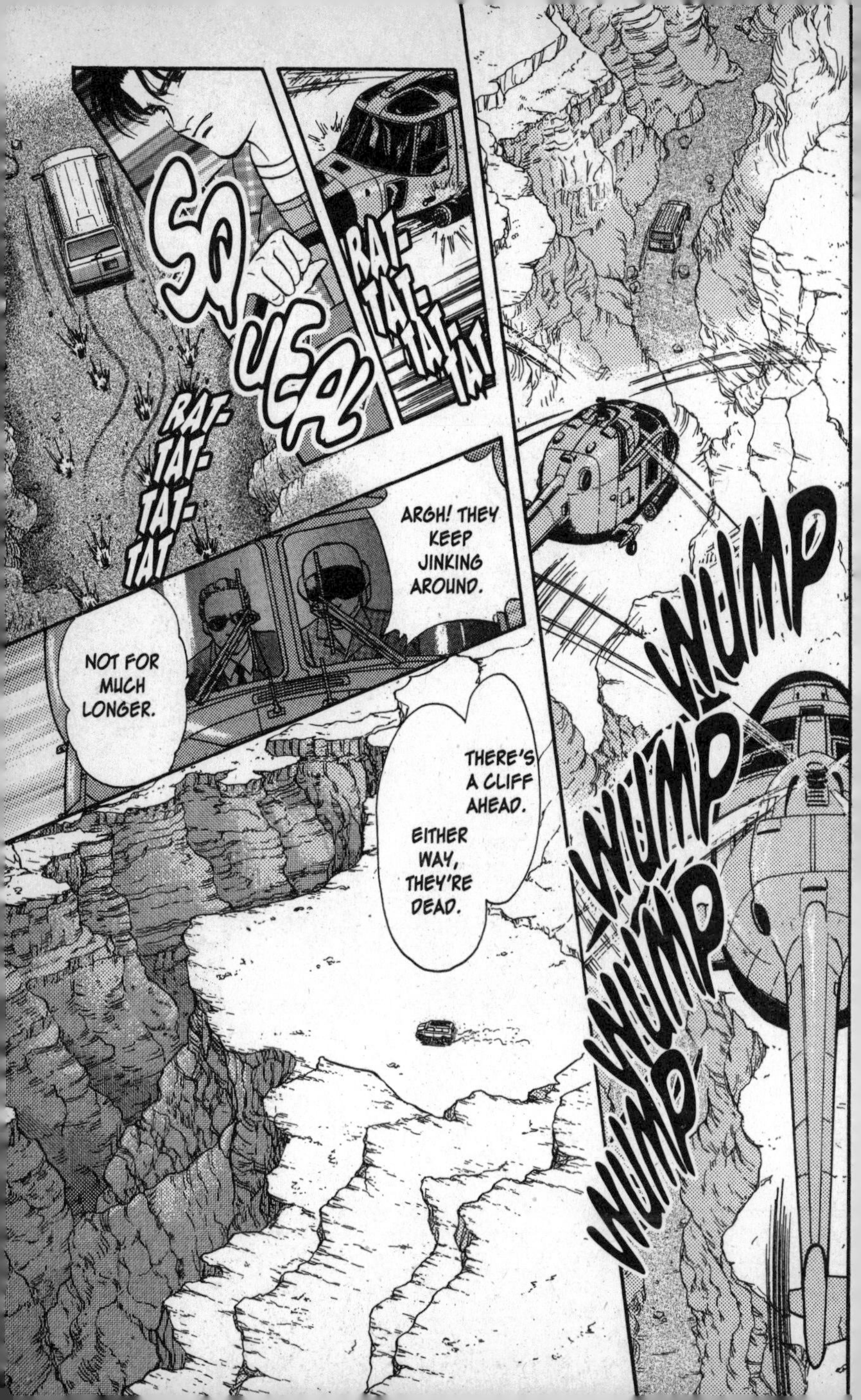
WUMP
WUMP
WUMP
WUMP
RAT-TAT-TAT-TAT
SQUEAL
RAT-TAT-TAT-TAT
ARGH! THEY KEEP JINKING AROUND.
NOT FOR MUCH LONGER.
THERE'S A CLIFF AHEAD.
EITHER WAY, THEY'RE DEAD.

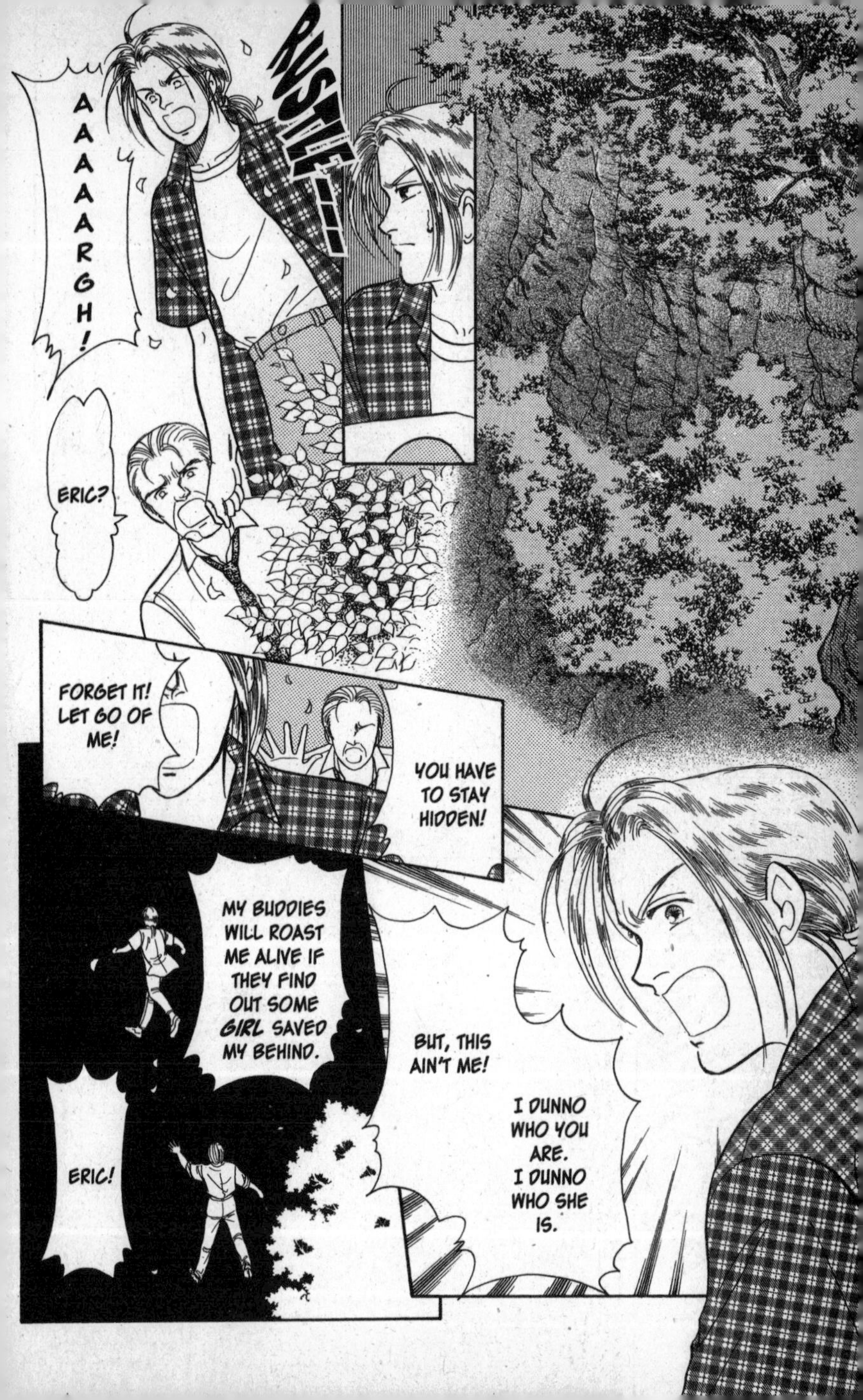
RUSTLE...
AAAAARGH!
ERIC?
YOU HAVE TO STAY HIDDEN!
FORGET IT! LET GO OF ME!
MY BUDDIES WILL ROAST ME ALIVE IF THEY FIND OUT SOME *GIRL* SAVED MY BEHIND.
BUT, THIS AIN'T ME!
I DUNNO WHO YOU ARE. I DUNNO WHO SHE IS.
ERIC!

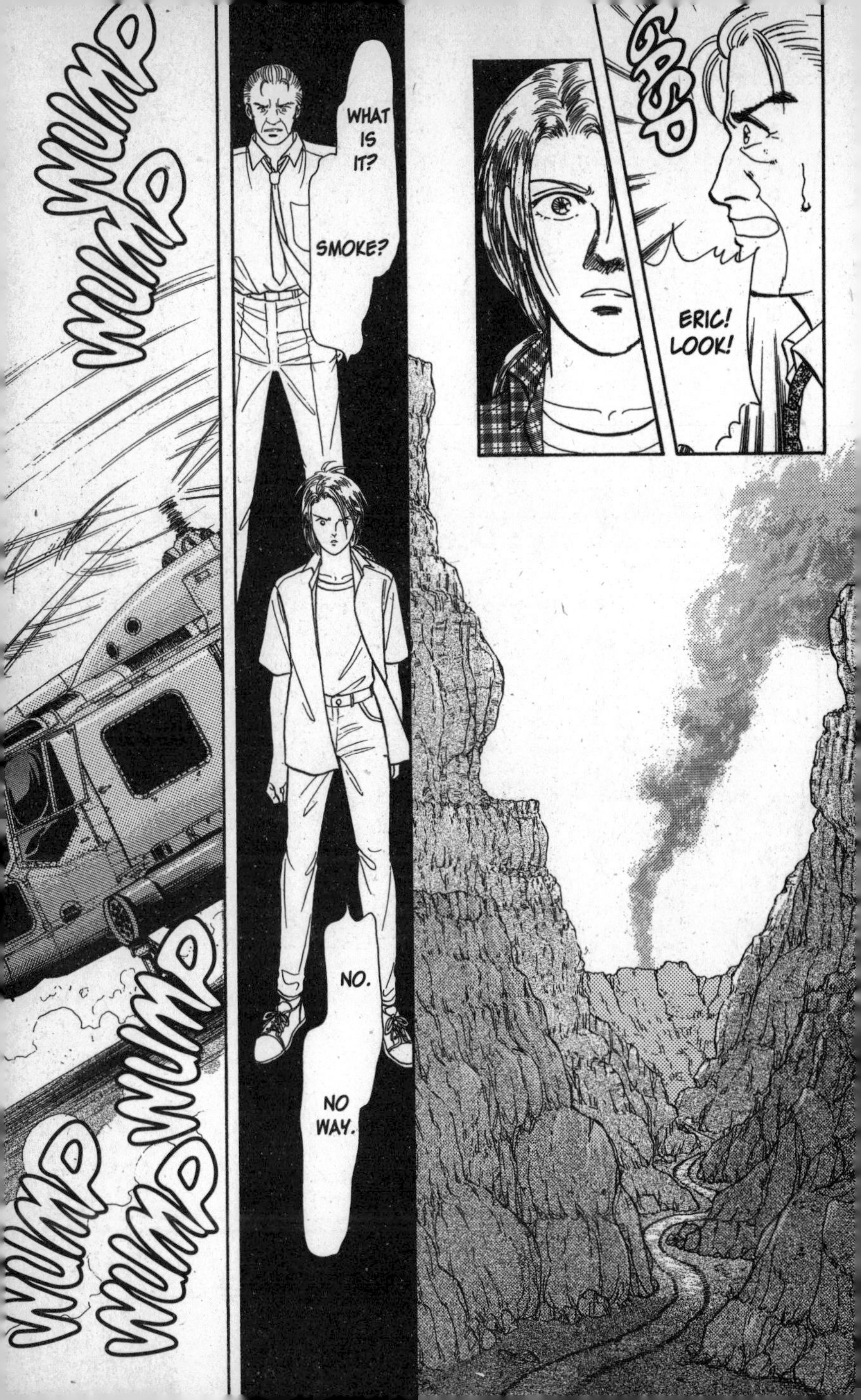
GASP
ERIC! LOOK!
WHAT IS IT?
SMOKE?
NO.
NO WAY.
WHUMP WHUMP
WHUMP WHUMP
WHUMP WHUMP

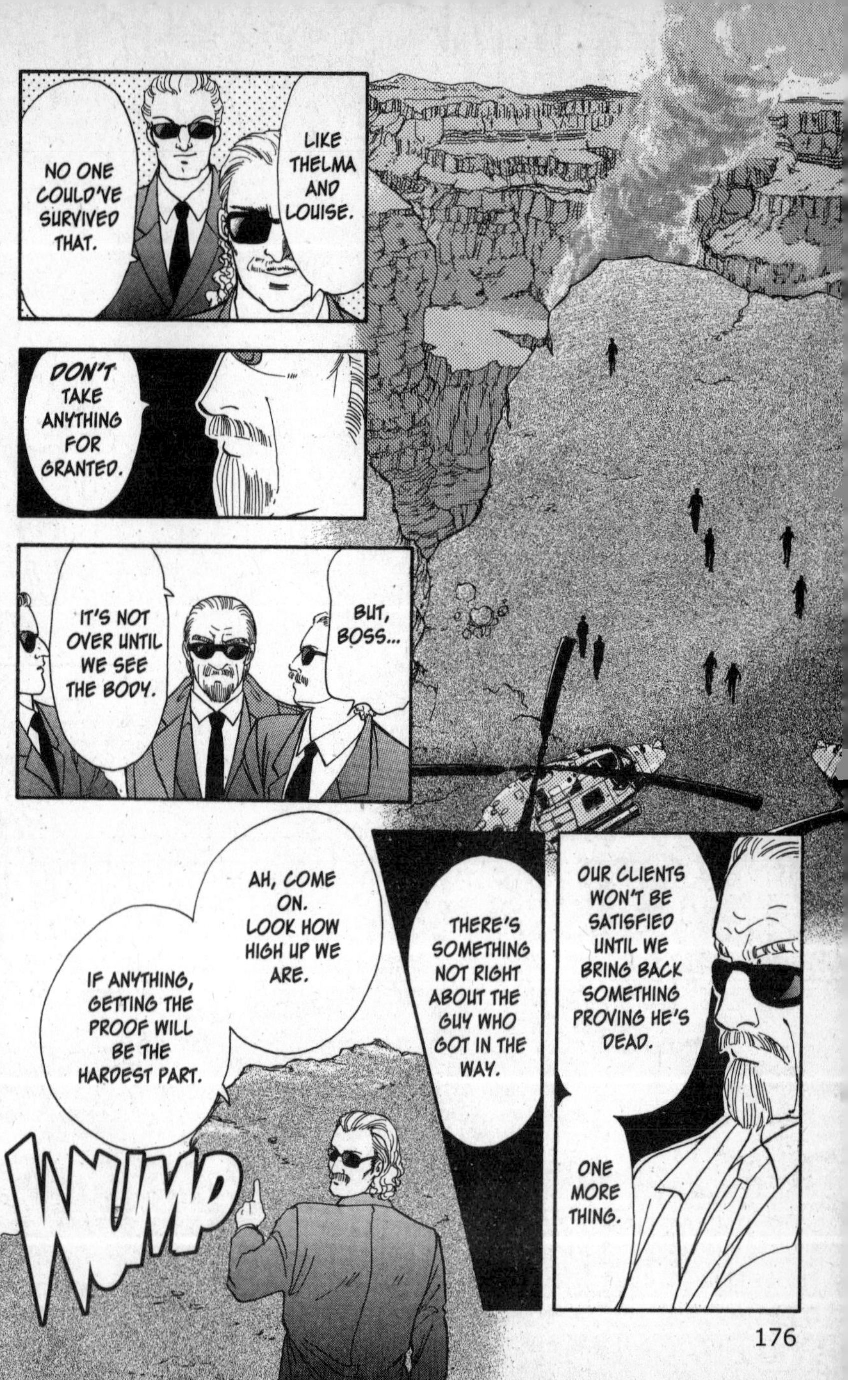
LIKE THELMA AND LOUISE.
NO ONE COULD'VE SURVIVED THAT.
DON'T TAKE ANYTHING FOR GRANTED.
BUT, BOSS...
IT'S NOT OVER UNTIL WE SEE THE BODY.
OUR CLIENTS WON'T BE SATISFIED UNTIL WE BRING BACK SOMETHING PROVING HE'S DEAD.
ONE MORE THING.
THERE'S SOMETHING NOT RIGHT ABOUT THE GUY WHO GOT IN THE WAY.
AH, COME ON. LOOK HOW HIGH UP WE ARE.
IF ANYTHING, GETTING THE PROOF WILL BE THE HARDEST PART.
WUMP

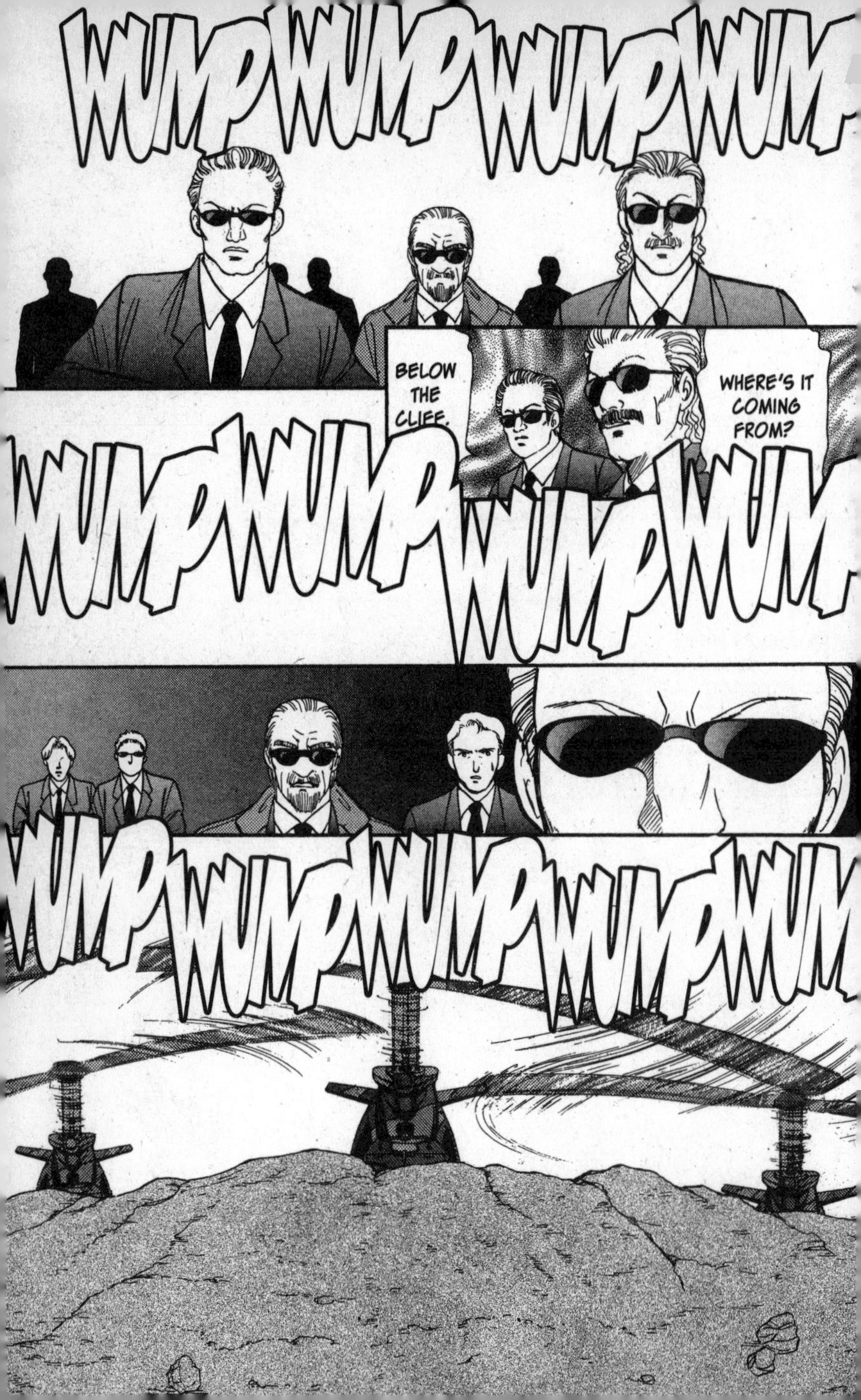
WUMP WUMP WUMP WUM
WHERE'S IT COMING FROM?
BELOW THE CLIFF.
WUMP WUMP WUMP WUM
WUMP WUMP WUMP WUMP WUM

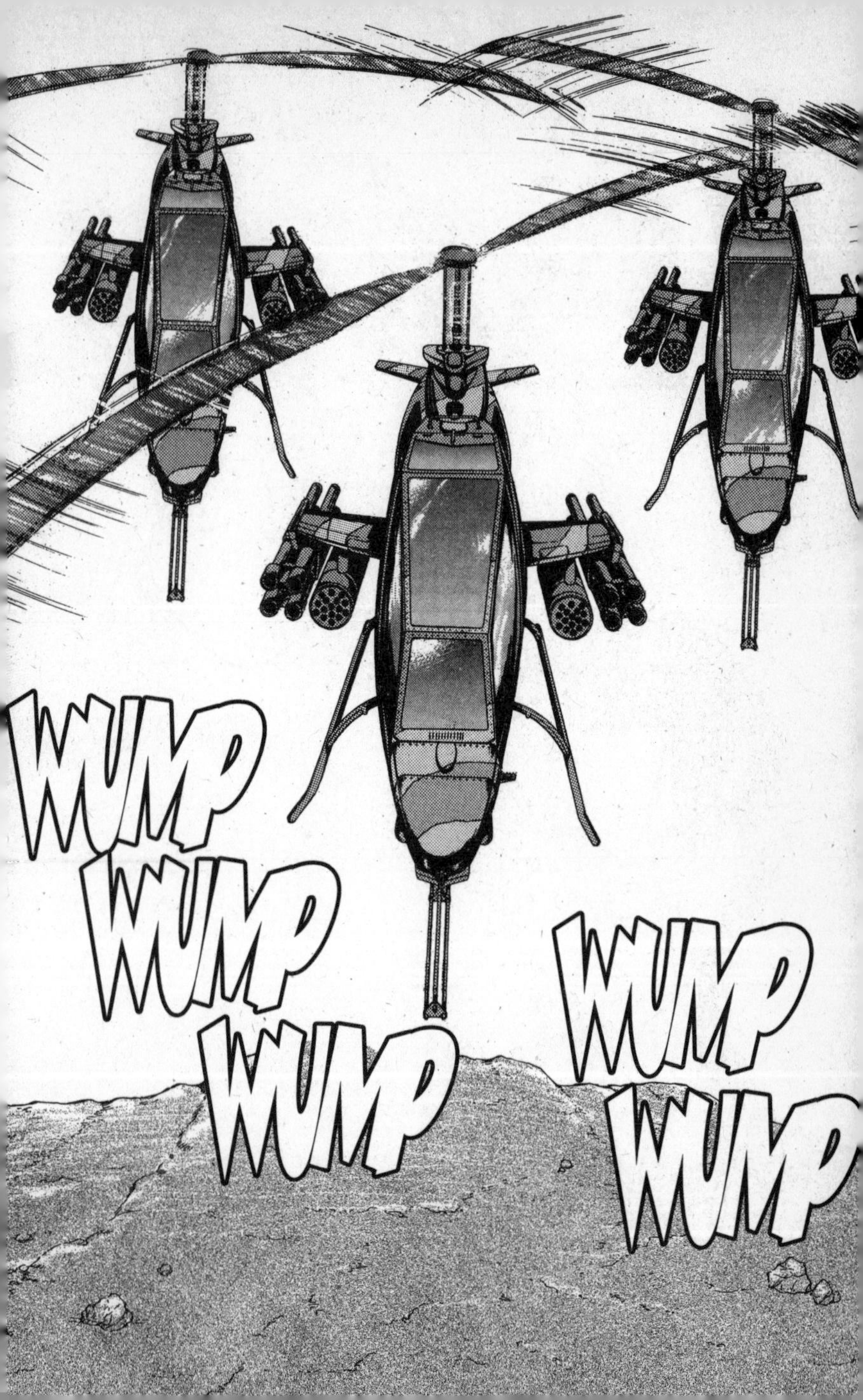
WUMP
WUMP
WUMP
WUMP
WUMP
WUMP

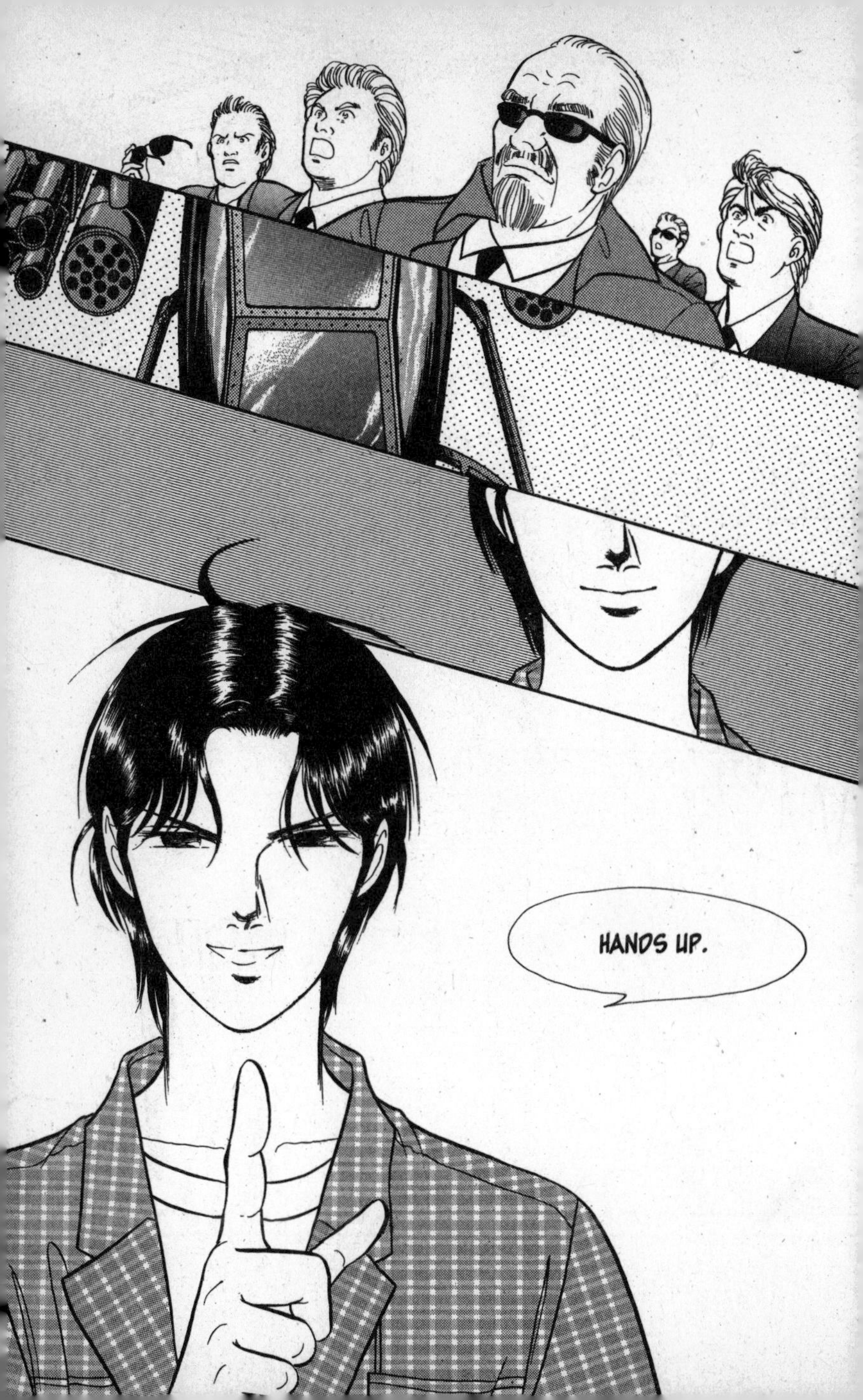
HANDS UP.

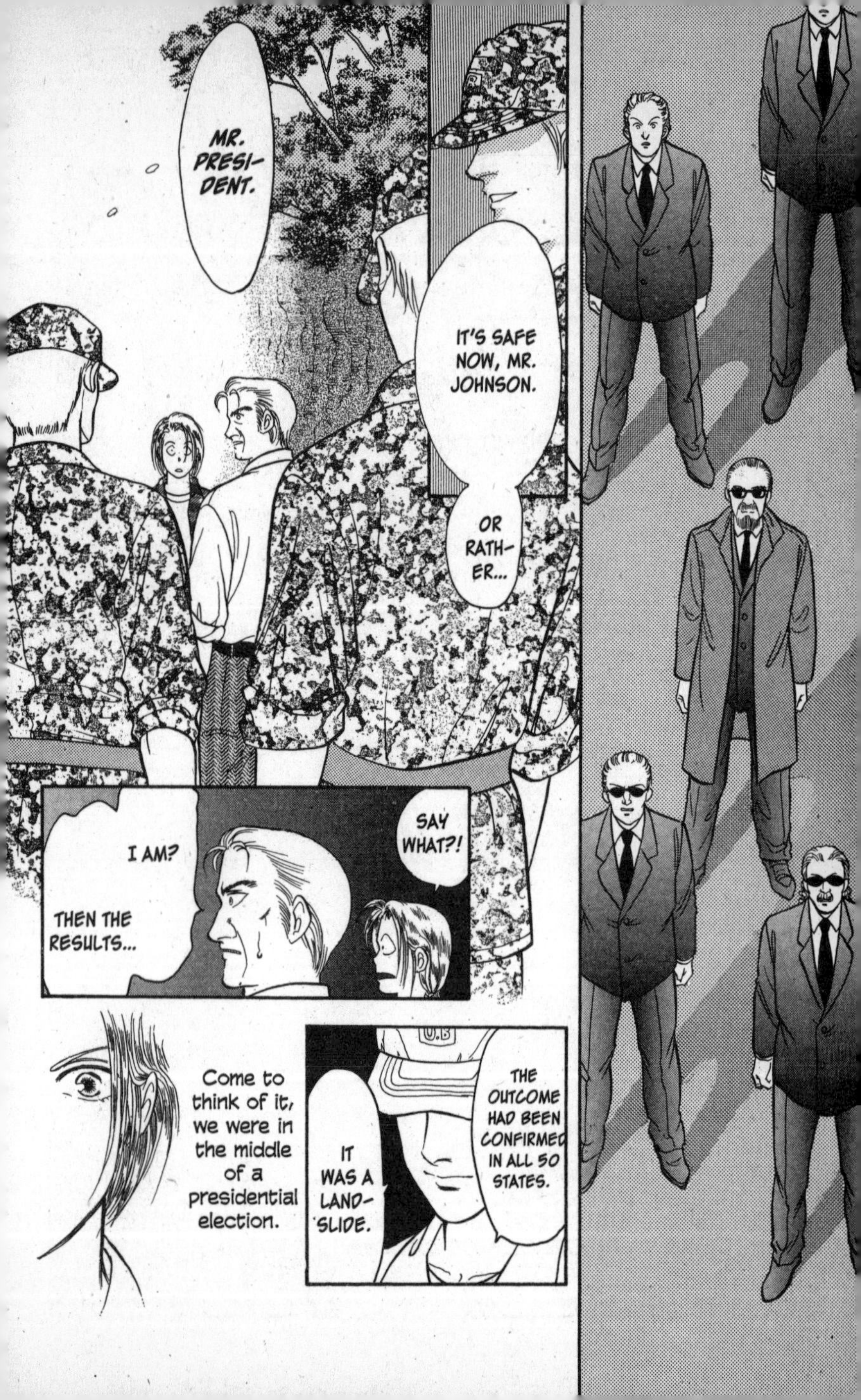
IT'S SAFE NOW, MR. JOHNSON.
OR RATHER...
MR. PRESIDENT.
SAY WHAT?!
I AM?
THEN THE RESULTS...
THE OUTCOME HAD BEEN CONFIRMED IN ALL 50 STATES.
IT WAS A LANDSLIDE.
Come to think of it, we were in the middle of a presidential election.

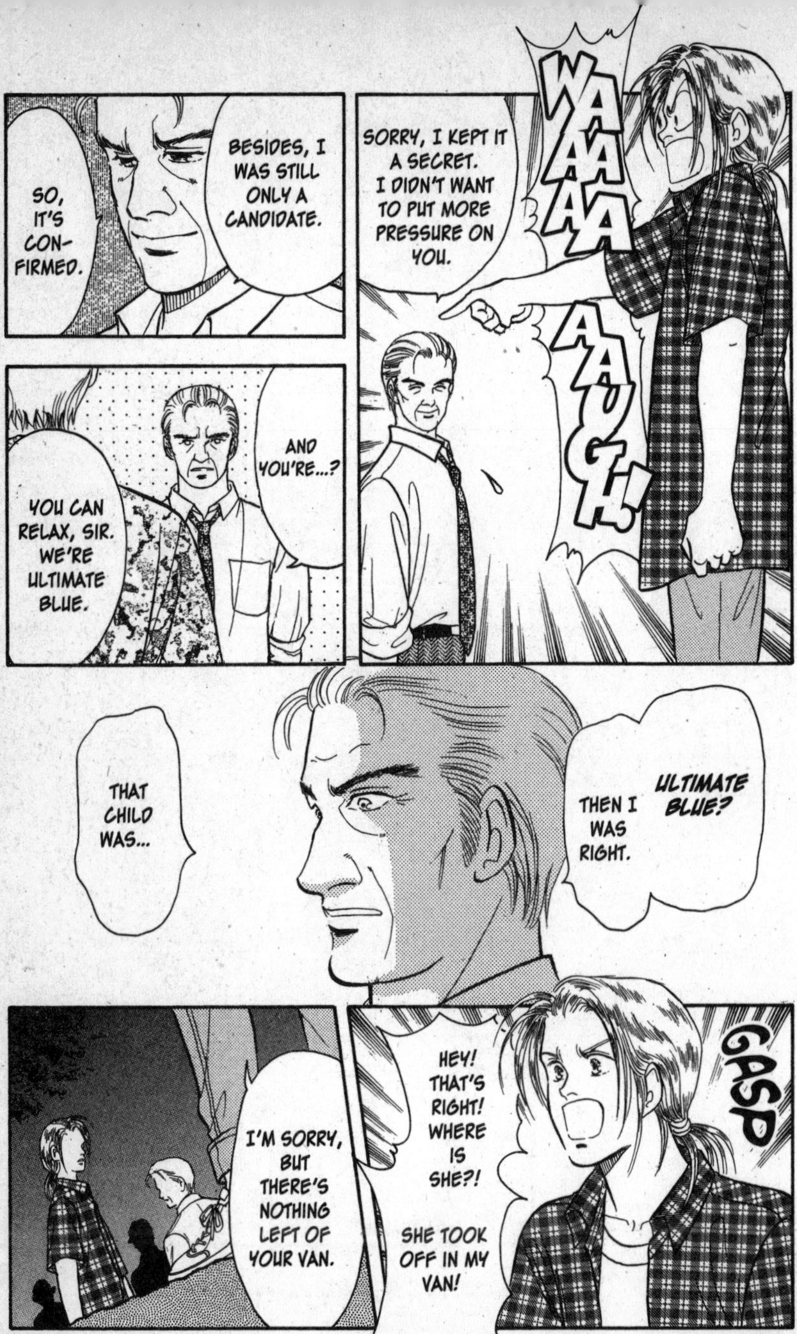
WAAAAA
SORRY, I KEPT IT A SECRET. I DIDN'T WANT TO PUT MORE PRESSURE ON YOU.
AAUGH!
BESIDES, I WAS STILL ONLY A CANDIDATE.
SO, IT'S CONFIRMED.
AND YOU'RE...?
YOU CAN RELAX, SIR. WE'RE ULTIMATE BLUE.
ULTIMATE BLUE?
THEN I WAS RIGHT.
THAT CHILD WAS...
GASP
HEY! THAT'S RIGHT! WHERE IS SHE?!
SHE TOOK OFF IN MY VAN!
I'M SORRY, BUT THERE'S NOTHING LEFT OF YOUR VAN.

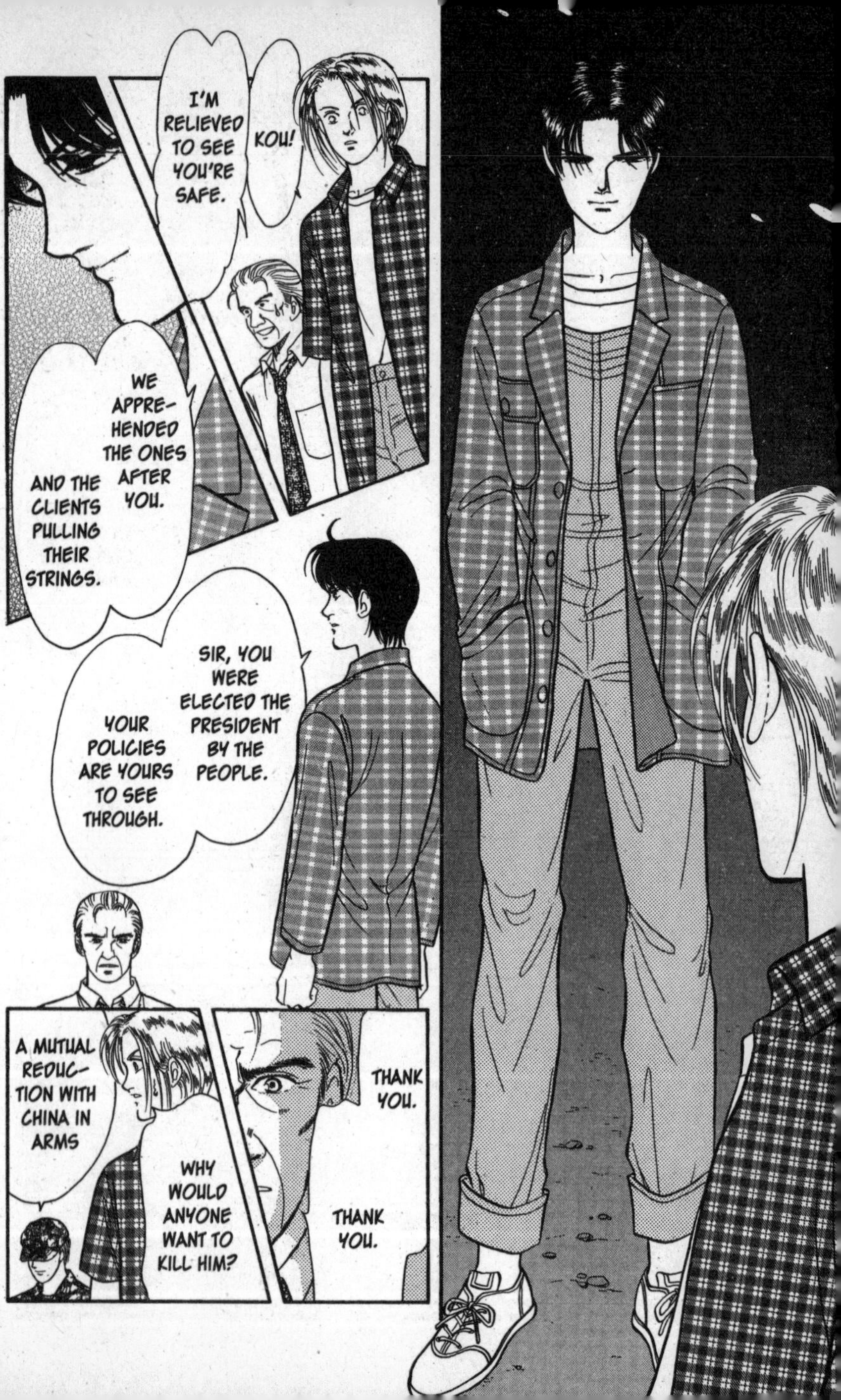
KOU!
I'M RELIEVED TO SEE YOU'RE SAFE.
WE APPREHENDED THE ONES AFTER YOU.
AND THE CLIENTS PULLING THEIR STRINGS.
SIR, YOU WERE ELECTED THE PRESIDENT BY THE PEOPLE.
YOUR POLICIES ARE YOURS TO SEE THROUGH.
THANK YOU.
WHY WOULD ANYONE WANT TO KILL HIM?
THANK YOU.
A MUTUAL REDUCTION WITH CHINA IN ARMS

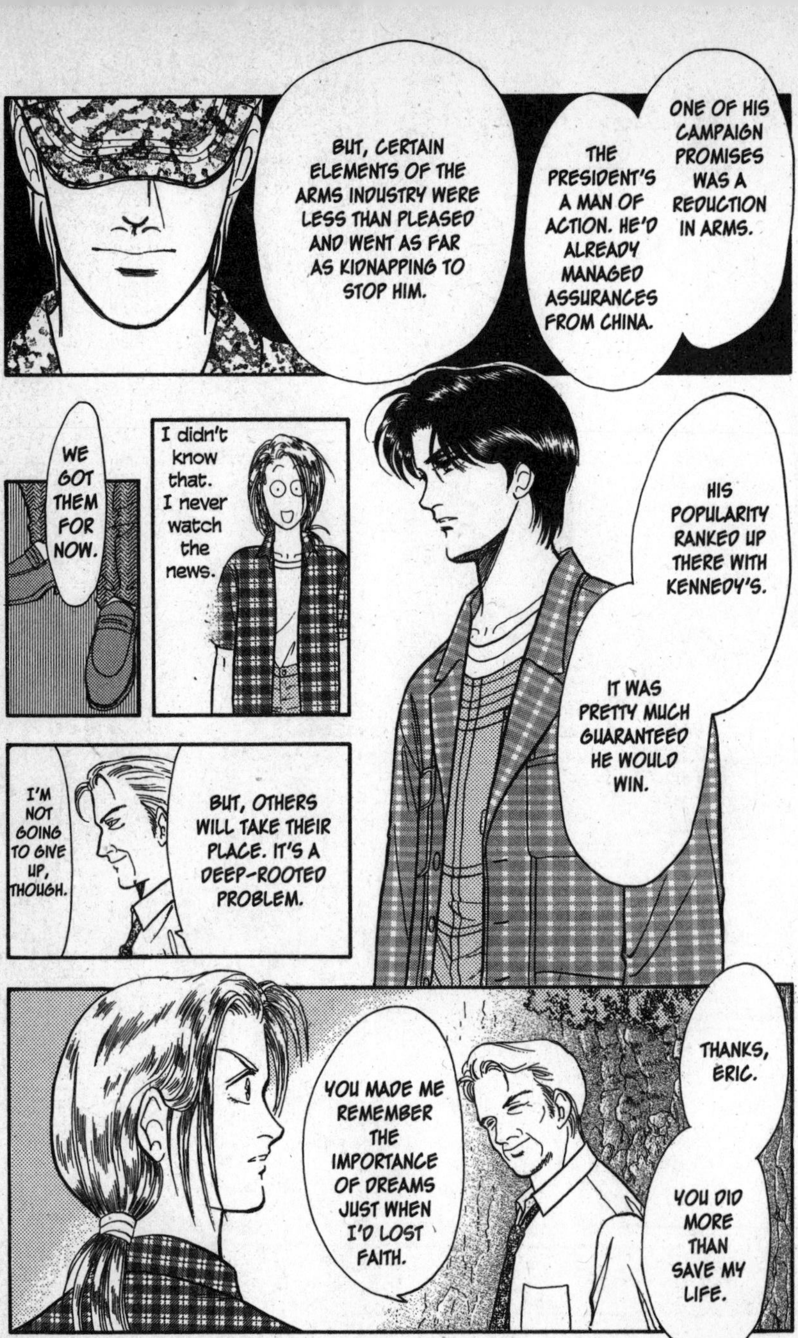
ONE OF HIS CAMPAIGN PROMISES WAS A REDUCTION IN ARMS.
THE PRESIDENT'S A MAN OF ACTION. HE'D ALREADY MANAGED ASSURANCES FROM CHINA.
BUT, CERTAIN ELEMENTS OF THE ARMS INDUSTRY WERE LESS THAN PLEASED AND WENT AS FAR AS KIDNAPPING TO STOP HIM.
HIS POPULARITY RANKED UP THERE WITH KENNEDY'S.
IT WAS PRETTY MUCH GUARANTEED HE WOULD WIN.
I didn't know that. I never watch the news.
WE GOT THEM FOR NOW.
BUT, OTHERS WILL TAKE THEIR PLACE. IT'S A DEEP-ROOTED PROBLEM.
I'M NOT GOING TO GIVE UP, THOUGH.
THANKS, ERIC.
YOU DID MORE THAN SAVE MY LIFE.
YOU MADE ME REMEMBER THE IMPORTANCE OF DREAMS JUST WHEN I'D LOST FAITH.

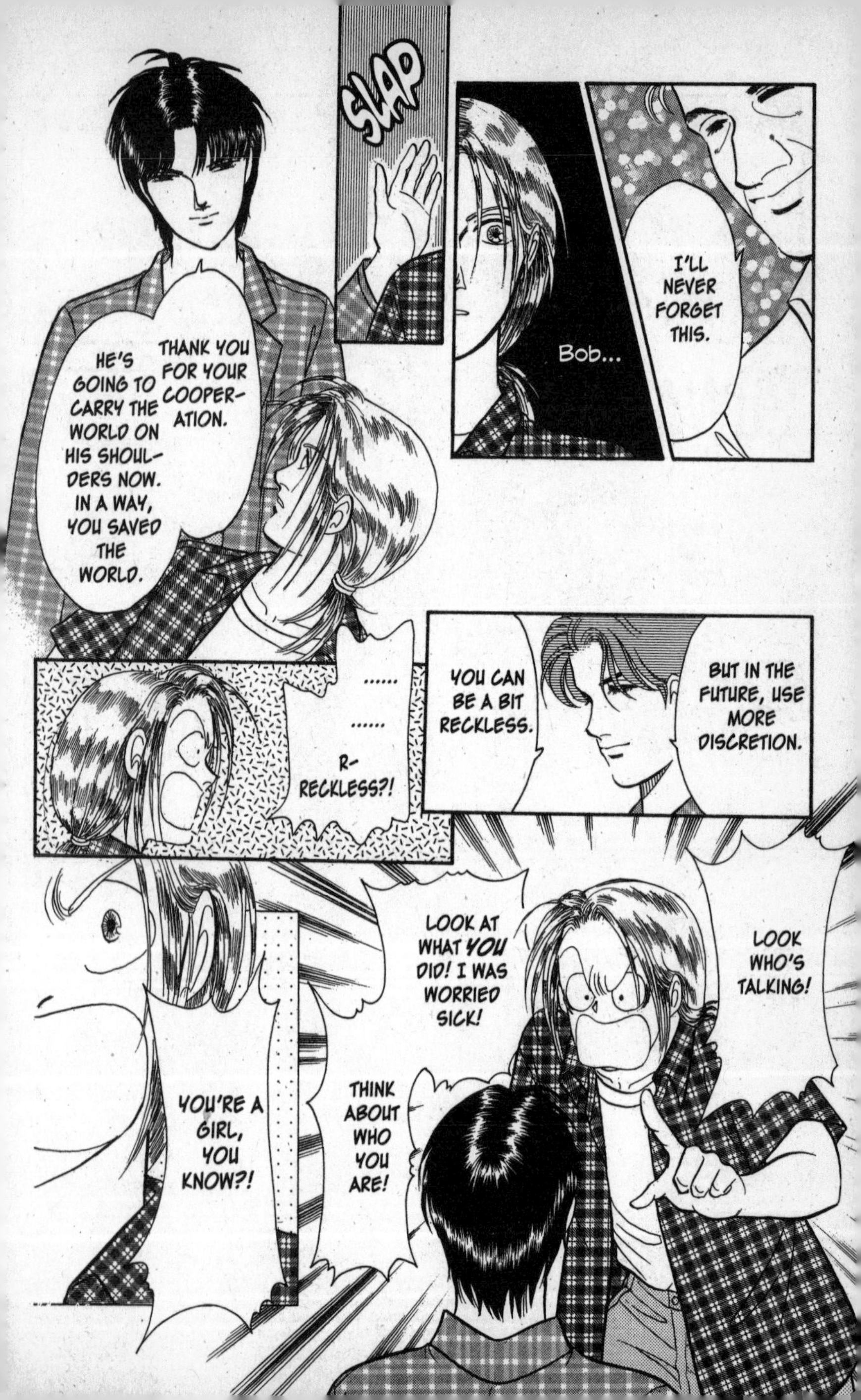
I'LL NEVER FORGET THIS.
Bob...
SLAP
THANK YOU FOR YOUR COOPERATION.
HE'S GOING TO CARRY THE WORLD ON HIS SHOULDERS NOW. IN A WAY, YOU SAVED THE WORLD.
BUT IN THE FUTURE, USE MORE DISCRETION.
YOU CAN BE A BIT RECKLESS.
......
......
R- RECKLESS?!
LOOK WHO'S TALKING!
LOOK AT WHAT YOU DID! I WAS WORRIED SICK!
THINK ABOUT WHO YOU ARE!
YOU'RE A GIRL, YOU KNOW?!

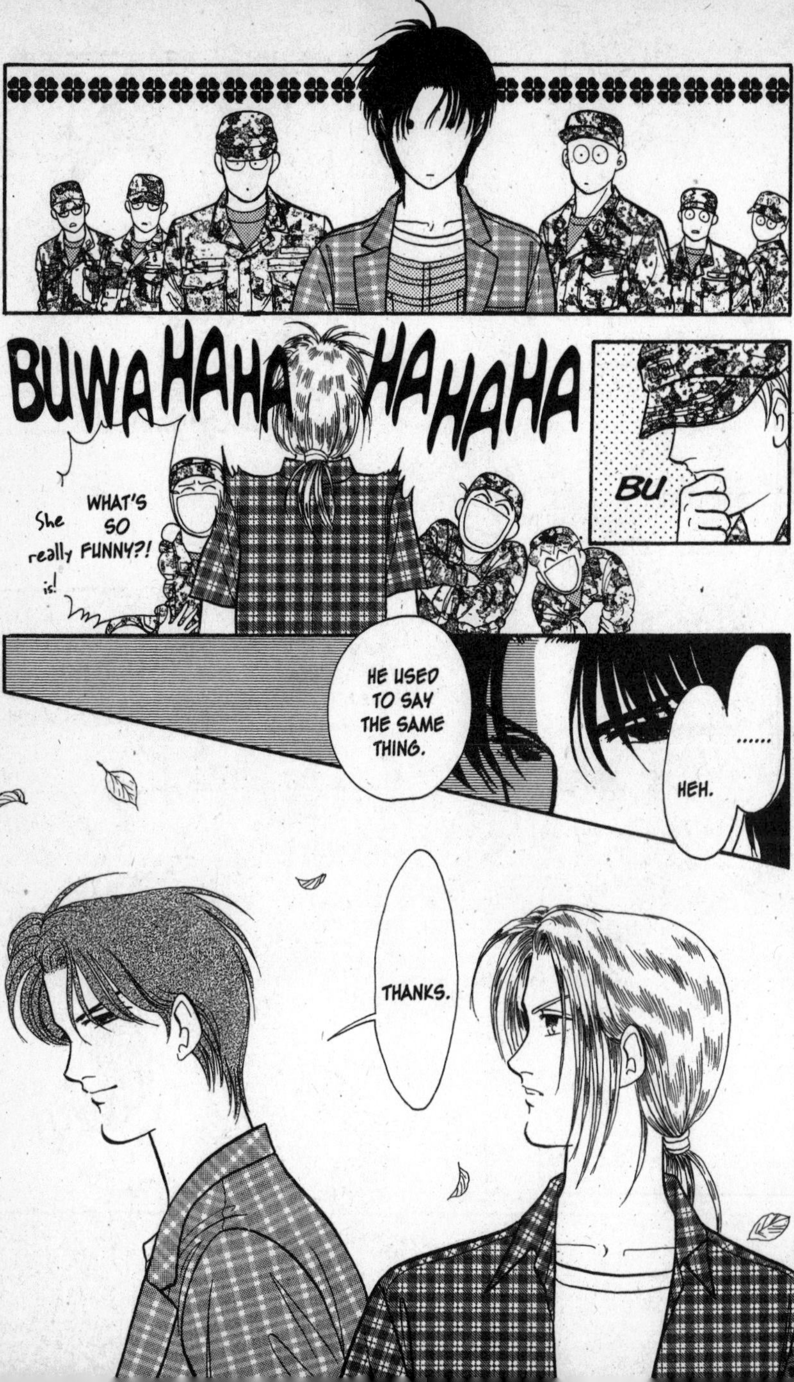
BU
BUWAHAHA HAHAHA
WHAT'S SO FUNNY?!
She really is!
......
HEH.
HE USED TO SAY THE SAME THING.
THANKS.

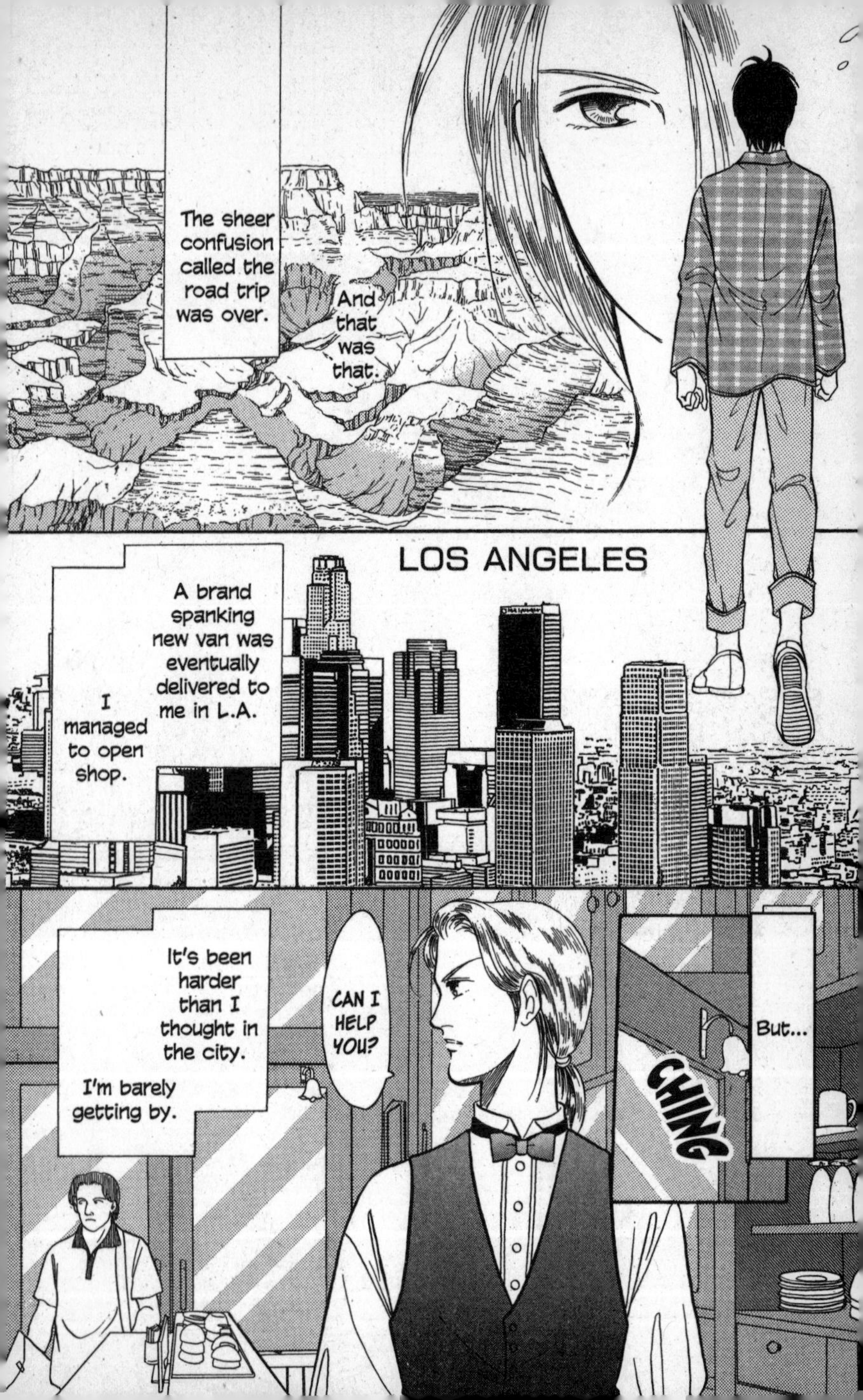
The sheer confusion called the road trip was over.
And that was that.
LOS ANGELES
A brand spanking new van was eventually delivered to me in L.A.
I managed to open shop.
But...
CHING
CAN I HELP YOU?
It's been harder than I thought in the city.
I'm barely getting by.

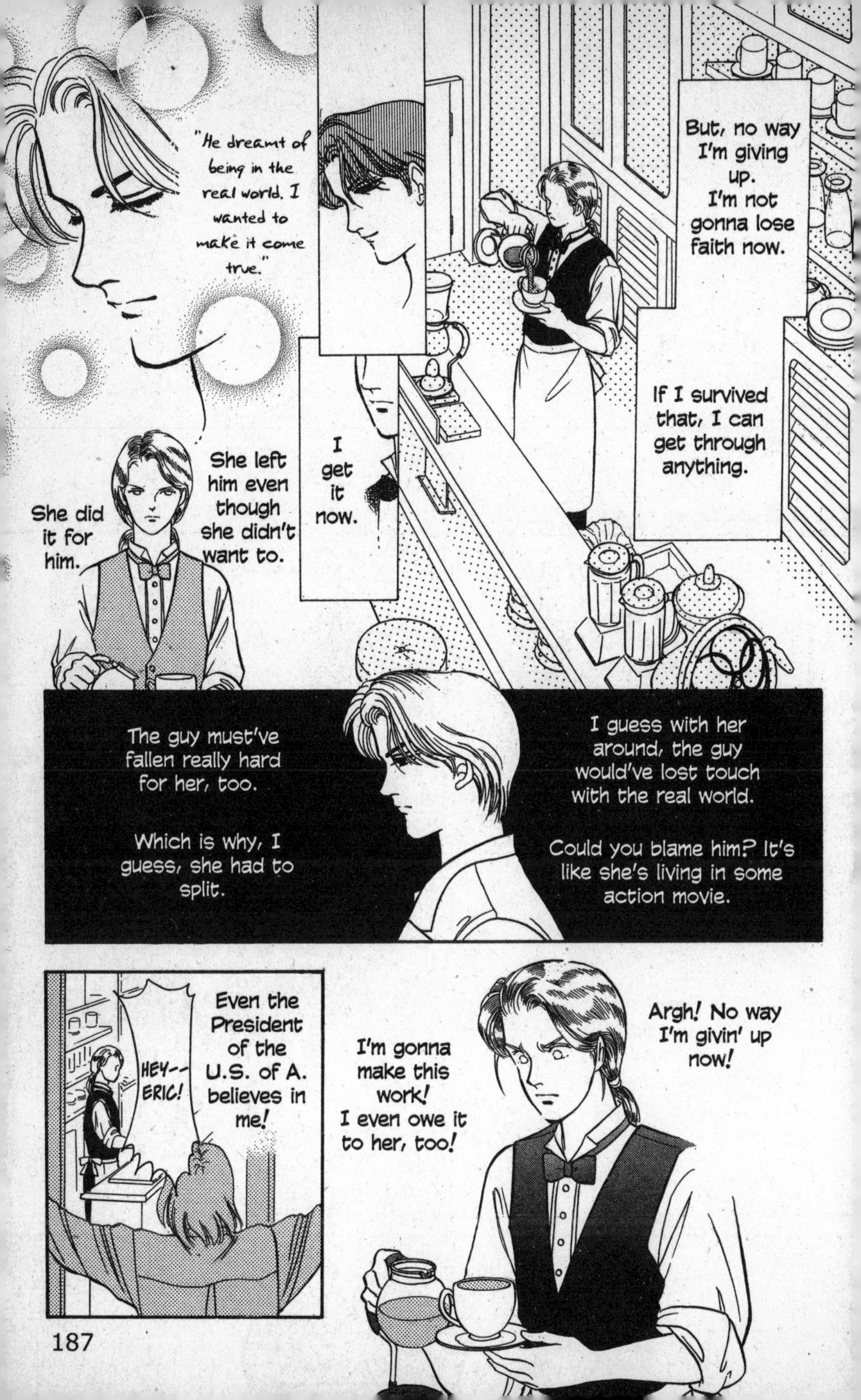
But, no way I'm giving up. I'm not gonna lose faith now.
If I survived that, I can get through anything.
I get it now.
"He dreamt of being in the real world. I wanted to make it come true."
She left him even though she didn't want to.
She did it for him.
I guess with her around, the guy would've lost touch with the real world.
Could you blame him? It's like she's living in some action movie.
The guy must've fallen really hard for her, too.
Which is why, I guess, she had to split.
Argh! No way I'm givin' up now!
I'm gonna make this work! I even owe it to her, too!
Even the President of the U.S. of A. believes in me!
HEY-- ERIC!

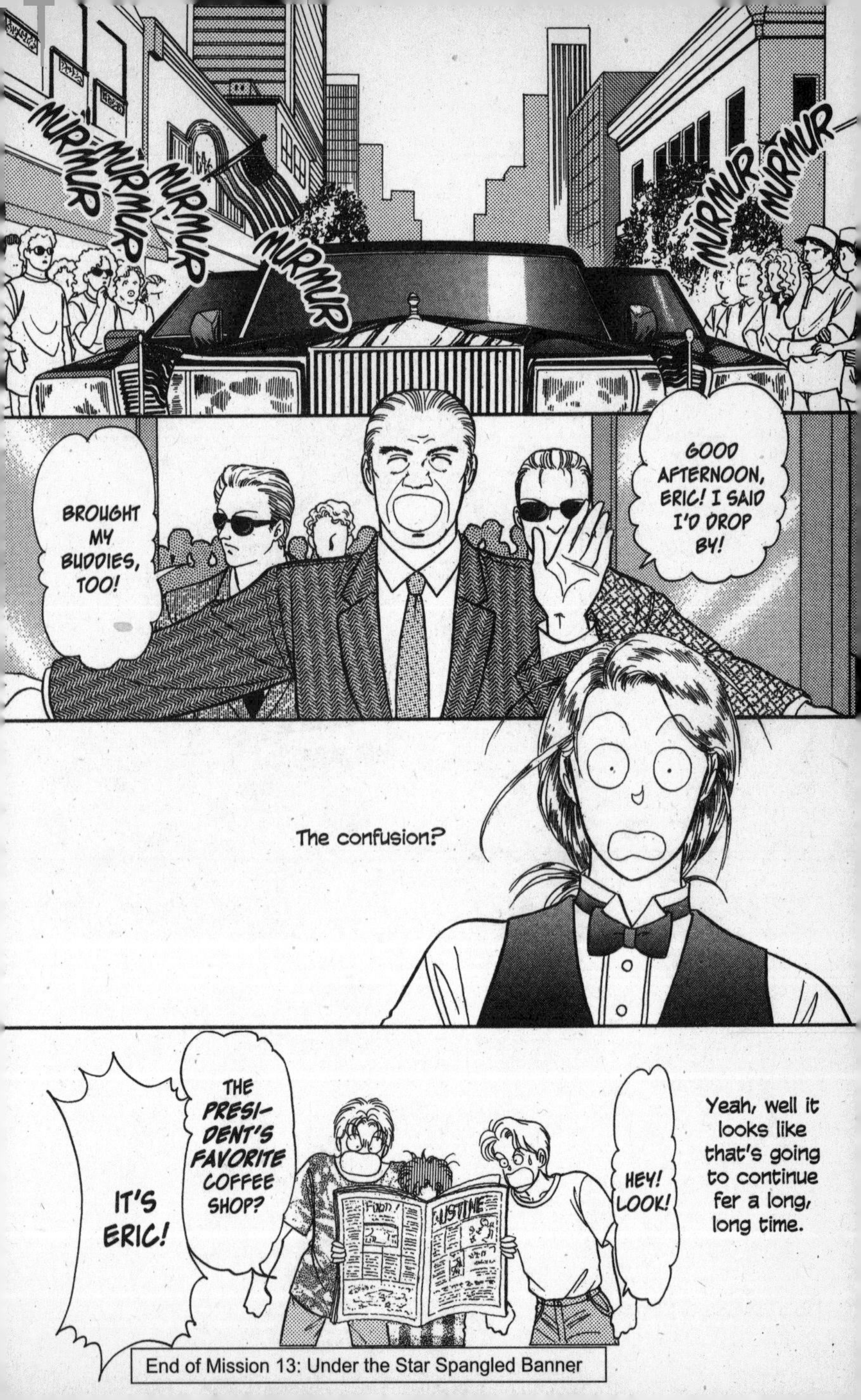
MURMUR MURMUR
MURMUR
MURMUR MURMUR
MURMUR
GOOD AFTERNOON, ERIC! I SAID I'D DROP BY!
BROUGHT MY BUDDIES, TOO!
The confusion?
Yeah, well it looks like that's going to continue fer a long, long time.
HEY! LOOK!
THE PRESIDENT'S FAVORITE COFFEE SHOP?
IT'S ERIC!
End of Mission 13: Under the Star Spangled Banner

End of Musashi Number Nine 6

cmx

In the next
volume of

MUSASHI # 9

Volume 7

By
Miyuki Takahashi

Available in May

A deadly virus and the
glamour of the Academy
Awards ® define the
extremes of Nine's latest
exploits. The young spy
also finds herself back in
Japan where an old
friend" awaits. Memories
are stirred and new
hopes kindled, further
complicating a mission
that's already a race
against time.

cmxmanga.com

Jim Lee
    Editorial Director
John Nee
    VP—Business Development
Hank Kanalz
    VP—General Manager, WildStorm
Paul Levitz
    President & Publisher
Georg Brewer
    VP—Design & DC Direct Creative
Richard Bruning
    Senior VP—Creative Director
Patrick Caldon
    Executive VP—Finance & Operations
Chris Caramalis
    VP—Finance
John Cunningham
    VP—Marketing
Terri Cunningham
    VP—Managing Editor
Stephanie Fierman
    Senior VP—Sales & Marketing
Alison Gill
    VP—Manufacturing
Rich Johnson
    VP—Book Trade Sales
Lillian Laserson
    Senior VP & General Counsel
Paula Lowitt
    Senior VP—Business & Legal Affairs
David McKillips
    VP—Advertising & Custom Publishing
Gregory Noveck
    Senior VP—Creative Affairs
Cheryl Rubin
    Senior VP—Brand Management
Jeff Trojan
    VP—Business Development, DC Direct
Bob Wayne
    VP—Sales

KYUBANME NO MUSASHI Volume 6 © 1996 by Miyuki
Takahashi. All rights reserved. First Published in Japan in
1996 by AKITA PUBLISHING CO., LTD., Tokyo.

MUSASHI #9 Volume 6, published by WildStorm
Productions, an imprint of DC Comics, 888 Prospect St.
#240, La Jolla, CA 92037. English Translation © 2006. All
Rights Reserved. English translation rights in U.S.A.
arranged with AKITA PUBLISHING CO., LTD., Tokyo,
through Tuttle-Mori Agency, Inc., Tokyo. The stories, charac-
ters, and incidents mentioned in this magazine are entirely
fictional. Printed on recyclable paper. WildStorm does not
read or accept unsolicited submissions of ideas, stories or
artwork. Printed in Canada.

 DC Comics, a Warner Bros.
Entertainment Company.

Translation and Adaptation by
Tony Ogasawara

William F. Schuch — Lettering
Larry Berry — Design
Thierry Frissen — Additional Design
Jim Chadwick — Editor

ISBN: 1-4012-0857-6
ISBN-13: 978-1-4012-0857-8

FLIP IT!!

All the pages in this book were created—and are printed here—in Japanese RIGHT-to-LEFT format. No artwork has been reversed, so you can read the stories the way the creators meant for them to be read.

RIGHT TO LEFT?!

Traditional Japanese manga starts at the upper right-hand corner, and moves right-to-left as it goes down the page. Follow this guide for an easy understanding.

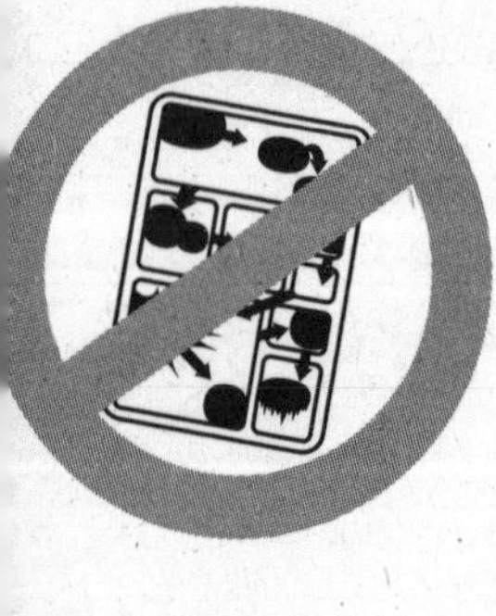
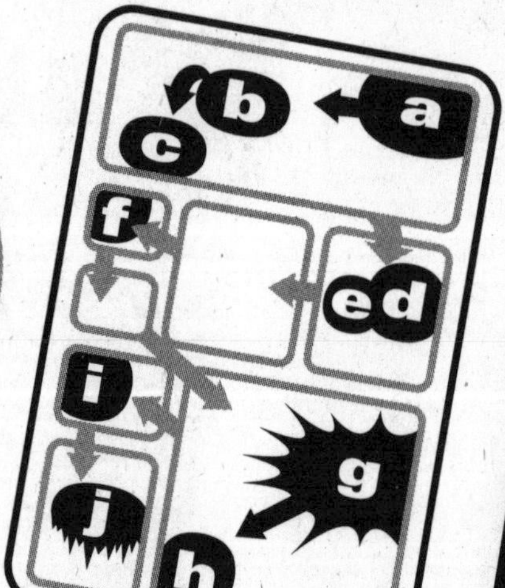
a
b
c
ed
f
g
h
i
j

Catch the latest at cmxmanga.com!